DOUGLAS COLLEGE LIBRARY

D0722211

PN
2287
L285
M29

Laurel & Hardy

Laurel & Hardy

Text by
John McCabe

Compiled by
Al Kilgore

Filmography by
Richard W. Bann

E. P. Dutton • New York

DOUGLAS COLLEGE LIBRARIES

The authors are particularly grateful to:
John Carroll who dragged John McCabe, a doubting child,
to his first Laurel and Hardy film; and to Mamie Beyer, who
carried her nephew Al Kilgore into a theatre, at an age too
young to doubt, for his first Laurel and Hardy encounter.

Acknowledgments
Our thanks to: Dick Baldwin, Kent Eastin (Blackhawk Films), Chris T. Fatta
(Olympia USA Inc.), Phillip Feiner, Roy Frumkes, Debbie Gelbspan,
Herb Gelbspan, Harry Jones of WCCO-TV, St. Paul-Minneapolis, Minnesota,
Gary Kaskel, Linny McCabe, Byron Paul, W.T. Rabe, Robert L. Rosen,
Al Schoonmaker, Stanley Simon, Mae Woods, Jordan Young,
the late Robert Youngson and Al Dahlem.

Designed by Harry Chester, Inc.

Produced by Richard Feiner and Company, Inc.
Copyright © 1975 by Richard Feiner and Company, Inc.
by permission of Hal Roach Studios, Inc.
All rights reserved. Printed in the U.S.A.

First Edition
10 9 8 7 6 5 4 3 2 1

United States rights exclusively controlled by Richard Feiner
and Company, Inc.; all other territorial rights exclusively
controlled by Overseas Programming Companies, Ltd.

No part of this book may be reproduced without the express
written permission of the copyright proprietor. All rights
other than this publication are specifically reserved by
Feiner/Overseas as recorded in the Copyright Office of the
United States of America, Volume 1445 Pages 417-425 and
Volume 1511 Pages 226-230-A.

No part of this book may be reproduced or transmitted in any
form or by any means, electronic or mechanical, including
photocopy, recording, or any information storage and
retrieval system now known or to be invented, without permission
in writing from the publishers, except by a reviewer who wishes
to quote brief passages in connection with a review written for
inclusion in a magazine, newspaper, or broadcast.

Published simultaneously in Canada by Clarke, Irwin & Company
Limited, Toronto and Vancouver.
ISBN 0-525-14395-5
Library of Congress Catalog Card Number: 75-10078

Contents

For Stan and Ollie

Marcel Marceau

I have no favorite Laurel and Hardy film. They all glow of mastership and grace and style. The films were not of equal merit, of course; maybe *Fra Diavolo* had the greatest unity of them all. It was sort of a funny Robin Hood. Stan and Ollie were launched in that film like two characters coming from another planet—like Don Juan and Leporello, Don Quixote and Sancho Panza, Don Juan and Sganarelle, the Four Musketeers—and the three Marx Brothers. Like these, Laurel and Hardy were unique and they were partnered—one being the counterpart of the other.

Chaplin and Keaton were alike in that one was at odds with the police and Victorian society; the other was at odds with props, women, or the absurdity of life itself. The first a Shakespearean fool, and the other a Greek or Roman mime philosopher and moralist.

Stan and Ollie were, of course, very much alike: two fools of God—two wonderful clowns at odds with themselves in the framework of a Victorian society which we still inhabit in many ways. They knew how to slide over a banana peel, how to make reality absurd. They encountered women, props, animals, logic, and a ludicrous society. They dealt with cops and cars and trains and threw custard pies. They were combined theatre and music-hall pantomimists, serving the comedy film as godfathers during a golden age when everything seemed possible and where actions spoke louder than words. They did it with style, grace, and naïve foolishness. They knew beautifully how to contrast characters, and what those characters meant. Ollie was the older, wise brother, the fatherly figure trying to prevent Stan from meeting the catastrophe, but he was always trapped himself; and yet he always had a gentle way of getting out of a situation, even when he was outraged or full of despair. Even when he was in trouble with Stan, fighting him, Ollie kept his gentleness.

They were both the victims of Stan's foolishness, and their sweet-sour battle kept them inseparable. We cannot conceive them one without the other, and like the yin and yang in Chinese philosophy, they are the black and white of life. They evoke our own absurdities, which make us laugh instead of cry; they remind us that if life is a tragedy for men who think, it is a comedy for those who feel—like most of *us* who believe that there is an answer for every question, even the unsolved—because there is an endless end to every situation. Laurel and Hardy knew that it was essential never to really end their films because they knew we would meet them in new adventures each time, and would not a real ending be a tragedy for their glorious buffoonery? They did light comedy with the style and grace and finesse of great clowns—which indeed they were. They combined awkwardness and graceful balletic movements—with beautiful lightness as Ollie's keynote, and slow-motion grace as Stan's. Their timing was exquisite.

In a way, Stan and Ollie exist to convince us that, like the Greek and Roman pantomimists and the commedia dell'arte actors, the fools of God are still well and alive forever. And they are alive as long as there will be societies and men dwelling in a world full of contrasts where violence, dreams, frustrations, and joys cling together in an inseparable battle of light and shadow. But Stan and Ollie preferred to believe that life is sweet despite the fact they knew what brutal faces our good world presents to us. Therefore they will be forever enjoyed by the child in us all; and they will so remain with all men who believe (like myself) that it is necessary to laugh at ourselves whenever we slide over a banana peel or get kicked on the bottom. Therefore, long live Stan Laurel and Oliver Hardy—our brothers, our friends!

Orson Bean

My name is Orson Bean, Harvard '48, Yale, nothing. I'm an enormous fan of Laurel and Hardy. Recently, in France in a survey, Laurel and Hardy were picked as the country's favorite comedians—even over Charlie Chaplin. Sometimes people are amazed to hear something like this because while they think of Laurel and Hardy as amusing they don't think of them as great. Somehow Laurel and Hardy have missed having snob appeal until relatively recently. People like W. C. Fields and, of course, Chaplin and Buster Keaton are idolized as great masters, and Laurel and Hardy are looked at as just funny fellows. But there has been a small, growing group of people who think that Laurel and Hardy are the greatest. This is one of the reasons for the emergence of the group I cofounded, The Sons of the Desert.

Jack Benny

Laurel and Hardy were two very funny gentlemen. Their humor will always be great because they do not rely on jokes. Instead, by placing themselves into basic situations and then having something go wrong, they are understood by people of all ages and all walks of life. They have been, excluding Charlie Chaplin, the most popular—and the most universal—comedians. Jokes may become outdated, but the type of comedy Laurel and Hardy did will always live with us.

Peter Bogdanovich

Who couldn't like Laurel and Hardy!! My favorite film is *Big Business,* I think.... The one I usually like best is the one I've seen most recently. After all, they were almost always at least wonderful.

Lenny Bruce

Another two guys that were great—Laurel and Hardy. Visual kind of comedy—great. Laurel and Hardy make Bud Abbott and Lou Costello look like... well, the comparison is like a Rolls-Royce with a Volkswagen, you know. You remember Lou Costello. The fact that he's passed away doesn't make him a better comedian.... His concept of comedy was humility, you know (*shouting in a high-pitched voice*), the little-boy kind of thing. Similar to Jerry Lewis who's a complete farce, you know (*does a quick imitation*), so he doesn't make it at all. But the relationship that Laurel and Hardy had was so delightful. And such a hard thing to do. There, if you watch them and start to analyze, is a love between two men that never smacks of any homosexuality. It's a delight, you really feel a sincere love there. They slept together in bed, but there was never anything lascivious or lewd. It was just a nice, simple light thing. With Stan saying (*imitating*), "We've got to shuffle off to Buffalo, Ollie, or we'll get in a whole lot of trouble." And the other guy so pompous all the time with, "Will you stop that, stupid?," with great takes to the camera. And also very ludicrous. You know the fat one would go, "All right, you stupid over there, how do you spell needle?" "Oh, well, needle is n-e-i—" "There's no *i* in needle." "Then you must have got hold of a bad needle." Completely wacked out, you know. But they're nice.

Eddie Cantor

It is their seriousness that strikes me most forcibly. They play everything as if it might be *Macbeth* or *Hamlet.* That, to me, has always been a true sign of comic genius. In addition they have two very important things going for them: one is the utter frustration of Hardy; and the other is the one-beat-behind-every-other-person's-thinking of Stan. He was always late, and always wrong, but underneath that frightened face, we always get the idea that he loved Ollie.

Hans Conried

It's interesting that Laurel and Hardy were never really publicized. Evidently publicity was not as effective as it should have been at that time, and they were—particularly in this country where they worked most—least appreciated. They did well. Financially they were a success, but actually the critical awards did not come to them. In Spanish-speaking countries, they were enormous. In England, they were regarded highly... In our craft, the presumption on their part of what we call telegraphing—letting the audience know what's coming—was astonishing. Laurel and Hardy would really telegraph a joke. You could see it coming three minutes before! One would tell the other, "loosen your suspenders," and the pants would come half down. Then, "extend the belt line," and he would draw the pants forward. And then you would *know* that he was going to reach over and get that bucket of cold water and dump it down the front of the other's pants. And *that* presumption no other clown, no other comedians, would have dared take.

Lou Costello

They were the funniest comedy team in the world.

Leslie Halliwell
(Author of *The Filmgoer's Companion.*)

Times were bad in the 1930s, all over the world, and working-class people depended heavily on jokes. Especially in the north of England, it seemed that a good laugh would help to blow away all the hardships that unemployment brought, and there were cinemas that thrived, at fourpence a time, on showing nothing but comedies, presenting in effect a repertory of famous star comedians: Gracie Fields (yes, getting laughs then), Leslie Fuller, Leon Errol, Duggie Wakefield, Will Hay, George Formby, Frank Randle, Buster Keaton, Arthur Askey, Jack Hulbert, Ralph Lynn and Tom Walls, Wheeler and Woolsey, and a score of others. We enjoyed them all, thoroughly. But our affection and love were reserved for one particular couple, two middle-aged, dark-suited, bowler-hatted fellows who strode regularly and cheerfully into our lives like visiting foolish uncles, accompanied by a silly tune called "The Dance of the Cuckoos."* They made a few features, but were most often seen in shorts of two or three reels, shorts which were advertised in letters as big as the feature and which, after a run in the town center, were fought for by all the suburban cinemas so that you could probably, as a regular cinema-goer, arrange to see each one five or six times if you liked. We remember that the ABC's publicity man once hit on a particularly happy turn of phrase. "In addition," the advertisement read, "we have pleasure in presenting our dear old friends, Mr. Laurel and Mr. Hardy." That was all. Not even the title of their latest adventure was given: it wasn't necessary. Stan and Ollie were funny and sympathetic whatever they were doing, even if, like members of the family, they were just being themselves. Nice, gentle, simple people were Stan and Ollie, and it did us a power of good every month or so to renew our acquaintance with them....

*Also known informally as "The Ku-Ku Song."

...Once seen, Stan and Ollie could never be forgotten, for they were satisfyingly all of a piece...Is there really less to savor in the adventures of this pair than in such acknowledged classics as Quixote or Boswell or Pickwick?

T. Marvin Hatley

(Musical director for Roach, composer of Laurel and Hardy's theme "The Dance of the Cuckoos," and much of their other music.)

A long time ago—those happy days. The Roach lot was a small one, and everybody knew each other and *liked* each other.

I knew Stan and Babe well, of course—Stan better than Babe because Stan was very much on the creative end of things. Also, Babe was much more of a private man than Stan. As is fairly well known, Stan was the principal source of the Laurel and Hardy gags. And what a pleasant, friendly, sympathetic man he was! Stan had what you could call a *sweet* personality, very humble. We had the boys over to our house several times. I remember when my wife was serving one of her deservedly famous spaghetti dinners to the boys, she naturally set down a big dish of it before Babe and a smaller dish before Stan. She went out to the kitchen and when she returned, the plates were switched. Stan had the big one, Babe, the small one. I guess Babe was trying to lose weight.

Whenever they played any musical instruments in the films, I'd play for them. I can play any instrument in the orchestra, more or less—so if Stan played the tuba, I'd record the tuba, or if Babe played the piccolo, I'd do that. In *Saps at Sea,* I did the trombone for Stan. I was *on* camera playing the accordion in *Bonnie Scotland.* I'd teach the boys how to hold the instruments so it would look good.

It was such fun. Stan and Babe used to call me down on the set to play for them between takes. Stan loved to sing the old English songs. I'd play the piano for him—and Babe would join in and sing tenor. Happy days.

Patsy Kelly

It would take me about 25 years to tell anyone why I love Laurel and Hardy. Number one, I had the great privilege and honor of working with them on the great Hal Roach lot. I knew them both, as well, and in addition to being two of the funniest men who ever lived, they were the kindliest. Not to like Laurel and Hardy you would have to be very much nuts, because they were absolutely wonderful, both off and on screen. Stan was an absolute genius. How they helped Thelma Todd and me when we were making our pictures! They would come on the set, tear up our indifferent scripts, and give us all sorts of practical suggestions—do this, do that—and the results were wonderful. Everybody on the lot loved those two great, great men. When I worked with them on *Pick a Star,* I was scared to death, a little bit in awe, but no need to be. They were so marvelous to me. As to my favorite film of theirs, it was *Swiss Miss.* The business of carrying the piano over the bridge and meeting the

ape—I must have laughed at that for about six months. If I ever got blue, I'd think of that, and that was it—happy again. I must have seen it 100 times. There is a cliché still floating around, and it's still true, and I apply it to Laurel and Hardy: the bigger they are, the nicer they are.

Danny Kaye

BOB HOPE: Ladies and gentlemen...To present an Honorary Award for the Academy...and one with special meaning for those of us who live by laughter...a man who has lived with the best of it....Mr. Danny Kaye.

(*Applause.*)

Music: Kaye play-on—"Anatole of Paris." (Kaye enters.)

KAYE: Ladies and Gentlemen: When the fat man with the derby hat and the tall, thin man with the sad face first came on the screen together, it was way back in 1926. They made the world laugh for 24 years—24 years—and they made us laugh because in them, we kind of saw ourselves: ridiculous, frustrated, up to our necks in trouble—but nevertheless, ourselves. Oliver Hardy delicately tipped his derby hat with his pudgy little fingers and left us a little while back. But the thin, sad-faced one, from whose fertile mind sprang many of the universally humorous notions that have been borrowed so freely by the comedians who have followed—he's still with us. Unhappily, he isn't well enough to be here with us this evening, but I'm very proud indeed to have been sent forth from the Board of Governors with this Award for creative pioneering in the field of comedy—presented to one of the really great men of our chosen profession, Mr. Stan Laurel.

Presented by. Danny Kaye
Academy Awards
1960

Jesse Lasky, Jr.

I have a lot of feelings about them. My wife, Pat Silver, knew them much better than I did. She was a neighbor of Stan Laurel. She said that he was the kindest, most creative, wonderful man that she had ever known. She worked very closely with him on the first live television series that was ever done in Hollywood, called *Mabel's Fables,* which she wrote, produced, and starred in. It was nominated for an Emmy award. He contributed only as a friend and neighbor. He helped her out of the experience and the techniques of British pantomime...Stan and Babe were kind, gentle, and wonderfully warm...

I think, with the glories that are showered on the Bob Hopes of our time, what a pity that some of this wasn't contributed to Stan Laurel. And maybe the only way that people are rewarded is to form close affiliations with the White House. I don't know . . . I don't want to sound bitter about this, but I think that some people have been honored to the eyeballs, and others have been neglected terribly.

George Marshall

These were two wonderful men. Stan was so marvelous, so creative. He was always very close to the director, and when he came up with some of those superb inventive gags of his, it was always something which improved the picture tremendously. He helped the picture build. In the days I worked at Roach, we did the shooting in strict continuity. This, of course, was a lot more expensive than the usual process of shooting all the kitchen scenes at one time, all the porch scenes at one time, and so on. But we realized that, for *us*, we really had to go from one gag to another naturally, gag number two frequently springing out of gag number one. So there was a natural evolution there in the Laurel and Hardy pictures we did. They grew organically. Of course one *could* shoot out of sequence and make the tie-ins later if one so desired, but it was more fun doing it the direct way we did—growing sequence by sequence. That is why I think those pictures, for all their incredibilities, are so natural. And having Babe and Stan in them made them so good.

Groucho Marx

You ask me if I find them funny. I don't find them at all these days, but when I do, I find them funny. And I find them funny, among other reasons, because Stan Laurel had a skinny neck and Oliver Hardy a fat stomach. As to why they are *really* funny, I leave that to the professors and the savants. I gave up trying to find out why people are funny a long, long time ago.

Romeo Muller
(Prominent television and film writer.)

Why do I like Laurel and Hardy?

Like is a totally irrelevant word. Even *love* is inadequate. I revere clowns. A great comic personality is the most human of all artistic creations: for humanity, really, is not much more than a rather disorganized parade of all the "little fellows" whom the great clowns represent. And, to me, Laurel and Hardy are the most human of all. They seldom win. Most of us seldom win.

Stan and Ollie are a part of me: Like them, I stumble from one "nice mess" into another. And when I come up with some improbable solution, the Stan in me always agrees with an enthusiastic "That's a *good* idea!" The Ollie reassures with a hearty "It coitainly *is!*" And off I go again.

Chaplin, Keaton, Lloyd, and the others usually come out on top for the final fade-out. Very gratifying. But I somehow know that, unlike Charlie, I am never going to clean up Easy Street; I'm never going to strike gold, reform Tomania, capture the Kaiser, or walk off into the sunrise with a smiling Paulette Goddard. It is far more likely that, after all my good intentions have gone awry, I'll end up flattened between two streetcars or up to my ears in that astounding mud puddle which always awaits halfway down the block.

But, like the boys, I know that one way or another I'll always be back with more "good ideas"—dead certain that I'll get that piano to the top of the hill.

Yes, Laurel and Hardy mean a lot to me. In days like these, when the illusion of "winning" seems so all important, they make the inevitability of losing—and then continuing—so touching and sublime.

George Stevens

I have a deeply warm spot in my heart for Stan and Babe—as artists and as men.

They were very important to me because as I was coming into the film world, so were they—and we learned together. I was 21 when I started with them. The people at Roach kiddingly referred to me as the Jackie Coogan cameraman because of my youth—and I *was* young.

It was a wonderfully warm world there at Roach's. Laurel and Hardy were especially warm: they didn't dislike anyone. No jealousies there. Babe Hardy was my closest friend in the world at that time; indeed, it was in his house that I first met the girl who became my wife.

Some time before beginning at Roach, I had seen Stan work, and I thought he was one of the unfunniest comedians around. He wore his hair in a high pompadour and usually played a congenital dude or slicker. He laughed and smiled too much as a comedian. He needed and wanted laughs, so much that he made a habit of laughing at himself as a player, which is extremely poor comic technique. How he changed! In those very early days he was obviously searching for a workable form and formula.

I photographed one of the first films Stan and Babe did for Roach, *Slipping Wives*. Then I was cameraman on some of their others of note, *Sugar Daddies, The Second Hundred Years, Hats Off, Putting Pants on Philip, Battle of the Century, Leave 'Em Laughing, The Finishing Touch, Their Purple Moment*—and those two classics, *Big Business* and *Two Tars*. I did over 25 of their films, and the atmosphere while making them can best be put in the phrase "No sweat." It was *all* fun.

Nobody at the studio imagined Stan and Babe were going to catch on so powerfully. When they made their first hit, *The Second Hundred Years*—a film which required them, as convicts, to shave off their hair—the studio waited anxiously for the hair to grow again so they could start the next one and cash in on their new popularity. Finally, after about three impatient weeks of waiting, the studio said to hell with the hair, we'll go with the next picture anyway.

It's interesting how the very fact of architecture would help shape the films. Then popular in California were duplexes with two contiguous doors, and they could evoke all kinds of contrasts and comedic comings and goings. I recall especially the double duplex with *four* doors set together with which we had so much fun in *Hats Off*. We would take the comedy right to homes in the area.

Today whenever I drive through Cheviot Hills, I keep looking for the home we wrecked in *Big Business.* It's probably still there on one of the side streets.

Two Tars we shot on what was then a country road right in front of the Santa Monica airport. That smashing-cars sequence took us only five or six days to shoot. We really did a lot in little time then, and without any idea that it was such great comedy. We did get an inkling of that, though, when we previewed *Two Tars* at the Oriental Theatre on Sunset. We ran the film, and the audience wouldn't let it go. They cheered, and applauded, and applauded—an altogether astounding reaction, it seemed to us at the time. That audience kept clapping until the theatre manager was forced to forgo the feature film (with a very famous star in it, I recall) and run *Two Tars* over again.

As to their work together, Stan was the story man, Babe was the golfer, and Babe liked it that way. One day I walked into the projection room at Roach's, and Stan was the only one there. He was watching some Laurel and Hardy rushes, and as he watched, he howled with laughter. I recall his feet were in the air; he was bicycling them furiously in a reaction of utter merriment. He knew what was good; there was no need for fake modesty. He laughed especially at Babe, and that not only because Babe was such a superb comedian but because Stan had the chance that creative people get so rarely—of seeing his own ideas not only brought to life but brought to life more magnificently than he had ever dared to dream they would be.

There was an economy drive at Roach's about 1930, and a wonderful man there, Ben Shipman, had the unhappy job of firing me. Oddly, this was regarded in a way as my good fortune because during these months everybody on the lot could get only a certain portion of their salary. For reasons of economy, a chunk of your salary was always kept back, to be paid sometime in the future, or, as in my case, when one left the organization. So I got quite a bit of money and the Roach gang told me *I* was the lucky one and that I simply had to throw a party to celebrate.

When I left Roach, Stan gave me a book as a farewell gift. It was evidently something of a Bible for him, *Clowns and Pantomimes* by Maurice Willson Disher. I do no injury to Stan by saying he was not a man for books, but this one he loved and had studied thoroughly. It was a view of comedy from Grock down to the then moderns. The losing of this book was one of the very real disappointments of my life.

I never saw a Laurel and Hardy film I didn't like or one that didn't have something marvelous in it somewhere. (I didn't see many of their later films.) As my career went along, I found comedy wasn't for me—except, that is, their comedy. As time went on, I left comedy, but Laurel and Hardy never left *me.*

Arthur Treacher

Laurel and Hardy were splendid. They were low comedy—broad comedy, if you like—yet very subtle. The thing that made them so good, so important to comedy, is that they played farce comedy in complete sincerity. That is the heart of farce, isn't it? I mean they played it dead straight. It was important to them, what they said. In farce you've got to get people in trouble, you know, and one must play it very straight. There are very few people who can do that anymore. Laurel and Hardy did—and I think they were delicious.

Dick Van Dyke

I first saw Laurel and Hardy when I was about six or seven years old. Thereafter I'd go to the movies every Saturday to see them, sitting right through all afternoon and evening performances until my mother'd come and get me out. Believe it or not, when I was a child I looked exactly like Stan Laurel. Maturity has changed me, but then we were identical. Indeed my *father* looked like Stan too, same ears and all. Everybody in our family did impressions of Stan. And it just happened that I married a woman with a long chin, with a smaller nose than mine, who looked quite a lot like Stan. Obviously I didn't marry her for that reason, but our four children look rather like Stan, too. So that there are *still* a lot of Laurel impressions in our family.

I couldn't really say precisely why Laurel and Hardy's humor attracts me so strongly or why I think they are so funny. But I do have one theory—that there was a hierarchy there: one in power, and the other beneath him, as in all human relationships. But the difference between the one in power and the one not in power was so small that sometimes they tipped the scales over and Stan took charge. This went back and forth, and I think there was something in that which made people laugh.

Another thing: Laurel and Hardy were really a love story—one of the greatest there ever was. I think the basis for their longevity in films was that they obviously loved each other very much. That is what sustained those movies in between the gags. Of course, like children in a fit of pique, they would hit each other, but never to hurt. Their trust and their love was childlike, with a basic underlay of innocence.

There was something almost Christian about the faith and the love they had for each other. They lived life the way it's supposed to be lived, and they showed us it doesn't work—at least not in Western culture.

I never cried at a Charlie Chaplin movie. Everyone else did but I never did. As a child I remember seeing a Laurel and Hardy film in which they had to be separated—and I cried. I don't think anyone has ever worked with children the way Stan and Ollie did. In *Pack Up Your Troubles* everyone wanted to take the little orphan girl away from them and put her in a home. When the boys ran from the law, protecting her—those scenes with the child showed me how much of a childish point of view Stan and Ollie had, particularly Stan and the little girl. They were on the same level, the same level of honesty and sweetness. There was a wholesomeness about it, and surely that's why we as children identified with him.

I consider Stan the greatest of film comedians. The reason is a very simple one. First of all because he got more laughs, both as a performer and as a creator of gags, than almost anybody else in film comedy. Not even Chaplin gets as much laughter, pure *laughter*, as Stan does. Chaplin is great, a genius—but with Chaplin I can always see the technique showing. Lord knows it's great technique, and I admire it very much—but with Stan the technique never shows. *Never.* And that to me is proof that he is a better craftsman than Chaplin —an infinitely better craftsman.

Alphabetical Listing of Laurel & Hardy Film Titles

Preview

This book is offered with an awareness that no single volume can serve as encyclopedic survey of Laurel and Hardy. Nevertheless, the authors are confident that the material covered bears at least the imprimatur of accuracy because of our total access to all Hal Roach Studios files and records. Indeed, most rewardingly, we have had total access to Hal Roach himself, the man ultimately responsible for the creation of Laurel and Hardy—and, praise be, still vigorous in his eighties.

What this book offers is a pictorial overview of the greatest comedy team in film history, together with all pertinent statistics and supplemental information necessary for an understanding of their career. These pages should also serve as a guidebook for those who have seen the films, either soon or late, and who wish their memories of Laurel and Hardy's world reinforced.

Laurel and Hardy were joined by accident and grew by indirection. When they began work as a team at Hal Roach Studios in 1926, they retained pleasant memories of their first professional connection, *Lucky Dog*, a comedy produced by G. M. "Broncho Billy" Anderson in 1917. That was a purely one-film association, and there was little reason at that time for Stan Laurel to think of Oliver Hardy as a possible partner. In fact, then and for some time after, Stan resisted the idea of any potent laugh maker sharing star billing with him. This was the instinctive fear of any performer of that period who had gone through much travail in order to insure an indelible reputation. It is sometimes not realized by those outside show business that performers' touchiness about matters of billing is, on the whole, justified. Vanity is not the basis of this concern but, rather, the understandably deep apprehension of being supplanted by a rival in a profession where security shifts as the sands. Thus Stan Laurel was not by nature inclined to welcome the incursion of Oliver Hardy as a partner in his films. Indeed, in the early 1920s when Stan was making two-reelers for a progressive producer, Joe Rock, Rock made the suggestion that Hardy be made a permanent member of the comedy stock company supporting Stan. Stan resisted this purely out of the traditional apprehensions that a clever comedian "supported" by another clever comedian might find that designation altered to "supplanted." Consequently, the team of Laurel and Hardy did not come into existence for yet another few years.

When it did, the catalyst for the joining was the brilliant director and producer, Leo McCarey, who by the mid-1920s was integrally involved in the creative functions of the Hal Roach Studios. Roach had a unique talent for finding talent—for confirming it and giving it essential opportunities to grow. Born at Elmira, New York, in 1892, Roach had more or less drifted through early life holding a wide range of jobs in a variety of places until he arrived in California in 1913. Immediately he got a job as a cowboy in several Western films for Universal Pictures. Soon aware of the moneymaking potential in what was just then commencing to be the Golden Age of Comedy, Roach founded his own small producing unit and, by judicious use of the talent he found everywhere about him, became a leading film comedy producer by 1920.

In Leo McCarey, Roach had discovered a man with unique abilities for the work in hand. Classic comedy film (Chaplin excepted) is usually not crafted virtuoso style. It is more frequently a compound of gagmen, directors, performers, and special-effects men. Leo McCarey at one time or another had served in all these areas. In supervising many of the films made at the Roach Studios, McCarey wore a great number of creative hats, and not the least of these was that of talent scout. He had seen the work of Oliver Hardy and Stan Laurel at various times during the years immediately following World War I, and when he learned that by a stroke of serendipity both men were under contract to Roach in 1926, he began to assess their qualities for possible teaming. The backgrounds of both men fascinated him.

Stan

Arthur Stanley Jefferson was born June 16, 1890, in Ulverston, a northern English town close to the Scottish border. His father, Arthur J. ("A.J.") Jefferson, was a total showman, having served as actor, director, playwright, manager, and all-around theatrical entrepreneur in many English cities. His wife, Stan's mother, was Madge Metcalfe, an actress of distinction in the rather dreadful plays A. J. wrote across the years. Yet for all their florid excitements, A. J.'s melodramas were great audience pleasers and utterly typical of their day. They

13

Absolute unknowns at the time, Stan Laurel and Charlie Chaplin on their way to the United States during the 1910 tour of the Karno Pantomime Company. Left to right, rear: Al Austin, Fred Palmer, Bert Williams, George Semon, Frank Melroy; center row: Stan, Fred Karno, Jr., Charlie Chaplin (sporting the life preserver of their vessel, S.S. *Cairnroma*), Arthur Dandoe; first row: "Mickey" Palmer, Mike Asher, Amy Minister (who was to marry Alf Reeves, the company manager and, later, Chaplin's), ship's captain.

were the staple fare at the theatres A. J. owned, but Stan rarely watched them. He went only to the early part of each evening's program, to the curtain raiser: the farce or one-act comedy sketch that invariably preceded the evening's chief offering.

A. J., knowing firsthand the career perils of an actor's life, made a point of encouraging Stan to think of theatrical management as a future. He thought he had something to offer the boy, because after years of touring the Jefferson family settled down in Glasgow where A. J. leased the prestigious Metropole Theatre. Stan, at the gentle insistence of his father, became an assistant manager there with the tacit understanding that he would one day take over the Jefferson enterprises. But the youngster had a different plan in mind.

Years later, in speaking of his schooling, Stan said,

I was more or less born a comedian, I think. I can't recall a time when I wasn't kidding around in class (or out of it), and that, perhaps more than anything else, made me the dreadful student that I was. In my earlier days, Dad and Mum were always on the move, and I spent much time in boarding schools where I suspect I found relief from loneliness in being the class clown. This must have been an inborn talent inherited from my dad who, although he acted principally in melodramas, loved and wrote comedy and acted in farces as well. I was much interested, by the way, in getting a copy of my birth record from Somerset House, which a fan sent me not long

ago. In addition to all my birth statistics, I notice that my dad put down for his occupation: "Comedian." Seeing that pleased me very much.

As a schoolboy, I was even encouraged by the teachers to be funny. One of the masters particularly, a man named Bates, used to invite me down to his room at night where he and other teachers would get together over several spots of whiskey and let me entertain them. I enjoyed that, but I'm very much afraid it affected my progress as a scholar. In any case, my boyhood idols were people like Dan Leno, the great music-hall comedian, who could be droll and ridiculous and pathetic all at the same time. I made up my mind not long after we moved permanently to Glasgow that I would become a professional comedian even though I suspected my dad would not approve.

In 1906 Stan crafted a comedy act largely derived from favorite music-hall comedians he had seen, and so armed, requested an audition at A. E. Pickard's Glasgow Museum, a miscellaneous penny gallery and peep show which boasted a tiny theatre in back. Pickard, an old friend of A. J.'s, assuming that the boy came to him with parental approval, gave Stan the chance to present his wares to a scanty audience one May evening. By pure accident A. J. decided to visit Pickard's that night and what he saw both appalled and delighted him. He was distressed that Stan's act—a weird mélange of songs, jokes, and unintentionally eccentric dancing—

14

was completely unoriginal. But A. J. was greatly taken with his boy's easy grace and skillful pantomime. It made the thirdhand material quite palatable. In taking a curtain call, Stan bowed graciously to his minuscule audience and froze with horror when he saw his father leaning against the rear entrance to the theatre.

He need not have worried. A. J. had not realized the depth of Stan's feelings for the stage. Forthrightly, he gave his son the most practical form of encouragement in his power: he cast about among his friends in "the profession" for performing opportunities. One of A. J.'s friends, the producer of Levy and Cardwell's Pantomime Company, hired Stan as assistant stage manager, callboy, and supernumerary. In 1907, Stan's first year on tour, the company performed *Sleeping Beauty,* and Stan gradually worked his way up the ladder of supporting roles until he became featured comedian. For several seasons he played in almost every kind of theatrical enterprise—as actor in melodrama and farce; as dancer/comedian in music hall—until he found work with a group that afforded a fitting milieu for his talents —the Fred Karno Company. Karno, a man with a lust for laughter, organized a series of theatrical troupes that specialized in wordless plays—total pantomimic presentations in which various vignettes of English life were presented in rich comic style.

When Stan joined the leading Karno troupe in 1910, he reveled in the opportunity to use his total bodily instrument for laughter's sake. This was acting which blended the craft and the art of a circus clown, Shakespearean buffoon, and ballet dancer. Karno's was the most thoroughgoing school of comedy any comic could wish for, and the richness of Karno's performing talent can be verified by mentioning the name of but one of its leading comedians, Charles Spencer Chaplin, then an unknown. Karno was so impressed with Stan that he made him Chaplin's understudy on the company's first American vaudeville tour late in 1910.

Stan quickly became Chaplin's closest friend in the company, and the two shared living quarters all during the long tour through the United States on the prestigious Sullivan-Considine circuit. In addition to understudying Chaplin, Stan at one time or another played almost every role in the company's feature attraction, *A Night in an English Music Hall.* It was in this act that Stan's superb pantomimic skills were given their fullest opportunities to mature and structure themselves. When the Karno troupe was reengaged to tour America in 1912, Stan again understudied Chaplin, luxuriating in the assignment. During this tour Chaplin was tapped by Mack Sennett for films, and the Karno company's bookings dwindled in consequence. All the actors were given the option of a return ticket to England or severance pay on the spot, allowing them to stay in the States and look for work. Stan chose to stay, going into American vaudeville in the guise of—Charlie Chaplin. Together with Alice and Baldwin Cooke, Stan did a three-act that featured himself as the newly popular Chaplin tramp. "I had little trouble doing Charlie," Stan said. "His movements and his walk were in my bones."

Stan spent more than a decade as a vaudevillian either with the Cookes or as a double-act with an Australian dancer-singer, Mae Dahlberg, who suggested to Stan (after he said he was worried because his name contained 13 letters) that he change his surname to Laurel. He did so, and she assumed the name as his common-law wife. Mae Laurel was unable to obtain a divorce from her spouse in Australia and, as many vaudeville partners did at the time in order to consolidate expenses, she and Stan became a team in every

sense. It was a decision he was later to regret, but at the time, as he said later, "it seemed a hell of a fine idea." After the wearying tensions of what seemed an unendingly peripatetic life, Stan was relieved to find a real home in Los Angeles in 1926. It was the year he signed his first long-term contract with Hal Roach.

"Babe"

Norvell Hardy—the Oliver was added later—was born to a distinguished Georgian family on January 18, 1892. In his natal city, Harlem, Norvell's dad, Oliver, was a leading figure—a popular lawyer and politician. Mr. Hardy died when Norvell was young and the family was forced to live on slim resources. They moved to nearby Madison, Georgia, where Mrs. Hardy bought a small hotel. The boy, too young to work, developed there a habit which was to remain with him the rest of his life.

"As a child," he said in later years,

I got into a habit that I still have. One could call it lobby watching. I sit in the lobby of any hotel where I stay and I just watch people. I like to watch people. Once in a while someone will ask me where Stan and I dreamed up the characters we play in the movies. They seem to think that these two fellows aren't like anybody else. I know they're *dumber* than anyone else, but there are plenty of Laurels and Hardys in the world. Whenever I travel, I still am in the habit of sitting in the lobby and watching the people walk by—and I can tell you I see many Laurels and Hardys. I used to see them in my mother's hotel when I was a kid: the dumb, dumb guy who never has anything bad happen to him—and the smart, smart guy who's dumber than the dumb guy only he doesn't know it.

Young Norvell derived his first name from his mother's maiden name, a potent one in his area of the South. Following his father's death, he honored that memory by becoming Oliver Norvell Hardy. Family pride was deeply impregnated in the boy, and when years later in films he would occasionally use his full name in self-introduction, it was always done with a sense of prideful dignity even if the circumstances were humorous. "I like the sound of my name," Hardy said on occasion, "and one thing I want to emphasize. I never use my name to make fun of it. I'm proud of my name—all of it." 15

The early life of Oliver Hardy is vividly recalled by his sister, Mrs. Elizabeth Sage of Atlanta. "Norvell was the baby of the family," she recalls.

He was really a beautiful boy, had such a handsome face. In fact, I think he was handsome all of his life even if he was heavy. He did use to eat a lot as a boy, he was awfully fond of his food. I can remember that he weighed 250 pounds at the age of 14. That was when he was sent away to military school at Milledgeville. He didn't like it there because all the boys used to make jokes about fat boys, and he didn't like it one little bit. But even at that, he had the sweetest disposition, and he was always such a sportsman about everything. He could stand up to a lot of kidding and he could hand out the kidding, too. And he had a mind of his own. I can remember a few times that, when he was at military school during the drill period, he would just get so tired that he would simply lie down flat on the ground and not budge an inch. They just couldn't move him! He was tired and that was that! The headmaster at the academy (he was a great friend of Mother's) used to call him "the funniest boy in the world." At commencement exercises one year, the undergraduates put on a "Who Killed Cock Robin?" skit. At the climax of the skit, when the chorus came out singing "Who Killed Cock Robin?," Norvell came out in costume and sang in his glorious tenor voice, "I killed Cock Robin! I tolled the bell because I could pull the rope. *I am the bull!*" And, there he was, so big and with such a lovely voice that it just broke up the proceedings right there. Everybody just leaned back and howled. He was such a funny thing and such a dear thing. Even at that time he displayed a wonderful stage presence and personality.

He could get angry, though. He would take kidding about his size but only up to a certain point. Back home he was always asked to umpire the local baseball games because of the good show he put on. There used to be a saying around town that they'd close the banks to see Norvell umpire. Well, sometimes he would make some decisions that weren't popular with the crowd and the crowd would start calling him Fatty and Fats, and Norvell would just stomp off and threaten to go home if the crowd kept on. They never let him go. He was the life of the town.

As I said, he always ate a lot. Once he ran away from military school because he said they didn't feed him enough. He refused to go back until his mother had made him 20 baking-powder biscuits, which he ate at one sitting! I think that maybe he always ate so much because he missed the father he lost when he was ten.

At the age of eight and under careful supervision, Oliver was given permission to join a troupe of entertainers, Coburn's Minstrels, who had heard of his charming voice. He toured with them for a few weeks but, despite the great success he met as a boy soprano, homesickness drove him back to the family. For a time he was a serious student of voice at the Atlanta Conservatory of Music. However, he did not think of becoming a professional entertainer until years later, when his career as a law student at the University of Georgia was aborted by lack of interest. In 1910 when the Hardys moved to Milledgeville, 18-year-old Oliver entered the world of films—via the box office. That year he opened the first movie theatre ever to be operated in Milledgeville, and he sustained the operation until 1913.

Watching the many short comedy films that played his theatre convinced Oliver that his abilities as something of a town jester could be put to profitable use. Besides, that kind of work looked like *fun,* and Oliver Hardy was wedded to fun. In 1913 he gave up the theatre and went to Jacksonville, Florida, home of Lubin Motion Pictures, and almost immediately found work as an actor. For the Lubin one-reel comedies he was always cast as a "heavy," the villain with impossibly dark brows and bushy moustache who was always properly chastised 40 seconds before fade-out. It was at this time that he received his permanent nickname. Along with most of the Lubin studio personnel, Oliver had his hair cut at the shop of a voluble Italian barber. This gentleman had decidedly epicene qualities, and he greatly enjoyed patting powder into Oliver's freshly shaved cheeks, murmuring "Nice-a bab-ee. Nice-a bab-ee." The actors picked it up, eventually selecting "Babe" as the Hardy cognomen.

For five years Babe worked in Florida and occasionally in New York for Lubin, Vim Comedies, and Edison Pictures. By the end of 1918 he had moved permanently to California where he supported prominent comedians like Jimmy Aubrey, Billy West, and Larry Semon. Mostly free-lancing, he found his way into many films and made the acquaintance of Leo McCarey on the Roach lot. By 1926 Babe was under long-term contract to that studio.

"The Boys"

"I never much referred to them as Stan and Babe, Stan and Ollie or Laurel and Hardy," said Leo McCarey.

Really, to me they were always The Boys. By the time I got engrossed with the possibility of their being a team, they had become almost like my sons—or maybe my *brothers* would be a little more accurate. My crazy brothers from the next town over.

By 1926 Stan was pretty fed up with vaudeville trouping, and he welcomed the job at Roach's not only because it gave him a permanent and well-paying base but also because he was most welcome there as a gagman and director, in addition to his status as a performer. In fact, he did so well as a creative person behind the camera that he actually gave up acting and didn't mind it a bit. Hardy was performing, of course, and he enjoyed it very much. We had a very good stock company of comedians there in 1926, all of them about equal in talent, so rather than featuring or starring one or two of the top best, we labeled our pictures the Comedy All Stars series. Stan was directing one of these films, *Get 'Em Young,* and Babe Hardy was playing the butler in it. One evening, Babe—who was a very good cook—scalded himself severely while preparing a leg of lamb—and the studio asked Stan to step in and replace Babe.

Stan resisted because he was enjoying work behind the camera but eventually the head of production, a very clever man named F. Richard Jones, who had taught Stan many things about moviemaking, persuaded Stan to play the role. Persuaded him with an increase in salary, I might add. Jones saw Stan's great potential as a performer, and by 1927 Stan was reconciled to being a comedian essentially, although he certainly never gave up his function as a gagman. Nineteen twenty-seven is when I come into the story. When I contributed—as I always did—to the gag and story sessions of the Comedy All Stars, I commented time to time on the particular suitability of Hardy as Stan's comic foil. They seemed to fit so well together, I said—not only because they were such contrasting figures but also because they seemed to have this solid instinct that only top-flight comedians have of the *reality* underlying a gag. They were both superb actors, of course, and could have played serious stuff quite easily—and very well.

So, I encouraged their getting larger parts in the films. Gradually, their parts grew larger and the parts of the other players grew smaller. This was the evolution of the team of Laurel and Hardy.

Their partnership flourished all those many years for lots of reasons, but it is important to remember that once they began to move forward together as a unit, they had the great good fortune to have as half of their membership one of the greatest gagmen of this or any other century. Stan was a comedy genius, and although he certainly used gagmen and employed directors, *he* was really the creative spirit behind the making of their pictures. Fortunately, Babe didn't care too much about structuring the gags and the like—even though he did help at times. I say "fortunately" because if they were both highly creative in that way discord might have arisen. But it never did. They were in harmony right from the very start, and they maintained that harmony right up to the end.

The Films

Laurel and Hardy made 105 films.* A pictorial survey of these follows, in release-date sequence, together with basic plots and gag highlights. The photographs used are mostly studio publicity pictures, shot by a still photographer either just before or just after the actual shooting of the movie scene depicted. We have tried to use production stills as much as possible, for two reasons: first, they are infinitely better photographically than frame blow-ups with their grainy murk; second—and vitally—the Roach still photographer stayed very close to the cinematographer. (See note on page 317.) Because a still photograph has a slightly different rubric of placement and lens scope from a movie frame, the scenes represented here are a bit different from the same scene as it appears in the film. Moreover, there are odd times when the stills are deliberately unrepresentative of anything in the film. These stills (which are so designated in the text) were made for two reasons. First, when some stills were sent out before film release, the Roach Studios did not want to tip their hand and give away a perfectly good gag, so they posed a stimulating still quite unlike the action occurring at that point. Second, some stills were posed on the spur of the moment purely to accommodate a gag Stan or someone thought of for the characters. But, in general, these stills show the actual progress of the story.

Each film summary begins with an evaluation of the film's worth, using the following symbols:

Excellent

Above average   Average   Below average

*Laurel made 76 films without Hardy (1916-1928); Hardy made 213 films without Laurel (1914-1928, 1939, and 1950).

Since these ratings are made by the authors—individuals shamelessly devoted to Laurel and Hardy—there is an inevitable amount of inbuilt prejudice. Notwithstanding, the authors claim a certain selectivity by registering themselves as Laurel and Hardy buffs, *not* as Laurel and Hardy fans. The distinction is a very real one. Fans are massively infatuated with their love object; buffs are by their very nature selective and critical— sometimes contentiously so. Or to put it another and perhaps more cogent way: buffs tend to type their letters of admiration; fans *always* scrawl theirs in pencil or battered ball point on lined paper.

It is hoped that these evaluations will be of practical value to those Laurel and Hardy buffs—and fans—who wish to rent or purchase the films for home use and who have forgotten or never learned the comparative artistic value of each. It is, of course, a source of great comfort to all admirers of Laurel and Hardy that the majority of the films are available for purchase in either 8mm or 16mm. The best source for such purchases is Blackhawk Films, Davenport, Iowa, 52808. A postcard asking for their catalogue will receive a prompt reply from Blackhawk, the exclusive licensee of Hal Roach Studios.

The Laurel and Hardy World

We wonder what a person who has never seen Laurel and Hardy might make of these pages. His reaction would probably be obliquely similar to that of a non-reader of music confronting the score of Beethoven's Fifth Symphony. The words "Well, here's another fine mess you've gotten me into!" seen coldly in print can no more suggest Ollie's frustrated and warmly astringent rendering of them than the notes G, G, G, E on paper can reproduce the majesty of Beethoven's utterance.

In looking at the Laurel and Hardy canon, film by film, it is not by any means our intention to recount the plots exegetically, describing every gag or comic moment in full nuance. Words cannot do that. Because our purpose is to serve largely as a focus of memory, and because we wish to be evocative of the spirit rather than the detail of Laurel and Hardy's world, we must immediately foreclose on those who have never seen at least a representative sampling of the films. We are, however, hopeful that nonviewers will at least become aware of the general ambience of Laurel and Hardy's comedy, an awareness (we should hope) conducing to the viewing experience.

There is a basic Laurel and Hardy vocabulary of phrase, gesture, and movement one learns to treasure after repeated viewing. It is mostly repeated viewing that warrants loving and finding funny (and oddly moving, on occasion) Stan's cry or Ollie's look of long-suffering made directly into the camera. Again—therein lies the inadequacy of print and still photograph in fully evoking Laurel and Hardy's world. But let us try.

Stan and Ollie are two supremely brainless, eternally optimistic men, almost brave in their perpetual and impregnable innocence. They certainly have been known to break the law, but almost never with malice aforethought. Their integral selves are probably defined by Cardinal Newman's description of a gentleman as one who never knowingly inflicts pain on another. Stan and Ollie hardly ever inflict pain—and then only when the laws of comedy—gently, in their case—demand otherwise.

If, as Hal Roach insists, all great comedians are essentially babylike, Stan and Ollie eminently qualify. Their childlike charm is embedded in innocence and possesses a characteristic we do not automatically grant all children. That characteristic is niceness. One hesitates to define a nice person because the word has multiple meanings, especially the unpleasant connotation of "milk sop." Stan and Ollie are certainly nice but with full masculine authority. On occasion they do go out on the town in the hope of seeing hootchy-kootchy girls, and at one point in his career Ollie must sadly confess—to himself, in a mirror—that he has "pulled a wild party." Stan can become weavingly, lip-smackingly besotted. Yet the inherent flavor of niceness as commonly understood, of truly sturdy innocence, permeates their world and is their unchanging base.

The Laurel-and-Hardy persona is partially defined by certain comic devices, pet phrases, and pantomimic bits. These are used, but rarely overused, in the films, and come to be character identifications every bit as explicit as the idiosyncrasies of your old Uncle Al. "Visual" comedians (as distinguished from "stand-up" or "talking" comedians) necessarily employ a pantomimic base for their work. They must project their entire bodily instrument to create comedy. Laurel and Hardy had an inbuilt physical contrariety to aid them and they enhanced this ludicrousness with little touches, being very careful never to desert reality. Stan kept his hair short on the sides and back but let it grow long on top to create a natural fright wig through his inveterate gesture of scratching his noggin at moments of shock or wonderment and simultaneously pulling up his hair. To achieve a flat-footed walk, he removed the heels from his shoes (usually Army shoes) and allowed himself to lope along in a wide-spaced step, arms swinging in an eccentric rhythmic cadence. When talking with Ollie, he would frequently look at his pal's forehead instead of his eyes, thereby enhancing his out-of-this-world coloration.

Other Laurel mannerisms:

The eye-blink. Instead of doing the conventional comic "take" of other comedians who rear back in a reaction of astonishment, Stan "takes" very slowly by closing his eyes for a long second, then opening them wide as if his lids had just come unglued. He next arches his eyebrows wide, then narrows them again in a desperate simulation of thought.

Arm-fold-fall. When confronted with a naughtiness he has committed, Stan frequently attempts to fold his arms in defiant self-bolstering. But he is unable to complete the action. He forgets how to hold the pose, and his arms drop helplessly, leaving him even more naked unto his enemies.

The cry. The most tangible evidence of his character's essential childishness, Stan's cry is a full-fashioned lamenting, with eyes screwed up tightly, face contracted in pain, as he wails in babyish high pitch. One of his character's most potent laugh getters, it was, nevertheless, of all Stan's mannerisms, the only one he disliked doing. He retained it simply because it worked.

The rhetoric strangle. When Stan gets into the perilous environs of ratiocination, he is initially bold, then falters and falls. He is capable of formulating sensible thoughts, coming up occasionally with a very good idea, an idea that he explains succinctly to his partner. "Let

18

me have that again," says Ollie, and Stan does—but by this time his brain can hold no more. He delivers his original concept in language so subverted from its original form that it now resembles a scrambled Scrabble board. "I know exactly what you mean!," says a delighted Ollie. (For examples, see *Oliver the Eighth* and *Towed in a Hole.*)

White magic. Stan's cherubic otherworldliness is given comic underscoring by his unbidden forays into magic of a kind children particularly adore—the sudden eruptions of the impossible done with the greatest kind of coolness. When, for example, in *Way Out West,* Stan needs a flame he simply ignites his thumb, holding his clenched fist as if it were a cigarette lighter. He does this with an ease and naturalness that infuriates Ollie to the point of incoherence.

Ollie has equally indelible hallmarks of characterization. In guiding his dumb pal through life's perils, he asks only one recompense—the recompense he firmly believes his greater bulk entitles him to: he must come first. The "You-after-me-Stanley" syndrome is always operative because, in Ollie's simpleminded view, he is not only bigger but considerably smarter than his pal. That this last is palpably untrue and that his insistence on priority inevitably leads to a personal indignity never deters Ollie in the slightest. Ollie is the inevitable leader, he feels, and whatever Ollie feels he feels totally.

Other Hardy mannerisms:

The tie-twiddle. When Stan and/or Ollie commit a faux pas, Ollie has enough understanding of the niceties of life to realize that an acknowledgment must be made. Beaming embarrassment, he coyly wiggles his tie in a propitiatory flutter at the injured party. This is usually accompanied by a melodic titter, which he fondly—and incorrectly—assumes is ingratiating.

The camera-look. Although he does "takes" in the conventional sense—and beautiful they are, too, with feet bursting akimbo and arms wildly flailing—Ollie, like Stan, tends to make his reactions quiet and heartfelt. When he looks into the camera after a Laurel foul-up that has literally brought the ashes down on his head, Ollie takes us into his confidence—sometimes sadly, sometimes with soul-deep resignation, sometimes with glaring frustration. Early in their days as a team, Stan recognized the value of the camera-looks as moments of accommodation to the duration of laughs in the movie house. In editing the films, Stan—by means of intensive previewing of the films in small towns near the studio—discovered the advantage of using Hardy's camera-looks as "holds." In the theatre, a comedian very soon learns how to "hold." When he gets a laugh, he does not begin to speak his next line until the laughter dies. At times a laugh can last for 10, 15, or more seconds. If the comedian "walks through" his laugh, if he speaks during it, his next speech is lost. After sneak-previewing their films and clocking the average duration of strong laughs, Stan took the film back to be edited, either extending or diminishing the footage of Ollie's camera-looks. Thus the "holds" became perfectly functional and the camera-looks insured that dialogue was not buried by laughter.

The derby at rest, the signature. Like a knight proudly holding his plumed helmet, Ollie, after doffing his hat grandiosely, consigns it in a rococo sweep to the curve of his left arm. This is usually the prelude to his superb use of any writing instrument. When Ollie takes a pen in hand, it is celebration, a joyous occasion. After several baroque flourishes in the air, he signs his name as Napoleon must have done—with exquisite pleasure in being just who he is and so identifying that wonderful self. After Ollie signs his name, he pauses, lifts the pen lightly, and then thrusts the nib down sharply to make a period indelible through eternity.

Inescapably, the ideogram for Laurel and Hardy is a pair of derbies. The quasi-British formality of this headgear is in perfect consonance with their bone-bred politeness. Whatever else they are, they are gentlemen—Mr. Laurel and Mr. Hardy. "I'm Mr. Hardy," Ollie properly introduces them (usually to those who couldn't care less), "and this is my friend, Mr. Laurel."

As gentlemen go, their gentleness is literal, and its confrontation with rude adversity provokes that genuinely undefinable thing called laughter. No one—George Meredith and Henri Bergson notwithstanding—has ever satisfactorily explained laughter and the prime emotion (if there is one) underlying it. Whatever that emotion (cognition? certitude?) might be, and whatever Laurel and Hardy's connection with it, there is strong suspicion among many who love film comedy that it has an elemental, kissing-cousin connection with love.

The Roach Years

Laurel and Hardy were unique—literally inimitable. People ask me why I never made another Our Gang series. It's for the same reason I've never produced another Laurel and Hardy series: people like that aren't around anymore.

Laurel and Hardy were absolutely in a class by themselves, and the wonderful thing about it is that their comedy still holds up today, holds up better than most comedy then—forty or fifty years ago.

Babe Hardy was a very good comedian *and* actor. Moreover, all those gestures and mannerisms were things he developed himself. He wasn't interested in the production end as Stan was. Stan was also a writer and director for us and he enjoyed that just as much as performing. Except for Chaplin, there was no better gagman in the business than Stan Laurel. He could always get the most out of every single gag.

There are many reasons why Laurel and Hardy were a great comedy team, but one of the basic reasons is that each was a perfect straight man for the other. Each was individually brilliant as a comedian, yet each could serve as foil for the other. They complemented each other perfectly. Also, you could shoot a gag with one of them, then cut to a close-up of the other, and *his* reaction always got *another* laugh. So you got two laughs instead of just one.

Basically the Stan and Ollie characters were childlike, innocent. The best visual comedians imitate children really. No one could do this as well as Laurel and Hardy, and still be believable. We always strived for that, and we sure must have succeeded—because the world is still laughing at them.

HAL ROACH

The Hal Roach Studios.

Hal Roach's office.

At the heart of the Roach lot, Lake Laurel and Hardy — into which our heroes were dunked more than any others in the course of duty.

Stan's Cheviot Hills, California, estate, 1935.

The Roach back lot.

Stan's recreation room, Cheviot Hills, California. Among the autographed pictures: Babe; Mae West (she always wanted to do a film with Laurel and Hardy); Harry Langdon; Lawrence Tibbett; Charley Chase; and Stan's father, A.J. Jefferson.

Street view, the Roach back lot.

Another street view, the Roach back lot.

Another view, Stan's recreation room. Among the pictures: the 1932 British tour, Stan and Babe with an American Legion bigwig; Stan's dad; Stan and Babe with Buster Keaton and Jimmy Durante; Stan and Babe with Joan Crawford and Douglas Fairbanks, Jr.; stills from *Slipping Wives* and *Babes in Toyland;* Stan in vaudeville days.

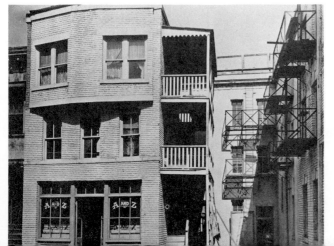

LUCKY DOG

1917

Sunkist (Sun-Lite) Comedy Series / Two reels / Silent / Released 1917-1919 by Metro / Produced by Gilbert M. (Broncho Billy) Anderson as a pilot film / Directed by Jess Robbins.

Brash young man accused of dognapping Stan Laurel / *The girl in Laurel's dream* Florence Gillet / *Masked bandit who confronts Laurel* Oliver Hardy.

The plot of this very slight film can be summed up concisely: Stan finds a stray dog; enters it in a dog show; the owners appear, and he is accused of dognapping. He is forgiven.

Ollie's role, only a bit, is limited to a brief comic-menace encounter with Stan, the star of the film. Chasing his runaway satchel down the street—the dog is inside—Stan captures his quarry at the very spot where stock comic-villain Hardy is waving his gun at a holdup victim. Mistakenly stuffing the loot in Stan's pocket, the bandit releases his frightened victim and spins around to confront the astonished Stan. Enraged, Ollie begins to bounce Stan around like a Yo-Yo. On this enlivening note, they share words on the screen for the first time. Ollie says, by way of a title card, "Put 'em both up, insect, before I comb your hair with lead."

Ollie grabs the wad of money from Stan but Stan, more annoyed than scared, tricks Ollie, snatches the money from him, kicks his burly assailant in the fundament, and scoots off down the sidewalk. Stan scampers through a hole in the fence, and Ollie attempts to follow, getting stuck in the process. Delighting in his opponent's predicament, Stan climbs back over the fence and plants a hearty kick on Ollie's expansive rear end before running off down the street.

Glen Tryon Series / Two reels / Silent / Released December 26, 1926, by Pathé Exchange / Produced by Hal Roach / Directed by Fred L. Guiol / Titles by H.M. Walker / Story by Hal E. Roach.

Orville Glen Tryon / *Mother* Charlotte Mineau / *Father* Rube Clifford / *Sister* Sue O'Neil/Molly O'Day / *Theda Bara* Herself / *Our Gang* Mickey Daniels, Scooter Lowry, Allen (Farina) Hoskins, Jackie Condon, Jay R. (Skinny) Smith, Johnny Downs, Joe Cobb / *House Detective* Oliver Hardy / *Em, Hardy's wife* Edna Murphy / *Imbibing trashman* Jerry Mandy / *Hotel dress extras* Ham Kinsey, Ed Brandenberg, Jack Hill* / *Starving actor* Stan Laurel / *Bit* Al Hallet / *Conductor* Stanley (Tiny) Sandford** / *The Hal Roach Bathing Beauties* Themselves.

*Working in first of his 34 films with Laurel and Hardy.

**Working in first of his 23 films with Laurel and Hardy.

A country boy named Orville (Glen Tryon) and his family go to Hollywood to pay a mortgage debt. These rustics, like most visitors, go on a sightseeing tour and are treated to glimpses of such diverse Hal Roach stars of the time as Our Gang and Theda Bara. Orville sees what seems to be a movie unit filming on location in front of a bank. This is actually a holdup gang's ruse—which duly fails—but simple Orville never catches on. He gets innocently involved with a transvestite in a lengthy chase leading to the Hollywood Hotel. Variations on the chase only end when the film does.

Ollie (wearing a voluminous moustache) has an extended role as the hotel detective, spending most of his time in a bathtub or out of it, wearing a towel, continually hounded by his jealous wife. Stan has only one scene, late in the film, introduced by a title identifying him as a starving actor too hungry to sleep and too wobbly to get up. (Stan's makeup is akin to that of Laurel and Hardy's later foil, James Finlayson.) Ollie does not appear in the scene.

DUCK SOUP

1927

(no rating—film currently unavailable for screening)

All Star Series / Two reels / Silent / Released March 13, 1927, by Pathé Exchange / Produced by Hal Roach / Directed by Fred L. Guiol / Titles by H.M. Walker / Story based on a sketch written by Arthur J. Jefferson (Stan Laurel's father), entitled *Home from the honeymoon.*

Actors appearing in the film (role names not known) Stan Laurel, Madeleine Hurlock, Oliver Hardy, William Austin, Bob Kortman. (Reworked into *Another Fine Mess* three years later.)

[The authors are delighted (a word we never overuse) to have our friend, William K. Everson—one of the doyens of film scholarship—as guest commentator for a so-called lost Laurel and Hardy film. The lost is now found, thanks to Bill's indefatigable researches. We need hardly say, but do so gladly, that Bill Everson's book, *The Films of Laurel and Hardy,* has introduced thousands of people to the pleasures of revisiting our two heroes by way of the still photo and cogent commentary. Herewith—Bill.]

Finding one of the sparse handful of still-missing Laurel and Hardy comedies is somewhat akin to unearthing the Holy Grail (and of somewhat more practical and cultural value), so it was in a state of some anticipation that I sat down in the summer of 1974 to look at the first "new" Laurel and Hardy I'd seen in some ten years: a print (with French titles) of *Duck Soup.* Admittedly, the fact that it was a Pathé—and an early one at that, rather than an M-G-M—worked against expectations of it turning out to be a classic, and indeed its values *are* more academic than comedic.

The few very scattered U.S. references (one could hardly call them reviews) turn out to be less than reliable. In toto, they suggested that it was all slapstick and nothing else (not true at all), that it was a Stan Laurel comedy in which Hardy merely appeared (more understandable, since obviously contemporary reviewers knew Laurel as a solo comedian, whereas Hardy they hardly knew at all), and—this from later references—that segments of the film later formed the basis of their talkie three-reeler, *Another Fine Mess.* The last is perhaps the understatement of all time, since it is an exact blueprint for *Another Fine Mess,* and few of their remakes ever followed an original so carefully.

Duck Soup and *Slipping Wives* were both made very late in 1926, and copyrighted early in January of 1927. It would be interesting to know which film was actually produced first, but in any case *Duck Soup* is astounding in that Laurel and Hardy already appear *as a team,* and in their familiar (if not too frequently exercised) roles of hoboes on the run from the law. Admittedly, in deference to Laurel's greater status as a comedian at that time, he does get the lion's share of the comic footage, but the plot, and the action, is built around their teamwork. With all the accolades heaped on Hal Roach for having the wit to leave Laurel and Hardy pretty much alone to develop their own brand of comedy, perhaps it's time to add a genial reprimand, too, for being so slow on the uptake and not realizing from the very beginning what tremendous potential these comedians had *as* a team.

Since much of the humor of the story is essentially verbal, it's understandable that the sound remake would be funnier. Laurel and Hardy's timing and delivery were always much funnier than the content of the lines themselves, and Laurel—masquerading as a maid, and tilting with the lady of the house—can't deliver as effectively through silent subtitles. Moreover, in the late 1920s and early 1930s the comedians had plenty of time to polish and hone their routines to perfection, so that by the time of *Another Fine Mess,* everything was working like a precision watch, the weaker gags eliminated, the stronger ones expanded. Nevertheless, the silent *Duck Soup* does have some advantages over its remake.

It's the story, of course, of the two pals pursued by the law, taking refuge in a millionaire's mansion. The millionaire having fortuitously left on a vacation, and the staff is away, Oliver masquerades as the master of the house and Stan as his maid—all of this being done for the benefit of prospective new tenants, to explain their own presence in the house, and to prevent their being forced to leave and wind up in the still-waiting arms of the law.

In the remake the boys have really done nothing to cause them to fear the law. Laurel has rather tactlessly offended a policeman, but that is all, and their pursuit by the cops is merely a device to get them into the house, and the plot proper underway.

In *Duck Soup,* however, even though the prologue is likewise merely a device to get them into the house, 23 there's a little more substance to it. The boys are vagrants, and the sheriff (Bob Kortman) is seeking to round them up and put them to work fighting a forest fire. Thus their flight is occasioned both by fear of arrest and by actual danger, and because this threat is never removed, there is a much more positive reason for their taking over their new roles and staying in the house. Since most of the action takes place indoors, a little more care than usual has been taken with the interior sets, and *Duck Soup* is a rather good-looking production, slightly above the average standards of the Pathé-Roachs. A further asset: the opening and closing chase scenes through the streets of Hollywood and Los Angeles are longer in the silent version, and perhaps because Hollywood itself gets more attractive and less built-up the further one goes back in time, these street scenes are more interesting, although the reasons undoubtedly stem more from geographical history and nostalgia than from art.

One major drawback in the silent version is the physical appearance of Hardy. As the hobo on the run, he wears a heavily exaggerated "unshaven" makeup, similar in effect to the totally black chins and jowls sported by villains in comedies of a much earlier day. In his masquerade as the colonel he maintains this makeup. Although the incongruity of a dapper, well-dressed, floridly gesturing colonel with an unshaven chin might be good for a single gag, it doesn't work when sustained throughout the film. All of Hardy's grace and eloquence is minimized by the ugliness of that chin. That element of course is totally missing from the remake. In fact, in all of their later comedies, the boys used the condition, tattered or otherwise, of their clothes to indicate their economic status. Their faces were left as clean canvases on which they could paint all the nuances of their pantomime. Unshaven chins put in rare appearances only for establishing or wrap-up gags.

The "plot" of *Duck Soup* is a simple one, little more than a single situation. In *Another Fine Mess,* even with the benefit of some funny dialogue exchanges (especially the coy "girl-talk" between Laurel as the maid and the new mistress of the house, Thelma Todd), it was stretched rather beyond the limit at three reels. *Duck Soup* is paced rather better at the traditional two reels, and indeed might seem a much funnier film on its own merits if the remake did not exist and we did not automatically judge *Duck Soup* both as a revamping of a vocal music-hall sketch (which it was) and as a prelude to an equally vocal sound comedy in which even such details as Hardy's constant mispronouncing of the new tenant's name (Lord Plumtree), and his lordship's effeminate cackle, depend on that ubiquitous sound track.

If not a classic in itself, *Duck Soup* is certainly a landmark comedy, positively establishing that although the Laurel and Hardy partnership obviously added polish and bits of business through the years, the basics of their liaison were there from the beginning, whether by instinct, accident, or design. The mystery now is why the retrogression in the later 1927 films? Films like *Flying Elephants,* in which they were split up and not given teamwork comedy, almost reduce their work to a kind of infancy that would progress with remarkable rapidity to maturity in only a year or so. But *Duck Soup* proves that they actually bypassed any infancy stage, and *started out* on a level of fairly enterprising adolescence.

Now, how about *Hat's Off?* Does anybody have any good connections at the People's Film Archive of Outer Mongolia, or the Film Study Centre of Inter-Urban Borneo?

WILLIAM K. EVERSON

SLIPPING WIVES

1927

All Star Series / Two reels / Silent / Released April 3, 1927, by Pathé Exchange / Produced by Hal Roach / Supervised by F. Richard Jones / Directed by Fred L. Guiol / Direction assistance by Lewis R. Foster / Photographed by George Stevens / Edited by Richard Currier / Titles by H.M. Walker / Story by Hal E. Roach / Costumes by Will Lambert.

Wife Priscilla Dean / *Leon, the artist husband* Herbert Rawlinson / *Delivery man, Ferdinand Flamingo* Stan Laurel / *Jarvis, the butler* Oliver Hardy / *Hon. Winchester Squirtz* Albert Conti. (Working title: *Her House Sheik.*) (Reworked into *The Fixer Uppers* eight years later.)

Opening title: **"The story of a drifting husband and wife who no longer talk to each other –they bark."**

Leon, an artist (Herbert Rawlinson), title-described as "He wanted to do something big, so he painted an elephant," mostly ignores his wife (Priscilla Dean). A mutual friend, Winchester Squirtz (Albert Conti), urges the lady to hire a gigolo, thereby fanning the ebbing flames of Leon's desire. The front doorbell rings and Priscilla's butler, the haughty Jarvis (Oliver Hardy), answers to admit a paint delivery man, Ferdinand Flamingo (Stan). Refusing to use the servant's entrance, Ferdinand hands over the paint and a tussle ensues, ending with Jarvis falling messily into the paint. Priscilla comes to insist that Jarvis stop his playing and "see what the young gentleman wants."

Ferdinand is deemed by Squirtz just dumb enough to act as the cardboard lover, but Ferdinand refuses until money speaks. Ferdinand believes Squirtz is Priscilla's husband. Jarvis, directed to see that Ferdinand is properly attired, insists he take a bath first. Ferdinand resists, tries to escape the pursuing butler—who winds up, fully clothed, in the waiting bath. Enraged, he dumps Ferdinand, also fully clothed, into the tub.

That night Ferdinand is introduced to the household as a weekend guest—one Lionel Ironsides, noted writer of fairy stories. Asked by Leon to expatiate on his latest, Ferdinand says it is about Delilah and her "gink," Sampson. Ferdinand rises to tell his story graphically. (This superb Laurel pantomime rivals, even surpasses, Chaplin's excellent David and Goliath sequence in *The Pilgrim,* made four years earlier.) Titles complement Ferdinand's pantomime: "Then one night, Sampson stepped out with a cousin from Omaha, and the next day he was very sleepy. Then along came this dame Delilah—she was a lady barber." This is followed by a pantomime of the haircutting, Sampson's awakening, and walking about with wobbly legs. "Then came 40,000 Philadelphians and poked out his eyes. Then Sampson gets his strength back. He's sore as an owl and wants to clean house." Ferdinand next uses his own strength to knock down two large vases, which conk him on the head.

In an aside Priscilla tells Ferdinand he is being paid to make love to her, "make a fuss over me." He does so but only in the presence of the inattentive Leon, whom Ferdinand believes to be only a family friend.

24

Later, seeing Priscilla kissing Leon, Ferdinand gets him on the side and says, "Isn't she a red-hot mamma? Her husband must be an awful sap." Leon agrees.

At bedtime, looking through a keyhole and seeing Leon kissing his wife, Ferdinand—apprehensive as Squirtz walks by—rushes in, warns Leon that Priscilla's husband is outside. Priscilla tells Leon of her subterfuge, and he rushes out after Ferdinand with a shotgun, shouting "I'll kill the home wrecker!" Running into a room where Ferdinand is hiding, Leon says confidentially to him, "Get out, I'm only trying to make my wife think I'm jealous." Ferdinand leaves, Jarvis follows him with his shotgun, saying "I'll get him on the wing." Leon tries to stop Jarvis, a chase follows, and both Leon and Priscilla try to stop Jarvis from shooting Ferdinand—fade-out.

Love 'Em and Weep

1 1927

All Star Series / Two reels / Silent / Released June 12, 1927, by Pathe Exchange / Produced by Hal Roach / Directed by Fred I. Guiol / Titles by H.M. Walker / Story by Hal E. Roach.

Finlayson's sweetheart Mae Busch / *Finlayson's aide, Romaine Ricketts* Stan Laurel / *Titus Tillsbury* James Finlayson* / *Judge Chigger* Oliver Hardy / *Mrs. Aggie Tillsbury* Charlotte Mineau / *Laurel's wife* Vivien Oakland / *Finlayson's butler* Charlie Hall** / *Hardy's wife* May Wallace / *Walter* Ed Brandenberg / *Gossip* Gale Henry. (Working title: *Better Husbands Week.*) (Remade as *Chickens Come Home* four years later.)

*Working in first of his 33 films with Laurel and Hardy.

**Working in first of his 47 films with Laurel and Hardy.

(Working title: *Better Husbands Week.*) / (Remade as *Chickens Come Home* four years later.)

Opening title: **"Ancient proverb—Every married man should have his fling—but be careful not to get flung too far."**

An absolute blueprint for their later sound film, *Chickens Come Home* (1931), there is no point here in detailing the plot of what is to grow into a quite superior remake. Some of the differences, however, are worth noting at this point.

The story is the same: a happily married businessman is visited by an old flame who threatens blackmail. She visits his home and creates a havoc of embarrassment and near disaster.

Key differences between *Love 'Em and Weep* and *Chickens Come Home* are: the first film is shorter, its gags, although essentially the same as the later film, are less subtly done, and, above all, the comedy in the first film is not fully in the hands of Laurel and Hardy.

In *Love 'Em and Weep,* for instance, the businessman is played amusingly but in a single dimension of frenetic over-reaction by James Finlayson; and Babe Hardy (in the role of a guest at Fin's) is artistically suppressed by bushy sideburns, glasses, large moustache—and the fact that he has absolutely nothing to do. In *Chickens Come Home* Hardy takes over the Finlayson role, infusing it with his many comedic nuances. In the sound remake Finlayson becomes a blackmailing butler, and is excellent because his strenuous mugging befits his single-note role. Stan plays the same part in both films—a friend of the businessman—and is excellent in both appearances.

Why Girls Love Sailors

1927

(no rating—film currently unavailable for screening)

All Star Series / Two reels / Silent / Released July 17, 1927, by Pathé Exchange / Produced by Hal Roach / Directed by Fred L. Guiol / Titles by H.M. Walker / Story by Hal E. Roach.

Girl's lover, the hero, a young gob Stan Laurel / *Seafaring Petty Officer Leggit* Oliver Hardy / *Bemused bit* Bobby Dunn / *The moneylender* Sojin / *The girl, Delamar* Anna May Wong / *The admiral* Eric Mayne. (Burlesque on the seagoing genre established the previous year with the popularity of Douglas Fairbanks' *The Black Pirate*, James Cruze's *Old Ironsides*, and two William Boyd features, *The Volga Boatman* and *The Yankee Clipper*.)

Ollie, a rough sea captain, kidnaps Stan's girl friend and takes her to his ship. Unable to best the captain physically, Stan uses the strategy of disguising himself as a vamp to get aboard. Ollie's jealous wife appears on the scene to confront her husband, giving Stan the opportunity to steal off with his sweetie.

The foregoing summary of this long-lost film was all that Stan Laurel could remember of it many years later. One of the few stills taken during the making of the film shows Stan in female attire, confirming at least in part Stan's description.

However, a summary of *Why Girls Love Sailors,* as originally projected, has recently been found among the papers of the film's director, Fred Guiol. This manuscript—it must be emphasized—is not a cutting continuity (the actual record, shot by shot, of the complete and edited film) but is only a general projection of story line yet to be filmed—a story line in which Stan nowhere appears in female guise. Indeed, this entire story line is markedly different from the summary Stan gave of it.

The projected Guiol story has Stan as a young gob aboard a U.S. battleship lying off the China coast. In a nearby port is an exquisite Chinese girl (to be played by Anna May Wong). In love with Stan, she is waiting anxiously for him. But the girl is kidnapped by a villain-ous moneylender who wants to marry her. Stan and his close friend—a petty officer played by Babe—have come to town earlier. After comic dalliance at a restaurant, Stan sees his girl friend being abducted by the villain. He follows her and with true Douglas Fairbanks gusto rescues her through strategic manipulation of fireworks. Ollie, separated from Stan during the girl's kidnapping, finally arrives on the scene with a contingent of U.S. Marines and all is well.

Thus, Guiol's summary of what he wanted to film. Whether his plans were realized in whole or in part or whether Stan's memory is accurate can be determined only when the film is available for viewing. Up until now all prints seem to have vanished but one has recently been reported in the archives of Cinémathèque Française in Paris.

In 1954 Babe Hardy told John McCabe that during the making of this film one of the most durable Hardy trademarks, the tie-twiddle, was born. In a scene in which he opens a door and is met by water thrown in his face, Babe was momentarily distracted and could not think of what to do next. Realizing that some kind of comic reaction was expected, he decided to blow his nose with his sopping tie. But as he began the gesture, he realized it might prove offensive. Instead, he took the tie and wiggled it in embarrassment. Babe also told McCabe that the Hardy camera-look was developed in *Why Girls Love Sailors,* although its prototype can be seen embryonically in earlier films.

WITH LOVE AND HISSES ▬▬ 1927

All Star Series / Two reels / Silent / Released August 28, 1927, by Pathé Exchange / Produced by Hal Roach / Directed by Fred L. Guiol / Titles by H.M. Walker / Story by Hal E. Roach.

Cuthbert Hope Stan Laurel / *Top Sergeant Banner* Oliver Hardy / *Captain Bustle* James Finlayson / *Major General Rohrer* Frank Brownlee / *Soldiering rookie* Chet Brandenberg / *Finlayson's girl friends* Anita Garvin, Eve Southern / *Soldier sleeping next to Stan* Will Stanton / *Soldier with voracious appetite* Jerry Mandy / *Other soldier* Frank Saputo / *Girl friend* Josephine Dunn.

Opening title: **"There were cheers and kisses as the Home Guards left for camp—the married men did the cheering."**

Virtually plotless, this army situation comedy has Ollie as rowdy sergeant Banner (a title describes him as a bouncer in a café where the ambulance service is free). Stan is Cuthbert Hope, a sissy private, eternally weeping (so dumb, we are told, that he thinks "Taps" is a couple of smacks on a bass drum). James Finlayson is crusty Captain Bustle. Most of the film's gags erupt when two of the three rub rank against each other. Ladies' man Bustle chastises Banner when he tries to muscle in on Bustle's two girl friends. Banner, in turn, throws Cuthbert out of the luxurious train compartment belonging to the captain, hoping to have it himself. Bustle, again in turn, bullies the sergeant to be on his way.

At Camp Klaxon next day, during morning formation, dress-right-dress commands bring forth a stream of rather startling but very funny effeminate poses and gags by Cuthbert. (Stan is, in many ways, still portraying the aggressively silly character he created in his pre-Roach days. Here he is some months away from becoming the invincible-simpleton pal of Ollie.)

The soldiers are sent on a long march, and two miles from camp, exhausted, they decide on a swim. Cuthbert is ordered to watch the pile of clothes. The sergeant flicks his cigarette toward the clothing as he dives into the water. Cuthbert, wanting some fun, disrobes and chases the sergeant around the pond—as the clothes burn.

Back at camp the major general arrives for an inspection and an aggressive bugle call summons the troops back. The soldiers scramble out of the water to find their garments destroyed. Without clothes, they are forced to hide behind a large poster for Cecil B. De Mille's film, *The Volga Boatman,* which has convenient holes for them to stick their heads through. As they carry the poster away to cover themselves, a skunk appears to help them move even more swiftly toward camp. En route they upset a bees' nest. The bees profoundly disrupt the parade ground formation at camp. The last scene of the film shows the troops, the following day, marching past with swollen posteriors, and we are left with the information that all's well that ends swell.

All Star Series / Two reels / Silent / Released September 10, 1927, by M-G-M / Produced by Hal Roach / Directed by Fred L. Guiol / Photographed by George Stevens / Titles by H.M. Walker.

Cyrus Brittle James Finlayson / *Cyrus Brittle's lawyer* Stan Laurel / *Cyrus Brittle's butler* Oliver Hardy / *Cyrus Brittle's new brother-in-law* Noah Young / *Mrs. Brittle* Charlotte Mineau / *Daughter* Edna Marian / *Hardy lookalike* Eugene Pallette / *Hotel atmosphere extras* Jack Hill, Charlie Hall, Sam Lufkin* / *Fun house ticket taker* Sam Lufkin / *Girl in the fun house* Dorothy Coburn / *Bellboy* Ray Cooke / *Dog* Jiggs.

*Working in first of his 39 films with Laurel and Hardy.

Opening title: "The story of a millionaire oil man who was married and didn't know it—this will give you a rough idea what oil men are like."

Millionaire Cyrus Brittle (James Finlayson) has had a rough night. His affable butler (Oliver Hardy) is giving him an icy restorative. He will need it. Fin's new family is downstairs.

Fin finds, to his stunned surprise, that he got married the night before, and the bartender was best man. Here we meet, as described by title, the bride (Charlotte Mineau): "she came over as first mate on the Mayflower"; her brother (Noah Young): "has three bad habits—he steals things, he kills people, and eats with his knife"; and the bride's daughter (Edna Marian): "she cries every time her mother gets married." They look forward to shaking Fin down to his very last dollar.

Fin decides to call his attorney (Stan) who, a title tells us, "went through medical college, and came out a lawyer."

The butler is not accustomed to the manners of the brother; the brother is not accustomed to manners.

The bride glowers at her glowering groom.

The brother tells Fin, "You married my sister in the lion's cage last night!" Fin says, "It's all a mistake—I thought she was one of the lions."

The brother says $50,000 is the only way to correct the mistake—an appropriate moment for the lawyer to enter.

The butler attempts to remove the lawyer's hat a number of times but the gentleman's possessiveness is obsessive, until he enters the living room where, for no discoverably good reason, he gives up the hat.

The lawyer opens his briefcase, solemnly removes his laundry, and kicks it under the piano.

After looking the brother over carefully, the lawyer tells Fin, "That's one point in our favor." The brother backs up—with tangible support—his demand for $50,000.

Fin evades his bride and brother-in-law for a time but days later he is discovered hiding in a hotel. To get past the waiting brother-in-law, the lawyer "top-dresses" as a lady, mounts Fin's shoulders, and covers all with a dress coat. The butler proudly escorts "her" down the elevator.

A dog displays great curiosity about the odd-looking lady. The butler tries to fend him off.

On the street a curious cop starts to lift up the coat but the lawyer slaps his inquiring hands down, throwing the cop's cap off camera. They escape from the cop to a dance hall, and as the lawyer dances with the butler, a stranger dancing nearby, kicking heartily, causes Fin to reveal himself. (The brother, bride, and bride's daughter were added to this still for piquancy.)

Still suspicious, Fin's new family follows.

Fin and company flee to a fun house. Following them, the brother, bride, and daughter have rough weather going through the barrel section.

29

Hot in pursuit on the sliding platform.

The lawyer, butler, and Fin enter the big spinning barrel. (The brother, bride, and daughter were added to this still. In the film, they enter it after their quarry leaves, then experience their own mad spin-around.)

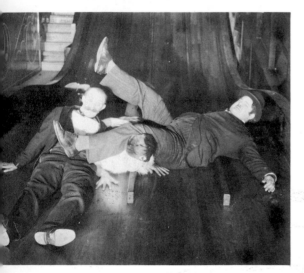

Fin, butler, and lawyer go down the slide into the bowl and try to climb out.

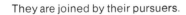

They are joined by their pursuers.

A bevy of pretty girls zooms down to join them. The final shot in the film is of the curious cop standing nearby, looking with suspicion at a couple walking past him. The lady is wearing a duplicate of the dress coat the lawyer is sporting. The cop lifts up the woman's coat; she swings on him, knocking him flat.

SAILORS, BEWARE!

All Star Series / Two reels / Silent / Released September 25, 1927, by Pathé Exchange / Produced by Hal Roach / Directed by Hal Yates / Titles by H.M. Walker / Story by Hal E. Roach.

Chester Chaste Stan Laurel / *Purser Cryder* Oliver Hardy / *Madame Ritz* Anita Garvin / *Man in robe* Stanley (Tiny) Sandford / *Society ladies aboard the S.S. Miramar* Viola Richard, May Wallace, Connie Evans, Barbara Pierce / *Baroness Behr* Lupe Velez / *Baron Behr* Will Stanton / *The other cabdriver* Ed Brandenberg / *Lady in easy chair* Dorothy Coburn / *Captain Bull* Frank Brownlee / *Roger, midget "son" of Madame Ritz* Harry Earles / *Man boarding boat* Charley Young.

Ollie, as the flirtatious purser aboard the ritzy S.S. *Miramar,* has only two important things on his mind—blondes and redheads. Dim-bulb Stan is a cabdriver who delivers Anita Garvin, a glamorous jewel thief, and her midget husband (dressed as a baby) to the dock. The larcenous Anita and her midget plan to board the luxury steamship and thrive as best they may. Stan's cab is inadvertently hoisted aboard as cargo. Thinking he has been kidnapped, Stan goes indignantly to the purser for satisfaction.

The ship's captain sternly informs Stan that any stowaway the captain doesn't murder, he puts to work. The surly Ollie is charged with the responsibility for seeing that Stan does not loaf. Dressed as a steward, Stan delivers drinks to the midget's room, an assignment that evolves into a protracted crap game with this extraordinarily precocious baby. The baby has the preemptive habit of rolling nothing but sevens. This, the funniest segment in the film, is made so primarily by Stan's shocked camera-looks, whimpering cry, Harry Langdon-like astonishment, and squints of incredulity (these last rather resembling those of James Finlayson).

There follows a slapstick pool-side sequence involving both Stan and Ollie, highlighted by Stan shoving a haughty Lupe Valez into the water. This is topped with Ollie's being doused by buckets of water from angry passengers trying to even the score with rampaging Stan. A ladies' card game follows, with Stan covertly sabotaging Anita's nefarious schemes. All the ladies' jewelry is stolen; and it is Stan, the honest cabbie, who cracks the thieves' racket by unmasking the "infant" in a bathtub. For a highly interesting if slightly unbelievable last scene, the angry midget beats up Ollie, illustrating the film's literal punch line.

All Star Series / Two reels / Silent / Filmed in black and white, but released with amber-tinted sequences / Released October 8, 1927, by M-G-M / Produced by Hal Roach / Directed by Fred L. Guiol / Edited by Richard Currier / Titles by H.M. Walker.

Little Goofy Stan Laurel / *Oliver Hardy* Himself / *Governor Browne Van Dyke* James Finlayson / *Dinner guest* Eugene Pallette / *Snarling prison guard* Stanley (Tiny) Sandford / *Countess de Cognac* Ellinor Van Der Veer / *Officers* Alfred Fisher, Charles A. Bachman, Edgar Dearing / *French Police Chiefs: Lecoque* Otto Fries, *Voitrex* Bob (Mazooka) O'Conor / *Prison warden* Frank Brownlee / *Lady preening herself* Dorothy Coburn / *Convict* Charlie Hall / *Dinner guest* Rosemary Theby.

(no rating—film currently unavailable for screening)

Opening title: "**Will Rogers says— 'Being in jail has one big advantage— a man doesn't have to worry about wearing his tuxedo.'**"

Little Goofy (Stan) listens fearfully to Big Goofy's (Ollie's) plan to break out of durance vile.

Apprehensively, they go down their man-made tunnel . . .

. . . and Stan sets his candle too close to his pal's posterior, shortly afterward declaring he smells burning ham.

But their tunneling is executed smartly—right into the warden's office.

Stan asks a fellow con how long he's in for. "Forty years" is the reply. "Mail this for me when you get out," Stan tells him solemnly, slipping the letter along.

The guard (Tiny Sandford) threatens Stan on several occasions as a result of mischance and inadvertence — Stan's, that is. (The boys' consignment to the rock pile is purely to dramatize this still. In the film they actually disport on a sandpile.)

They have another plan to escape but are forestalled.

Seeing painters leave for lunch, they turn their coats inside out and, buckets in hand, make an easy departure.

33

To forestall the suspicions of a cop on the beat, the boys paint everything in sight— the street, a car at the curb . . .

. . . a pretty girl's posterior . . .

Some hours later ("Four hours passed— one after the other," the title says), the boys, in disposing of their paint, dispose of it accidentally on the officer.

Two French police chiefs (their arrival in America is a secret to everyone but the press) are on their way to the prison as guests of honor. Stan and Ollie, not knowing who they are, board their limousines, evict them, assume their garments, and arrive at the governor's mansion on the prison grounds.

Under the frigid gaze of the butlers, the boys make several social gaffes, not the least of which is the fervid bussing of the butlers in what they consider true Gallic style.

Stan and Ollie bring hearty conviviality to their encounter with the society ladies at dinner. The ladies are slightly stunned but remain determinedly game in standing up to their eccentric manners.

At the clash of the dinner gong, the boys go into automatic lockstep as a dinner guest (Eugene Pallette) and the governor (James Finlayson) look on agog.

Stan picks up fruit salad on his knife, and when Ollie sternly warns him to use his fork, does so—attempting to stab a highly mobile cherry that defies subjection. He retrieves the cherry from the back of the hostess' gown, holds it up triumphantly, but it eludes him again, ultimately winding up in the governor's eye.

On an official tour of the prison, the "guests of honor" are confronted by the Frenchmen, and wind up again as permanent guests of the state.

CALL OF THE CUCKOOS

1927

Max Davidson Series / Two reels / Silent / Released October 15, 1927, by M-G-M / Produced by Hal Roach / Supervised by Leo McCarey / Directed by Clyde A. Bruckman / Photographed by Floyd Jackman / Edited by Richard Currier / Titles by H.M. Walker.

Papa Gimplewart Max Davidson / Mama Gimplewart Lillian Elliott / Love's greatest mistake Spec O'Donnell / The cuckoos Charley Chase/Parrott, Stan Laurel, Oliver Hardy, James Finlayson / Prospective house buyer Frank Brownlee / The "Wheelbarrow" Charlie Hall / House buyer Charles Meakin / Couples at the housewarming Leo Willis, Lyle Tayo, Edgar Dearing, Fay Holderness / Bit Otto H. Fries.

Opening title: **"There are two kinds of cuckoos—those who live in clocks ... and those who can't."**

Mr. Gimplewart (Max Davidson) is distracted by the shenanigans of some oddballs attending a training school for radio announcers next door. At this establishment, a title tells us, "The quicker they go daffy, the sooner they get a diploma." The prime cuckoos ...

... are four in number (Stan, Ollie, Charley Chase, and James Finlayson). They are seen briefly rollicking on the lawn in a wild pastiche of the William Tell story. The oddity of his neighbors is the impelling reason for Gimplewart to move to a new neighborhood. But his house is a complete disaster; virtually everything in it malfunctions. Even the floors are not level, and the Gimplewart piano ...

... almost crushes him before moving irresistibly through the house, down onto the sidewalk, and into a car parked at the curb. Gimplewart asks distractedly, "Is there anything else can happen?" The answer is affirmative. The four cuckoos, still mugging playfully, announce, "We've moved next door!"

Note: Stan and Babe appear with their heads shaved, the legacy of their previous roles as convicts in *The Second Hundred Years,* shot a few days before this film. "They were so tremendous in the convict picture," said George Stevens, "that the studio grew impatient waiting for their hair to grow in. Finally it was decided that there was no use in waiting. The boys were just too good to be kept inactive, so they were put almost right away into the next picture, brush cut and all."

HATS OFF

1927

All Star Series / Two reels / Silent / Released November 5, 1927, by M-G-M / Produced by Hal Roach / Supervised by Leo McCarey / Directed by Hal Yates / Edited by Richard Currier / Titles by H.M. Walker.

Stan Laurel Himself / Oliver Hardy Himself / Proprietor, Kwickway Washing Machine Co. James Finlayson / Customer at top of stairs Anita Garvin / Leggy lady on stairs Dorothy Coburn / Pedestrians involved in the free-for-all Ham Kinsey, Sam Lufkin, Chet Brandenberg.

Opening title: "**The story of two boys who figure that the world owes them a living— but is about thirty-five years behind in the payments.**"

After losing their jobs as dishwashers, Stan and Ollie see a tremendous job opportunity facing them in Finlayson's washing machine shop.

Curious, Stan takes the cover off a machine to see if it's working. It is— with Ollie and Fin receiving the benefits.

Ollie tells Stan to desist and Fin recovers as best he can.

The boys load a truck with a sample washing machine (Fin has urged them to sell door-to-door with product in hand), and in process of getting the machine up on the truck, they dump it on poor Fin a number of times. They take the machine to a four-door apartment complex. There follows a frantic session of door knocking: shifting the machine to another door after no one responds at the first; knocking at the second door, and shifting the machine back to the first door when it opens unexpectedly; reaching the first door, whereupon it shuts and the second door opens; shifting the machine back, but again arriving too late; and so on with doors number three and four. They finally **succ**eed in selling nothing.

They drive the truck past a high rise of terraced steps, and at its very top the boys see a lady (Anita Garvin) waving and shouting to them. "Come on up here," she says. The boys carry the washing machine up the long flight, but halfway up Ollie's hat falls off and Stan is sent down to get it from the bottom of the hill. The machine gets out of Ollie's grip and runs away down the steps. Painfully, they recapture the machine and bring it to the top. There the lady confronts them with a question, "Will you mail this letter?"

Ollie takes the letter and asks, "Would you be interested in the world's most synchronistical washing machine?" The lady is not interested; she explains she has her own Chinaman.

The boys carry the machine down, huffing and puffing as they go. They both stumble and their hats fall off. They recover them but discover they have put on the wrong ones. (This film is the apotheosis of the Laurel and Hardy hat-mixup gag, which occurs over and over again —almost to excess.) As they reach their truck, far below, the lady yells for them to return. Ollie, suggesting that maybe the Chinaman has sprained his back, directs Stan to go up and see what the lady wants. While Ollie has difficulty keeping the machine from rolling over him, Stan crawls painfully up the steps and, in the last throes of exhaustion, comes to the lady. Anita tells him, "I forgot to put a stamp on my letter." Stan motions for Ollie to come up, and when Ollie does so jubilantly anticipating a sale, Stan wonders why his pal is hauling up the washing machine.

In heaving exhaustion, Ollie arrives at the top with the machine, and begins his sales pitch. "No," says Stan, "she forgot the stamp—and *you've* got the letter." Anita offers Ollie the stamp, Ollie hits Stan in the nose and when Stan cries, Anita hits Ollie in the nose, yelling, "You're the kind of a man that always thinks of himself first." The boys start to carry the machine down and, following a hat mixup, sit aggrievedly on the steps.

They resume their labors but are distracted by a fair vision (Dorothy Coburn).

Chummily, the fair vision asks for a washing machine demonstration. "Where?," she is asked.

She points far up the steps, and Stan impetuously kicks the vision in her rear. She hits Ollie on the nose, threatens Stan, and walks indignantly up the steps. In another hat mixup, the boys kick each other's derbies down the street.

Ollie's hat lands on a street marker and, vengefully, Stan kicks it—winding up with a smashed toe.

Fin—and in sequence a number of other men—engage in a series of attacks on each other's hats. Stan knocks off Ollie's, Ollie knocks off Stan's, Stan knocks off Fin's, Fin knocks off a stranger's who intrudes, a new intruder knocks off the intruder's—until a stupendous free-for-all ensues. At its height, a steamroller accidentally flattens the washing machine. Even a policeman is caught up in the maelstrom.

Police reserves come to drive all away except Stan and Ollie who have, for the last time, for the umpteenth time, put on the wrong hats.

Note: No known print of *Hats Off* exists.

41

Do Detectives Think? ♠♠ 1927

All Star Series / Two reels / Silent / Released November 20, 1927, by Pathé Exchange / Produced by Hal Roach / Directed by Fred L. Guiol / Titles by H.M. Walker / Story by Hal E. Roach.

Ferdinand Finkleberry Stan Laurel / *Sherlock Pinkham* Oliver Hardy / *Judge Foozle* James Finlayson / *Judge's wife* Viola Richard / *The Tipton Slasher* Noah Young / *Detective agency supervisor* Frank Brownlee / *The Slasher's little pal* Will Stanton / *Juror* Charley Young / *Officer* Charles A. Bachman. (Working title: *Body Guards*.) (Reworked into *Going Bye-Bye!* seven years later.)

Opening title: **"This story opens with a lot of people in court—most of them should be in jail."**

Popeyed Judge Foozle (James Finlayson) sentences the burly and belligerent "Tipton Slasher" to death—adding gratuitously, "and I hope you choke!" The Slasher is not a nice man. A title tells us that he had "killed two Chinamen—both seriously." Enraged beyond measure, the Slasher says he will escape and cut out the judge's tonsils—without anesthetic. The Slasher does escape and makes his way to the Foozle mansion for retribution. The judge reads of the escape and phones for help from the detective agency where...

... the boss (Frank Brownlee) charges his two best men to go and guard Foozle well. These two are, as described in the titles, "Ferdinand Finkelberry—the second worst detective in the whole world" (Stan) and "Sherlock Pinkham—the worst" (Ollie). The boss explains that the Slasher will probably kill them but they'll be buried like heroes.

On their way to Foozle's the boys pass a cemetery this spooky, windy evening, and their hats are blown off among the tombstones. Ollie forces the weeping Stan to tiptoe through the long shadows and recover their errant derbies. This done, there follows the usual hat mixup: Stan, as we know he must, gives Ollie the wrong hat, then gives Ollie the wrong hat, then gives Ollie the wrong hat, and follows it all up by giving Ollie the wrong hat.

Meanwhile the Slasher subverts Foozle's new butler and takes his place in the household where, armed with huge knives, he bides his time for an opportunity to remove the judge from his tonsils. When the boys arrive, Ollie tries to impress Foozle by shooting an apple off Stan's head. The Slasher puts the boys to bed for a nice long sleep, and immediately prepares to slit Foozle's throat. The rest of the film is a series of stealthy prowlings, chases, and pratfalls around hallways, stairs, and doors. The Slasher now includes Stan and Ollie as intended victims, and when Ollie accidentally mixes it up with the killer, Stan handcuffs the culprit only to discover that the cuffs are actually on Ollie. But, through no efforts of his own, Stan finally captures the Slasher, and for safekeeping hustles him into the closet where Ollie is hiding. A police squadron arrives and drags the defeated Slasher away. Ollie emerges from the closet with two shiners he did not have before he entered his refuge. As the boys leave, a haughty Stan gives Ollie the wrong derby again for the final gag of the film.

Note: Here for the first time (in deference to their appearance as typical hard-boiled detectives of the time) the boys wear derbies, which ultimately are to become not only their perpetual headwear but their genteel and timeless escutcheon.

Putting Pants On Philip

1927

All Star Series / Two reels / Silent / Released December 3, 1927, by M-G-M / Produced by Hal Roach / Supervised by Leo McCarey / Directed by Clyde A. Bruckman / Photographed by George Stevens / Edited by Richard Currier / Titles by H.M. Walker.

Philip Stan Laurel / Piedmont Mumblethunder Oliver Hardy / Ship's doctor Sam Lufkin / Tailor Harvey Clark / Bus conductor Ed Brandenberg / The girl chased by Philip Dorothy Coburn / Culver City open-air crowd extras Chet Brandenberg, Retta Palmer, Bob (Mazooka) O'Conor, Eric Mack, Jack Hill, Don Bailey, Alfred Fisher, Lee Phelps / Officer Charles A. Bachman.

Opening title: "**The story of a Scotch lad who came to America to hunt for a Columbian half dollar—his grandfather lost it in 1893.**"

At the pier the ship's doctor (Sam Lufkin) gives Philip (Stan) a medical examination. Philip bites down on the thermometer tearfully, and breaks it.

Philip reacts energetically causing a gentleman nearby, Piedmont Mumblethunder (Ollie), to comment, "Imagine—somebody has to meet that!"

It is himself, Piedmont discovers to his horrified surprise, who is slated to meet the naïve Philip. As Philip's uncle, Piedmont has already been warned that the boy has an obsessive interest in girls. (The old Scotch gentleman in this still has been added for flavor.)

Piedmont asks Philip, "What can I do to entertain you? What are you interested in?" A girl walks by and Piedmont restrains his nephew.

Piedmont tells Philip he must walk in the rear. He explains, "Every man, woman, and child in this town knows me. You walk behind—stay behind."

Philip runs off after a girl, drawing a considerable crowd of interested spectators. After Piedmont catches him, Philip takes some snuff and his sneeze causes his prime undergarment to collapse.

The crowd increases, enjoying itself very much. Piedmont asks the crowd to cease laughing at his nephew.

A charming girl (Dorothy Coburn) that Philip has previously chased reappears, and Philip leers appreciatively.

Sternly, Piedmont hustles Philip along. Walking over a ventilator grille, Philip's kilt flies up, and two girls fainting at the sight make us aware that, as a nearby cop puts it, "This dame ain't got no lingerie on." Piedmont tells the policeman, "I'll stop this, officer. I'm gonna put pants on Philip—right now!" They go forthwith to the tailor's shop. The tailor (Harvey Clark) has never had an experience like this in all his career.

In taking measurements for Philip's inseam leg length, the tailor discovers Philip is morally affronted by the procedure. Such a thing could never happen in Scotland. As Philip says tearfully, "I never wore a set of pants in my life!"

As the battle to subdue Philip progresses, Piedmont tells the tailor to guard the doors. Piedmont is determined to get that inseam length, and he chases Philip into an inner room for that purpose. We see nothing of that scramble, but moments later Piedmont enters triumphantly, saying, "Thirty-three!" to the tailor. Philip, crying like a newly deflowered maiden, comes in to add, "The Bide-a-Wee Club shall hear of this—"

In a long sequence Philip once again finds the girl he has been chasing, and upon seeing her trying to get across a muddy corner, rips off his kilt and lays it down in the mud. "Just an old Scotch custom," he says gallantly, bowing low. She laughs, jumps across the kilt, and leaves. Piedmont observes, laughs, and, as Philip bends over to pick up the kilt, stops him peremptorily. Haughtily, Piedmont snaps Philip in the nose and says, "Just an old *American* custom." Piedmont steps on the kilt and descends into a huge mudhole.

THE BATTLE OF THE CENTURY ◼◻◼ 1927

All Star Series / Two reels / Silent / Filmed in black and white, but released with amber-tinted sequences / Released December 31, 1927, by M-G-M / Produced by Hal Roach / Supervised by Leo McCarey / Directed by Clyde A. Bruckman, and Hal Roach (uncredited) / Photographed by George Stevens / Edited by Richard Currier / Titles by H.M. Walker / Story by Hal E. Roach.

Canvasback Clump Stan Laurel / *Oliver Hardy* Himself / *Sewer worker* Dick Gilbert / *Dentist* George K. French / *Dental patient* Dick Sutherland / *Boxing referee* Sam Lufkin / *Thunder-Clap Callahan* Noah Young / *Ring announcer* Gene Morgan / *Bit* Al Hallet / *Woman who slips on pie* Anita Garvin / *Insurance agent* Eugene Pallette / *Woman at window* Lyle Tayo / *Delivery man* Charlie Hall / *Pie victim boarding auto* Dorothy Coburn / *Ringside spectators* Ham Kinsey, Bert Roach, Jack Hill / *Warring pedestrians* Bob O'Conor, Ed Brandenberg, Dorothy Walbert / *Fruit vendor* Charley Young / *Dignified dowager with lorgnette* Ellinor Van Der Veer.

The referee introduces the powerful pug, Thunder-Clap Callahan (Noah Young), wh[o] bows to hearty applause, and his opponent, Canvasback Clump (Stan), who bows to rapturous boos. His manager (Ollie) reminds Stan that his weak spot is his stomach, adding, "If we win, we get $100. If we lose, we get $5. That's a difference of $1,500."

Opening title: "**The big fight—ringside seats extended as far west as Honolulu.**"

Noah rushes at Stan, and Stan, quite accidentally, knocks him out. The referee shrinks back in apprehension.

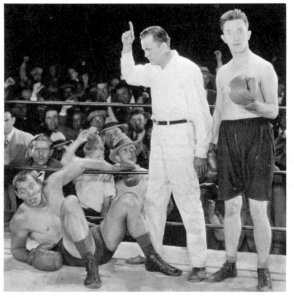

The referee refuses to begin the count until Stan goes to a neutral corner. Stan, who doesn't know what the word *corner* means, let alone the word *neutral,* remains in place—and Noah is saved by the bell. Stan is floored, Ollie faints, and Noah says to the referee, "You don't need to count; it's getting late."

In the park a shrewd insurance agent (Eugene Pallette) tells Ollie, "For $5, you can insure that fellow. Then if he gets hurt, you get the money." Ollie gets $5 from Stan's hat and gives it to Eugene. Ollie borrows a pen from Stan but has difficulty opening the top. When he does, out spurts a fat jet of ink. The policy is bought by Ollie, who signs it after dipping the pen in the ink on his nose.

Stan, slipping on a banana, complains that this accident could have hurt him. Inspired, Ollie grabs a banana skin and attempts to throw it on the sidewalk at strategic points as they stroll along.

But the banana peel causes a cop to fall, and Ollie is horrified.

Ollie quickly hands the banana to Stan, and the cop hits Stan on the head. Pointing to the bump, Ollie says to Stan, "I'll get $1,000 for that pineapple." (Eugene Pallette is not in this scene. He was brought in by the still photographer to liven up the photograph.)

The banana peel is still on the ground, and a pie vendor (Charlie Hall) comes out of a shop and slips on it. Then begins a reciprocal destruction sequence between Charlie and Ollie, culminating with a pie in Ollie's face. Person after person enters the cascading battle, with Charlie's pie wagon serving as the arsenal for the onslaughts.

A man in a dental chair gets an open mouth full of pie; a man hit by a pie falls jackknifed into a garbage can; a woman putting out a flowerpot receives a pie; a dowager sitting in a limousine gets one; a mailman reaching in his mailbox finds a pie; a pretty lady (Anita Garvin) slips on a pie, lands in it, and exits shaking the pie from her derriere. An officer sees Stan and Ollie chortling at the sight of all this. He asks them if *they* started the pie fight. Ollie asks, "*What* pie fight?" The pie fight surges to new dimensions; the cop finally gets *his* pie in the face, and he chases Stan and Ollie down the street.

Note: Only the pie-fight sequence of *The Battle of the Century* is extant.

LEAVE 'EM LAUGHING

▄▟▗ **1928**

All Star Series / Two reels / Silent / Released January 28, 1928, by M-G-M / Produced by Hal Roach / Supervised by Leo McCarey / Directed by Clyde A. Bruckman / Photographed by George Stevens / Edited by Richard Currier / Titles by Reed Heustis / Story by Hal E. Roach.

Stan Laurel Himself / *Oliver Hardy* Himself / *Traffic cop* Edgar Kennedy / *Landlord* Charlie Hall / *Nurses* Viola Richard, Dorothy Coburn / *Dental patients* Stanley (Tiny) Sandford, Sam Lufkin, Edgar Dearing, Al Hallet / *Dentists* Jack V. Lloyd, Otto Fries / *Irate motorist* Jack Hill. (Working title: *A Little Laughing Gas.*)

Opening title: "**What's worse than an aching tooth at three in the morning? Two of them.**"

Ollie tells Stan that he'll pull the tooth for him in the traditional do-it-yourself mode. It fails.

Their landlord (Charlie Hall) tells them all this ruckus is forcing him to evict them in the morning. Stan is belligerent in his agony, and everybody gets assaulted in the process—even the bed.

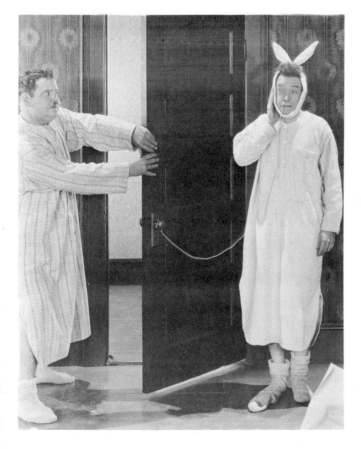

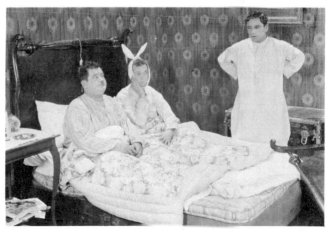

A title reads: "Where brave men's hearts go pit-a-pat—the dentist's office." Stan overhears a patient saying, "This dentist broke my brother's jaw yesterday!" Shortly after, a patient is carried out of the dentist's room on a stretcher.

Another patient runs out of the room only to be run to the ground by the dentist (Jack V. Lloyd) and his nurses (Viola Richard and Dorothy Coburn).

Stan is finally coerced into the chair of pain . . .

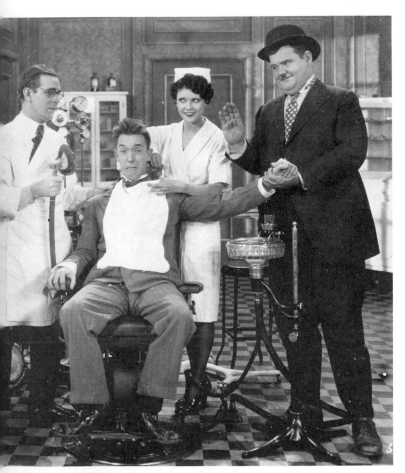

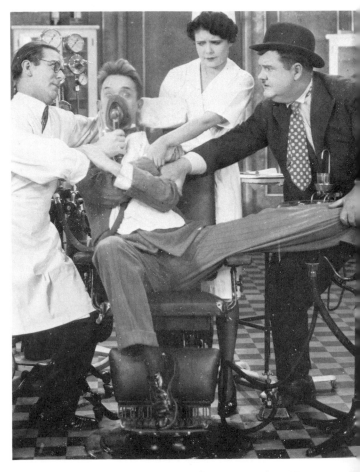

. . . and is attacked with a gas mouthpiece. He fights valiantly and Ollie tells the others to leave them alone, "and when I get him in the chair, sneak up on him." The dentist and nurses leave.

Ollie demonstrates to Stan that there is nothing to it—"It's as easy as pie! Just relax!"—by getting in the chair himself. Meanwhile, one dentist tells the other, "I'm all in. Will you pull a tooth for that guy in the chair?"

The other dentist (Otto Fries) goes briskly to the chair, quickly chloroforms Ollie and extracts his tooth, then gives the tooth and the pincer to Stan.

Stan is stunned at this quick turn of events. When Ollie awakes, he sees Stan holding the pincer and his tooth. He throws Stan down mercilessly in the chair and gives him ample dosage of laughing gas, at the same time getting a liberal portion of it himself.

By the time they get outside and start their car, the nitrous oxide is at work and they succumb to laughter. They crash into a taxi and roar appreciatively.

They get into the middle of the street and cause a traffic jam. A cop (Edgar Kennedy) tries to straighten things out but the boys fail to respond to Edgar's directions. The car stalls and Stan tells Edgar, "Wind it up!" Edgar cranks the Ford . . .

. . . and in the process, his belt falls off, followed in turn by his pants. The boys back up into a car, and its driver argues heatedly with them. Edgar forces the man to back up, and motions the boys to go ahead. Instead, hooting happily, Stan and Ollie back up, running over Edgar. Edgar dusts himself off, comes over to the boys, slowly. Ollie slaps him, Edgar slaps Ollie—the boys howling with laughter all the while.

"You're practically in jail right now," Edgar tells them. He gets in the driver's seat and backs up, again crashing into the car behind them. After getting the car in and out of another traffic jam, Edgar drives the boys and himself past a sign saying Street Closed. They zoom around the corner— into a mudhole. The car sinks into the mudhole as Stan and Ollie chortle merrily.

FLYING ELEPHANTS

All Star Series / Two reels / Silent / Released February 12, 1928, by Pathé Exchange / Produced by Hal Roach / Directed by Fred Butler, and Hal Roach (uncredited) / Titles by H.M. Walker / Story by Hal E. Roach.

Little Twinkle Star Stan Laurel / *Mighty Giant* Oliver Hardy / *Gorgeous "wrestler"* Dorothy Coburn / *The other fisherman* Leo Willis / *Hulking cavemen* Stanley (Tiny) Sandford, Bud Fine / Part cut from final release print: *Stone-Age lovely* Edna Marian. (The seemingly irrelevant title derives from a brief animated sequence that does indeed depict flying elephants.) (Working titles: *Were Women Always Wild?* and *Do Cavemen Marry?*)

Note: The Pathé releases were advertised in the trades as having but one star, Stan Laurel, even though M-G-M All Star Comedies concurrently issued were giving twin billing to Stan Laurel and Oliver Hardy.

Opening title: **"6,000 years ago all men were forced to marry or work on the rock pile—that's why it was called the Stone Age."**

In this loosely constructed but delightfully bizarre film Stan and Babe give essentially solo performances, appearing together only briefly (but affectionately) during the closing sequence.

King Ferdinand has decreed that all males between 13 and 95 must marry within 24 hours under penalty of banishment or death—or possibly both. The first of the story's three principals we meet is Ye Aged Saxophonus (James Finlayson), a wizard, who drives "Ye Firste Ford" and has a throbbing toothache. He also has a pretty daughter, Blushing Rose (Viola Richard), described as "a goodly wench withal." Our second principal comes into ken shortly after—a mighty giant (Ollie)…

…a behemoth of courtly manner and gesture who considers himself a prime ladies' man despite their contrary opinion. For small talk he is given to interesting observations like "Beautiful weather—the elephants are flying south." A trick shot verifies the statement. Our third protagonist…

…is Little Twinkle Star (Stan), a pristine pansy, who revels in skipping along from hilltop to hilltop doing the scissors kick, scattering flowers and love couplets as he goes. On learning that he must find a wife, the virginal Stan hails a gorgeous creature (Dorothy Coburn)

and tries to haul her off to his cave. Failing to win his wrestling match with her, he sets out after Blushing Rose. When Saxophonus wants to know how he intends to provide for her, Stan announces that he is a shootsman: he shoots fish, sardines a specialty. In a brilliant display of pantomimic agility Stan gets in the water, club at the ready, snatches a convenient fly from the air, carefully placing it on the water as bait; instantly, an equally convenient fish passes by and snaps at the dead fly. Stan swipes at the fish with his club, captures it beautifully in his hands, and tosses it on the beach.

In the interim Saxophonus' toothache has grown worse. Ollie decides to help him by tying the tooth to a large boulder and throwing it over a precipice. Saxophonus travels all the way down with the boulder but the trip was worth it: the tooth is extracted. Saxophonus introduces Ollie to Stan, and after rubbing noses, the two discover they are rivals for Blushing Rose. A goat conveniently bumps Ollie off a cliff, leaving Stan with his bride-to-be. But Stan, Rose, and Saxophonus have their problems too—a bear that chases them off into the final fade-out.

The Finishing Touch

1928

All Star Series / Two reels / Silent / Released February 25, 1928, by M-G-M / Produced by Hal Roach / Supervised by Leo McCarey / Directed by Clyde A. Bruckman / Photographed by George Stevens / Edited by Richard Currier / Titles by H.M. Walker.

Stan Laurel Himself / *Oliver Hardy* Himself / *Officer* Edgar Kennedy / *The nurse* Dorothy Coburn / *The owner* Sam Lufkin.

Opening title: "**The story of two boys who went to school for nine years—and finished in the first reader.**"

Stan and Ollie are in the building trade—professional finishers. A title reads, "They can finish a thing that hasn't even started." The owner of a half-completed house (Sam Lufkin) tells the boys he will give them $500 if they finish the home by noon next Monday. "For $500," Ollie tells him, "we'd finish by noon today!" As the boys noisily prepare for work, a nurse comes out of a nearby hospital and pleads with the cop on the beat, "You've got the authority. Make them stop that noise!"

The cop (Edgar Kennedy) tells them, "If you must make a noise, make it quietly." Stan shushes Ollie, and Ollie says, "Don't s-s-h-h so loud." Hunting for a board to bridge a way across to the house, Stan puts a thin board up, realizes it is not sturdy, and puts broken parts of a big board on top of it. Moments later Ollie walks across, it breaks, and he falls heavily. Later, we see Stan walking across our line of vision holding one end of a board; the board continues, and continues, and continues, and shortly after we see Stan walk across, supporting the other end of the board.

Ollie steps on some nails and orders Stan to pick them up. Stan puts them in the shovel with his hand, dumps them in the bucket with the shovel, and accidentally loses sight of the bucket by hooking it onto the shovel behind him.

Stan is ordered to sandpaper the door. Then the nurse enters, demanding, "Who's the big cheese here?" Stan points to Ollie, and the girl informs him, "You're gonna stop the noise—or I'm gonna pet somebody!" She pokes Ollie in the nose and steps over a board, which tips up and hits her. She walks back to Ollie, who is holding his nose, and punches him in the stomach. She pokes Stan who is prevented from retaliating by Ollie. The girl starts to pick up a hammer as Stan tears a piece of sandpaper. Stricken with embarrassment, the girl runs out quickly.

Ollie, preparing to do shingling, puts some nails in his mouth, takes a hammer, and walks out the door. He falls from the stairless doorway outside and swallows the nails. While inserting a window casing, Stan loses part of it and the window frame breaks over him. After shushing him, Ollie puts more nails in his mouth, grabs some shingles, and exits out the doorway from which Stan has just removed the box Ollie placed there for use as a step. Ollie falls and swallows the nails. Stan shushes him, Ollie kicks Stan and puts his step-box back by the doorway. Ollie steps on the box, which breaks.

The nurse (Dorothy Coburn) can only take so much. This time the cop gets it—right in the eye.

The Laurel and Hardy approach to industrial safety is catastrophically casual.

Ollie succeeds in shingling, principally the cop.

Ultimately, as a title tells us, "The house was finished—in spite of anything they could do." The owner is delighted, hands them the $500, and Ollie pontifically assures him, "She's built like Gibraltar." Then a bird flies onto the chimney, the chimney tilts and caves through the roof, the pillars fall off the porch, a window falls out, another window falls out. The owner demands his money, the boys toss it back and forth as he chases them, but he finally wrests it from Stan. Stan smears the man with paint.

They have a brick-and-rock throw.

The nurse comes into the middle of the fray, and a brick knocks her into the mortar. (Miss Coburn's stand-in appears in the still.)

Stan and Ollie give up bricks in favor of rocks. Seeing a rock under their truck's wheel—placed there as a brake—Stan grabs it, and Ollie struggles to get it from him. The truck rolls down the incline to the house and destroys it in one massive finishing touch.

FROM SOUP TO NUTS

1928

All Star Series / Two reels / Silent / Released March 24, 1928, by M-G-M / Produced by Hal Roach / Supervised by Leo McCarey / Directed by E. Livingston (Edgar) Kennedy / Photographed by Len Powers / Edited by Richard Currier / Titles by H.M. Walker / Story by Leo McCarey.

Stan Laurel Himself / *Oliver Hardy* Himself / *Mrs. Culpepper* Anita Garvin / *Mr. Culpepper* Stanley (Tiny) Sandford / *Cook* Otto Fries / *Maid* Edna Marian / *Haughty guest* Ellinor Van Der Veer / *Party guests* George Bichel, Dorothy Coburn, Sam Lufkin, Gene Morgan / *Dog* Buddy. (Reworked into *A Chump at Oxford* twelve years later.)

Opening title:
"Mrs. Culpepper is an idol to the snobs—and a pain in the neck to everybody else."

Mrs. Culpepper is planning a posh dinner party tonight, and two earnest members of the working class arrive at her front door. Their business cards read: "Laurel and Hardy—Waiters. All We Ask Is A Chance." Stan pulls at the bell cord, but Ollie imperiously takes over, pulls it himself—and it flies smartly out of the wall.

Ollie hands their letter of introduction to the maid (Edna Marian). Moments later, Mrs. Culpepper is reading it with more than a trace of incredulity:

Cooks' and Waiters
Association
3510 Lexington Avenue
EXPERIENCED HELP
FURNISHED

Dear Mrs. Culpepper—
These two boys are the best that we could furnish on such short notice. They are experienced waiters, but their experience has been in railroad eating houses.

With apologies—
H. A. Bradley

Mrs. Culpepper turns the boys over to the maid, who takes them to the kitchen. Ollie enters first, and Stan's forthright entrance behind him dumps Ollie's hat in the frosting bowl. Ollie has emphasized to Stan that he must keep his hat off in the house. Seeing the chef in his professional headgear, Stan removes it and, referring to his pal, says sharply, "He doesn't like it!" The chef and Stan engage in an on-off hat pull that culminates in breaking plates over each other's head.

At the table, Mrs. Culpepper attacks her fruit cocktail but is uncertain which utensil to employ. After essaying soup spoon and fork, she takes the proper spoon and tries desperately to keep a cherry on it long enough to reach her mouth. Farther down the table where Mr. Culpepper is sitting next to a lady guest, the Culpepper dog crawls between the lady's legs with a banana in its mouth. Seconds later, the lady punches Mr. Culpepper indignantly with her elbow and says "Be a *gentleman!*" Meanwhile, after continuing frustrations, Mrs. Culpepper gets the cherry on her spoon, but just as she is raising it to her mouth, her tiara falls over her eyes. At this point, Stan and Ollie make their entrance into the dining hall, Stan with the soup, Ollie with the plates.

Stan is not attentive, and Ollie wonders momentarily about the source of the moisture. Ollie directs him to put the soup down on the serving table, but Stan indicates he cannot because a large cake is there. Ollie picks up the cake and steps on the banana peel, which the Culpepper dog has just discarded on the carpet. Ollie falls into the cake, and throws the peel angrily away.

Ollie implies that Stan is at least partially responsible for this indignity. Stan, in handing the soup around, does not notice he is walking toward the banana peel Ollie threw away. Stan falls and soup sprays the host . . .

...Mr. Culpepper (Tiny Sandford), who uses Stan's shirttail to mop up. Stan pulls it away and takes out Culpepper's shirttail to wipe off his own coat. The host tries to punch him but Stan punches first and Mr. Culpepper departs in very high dudgeon.

Mrs. Culpepper (Anita Garvin) is still chasing the elusive cherry. As she does so, Ollie enters proudly with another cake, again slips on the displaced banana peel, and dives face first into the cake. Mrs. Culpepper again frenziedly attacks the cherry, again fails. Stan has a good idea. He puts a glass over the cherry, captures it, and hands it to her. Just as she is about to eat it, Stan gives her a congratulatory backslap and the tiara slams down over her eyes. Stan goes to the serving table as Ollie enters the room, victoriously serene, wheeling in a new cake on a tea cart.

Mrs. Culpepper hits the dinner chime and Ollie comes to ask "Did you gong, madame?" At long last, she gets the cherry on her spoon and almost in her mouth when Ollie hits the gong— the tiara drops again. Ollie lifts it up for her. "Serve the salad," she orders, "without dressing." Ollie leaves with his instructions, and her tiara falls again. Ollie goes to Stan and tells him, "Bring in the salad, undressed." Stan ponders this, broods a bit, then bursts into tears. The maid looks at him wonderingly, and he sobs out, "I have to serve the salad undressed." "I always serve it that way," she says. "What kind of a party *is* this?," Stan asks. After further footage of Mrs. Culpepper trying to snare the elusive cherry, Stan enters in his underwear, carrying the large salad bowl. At first no one notices him as he goes disgustedly from guest to guest putting the salad on their plates, but then Mr. Culpepper looks at him unbelievingly. "Can you imagine my embarrassment?," Stan asks him. Through all of this, Mrs. Culpepper is perfervidly trying to spear her cherry, the tiara inevitably collapsing again. She claps her hands and tells Stan to lift it up. He does so, she sees his dishabille and screams. As the guests rise in disorder, Ollie drapes a coat around Stan.

(No such scene occurs in the film, but it probably should have.) Mrs. Culpepper actually retains her dress but not her decorum. Ollie asks her, "How's that—perfect?" She slaps Ollie, who, losing his balance, spins along, finally crashing into the tea wagon, facedown in the cake. The tea wagon breaks.

You're Darn Tootin'

1928

All Star Series / Two reels / Silent / Released April 21, 1928, by M-G-M / Produced by Hal Roach / Supervised by Leo McCarey / Directed by E. Livingston (Edgar) Kennedy / Photographed by Floyd Jackman / Edited by Richard Currier / Titles by H.M. Walker.

Stan Laurel Himself / *Oliver Hardy* Himself / *Man from inside the ABC Restaurant* Sam Lufkin / *Worker in manhole* Chet Brandenberg / *Officer* Christian Frank / *Drunk* Rolfe Sedan / *Cross-eyed pedestrian* George Rowe / *Sister McPherson* Agnes Steele / *Bandstand musicians* Ham Kinsey, William Irving, Charlie Hall / *Orchestra leader* Otto Lederer / *Boarder* Dick Gilbert / *Passersby* Dick Gilbert, Frank Saputo. (Working title and British title: *The Music Blasters.*)

Opening title: **"The story of two musicians who played neither by note nor ear—they used brute strength."**

At a public concert, a title tells us, "The orchestra leader was making his farewell appearance—the public had been demanding it for years." At the conclusion of a piece, the conductor (Otto Lederer) taps his stand for the orchestra members to sit down after their bow. They do, except for Stan and Ollie who rise—in typical nonsynchronization.

Stan and Ollie are harmonious in being totally out of harmony with both the conductor and their fellow musicians. They are, in consequence, relieved of employment.

Back at their boardinghouse a note from their landlady tells them, "In the excitement of having a job, you have overlooked 14 weeks board bill." Stan cannot get salt out of his shaker; he unscrews the top, pours out a bit, and puts the top back on the shaker without screwing it tight. Ollie takes the salt, shakes it in his soup, and it all spills out. The same happens with the peppcr. Stan is about to take the top off the catsup bottle, but Ollie quickly places it on the floor. The landlady asks her little boy, Sturgeon, where he has been. "Down at the bandstand," he says, and when his mother asks him if the music was any good, he says, "It was great,"—indicating the boys—"after they was fired."

The landlady (Agnes Steele) orders them to *"go!"*

"Very well, sister McPherson," Ollie says in imitation of her high dramatic tone, "we *go!*"

They begin self-employment as street musicians...

...but the cop on the beat (Christian Frank) asks for their license. "We have no dog," Ollie says. But they leave anyway.

A drunk, seeing that the boys are having difficulties conducting each other, takes over the job. Stan and Ollie swing to with a will. Upstairs in a rehearsal hall, their conductor nemesis is rehearsing for yet another farewell appearance. He hears the cacophony below. At the conclusion of their number, Stan holds out a hat to the approaching policeman but the conductor fills the hat first—by pouring a bowl of water into it from above.

Departing to find a more appreciative audience, the boys walk across the street and Stan falls into a manhole. Ollie pulls him up; the workman below has not appreciated the unexpected company.

DANGER

Ollie, in turn, has difficulty avoiding the hole..

The boys keep losing either themselves or their instruments in the manhole until its rightful owner (Chet Brandenberg) gives Ollie a painful reminder to stay away. In internecine battle, Ollie breaks Stan's clarinet in two and throws it in the street. Stan knocks Ollie's horn into the street, where a truck squashes it flat.

In a rising crescendo of mutual affronts, the boys assault each other's ties, shins, handkerchiefs, stomachs, buttons, and clothing. A man comes out of the restaurant, and Ollie tells him what has occurred. The man hits Stan in the stomach; Stan kicks him in the shins. Another man comes over and pushes Stan, who kicks him in return.

Person after person enters the fray, reciprocally devastating each other's shins and vengefully pulling off each other's pants. The cop enters to restore order but Stan indignantly pulls off *his* pants. Seeing what has been done, the boys run off, pantsless. A fat man appears, shouting "I've been robbed!" The last scene is of Stan and Ollie, both attired in the fat man's pants, striding away in easy step, tipping their hats graciously.

THEIR PURPLE MOMENT

1928

All Star Series / Two reels / Silent / Released May 19, 1928, by M-G-M / Produced by Hal Roach / Supervised by Leo McCarey / Directed by James Parrott / Photographed by George Stevens / Edited by Richard Currier / Titles by H.M. Walker.

Stan Laurel Mr. Pincher / *Oliver Hardy* Himself / *Hardy's girl friend* Anita Garvin / *Laurel's girl friend* Kay Deslys / *Cook* Jimmy Aubrey / *Mrs. Pincher* Fay Holderness / *Mrs. Hardy* Lyle Tayo / *Cabdriver* Leo Willis / *Doorman* Jack Hill / *Night-club patron* Jack Hill / *Extra* Retta Palmer / *Waiters at the Pink Pup* Stanley (Tiny) Sandford, Sam Lufkin, Ed Brandenberg / *The suspicious gossip* Patsy O'Byrne / *Waitress* Dorothy Walbert / *Parts cut from final release print: Waiter* Edgar Dearing / *Officer* Edgar Kennedy / *Midget* Harry Earles / *Pink Pup atmosphere extra* Clara Guiol. (Reworked as *Blotto* two years later.)

Opening title: **"Dedicated to husbands who 'hold out' part of the pay envelope on their wives—and live to tell about it."**

Mrs. Pincher (Fay Holderness) has collected a big wad of grocery coupons—"Only 2,000 more and she gets a cream pitcher." Mr. Pincher (Stan) is described by the title as "A goodly man—the boldest thing he ever did was to whistle in the backyard." In handing over his weekly salary, he must account for a missing $3, a sum he insists he spent on the Chinese phonograph record he is holding. Actually he has secreted the money (with previous salary skimmings) in a card case secure in the secret compartment-inner pocket of the gent in the large photograph. Mrs. Pincher has actually seen Stan deposit the money there; furtively she takes all the money from the photograph, replacing it with her grocery coupons.

Mrs. Hardy (Lyle Tayo) suspects that her husband may be playing Stan's game of holding back part of their income.

Ollie confirms: "She found my hideout! She's a bloodhound!"

"My wife'll never find mine!," Stan asserts. "I'm a weasel!" Stan removes the fat billfold from the photograph without looking at its contents. The boys, deciding to live it up on Stan's money, tell the ladies they are going down to the bowling alley.

On their way to dubious pleasures, they encounter the town gossip, a lady of rock-ribbed suspicions.

As the boys pass the Pink Pup Café, they hear the manager (Tiny Sandford) address two lovely ladies (Kay Deslys and Anita Garvin) in distinctly unchivalrous language: "Which one of you dames is gonna pay the bill? That's what I wanna know!"

Gallantly, Ollie says, "Would you consider us too bold if we were to assume all responsibility?" The girls wouldn't mind a bit.

The cabby (Leo Willis) asks who is going to pay the taxi bill. Ollie, fortified by his memory of Stan's bulging billfold, says they will take on this obligation as well.

In entering the café, Kay falls accidentally, and Stan, her escort, spills over her. The gossip happens by and, deliciously enthralled at the sight, rushes off to tell Mrs. Pincher and Mrs. Hardy.

Anita and Kay have been deserted by two deadbeats, and Kay indicates what lies in store for anyone foolish enough to leave her stuck with the bill again.

After ordering huge steaks for all, the boys sit back to enjoy the floor show—a midget troupe doing a chocolate-soldier dance. Delighted with the performance, Stan calls the cigarette girl over and orders a plethora of favors for the little folk.

On discovering his wallet bulging with very pretty coupons, Stan wonders how long he can delay the final accounting. Ollie, meanwhile, has cordially invited the cabdriver to order up a big steak.

As the lights lower for more of the floor show, Stan passes the billfold over to Ollie who recognizes their serious predicament. They both try to slide down out of their seats and sneak away, but Stan's contortions cause a waiter to trip and fall into a tray of mashed potatoes.

Their waiter brings a top-heavy bill and Ollie tells him to wait until the dance act now on the floor is finished. Stan shrinks down again trying to get out, and the waiter again falls over him, landing in another plate of mashed potatoes. Their waiter presents the bill once more; Stan and Ollie toss the billfold back and forth. Their waiter finally catches it and examines the contents in horror. The boys leave the table, evade their pursuing waiter, and duck into a booth—unaware of its occupants, their grim-visaged wives. The boys hide under the table; a waiter trips over them, getting a face full of mashed potatoes for the third time.

Confronted, Ollie "explains" that they were on their way to the bowling alley when Stan "dragged me to this den of vice!"

Angered, Stan throws a pie at Ollie who ducks, and Mrs. Hardy receives it.

A wild pie melee ensues between the Hardys, the Laurels, and the chef. As Stan starts to swing a chair, the waiter comes in with a tray of mashed potatoes and meets his inexorable fate. The waiter begins to throw mashed potatoes, and the headwaiter gets a face full. Ollie laughs and the headwaiter mashes a pie in Ollie's face.

Note: Stan's projected ending for this film was never used. As originally conceived, the boys were to flee their wives in the café, stumble into the midgets' dressing room, hastily put on some of their costumes, and walk out of the café on their knees. Several stills were taken of this sequence, but in the end the studio decided the pie fight made a funnier ending. These two stills are all that is left of a very funny idea.

Production Sidelight

SHOULD MARRIED MEN GO HOME?

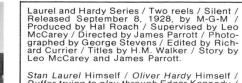

Opening title:
"Question: What is the surest way to keep a husband home? Answer: Break both his legs."

Laurel and Hardy Series / Two reels / Silent / Released September 8, 1928, by M-G-M / Produced by Hal Roach / Supervised by Leo McCarey / Directed by James Parrott / Photographed by George Stevens / Edited by Richard Currier / Titles by H.M. Walker / Story by Leo McCarey and James Parrott.

Stan Laurel Himself / *Oliver Hardy* Himself / *Duffer trying to play through* Edgar Kennedy / *Blonde girl friend* Edna Marian / *Brunette girl friend* Viola Richard / *Giant* John Aassen / *Muddy combatants* Jack Hill, Dorothy Coburn / *Lady golfer* Lyle Tayo / *Caddie* Chet Brandenberg / *Pro-shop manager* Sam Lufkin / *Soda jerk* Charlie Hall / *Mrs. Hardy* Kay Deslys.

Ollie and his wife (Kay Deslys) are weekend relaxing, reading the papers. They hear Stan approach; apprehensively they look out the window for him. Golf-togged to the nines, Stan clearly has a friendly game in mind. The Hardys duck back and hide as Stan knocks on the door. No reply. Stan slips a note halfway under the door: "If you are not in when I come back, I'll know you are out. Stan." About to go, he sees the note being pulled inside. The Hardys look out the window again; Stan sees them.

Resigned to their fate, the Hardys open the door. Stan, referring to divot-gouging on the turf, says, "I dropped in to see if you didn't want to dig a little golf!" Ollie says he and Mrs. Hardy have decided to stay in this morning. The three sit down—and wait. Stan livens things up by accidentally igniting an entire pack of matches, and as he rises, a window shade falls down. Trying to replace it, he gets on a cane chair with unfortunate results. Gesturing to the phonograph, he asks, "Do you mind if I play *The Maiden's Prayer?*" Ollie insists on playing it himself, pointedly saying that there is a right way and a wrong way to do a thing. He winds the Victrola too tightly, the turntable springs off—and Mrs. Hardy has had enough. She chases the boys out of the house. Before leaving, Ollie exchanges his pal's derby for a large rakish cap that keeps drooping down Stan's head for the rest of the film.

As they go, Stan dashingly leaps over the fence in a gazelle's gallop. Ollie, seeing his wife looking out the window, attempts to do the same. The entire fence goes down.

At the golf course they are told that only foursomes are allowed on the course today. The boys see two attractive young ladies (Edna Marian and Viola Richard), and a mild flirtation ensues. One of the girls asks, "Won't you bankers buy us a drink?"

They go to the soda fountain, and in checking the bankroll, the boys find it amounts to 15 cents. Ollie explains privately that 4 into 15 won't go—Stan must refuse a drink. After the others have ordered cherry sodas, Stan orders a malted milk. Following a brief conference, Ollie tries again, asking Stan heavily what *he* would like. Stan politely says he doesn't want any but one of the girls urges him to "join us." Brightly, Stan says, "Well, all right—put an egg in that malted milk." Ollie, infuriated, tells Stan *he* will know how to refuse. He does, but sneaks Stan's drink on the side. The bill turns out to be 30 cents. Ollie gives Stan the bill, with the 15 cents—and walks away. Stan, according to the title, "left his watch to square the 30 cents. It was that kind of watch."

Walking briskly to the first hole, Stan breaks stride frequently to pick up a number of vagrant golf balls.

Play begins. A burly golfer (Edgar Kennedy) impatiently pushes the dilatory Stan's ball aside and sets up his own. In bending over, Edgar loses his toupee. Stan picks it up, Edgar pulls it away from him, puts it on…

…takes a swing, hitting Stan right on the nose.

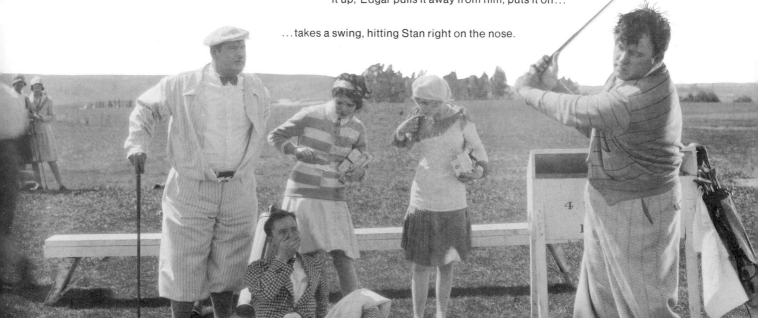

His ball landing near Stan's, Edgar comes over and gets into action, his toupee again falling off. Obligingly, Stan starts to pick it up, but accidentally grabs a flower-spouting divot. Without looking, Edgar brusquely snatches the divot and claps it on his head.

Edgar tries to avoid getting his feet in the mud when whacking his ball out of the mire, but Stan sanctimoniously shows him the golfing regulation stating that a ball must be played from where it lies. Edgar walks into the mud, hits the ball, knocking a mud clump into a young lady's face.

This begins a reciprocal-destruction melee among a number of the players—mud pie for mud pie—with Stan and Ollie uninvolved, until Ollie falls in. A bully comes over...

...and pushes Stan in. The boys feel something stirring under them, and it turns out to be...   ...Edgar coming up with his ball.

EARLY TO BED

🎩🎩🎩 **1928**

Laurel and Hardy Series / Two reels / Silent / Released October 6, 1928, by M-G-M / Produced by Hal Roach / Supervised by Leo McCarey / Directed by Emmett Flynn / Photographed by George Stevens / Edited by Richard Currier / Titles by H.M. Walker.

Stan Laurel Himself / *Oliver Hardy* Himself.

Opening title: "**9:00 a.m. to 10:00 a.m. That important hour when financial kings of American affairs open their mail.**"

Stan and Ollie are at the bottom of the financial ladder. But a letter arrives that tells Ollie he has inherited his uncle's fortune. To share in this plenitude, Stan becomes Ollie's butler.

One night Ollie comes home carrying (a title tells us) "just enough champagne to make his nose tickle." Ollie rings his bell, then hides. He repeats the jape several times.

At one point Stan comes out to look around for the miscreant bell ringer, and Ollie runs into the house, closing the door and peering out mischievously from the door panel.

Stan searches assiduously.

He spots the miscreant.

Ollie opens the door and Stan falls in. Upon recovering his dignity, he helps the master with his coat.

The master is a bit beyond caring.

Stan gets the idea that Ollie has been drinking. The dog is faintly bemused by all this.

Stan tries to get Ollie to bed but Ollie's romping spirits prevail. Ollie says he'll go to bed, but insists he must be caught first. Ollie falls over a pillow, Stan catches him, and a genteel wrestling match follows.

Worn out, Stan goes to bed, removes his dog from it, and finds the dog's last meal.

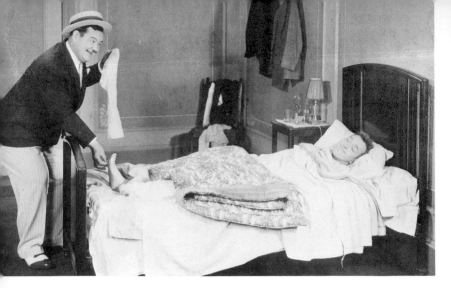

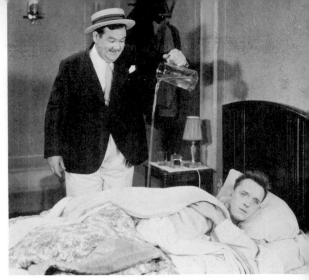

"Wake up! Take a look at my new spring outfit," shouts Ollie. Stan is beatifically at rest.

Ollie finds a more forthright way of waking him up.

Stan wants to quit his job; Ollie won't let him. Stan says, "I'll *make* you fire me," and he runs rampaging through the house, destroying as he goes, with emphasis on expensive vases.

Ollie joins in the onrush of destruction.

Stan falls face first into a cake.

"You're frothing at the mouth!," Ollie tells him.

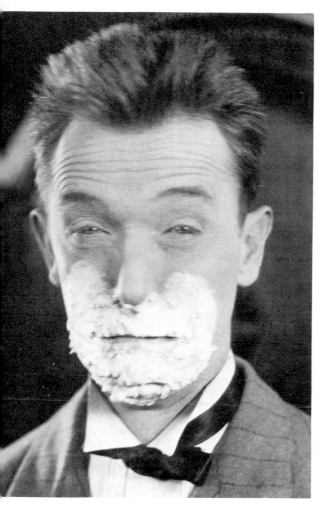

"You've gone mad!," he continues. Stan's reactions verify that somewhat.

Ollie tries to keep Stan from more precipitate destruction, but Stan, fully enraged, grabs a shovel and chases Ollie into the foyer where Ollie has erected a fountain bedecked with Hardy gargoyles.

Ollie dives down into the fountain and Stan flails at the emerging air bubbles. Uncertain that it is the master or just where the master is, Stan sits down on the fountain and considers. Ollie rises up from the water, knocks off one of the gargoyles, and substitutes himself, spewing out water pontifically. During protracted byplay, in which Stan hits various of the Hardy heads to test their aliveness, Ollie finally stands up laughing. He asks that they forgive, forget, and be pals again. They muss each other's hair affectionately. Then Ollie pushes Stan into the fountain and jovially hits him over the head with a shovel.

Production Sidelight

A posed, out-of-role still: Babe indicating that the pajamas are too ample even for him.

75

TWO TARS

1928

Laurel and Hardy Series / Two reels / Silent / Released November 3, 1928, by M-G-M / Produced by Hal Roach / Supervised by Leo McCarey / Directed by James Parrott / Photographed by George Stevens / Edited by Richard Currier / Titles by H.M. Walker / Story by Leo McCarey.

Stan Laurel Himself / *Oliver Hardy* Himself / *Brunette coquette* Thelma Hill / *Blonde coquette* Ruby Blaine / *Man whose fenders are ripped back* Charley Rogers / *Family motorists* Edgar Kennedy, Clara Guiol / *Man who flings rolled-up bedding at Stan* Jack Hill / *Shopkeeper* Charlie Hall / *Motorcycle cop* Edgar Dearing / *Truck driver* Harry Bernard* / *Straw-hatted pedestrian in early scenes* Sam Lufkin / *Moustachioed motorist in derby hat* Sam Lufkin / *Countryside motorists* Baldwin Cooke**, Charles McMurphy, Ham Kinsey, Lyle Tayo, Lon Poff, Retta Palmer, George Rowe, Chet Brandenberg, Fred Holmes, Dorothy Walbert, Frank Ellis, Helen Gilmore. (Working title: *Two Tough Tars.*)

*Working in first of his 26 films with Laurel and Hardy.

**Working in first of his 30 films with Laurel and Hardy.

After newsreel footage of the U.S. Navy steaming along in briny glory, we see Stan and Ollie in sailor garb driving down a city street. They are identified by a title as "two dreadnaughts from the battleship *Oregon.*" They have rented a car, and in holiday mood . . . almost smash into a pole supporting a gentleman (Sam Lufkin) who flays them verbally.

Ollie takes the driver's seat with the imperious statement, "The first rule of the road—always keep your eyes straight ahead!" As he explains this directly to his friend, he crashes into a lamppost and Stan says, "What's rule number two?"

The boys introduce themselves to two lovelies: "This is Ensign Laurel," and "Meet Secretary Wilbur" (the Secretary of the Navy in 1928). The lovelies (Thelma Hill and Ruby Blaine) try to extract the contents of an uncooperative gum machine. The machine explodes its treasures unexpectedly, causing Stan to slip to the ground after the shopkeeper (Charlie Hall) bops him in the gut. Then the girls, too, fall prey to the shifting ground.

After a glorious day (a title tells us the boys "telephoned the admiral to hold the fleet—they might be late") Stan, Ollie, and the girls come across a traffic jam caused by a road repair crew. Backing out, they are hit by a coupe driven by Edgar Kennedy. Ollie backs into him, ruining Edgar's radiator. Ollie again backs into Edgar's car, which in turn smacks into the car behind, breaking its headlight.

Edgar gets out of his car and kicks the boys' car. Stan reciprocates by tearing off Edgar's headlight.

Stan kicks Edgar's light into a nearby windshield, and that motorist breaks one of the girls' balloons, causing Stan to plaster the offender's head with cement.

The offender slashes Stan's and Ollie's tires, and the boys completely remove his wheels.

After Edgar pulls some hair off Ollie's chest, Ollie pushes Edgar into a car covered with camping equipment. Edgar and the camper argue.

Stan cranks his car, is then bumped by Edgar; Stan pulls off Edgar's radiator, and together the boys confront Edgar after he pulls off their rear fender. The boys rip off the top of Edgar's car. Edgar sinks down in dejection on his running board—which collapses.

During the brouhaha, a truck driver (Harry Bernard) throws a tomato that hits Stan in the back of the neck. A bespectacled bystander with a basket of tomatoes becomes the focus of Stan's revenge. Stan rubs tomatoes on his face and slams a hat down on the man's tomato-smeared head.

As the result of a nearby argument, a rolled tent hits Stan, which is followed by a grease-gun dispute between the girls and Edgar's wife.

Walking past a coupe, the driver (Charley Rogers) opens the door, accidentally hitting Ollie, who together with Stan revenges himself by assaulting a fender.

The boys are approached angrily by a camper (Jack Hill); Ollie pushes him out of the way, and the camper's roof baggage falls all over him. The camper throws material at the jeering crowd, and the crowd roars into battle. A traffic cop arrives, asks "Who started this?" Everybody yells, "They did!," pointing to Stan and Ollie. The cop arrests the boys and motions the cars to get moving. A melancholy parade of disabled cars begins.

One of the vehicles flattens the cop's motorcycle, after the boys sneak off. Jumping on Edgar's car, the cop says, "Follow them sailors." However, the boys have not quite gone. They back up suddenly, demolishing Edgar's car, spreading Edgar, his wife, and the cop over the roadside.

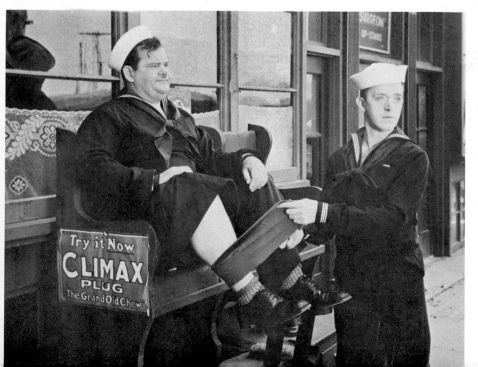

"EVERYBODY follow them sailors!," yells the oop. Cars pursue the boys into a railroad tunnel, but they back out suddenly as a train roars through. The final shot is of the boys emerging from the tunnel in their squashed car, swaying disastrously, as they painfully make their way along.

Production Sidelight

A deleted scene from the beginning of the film: The boys prepare to go out on the town.

HABEAS CORPUS

1928

Laurel and Hardy Series / Two reels / Silent, but with synchronized music and sound effects / Released December 1, 1928, by M-G-M / Produced by Hal Roach / Supervised by Leo McCarey / Directed by James Parrott / Photographed by Len Powers / Edited by Richard Currier / Titles by H.M. Walker / Story by Leo McCarey.

Stan Laurel Himself / *Oliver Hardy* Himself / *Professor Padilla* Richard Carle / *Officer Charles A. Bachman* / *Ledoux, the detective agent in butler disguise* Charley Rogers / Part cut from final release print: Graveyard custodian Lon Poff.

Opening title: "**Professor Padilla expected to startle the medical world with his new theory—that the human brain has a level surface—in some instances, practically flat.**"

A mad professor confides to his butler that he very much needs a body for scientific investigations. To the professor's house come two vagabonds (Ollie and Stan), anxious for a handout. Stan asks the butler (Charley Rogers), "Could you spare a piece of buttered toast?"

The professor thinks he can use the boys. He suggests they go to the graveyard and bring back a body that very night. Furtively, the butler, a detective in disguise, has warned headquarters that the professor has gone balmy again and is sending two men to the graveyard.

When darkness comes, the boys arrive at a street sign that they are unable to read. Stan wants to climb up the post and read it but Ollie bossily says *he* will do so.

He climbs up to read WET PAINT, and comes down indelibly marked by his misadventure.

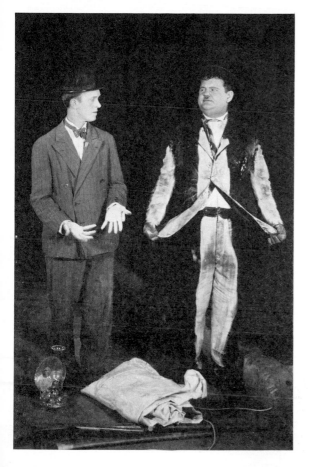

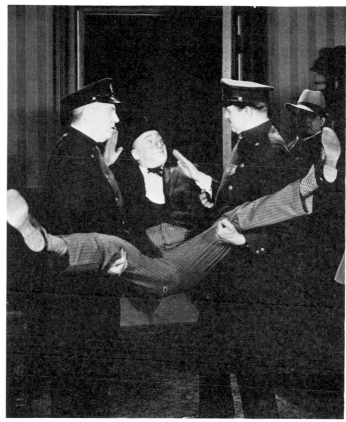

Meanwhile, the police have removed the professor (Richard Carle) to happier surroundings where some nice folks in white will take care of him.

After frightening a night watchman (a sequence deleted from final print of the film) and other difficulties, Ollie tries to jump over the cemetery wall but he crashes down *with* it.

As a detective watches off camera, Ollie helps Stan onto the grounds by pitching him into an open grave.

While Stan is commiserating with Ollie, who has inadvertently slammed a shovel on his own big toe, the detective creeps into the empty grave and crawls into a white sheet there. The boys return and haul him victoriously aloft.

Ollie tells his pal that quiet is a prime desideratum of their operation.

Oddly, the "corpse" they have abducted seems to be showing signs of life.

Ollie takes the pulsating sack, puts it on Stan's back, and they both walk off. The detective's feet break through and he walks companionably along behind Stan. Stan keeps hearing someone following him but every time he looks back there is no one there but his sack. The detective has fun by removing Ollie's hat, and finally grabs him by the face. Ollie runs away and falls into a mudhole at the curb; Stan jumps over it, but the detective falls in. Stan pulls Ollie out of the mud, and Ollie asks him, "Where's the remainders?" The detective climbs out and the boys rush 82 about in a frenzy of fear.

WE FAW DOWN

1928

Laurel and Hardy Series / Two reels / Silent, but with synchronized music and sound effects / Released December 29, 1928, by M-G-M / Produced by Hal Roach / Directed by Leo McCarey / Edited by Richard Currier / Titles by H.M. Walker.

Stan Laurel Himself / *Oliver Hardy* Himself / *One-Round Kelly* George Kotsonaros / *Mrs. Laurel* Bess Flowers / *Mrs. Hardy* Vivien Oakland / *Fighter's girl friend* Kay Deslys / *Kay's girl friend* Vera White / *Pedestrian* Allen Cavan. (British title: *We Slip Up.*)

Opening title: "**This story is based upon the assumption that, somewhere in the world, there are husbands who do not tell their wives everything.**"

The boys, spending an afternoon at home, would like to be spending it elsewhere—at a poker game.

The wives (Bess Flowers and Vivien Oakland) are playing cards, and the boys receive an alibi-establishing call from their poker cronies. Ollie pretends it's his boss.

Ollie tells the skeptical ladies, "That was the boss. He wants Stan and me to go to the Orpheum Theatre."

In retrieving a chubby lady's (Kay Deslys) hat from under a car, the boys vie with each other in gallantry. The car moves away as a street sprinkler comes past, and Stan and Ollie fall wet and prostrate. The hat is returned to Kay as her girl friend (Vera White) looks on. The girls invite the boys to dry off in their apartment.

While the boys gratefully take up the girls' offer, the Orpheum Theatre is burning, and so are Mrs. Laurel and Mrs. Hardy when they read about it in the late afternoon edition. The wives leave to hunt down their hubbies.

Over a convivial bottle of beer, the boys are titillated into making some modest whoopee.

After a skirmish with a neighbor who needs his sleep and resents the sounds of revelry, the door opens and in prances "One Round" Kelly (George Kotsonaros), Kay's boyfriend. He opens a knife.

Stan picks up a pie
and swamps Kelly.
The boys grab
their clothing and
go out the window.

As they descend to
the sidewalk,
happy in the
knowledge they've
made a clean
getaway, they fail
to see their
horrified spouses.

The wives secretly return home.
"Don't forget, we went to the
Orpheum," says Ollie. Ollie says to
Vivien when they come in, "Boy, what
a show we saw!" He disbelieves
her disbelief.

Ollie tells his doubting audience—abetted by a pantomimic assist from behind the sofa by Stan who has access to the Orpheum's newspaper ad—just how wonderful the show at the Orpheum was. He tells of a Russian dancer, not realizing Stan is describing a bicycle act. Ollie flounces about as a Russian dancer, causing the top of the piano stool to fall off. He sits down, to great discomfort.

Still describing the show, Ollie mimes a hula dancer and is horrified to read the headlines describing the Orpheum's demise.

Deflated, Ollie says, "It's a good thing we went to the Palace instead of the Orpheum." Stan goes into convulsions as the doorbell rings.

Vera is at the door, and says, "Here's your vest, big boy." Ollie is severely discomfited.

Vivien goes out, returns quickly with a shotgun, and the boys dash away. Next, there is a distance shot of two apartment houses as Stan and Ollie run between them. The girls chase the boys; Vivien shoots, and a number of men jump out of the apartment house windows in various states of undress.

LIBERTY
1929

Laurel and Hardy Series / Two reels / Silent, but with synchronized music and sound effects / Released January 26, 1929, by M-G-M / Produced by Hal Roach / Directed by Leo Mc-Carey / Photographed by George Stevens / Edited by Richard Currier and William Terhune / Titles by H.M. Walker / Story by Leo McCarey.

Stan Laurel Himself / *Oliver Hardy* Himself / *Store owner* James Finlayson / *Prison warden* Tom Kennedy / *Woman entering cab* Harlean Carpenter/Jean Harlow / *Worker at seafood dealer* Harry Bernard / *Cabdriver* Ed Brandenberg / *Getaway drivers* Sam Lufkin, Jack Raymond / *Officer* Jack Hill.

A group of titles and some newsreel footage devoted to stalwart Americans who have fought for liberty end with: "And even today—the fight for liberty continues." Stan and Ollie in prison garb try to elude a prison guard.

A falling branch fells the guard and the boys escape. They enter the cab of a henchman who has brought them civvies to wear. They dress hastily and in so doing put on each other's pants.

Leaving the cab, they run down an alley to exchange pants. A woman sticks her head out of a window and screams in horror. A policeman comes and the boys rush to a cab.

Unable to complete their transaction in the cab, they leave just as a man and woman (Jean Harlow) start to enter it. The couple reacts incredulously. The boys run to the rear of a fish market, and as they again begin to exchange pants, a crab, unseen, flips out of his box into Stan's pants. A man comes out of the door and stares at them. The boys hurry away, Stan in violent agitation caused by his mysterious visitor.

The boys come to the music shop of the redoubtable James Finlayson. Stan's crab-stimulated jumps wreak havoc with the records on sale.

Still needing privacy to exchange their pants, they come to a building construction site. In the "high and dizzy" tradition of Harold Lloyd, they obtain the requisite privacy atop the high girders.

Although they have finally exchanged pants, they are at the mercy of their own apprehensions—and of the *crab* who now inhabits Ollie's trousers. Unable to get down because the elevator is not available, they flail and wail wildly. Ollie thinks Stan is nipping at him; the ladder falls away; the elevator comes up unexpectedly. Standing beneath the elevator is a pursuing cop. The boys descend suddenly, march off, and the elevator rises to reveal the cop transformed to midget size.

WRONG AGAIN

1929

Laurel and Hardy Series / Two reels / Silent, but with synchronized music and sound effects / Released February 23, 1929, by M-G-M / Produced by Hal Roach / Directed by Leo Mc-Carey / Direction assistance by Lewis R. Foster / Photographed by George Stevens and Jack Roach / Edited by Richard Currier / Titles by H.M. Walker / Story by Lewis R. Foster and Leo McCarey.

Stan Laurel Himself / *Oliver Hardy* Himself / *Millionaire owner of Blue Boy painting* Del Henderson / *Officer* Harry Bernard / *Neighbor* Charlie Hall / *Owner of horse named Blue Boy* William Gillespie / *Man in buckboard* Jack Hill / *Sullivan* Sam Lufkin / *Henderson's mother* Josephine Crowell / *Stableboy* Fred Holmes. (Working title: *Just the Reverse.*)

At the fashionable Piping Rock Riding Academy the owner (William Gillespie) of the prize horse Blue Boy has evidence that two stable hands are overly zealous.

Ollie backs Blue Boy into the stable but his chum departs at the same time.

Stan, needing water for Blue Boy, turns it on, not noticing its focus.

Ollie grabs the bucket indignantly and says he'll fill it. Stan turns on the water and it pours through the bottomless pail.

The boys overhear two men discussing the latest news. "The famous *Blue Boy* has been stolen! There's $5,000 reward!," says one man. Stan and Ollie look at each other, then at the horse off camera. The man also tells them the address of *Blue Boy*'s rightful owner. Meanwhile, the *Blue Boy* the men have been discussing—Gainsborough's great painting—has been recovered by the police and the owner has been so informed by telephone. "Bring it right over," he tells the police. "Congratulations." 89

Unknowingly, Stan and Ollie take the horse to the painting's owner. Ollie comes into his front yard and sees the owner raising a window. "We've brought your Blue Boy," Ollie says. The owner throws down the front door key and says, "Take him right into the house." Bewildered, the boys do so. "These millionaires are peculiar," Ollie tells Stan. "They think just the opposite to other people," and with that he pantomimes a reverse turn with his hand, and Stan delightedly imitates it. (This becomes a running gag throughout the film.) Ollie goes on, "Even now he's taking a bath, an' it's only Monday." The millionaire, calling down from a balcony, says, "Put him on the piano, would you mind?" Stan, in the hall, hears the order, walks back into the room with Ollie and Blue Boy. "Now he wants his horse on the piano," he tells Ollie.

"Time out—while I think," says Ollie.

Blue Boy starts to eat a bowl of fern. Stan gets on top of the piano with the fern; the horse follows happily.

Stan jumps down. A second later so does Blue Boy. Upstairs the owner is puzzled by all the noise attendant upon putting a painting on the piano.

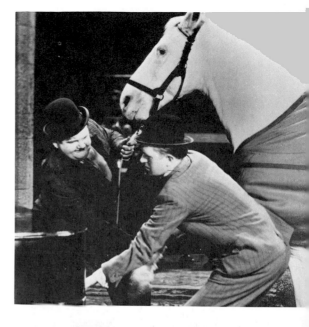

More direct ways of getting Blue Boy up are tried, including using Ollie himself.

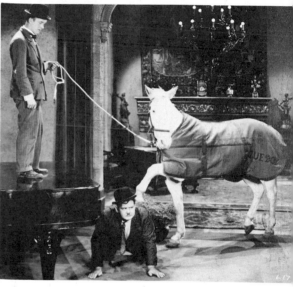

Blue Boy attains his domain, and a piano leg slips down. The boys try to lift up the piano, and Stan unintentionally uses Ollie as a means of support.

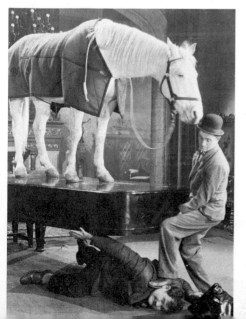

Ollie becomes part of the piano leg, but Blue Boy stands triumphant in his designated resting place.

A car is heard driving toward the house, and *Blue Boy*'s owner rushes out, telling the boys, "Pull the curtains—I want to surprise mother." The boys draw the curtains of the room. Two men bring in the *Blue Boy* painting. The owner returns with the lady, sees the horse on the piano, and chases the boys off with a shotgun. A detective who tries to stop him has been shoved against the picture. The lady asks if there has been any damage, and one of the detectives, pointing to the other cop whose head now emerges through the ripped painting, says, "No, ma'am—Sullivan is only stunned." A policeman brings the owner back and takes a smoking shotgun from him. "This man almost blew my brains out," says the cop indignantly. He turns, and we see his smoking posterior.

91

That's My Wife

1929

Laurel and Hardy Series / Two reels / Silent, but with synchronized music and sound effects / Released March 23, 1929, by M-G-M / Produced by Hal Roach / Supervised by Leo McCarey / Directed by Lloyd French / Edited by Richard Currier / Titles by H.M. Walker / Story by Leo McCarey.

Stan Laurel Himself / *Oliver Hardy* Himself / *Mrs. Hardy* Vivien Oakland / *Waiter at the Pink Pup* Charlie Hall / *Inebriate in soup altercation* Jimmy Aubrey / *Uncle Bernal* William Courtwright / *Waiter who falls in cake* Sam Lufkin / *Crooked waiter* Harry Bernard.

Opening title: "**There has been a serious misunderstanding in the Hardy family.**"

The misunderstanding has been *Stan* who, in the words of Mrs. Hardy (Vivien Oakland), ". . . dropped in to stay five minutes—he's been here for two years." Moreover, he eats grapes in bed.

Ollie pleads but Vivien is obdurate. "He leaves—or I leave." Without another word, she leaves—almost.

Ollie tells her that his Uncle Bernal won't leave them a dime if she goes. "What do I care for money?," Vivien asks grandly, sweeping out and knocking down a flowerpot.

She returns immediately, knocks down another flowerpot, and leaves for good. After a little altercation, Stan suggests that Ollie leave too. Reminded that it is, after all, Ollie's house, Stan decides to leave.

He goes upstairs to pack. Unexpectedly, Uncle Bernal drops by to meet Mrs. Hardy, whom he has never seen. And *if,* Uncle Bernal adds, "you are happily married . . . I'm going to set you up in a fine new home." Ollie says hastily that the little woman is upstairs right now, crazy to meet Uncle Bernal, and he'll bring her down this minute.

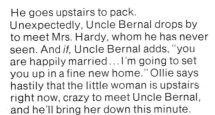

Ollie goes upstairs, convinces Stan that he must pose as Mrs. Hardy, and suggests the use of a doll's wig to help in the deception.

The dumbbell will also have to be used to effect total female contour.

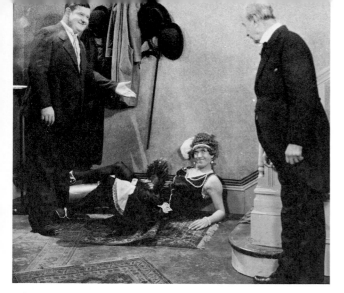

Ollie explains to Uncle Bernal (William Courtwright) that his wife, Magnolia Hardy, is not much to look at, "but what a clown," adding she'll be right down. As if to verify both statements, Stan falls downstairs.

After proper introductions, Uncle Bernal suggests a little dinner and dancing at the Pink Pup Café. Appalled, the boys realize they must suffer the experience.

At the Pink Pup, Ollie slips on the floor pulling Stan down with him, and the dumbbell escapes. Ollie hides it under their table, Stan's foot slips on it and he falls on the table.

The dumbbell rolls out on the floor, and a waiter (Sam Lufkin) carrying a large cake slips and falls—into the cake. Also caught in the fall (but for this still only) is a drunk (Jimmy Aubrey).

Sitting at another table, the drunk flirts openly with Stan. After a pelting exchange of sugar and bread between the two (with the sugar bowl hitting the waiter, again causing him to fall into a new cake he's carrying), Ollie overwhelms the drunk (now at their table) with a strategically applied bowl of soup. The drunk indignantly orders a bowl of soup to go, and when it comes, he goes with it.

Meanwhile, a rascally waiter steals a valuable necklace, lifting it off the neck of a lady patron. After the theft is discovered, the headwaiter says he will have everybody in the place searched. The thief drops the necklace down Stan's back. Feeling its presence, Stan tries to find it and tells Ollie, who also works to locate it. To facilitate the search, the boys get up to dance, wiggling as they go. Stan's way of wearing hose attracts some attention.

The dancers are aghast at Ollie's curious pawings of his partner.

Stan and Ollie go behind a screen to continue the search and are a bit more than embarrassed when a waiter removes the screen.

They go to a phone booth to search, but leave it shortly after a man comes to make a call. "Believe it or not," Ollie says to the man, "we were calling Philadelphia."

The necklace has been found on the floor, but the boys do not know it. The Pink Pup's MC introduces one of the evening's vaudeville turns—Garrick and Lucille in "The Pageant of Love." The curtain opens to reveal Stan and Ollie searching, scrambling on the floor.

Uncle Bernal has had enough of this unending unseemliness. "I'm through," he says, "I'll leave my money to a dog and cat hospital!" And he departs.

Ollie says to Stan, "I've lost my wife, an' my fortune—what next?" Whereupon some soup is poured over him by the drunk, who salutes smartly and says, "Lafayette, we are here!" He leaves, and the boys' chagrin changes to laughter.

LIF-9

BIG BUSINESS

1929

Laurel and Hardy Series / Two reels / Silent / Released April 20, 1929, by M-G-M / Produced by Hal Roach / Supervised by Leo McCarey / Directed by James Wesley Horne / Photographed by George Stevens / Edited by Richard Currier / Titles by H.M. Walker / Story by Leo McCarey.

Stan Laurel Himself / *Oliver Hardy* Himself / *Unreceptive customer* James Finlayson / *Officer* Stanley (Tiny) Sandford / *Householder who has no husband* Lyle Tayo / *Part of the neighborhood gathering* Retta Palmer, Charlie Hall.

Opening title: "**The story of a man who turned the other cheek—and got punched in the nose.**"

Stan and Ollie are selling Christmas trees in California. They stop at a lady's house, and she says she doesn't want any. Ollie asks reasonably enough if her husband wouldn't like to buy one? Coyly she admits she has no husband. To her great indignation, Stan asks, "If you *had* a husband, would he buy one?" At the next stop, Ollie resolutely ignores a sign prohibiting solicitors, pushes the bell, and is conked solidly on the head by a hammer.

They reach Fin's house and he coldly rejects their sales pitch.

He slams the door but their tree is caught therein. They ring the bell again, Stan pulls out the tree, Fin slams the door again, this time catching Stan's overcoat. The bell is rung again; Stan is freed and he begins the sales pitch once more. Fin slams the door, catching the tree again. The bell is rung once more, Fin throws the tree out of camera range, and the boys gather that maybe he really doesn't want to buy it. Stan gets a big business idea: perhaps Fin will order a tree for *next* year. Fin's reaction to this is to take a big pair of shears and cut the tree into several pieces.

Ollie cuts a few of Fin's scant hairs, Fin smashes Ollie's watch, Ollie tears the doorbell off the house. Fin calls the police department, and Stan cuts the telephone cord. Fin cuts off part of Ollie's shirt. These are the beginnings of a reciprocal destruction orgy that is to constitute the body of the film.

Fin rushes out to the boys' tin lizzie and begins to destroy their merchandise.

Stan swings a vengeful ax.

Fin pulls the door off their wagon.

The orgy intensifies. The boys attack Fin's house frontally. Fin watches incredulously.

Fin wrenches off the Ford's gas tank and throws it on the street. During this melee, a cop has arrived and sits across the street in his auto, taking careful notes on these proceedings.

The cop (Tiny Sandford) looks at Stan in disbelief. Fin has demolished the car, finally igniting the gasoline in which it is drenched. The house is in equally sad condition.

Mutual recriminations about who started the affair dissolve in pathos. Everybody sobs at the thought of it all, and the cop shoos away the crowd of neighbors who have collected. Stan gives Fin a Christmas cigar. The cop goes gulpingly back to his car, and as he turns around he sees Stan and Ollie laughing mischievously. The cop chases them down the street. Fin lights his cigar, which explodes, and he looks wrathfully at the group pounding off into the distance.

Note: There is no reason to suppose, as some people do, that these events happen in midsummer. Stan Laurel is the source affirming that it all occurs at Yuletide—in sunny California.

Production Sidelights

The aftermath: this production shot reveals how thoroughly the house was wrecked. The two men in the window are Roach studio employees—one of them the owner of the house (who was, incidentally, very well paid for the destruction).

UNACCUSTOMED AS WE ARE ∎∎∎ 1929

Laurel and Hardy Series / Two reels / All-talking / Released May 4, 1929, by M-G-M / Produced by Hal Roach / Directed by Lewis R. Foster, and Hal Roach (uncredited) / Edited by Richard Currier / Dialogue by H.M. Walker / Story by Leo McCarey.

Stan Laurel Himself / *Oliver Hardy* Himself / *Mrs. Hardy* Mae Busch / *Mrs. Kennedy* Thelma Todd / *Officer Kennedy* Edgar Kennedy. (Working title: *Their Last Word.*) (Reworked into *Block-Heads* nine years later.)

Note: This short represents the first talking or part-talking film Laurel and Hardy made. All subsequent productions (*The Tree in a Test Tube* excepted) were made with full sound. The silent films *Double Whoopee, Bacon Grabbers,* and *Angora Love* were made, in that order, before *Unaccustomed as We Are,* but shelved and held out of release while *Unaccustomed as We Are* was being rushed into circulation as the team's first talking picture. This and other shorts may have been adapted into silent prints with text titles to accommodate theatres not yet equipped for sound, but no special silent versions were filmed.

Opening title: "**The world over—a wife loves to have her husband bring a friend home to dinner—as a surprise.**"

Ollie brings Stan home to prove that Mrs. Hardy's cooking is a bit more than splendid. Mrs. Hardy (Mae Busch) indignantly spurns the opportunity of providing food for "all those bums that you happen to bring up here for dinner." She walks out, and Ollie faces up to cooking the meal himself.

Directed to set the table, Stan does so with minimal efficiency. He is thereupon directed to go into the kitchen and light the oven. He turns on the gas and comes out looking for a match.

Ollie says *he'll* light it, strikes a match, goes into the kitchen, and is blown out into the living room. In frustrated exasperation he lights another match, goes into the kitchen, and is blown out again. Mrs. Kennedy (Thelma Todd), the lady from across the hall, rushes in to find out what's wrong and volunteers to go into the kitchen. She rushes out with dress afire and Ollie pulls it off, replacing it with a tablecloth.

She starts to go back across the hall to put on another dress when she sees her husband (Edgar Kennedy), a tough-looking cop, just coming in. Mrs. Hardy returns at the same time. Knowing that a confrontation under these circumstances will be disastrous for everyone but Stan, Ollie hides Mrs. Kennedy in a trunk. Mrs. Hardy enters in a conciliatory mood—calling her spouse "Puzzoms"—but Ollie, anxious to get the trunk out of the apartment, assures his wife that she has "broken the camel's back once too often" and that he is packed and leaving for South America. "And I'm burning my bridges behind me!," he declares. Stan does not understand and Ollie repeats the statement. "Oh," Stan says, "I thought you said britches." As the boys move the trunk out, Mrs. Hardy grabs Stan and excoriates him unmercifully, asking him what he means by taking Ollie—"this poor little innocent to South America and advising him to burn his bridges, when he never even started a fire in his life?"

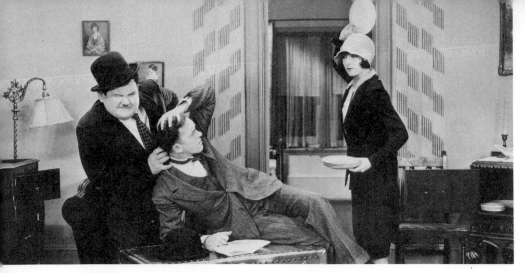

She hurls dishes at Stan...

...causing Officer Kennedy to come in and ask what's going on. (In the film, Kennedy does not see his wife.) Suffused with sobs, Mrs. Hardy storms off into her bedroom. Kennedy makes the boys drop the trunk—whence issues a scream —and he says, "Oh-h! There's a woman in the case, eh?" Kennedy calls Mrs. Hardy back and tells her he'll take the boys out, give them a good talking to, and in the interim she should fix them a nice little supper. She leaves gratefully as Kennedy directs Stan and Ollie to move the trunk to his apartment. This done, Kennedy erupts in laughter and tells the boys confidentially...

... that they simply must be more careful: "You fellows should go out on my beat with me some night to appreciate my technique. Now, come on, we will go to the wife and I will take the cluck out of the trunk and nobody will be the wiser.... You know we married men have got to stick together!" He hustles them back to Mrs. Hardy...

...and tells her that any time she wants peace and quiet to give him a call.

Distracted, Stan serves the spaghetti directly to the Hardy stomach. Meanwhile, Mrs. Kennedy, back in her own apartment, grimly gets out of the trunk. Returning, Kennedy goes to the trunk and stands over it, cooing, "Your dicky bird is waiting." Mrs. Kennedy steps out from behind a screen and says, "I'm a cluck, am I? Well, listen, you get a bit of my technique, dearie," and she heaves a vase at him. In the Hardy apartment the now-jovial threesome hear the din of battle across the hall, but Mrs. Hardy tells Ollie to ignore it: "That doesn't concern you in the least." Kennedy enters, stands glaring, and Ollie apologetically follows him into the hall. Ollie returns shortly, holding his nose, Kennedy reappears...

...and motions for Stan to come forth. Weeping, Stan goes out into the hall, and Kennedy shouts, "Quit your crying! Close your eyes! Shut 'em!" As Kennedy is about to swing on Stan, Mrs. Kennedy comes out into the hall with a huge vase and aims a fearful blow at Kennedy. Ollie and Mrs. Hardy hear a loud commotion. The door opens and Stan enters, whistling. He puts on his hat and leaves.

As he walks down the hallway, he turns and says, "Good-night, Mr. Hardy!" Starting down the stairs, Stan stumbles and falls. Ollie runs to the top of the stairway and looks down as the sound track carries the noise of a bouncing, resounding crash.

Note: Neither Laurel nor Hardy had ever spoken on the screen before—hence the film's title, a pleasant authentication of this fact.

DOUBLE WHOOPEE

1929

Laurel and Hardy Series / Two reels / Silent / Released May 18, 1929, by M-G-M / Produced by Hal Roach / Directed by Lewis R. Foster / Photographed by George Stevens and Jack Roach / Edited by Richard Currier / Titles by H.M. Walker / Story by Leo McCarey.

Stan Laurel Himself / Oliver Hardy Himself / Girl in cab who loses her dress Jean Harlow / Cabdriver Charlie Hall / Other cabdriver Ham Kinsey / Officer Stanley (Tiny) Sandford / Hotel desk clerk Rolfe Sedan / Man poked in the eye Sam Lufkin / Hotel manager William Gillespie / The Prime Minister Charley Rogers / Bellhop Ed Brandenberg. Note: Research has not disclosed the name of the actor who plays the Prince. Stan Laurel in 1960 could only remember that the actor was Erich von Stroheim's double.

Opening title: "**Broadway—street of a thousand thrills.**"

In a big, posh hotel just off Times Square, excitement is everywhere. The prince—of an unnamed but clearly semi-Prussian country—is coming. As he steps haughtily out of his taxi, his prime minister suavely dusts him off. Nearby, two highly untitled personages appear on the scene.

The front desk hears the lobby buzz: "There's the prince and his prime minister now!" Stan and Ollie, knowing nothing of this, advance to register, accepting the admiring crowd without question. Ollie signs with lordly mien; Stan flips the pen causing ink to bespatter a flapper's powder case. Coolly regarding the lobby while powdering herself, the ink smears her entire face.

Stan makes his usual determined X, and Ollie disgustedly pulls the pen from his hand, causing the ink to soil the register. Stan smiles triumphantly at his chum.

The hotel manager comes over and greets his "distinguished" visitors graciously. Ollie hands him a letter, which the manager reads with growing incredulity: "Dear Sir: Introducing your new doorman and footman. These boys are the best we could do on such short notice. There is some reason to believe they may be competent. Taylor, Secretary." Disgustedly, the manager calls a bellhop to take them away for proper attiring.

The genuine prime minister enters to announce the arrival in the lobby of the exalted one.

The prince enters, is about to be conducted to his suite, but at the open elevator he turns to the people in the lobby applauding him and says heartily, "And I am here to make what you Americans call—whoopee." As he is speaking, the open elevator, in defiance of every law save that of comedy, rises. Concluding his speech with a flourish, the prince turns and falls down into the muddy shaft.

The elevator returns to the lobby and Ollie, in doorman's attire, steps out grandly. The prince is brought up, enters the elevator, but steps out again to declaim, "This would mean *death* in my country." As he shouts this, the elevator rises again, the prince turns smartly and falls down the shaft once more. The elevator descends and Stan emerges, spiffily attired as a footman. The elevator goes up and the *prime minister* falls down the shaft. The boys go forward to their posts in front of the hotel.

Later, in the lobby, Stan helps a man put on his overcoat. Reaching deftly under the man's coat, Stan, in attempting to pull down the man's jacket, pulls off his shirt instead.

Inside, the lobby bellhop clicks a castanet to warn Stan and Ollie of some guests' departure. Ollie opens the door suavely, and a couple exits through the door opposite him. Ollie rushes to the other door, opens it, and a man comes out of the first door. Castanets. Ollie runs to the first door, opens it, and Stan stalks out. As Ollie continues to hold the door open, Stan opens the other door, a couple walk out and the man tips Stan.

Enraged, Ollie grabs the tip and tells Stan never to come through that door again: "*Crawl* under it." Stan cries. A cop (Tiny Sandford) enters, and Ollie, embarrassed, gives Stan his coin, then cleverly pulls it back. Stan misses it, Ollie throws it away, and it rolls down a sidewalk grate. The cop thunders to Ollie to retrieve it, but because he cannot, Ollie gives Stan another quarter.

Stan cheekily blows the whistle on Ollie's chest, and the taxi driver (Charlie Hall)— who had earlier come around when Ollie inadvertently blew it without cause—returns. This time he tells Ollie threateningly, "You blewed it again, sweetheart!" In mutual infliction of indignities, Charlie tears the visor off Ollie's hat; Ollie pulls Charlie's visor beneath his chin.

The cop enters the fray.

A glamorous lady (Jean Harlow) comes to visit the hotel. Stan unknowingly slams the taxi door on the train of her dress, and she walks away not realizing that the entire back of her dress has been pulled away.

The boys realize that Jean is in embarrassing straits, and Ollie rips off Stan's coat to wrap around her.

After further altercations with guests, Stan and Ollie leave, and the prince is covered with food thrown during a furore. He yells his defiance to the entire lobby, again standing in front of the open elevator. It rises; he inescapably falls down the shaft again. The elevator descends and Stan and Ollie emerge, walk out into the street and the ranks of the unemployed.

Note: In 1969 *Double Whoopee* received the distinction of being the first silent film in history to be transferred to sound, including voice synchronization. Chuck McCann, superb Laurel and Hardy mimic, provided both voices. Al Kilgore wrote the sound script and directed the dubbing. The film is awaiting release.

BERTH MARKS

1929

Laurel and Hardy Series / Two reels / All-talking / Released June 1, 1929, by M-G-M / Produced by Hal Roach / Directed by Lewis R. Foster / Photographed by Len Powers / Edited by Richard Currier / Story by Leo McCarey / Story edited by H.M. Walker / Introductory musical compositions by William Axt and Yellen and Ager.

Stan Laurel Himself / *Oliver Hardy* Himself / *Passengers* Harry Bernard, Baldwin Cooke, Charlie Hall / *Stationmaster* Pat Harmon / *Conductor* Silas D. Wilcox. (Working title: *In Vaudeville.*)

Opening title: "**Mr. Hardy told Mr. Laurel to meet him at the Santa Fe Station at a quarter of ten—but Mr. Laurel became confused and thought he meant 9:45.**"

The boys are a vaudeville team on their way to a booking. At the station, they walk on and off the scene alternately, just missing each other with undogged consistency.

After connecting, they listen to the conductor (Pat Harmon) call out the destinations of the next train. On hearing this resounding cry of unintelligibilities, Ollie is understandably frustrated. He asks the conductor if the train is going to Pottsville, and the conductor glares and tells him to keep his ears open. The conductor then repeats his gibberish incantation, mercifully adding, "and Pottsville."

The boys run for the train, which is now pulling out. Stan drops their music, and while they are picking it up, a passenger trips over their cello.

They make the train —just. Ollie asks Stan what they're going to do now that they've lost their music, and Stan brightly assures him that they can fake it. Glad that at least their instrument isn't lost, Ollie seeks out the conductor.

In taking a seat, Stan sits on a passenger (Sammy Brooks) who rises and shouts, "Say, what's the idea?" Ollie graciously explains that Stan didn't see the gentleman, which doesn't exactly endear the gentleman to either of them.

The boys run into the conductor (Silas D. Wilcox) who, on learning their destination, asks them what they are going to do in Pottsville. Ollie proudly assures him that they are a big-time vaudeville act. "Well," says the conductor with heavy ambiguity, "I'll bet you're *good.*"

Sitting down again, Stan has mangled a passenger's hat. (This still is unlike the actual footage in the film. The passenger finds his squashed hat after Laurel and Hardy leave the scene, but for the sake of a good still the photographer altered the action. The following two stills are similar rearrangements.)

Stan bumbles into a compartment containing a scantily clad lady who screams at the intrusion. Ollie pulls Stan out as a chunky man (Harry Bernard) walks by. The lady's husband (Charlie Hall), thinking the chunky man the nosy culprit, rips his coat up the back. The husband goes back to the compartment, and the chunky man, not having seen his assailant, turns slowly and sees a tall man (Baldwin Cooke) that he identifies as the coat-ripper. Chunky man attacks tall man. This chain-reaction antagonism spreads into the next car, from passenger to passenger.

The boys ponder the disaster they have inadvertently left in their wake.

Impecuniousness has forced them to share a single upper berth. They prepare to mount, Ollie first placing the cello under the seat. 107

Inevitable misalignments ensue.

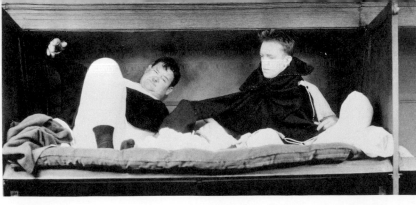

It had not occurred to Ollie that changing his clothes in the washroom was *de rigueur* for such travel. The resultant Laocoön-like entanglements are prodigious in their extensions.

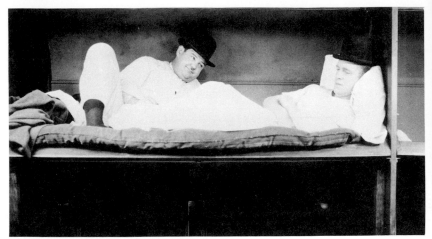

After mighty heavings and hoings, Stan is imperturbable as ever. Ollie almost admires his pal's resiliency. Just as Ollie, too, beds himself down comfortably, the conductor intones, "Next stop is Pottsville! All out for Pottsville!" Attired only in long johns, they make a mad dash out. Meanwhile, the camera follows the conductor as he walks through a car rampant with passengers ripping off each other's clothes in retaliatory frenzy. By the time the conductor reaches the car's end, his clothes are totally destroyed.

In Pottsville, Ollie asks where the "fiddle" is and Stan indicates it is still on the train. Mutual recrimination follows, Stan runs away as Ollie picks up a rock and konks him with it, then chases his chum into the distance.

MEN O' WAR

1929

Laurel and Hardy Series / Two reels / All-talking, sound on disc only / Released June 29, 1929, by M-G-M / Produced by Hal Roach / Directed by Lewis R. Foster / Photographed by George Stevens and Jack Roach / Edited by Richard Currier / Dialogue by H.M. Walker / Sound by Elmer R. Raguse / Introductory musical compositions by William Axt and S. Williams.

Stan Laurel Himself / *Oliver Hardy* Himself / *Soda Jerk* James Finlayson / *Officer* Harry Bernard / *Flirtatious brunette* Anne Cornwall / *Blonde feminine companion* Gloria Greer / *Bicycle rider* Pete Gordon / *Battling boaters* Charlie Hall, Baldwin Cooke / *Part cut from final release print: Lakeside diner at Hollenbeck Park* Rolfe Sedan. (The soda fountain routine is a reworking of the middle one third of *Should Married Men Go Home?*, made the previous year.)

At a park, Ollie and Stan have stopped to flirt with two lovelies (Gloria Greer and Anne Cornwall). Shortly before, a laundrywoman had dropped a female undergarment here. Ollie finds it and assumes one of the girls has lost it. Meanwhile Anne has lost her gloves, and Ollie approaches to ask the girls if they have lost anything. Anne, giggling, describes the article she has lost as white, odd-looking, buttoning on the side, easy to pull on—"you can just about imagine how I feel without them...And I just cleaned them with gasoline, too."

The boys are flabbergasted when a cop comes and returns the lost gloves to Anne.

Ollie hastily gives the garment to Stan who later consigns it to the bushes. The boys invite the girls for a soda, and Ollie tells them to "look the menu over and take anything in the world you want." The proprietor (James Finlayson) looks at the girls expectantly as Ollie takes Stan outside to explain a matter of finance. They have only 15 cents between them, enough for only three drinks (this is early 1929!), but Ollie has an idea. He says to Stan, "When I ask you to have a drink, you refuse." They return, and when Ollie asks what they all want, the girls order sodas, and Stan orders a soda. Disgustedly Ollie takes his pal away again, explains it once more, and returns. Again Stan orders a soda, and again Ollie takes him aside: "Can't you grasp the situation? You must refuse!" "But you keep *asking* me," Stan says plaintively. The message penetrates, Stan says he doesn't want any, but Anne encourages him not to be a piker. "All right," says Stan, "I'll have a banana split." Ollie insists he and Stan will split a soda. The girls order cherry and chocolate, Ollie orders sassafras. Stan says, "'I don't like frassasass," but Ollie orders it anyway.

Fin prepares the sodas. Ollie tells Stan to go ahead and drink *his* half. Stan drinks the entire soda and Ollie asks him sadly why he did it. "I couldn't help it," says Stan. "My half was on the *bottom*."

The check, unexpectedly, comes to 30 cents. "It's your party," says Ollie, handing the check over to Stan, "and I am going to let you pay the check." Ollie takes the girls outside and Stan, greatly worried, takes a chance on the slot machine, coming up a winner.

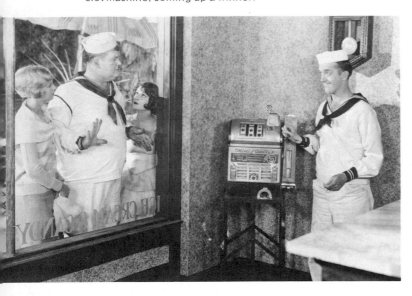

Fin rents them a boat and Stan assumes total proprietorship.

Ollie comes in and Stan begins to row—in a circle. Ollie demands an oar, and they start rowing the boat from the same side—the boat again circling. Ollie puts his oar on the other side of the boat and Stan does likewise. Again they circle.

"Now when I pull—you push!," Ollie tells him. The result: another circle.

They swat at each other with oars. Charlie Hall's canoe bumps their boat and Stan throws a hat full of water in Charlie's face. Charlie does as much for Ollie, and Ollie begins to swat Charlie with a pillow. Ollie breaks Charlie's oar in two, and Stan pushes Charlie into the water. Charlie returns to the boat and starts pillow-swatting also. Another canoe with a man and a girl in it rows by and a pillow from the boys' boat hits the man, knocking him into the water. A man and a girl in yet another canoe run into the first canoe, throwing the man and girl into the water.

An effluence of reciprocal destruction begins, mounting from strength to strength, until all the antagonists are in Stan's and Ollie's boat. Meanwhile, we periodically see Fin on the bank in frantic "takes," mugging horrendously. A cop comes into the scene, asking what the matter is. "Look at them—they're wrecking my boats!," yells Fin.

Fin and the cop get into the boat to pacify the combatants. The boat sinks and water covers all.

PERFECT DAY

1929

Laurel and Hardy Series / Two reels / All-talking, sound on disc only / Released August 10, 1929, by M-G-M / Produced by Hal Roach / Directed by James Parrott / Edited by Richard Currier / Story by Hal E. Roach and Leo McCarey / Story edited by H.M. Walker / Incidental music scoring was added for a 1936 reissue (originally there was no music track on this film) with compositions added by Marvin Hatley, Nathaniel Shilkret, and Le Roy Shield.

Stan Laurel Himself / *Oliver Hardy* Himself / *Uncle Edgar* Edgar Kennedy / *Mrs. Hardy* Kay Deslys / *Mrs. Laurel* Isabelle Keith / *Friendly neighbors* Harry Bernard, Clara Guiol / *Next-door neighbors* Baldwin Cooke, Lyle Tayo / *Parson* Charley Rogers / *Dog* Buddy. (Working title: *Step on It.*)

The Hardys and the Laurels are preparing for a picnic; the ladies busily aflutter with odds and ends and the men making the sandwiches. Unfortunately, the way to the kitchen is through a swinging door, which pushes Stan into Ollie, knocking a heaping tray of sandwiches considerably awry. The boys do some mutual shoving against each other, which upsets the wives (Kay Deslys and Isabelle Keith), but they remind the boys that it is the Sabbath, a day of peace. Sheepishly, the boys agree that there will be no more arguments. The sandwiches are salvaged but once again are spilled all over the floor when Ollie tries to pull their dog off the gouty foot ...

... of Uncle Edgar (Edgar Kennedy), who is going to the picnic under protest. As the gang prepares to depart, the neighbors along the street wave and shout, "Good-bye! Good-bye!" The picnickers return the cheery farewell. The motor starts—and the left rear tire runs over a nail and flattens. Everyone has to get out while the tire is changed. Edgar sits on the running board, laughing sardonically. Stan accidentally steps on Edgar's foot; he yells. Edgar puts his foot on the running board; Ollie shoves Stan again; Stan sits on Edgar's foot; he yells. Edgar holds his foot up; Stan slams the car door on it; Edgar yells. The tire jack is knocked over on Edgar's foot; he yells. The nail is pulled from the tire.

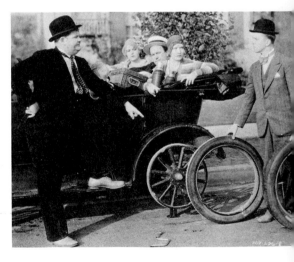

While he puts on the spare, Ollie directs Stan to hook the old one on back. Once all is in order, Ollie starts the car, releases the brake—and the neighbors cry, "Good-bye! Good-bye!" The picnickers chorus, "Good-bye! Good-bye!" But the car doesn't move—for an excellent reason—the jack is still supporting the axle. Stan lowers the jack; the *new* tire is flat. Ollie grabs the jack from Stan, throws it away angrily—and a crash glass is heard from the house next door.

A neighbor (Baldwin Cooke) grimly walks over with the jack and hurls it through the car windshield.

With equal grimness, Stan picks up a brick, slowly walks over to the neighbor's house, and throws it through a window. The neighbor determinedly walks over to the Hardys' house and pitches the brick through *their* window.

Stan and Ollie have taken off their coats to continue the duel more actively when they congeal in horror, looking down the sidewalk. They hastily put their coats on and run to the car. Seconds later, a parson strides by sanctimoniously. The boys find they have put on each other's coats, and once this is righted, they are set to drive off. "Good-bye! Good-bye!" "Good-bye! Good-bye!" Now the starter won't work so Ollie must crank the car, which he does to no avail. Testily, Ollie instructs Stan to throw out the clutch— and Stan does so literally, on the street. The cranking works, the car starts. "Good-bye! Good-bye!" "Good-bye! Good-bye!" Ollie waves...

...and smoke pours out of the motor. Stan picks up a nearby hose and aims it unsteadily, spraying Ollie liberally.

Friendly neighbors from across the street (Clara Guiol and Harry Bernard) watch the conflagration in horror.

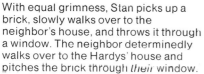

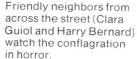

The unfriendly neighbor walks over and demands his hose. (Again, the microphone boom.) Ollie pushes Stan angrily against the car and the motor starts. The boys eagerly climb aboard. "Good-bye! Good-bye!" "Good-bye! Good-bye!" The car actually leaves, drives past a sign indicating a closed road, and moves across a muddy pool. As the car slowly sinks into the black morass, the picnickers look back at their neighbors and shout, "Good-bye! Good-bye!," until mud covers all.

113

Production Sidelights

Stan with his daughter, Lois, Jr., age two, and Babe, on the set of *Perfect Day*.

James Parrott, director of 21 Laurel and Hardy films, with his boys, circa 1930. Lake Laurel and Hardy (the Roach lot's pool) and a sturdy Model T as background.

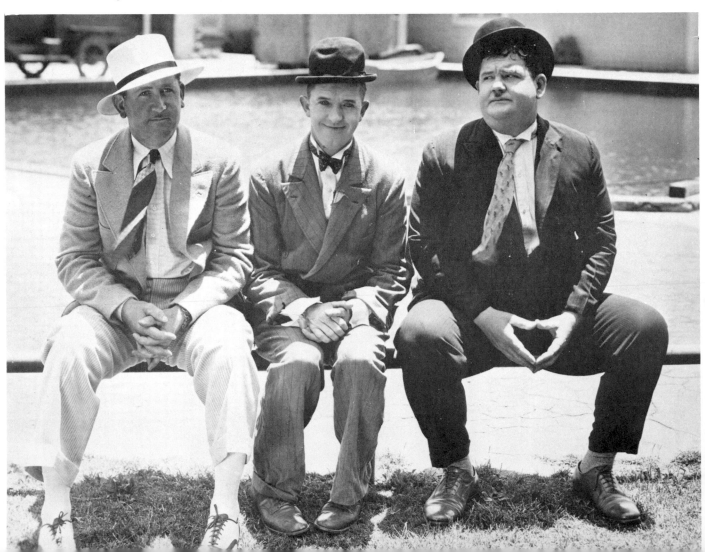

THEY GO BOOM

1929

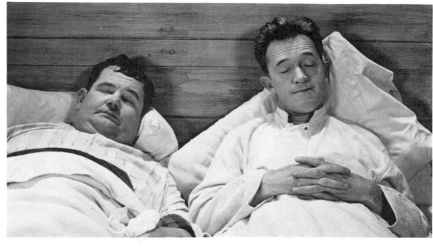

Laurel and Hardy Series / Two reels / All-talking, sound on disc only / Released September 21, 1929, by M-G-M / Produced by Hal Roach / Directed by James Parrott / Edited by Richard Currier / Story by Leo McCarey / Story edited by H.M. Walker / Introductory musical compositions by William Axt and S. Williams.

Stan Laurel Himself / *Oliver Hardy* Himself / *Landlord* Charlie Hall / *Officer* Sam Lufkin. (Working title: *The Sniffles.*)

Opening title: **"Mr. Hardy had the sniffles—his carburetor hadn't been right for days and days."**

Stan's wheezing, whistling snore arouses his partner. Ollie sneezes and the window shade rattles up. "Pull the curtain dowd!," Ollie commands in head-stuffed tones. Stan tries to a number of times, finally tying it down, but in getting back in bed he unthinkingly pulls the covers off Ollie. Ollie pulls them back, sneezes again—sending the shade back up once more. It falls off. Ollie sneezes again . . .

. . . this time huffing their fraternal motto, "Smile All the While," down onto his head. Stan asks Ollie why he doesn't stop sneezing. "Why," Ollie says, "I'm liable to die of ammonia."

Ollie tells Stan to hang the motto up, but in so doing the nail is driven into a wall water pipe. The water spouts out, hitting Ollie in the back as he lies abed. Uncertain of the source, he looks incredulously at the camera.

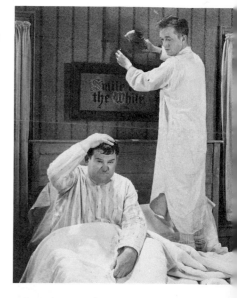

He turns over and the water pours down on his chest.

Sodden, Ollie says, "You've done it now. I've got ammonia." Directed to make Ollie a footbath, Stan carries a washbasin into the kitchen, on the way getting his sweat sock stuck on a stray piece of flypaper. It pulls the sock off. The bottom of the sock is now a glutinous, impermeable mass of adhesive. But Stan has a brilliant idea: he will simply wear the sock turned inside out.

Stan prepares the footbath by pouring in some odd-looking powder; Ollie asks what it is. "Why, it's mustard," Stan says. "I once used it when I had the measles. It cured me in no time." The powder sets Ollie to sneezing again, furiously. Stan pours in the hot water . . .

. . . and begins to stir it vigorously with a broom end. The other end hits Ollie and he wrenches it away. Stan goes out for some tempering cold water. Returning, he trips on the rug, spilling the water on Ollie; the pail hits the wall motto, which in turn smacks Ollie on the head—and the water pipe starts spewing again.

Ollie plugs up the leak and, in trying to hit Stan, jumps off the bed—into the boiling-hot water. Stan pours cooling water in the tub and Ollie immerses his feet in the mustard, which is now the consistency of congealed oatmeal.

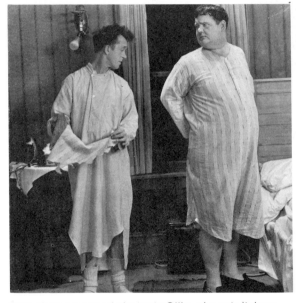

Stan gives a mustard plaster to Ollie, who sets it down while he wipes his feet off. That done, he asks for the plaster, and learns that Stan just gave it to him. Clearly, he must have set it down somewhere. He did—and unwittingly sat on it. Stan grabs for the plaster, eliciting a shocked what-are-you-trying-to-do look from Ollie. Finally, realizing where the plaster is, Ollie tells his pal to take it off. In doing so, Stan tears off half of Ollie's night shirt. Ollie looks at the camera with embarrassment, sees an open blind behind him, pulls it down quickly, and goes into the kitchen.

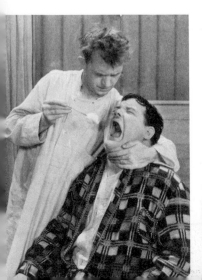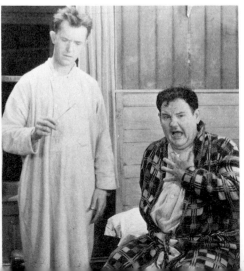

Soaking some cough medicine on a big swab, Stan dexterously puts it down Ollie's throat . . .
and pulls up only the stick.

  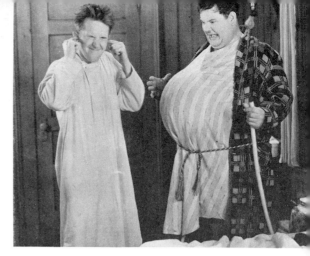

In the altercation, Stan pushes Ollie down on the bed, deflating the air mattress.

Ollie blows it up with vigor, creating a formidable bulge in one spot. Stan falls on it . . .

. . . and all the air backs up dramatically.

Their landlord (Charlie Hall) condemns Ollie for all the noise: "Why don't you be quiet like *he* is?," he says, pointing to Stan. Charlie glowers at Ollie and bids a gracious good-night to Stan.

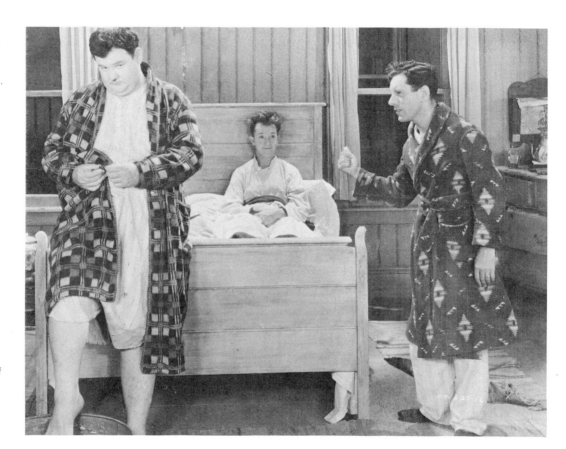

Ollie gets the inspired idea of taking the hose of the deflated mattress, attaching it to the gas outlet on the wall, and turning it on. The mattress grows amply in the process. Ollie jumps in bed, which knocks Stan out on the floor.

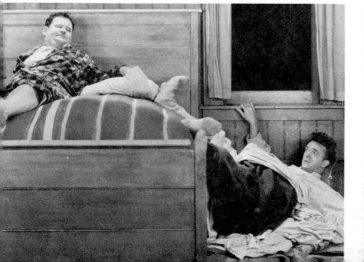 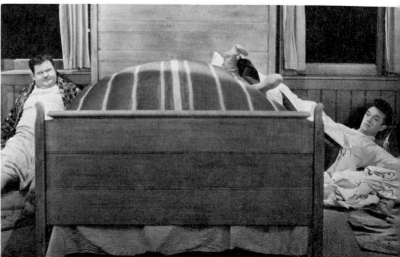

Ollie throws a pillow at Stan, which showers feathers everywhere—just as the landlord opens the door. Both the boys jump in bed, but Ollie falls out, and Charlie walks over and kicks him in the rear. Ollie pushes Charlie out of sight—there is a tremendous offscreen crash . . .

. . . and Charlie reveals the closest kind of contact with the washtub. He has had a mustard glop treatment. He tells the boys they must leave at once.

Ollie tells Stan the best thing they can do at the moment is to get in bed and pretend they are asleep. This may convince Charlie they are good boys. As Ollie gets in bed, his bathrobe catches on the gas switch, turning it on. Gradually the mattress starts to balloon—and levitate.

The mattress goes as high as it can. "I feel just like I'm floating," says Ollie. When the boys realize where they are, panic begins. The door opens and Charlie and a cop (Sam Lufkin) enter. Charlie flees. Ollie is about to sneeze, Stan pleads with him not to. But he does, the mattress explodes . . .

and a man from upstairs comes through the ceiling. Charlie comes back with more cops, demanding that the boys be thrown out. Ollie sneezes again, and plaster settles over all.

BACON GRABBERS

■ ■ ■   1929

Laurel and Hardy Series / Two reels / Silent, but with synchronized music and sound effects on disc only / Released October 19, 1929, by M-G-M / Produced by Hal Roach / Directed by Lewis R. Foster / Photographed by George Stevens and Jack Roach / Edited by Richard Currier / Titles by H.M. Walker / Story by Leo McCarey.

Stan Laurel Himself / *Oliver Hardy* Himself / *Playful debtor, Collis P. Kennedy* Edgar Kennedy / *Mrs. Kennedy* Jean Harlow / *Truck driver* Charlie Hall / *Construction worker* Bobby Dunn / *Sheriff* Eddie Baker / *Man who delivers attachment papers* Sam Lufkin / *Officer* Harry Bernard / *Stunt double for Stan Laurel* Ham Kinsey / *Stunt double for Oliver Hardy* Cy Slocum / *Dog* Buddy.

Opening title: **"The Northwest Mounted always get their man—but—the Attachment Squad of the Sheriff's Office get everything from a grand piano to the Grand Canyon."**

Attachment men ("bacon grabbers" in the slang of the 1920s) were noted for their acuity; Stan and Ollie, new to the force, are noted for their vacuity. The sheriff orders them to attach the radio of a notable local tough guy who has failed in his installment payments.

The boys come to the house of the tough guy (Edgar Kennedy) and find him mowing the lawn. Ollie explains courteously that he has a little paper for Edgar but when he turns to get the summons from Stan, it has been misplaced, and Edgar runs in the house, barricading himself.

Ollie borrows a Great Dane from a boy who assures him that the dog is vicious; indeed, has been raised on raw beef. Ollie takes the dog up to the house to intimidate Edgar, who shows the Great Dane a toy dog. The Great Dane runs away in abject fear, dragging his new master across the street. "Change his diet," Ollie suggests to the boy.

While Stan guards the front door as he eats his lunch, Ollie sneaks around to the back and discovers Edgar leaving by the rear door. They scuffle and Ollie shouts for the summons. Stan runs to them but instead of placing the paper in Edgar's hand, deposits his sandwich there. Edgar runs into the back door and Ollie, anticipating an exit from the front door, runs out front. Stan has followed Edgar into the house and comes out the front door where Ollie serves him the paper. Ollie, directing Stan to remain in front, returns to the back door, again chases Edgar who dashes, unseen, out the front door. The inattentive Stan snaps to in time to serve the paper on the next person through the front door—Ollie. In a subsequent flurry among the three of them, Edgar is served the paper. He says, "Well, boys, that's service —now try an' get the radio," withdrawing into the house.

Seeing a man go up a ladder on a nearby building under construction, the boys take the ladder, and minutes later the builder steps off the roof to where his ladder had been, falling into a mortar box.

After a series of indignities mutually inflicted by the boys misplacing the ladder on Edgar's house, Ollie assures Stan, "The brains had better remain on the ground." Stan is forced to ascend. Edgar, leaning out a window, assaults Stan with a mop as Ollie strives to maintain the ladder's balance. His suspenders break, and a dog comes by and tugs at them. Edgar's mop falls on Ollie's head. Stan's hands on the windowsill are crunched by the dropping window. Stan reopens the window, pulling himself onto it, grabs the shade to balance himself, and the shade unrolls, causing Stan to fall from the window, hanging on to the shade for dear life. Ollie gets the ladder back under Stan who pulls vigorously at the shade, finally dropping it on Ollie.

Edgar sticks a shotgun out of the window into Stan's face, and they struggle, Stan getting his finger in the gun barrel. The window falls on Edgar, the gun goes off, and Stan falls. The bullet hits a fireplug, knocking the top off, and drenching a nearby cop. Stan and Ollie both fall to the ground and the sopping policeman confronts them. "We're trying to recover a radio for the sheriff's office," Stan explains; and Edgar comes out of his front door. The boys go into the house and the cop says he is going inside to phone for the wagon. The boys bring the radio out of the house as the cop goes in. Stan and Ollie set the radio down in the street, and after a round robin of kicks between them and Edgar, a steamroller comes along and runs over the radio. "There's your radio! Try an' get Havana!," taunts Edgar.

Mrs. Kennedy (Jean Harlow) comes forth and tells hubby, "I just paid for our radio, darling. We own it." The boys are laughing appreciatively at Edgar's discomfort when the steamroller continues along its way and thoroughly demolishes their car.

THE HOOSE-GOW

▪ ▪ ▪   1929

Laurel and Hardy Series / Two reels / Sound / Released November 16, 1929, by M-G-M / Produced by Hal Roach / Directed by James Parrott / Photographed by George Stevens, Len Powers, and Glenn Robert Kershner / Edited by Richard Currier / Titles edited by Nat Hoffberg / Story by Leo McCarey / Story edited by H.M. Walker / Sound by Elmer R. Raguse / Introductory musical compositions by William Axt and S. Williams.

Stan Laurel Himself / *Oliver Hardy* Himself / *Governor* James Finlayson / *Prison guard Stanley* (Tiny) Sandford / *"Gentleman over there," with apples* Leo Willis / *Cook* Dick Sutherland / *Women at governor's party* Ellinor Van Der Veer, Retta Palmer / *Prison camp officer* Sam Lufkin / *Prisoners* Eddie Dunn, Baldwin Cooke, Jack (Tiny) Ward, Harri Kinsey, John (Blackie) Whiteford, Ed Brandenberg, Chet Brandenberg, Charles Dorety / *Treetop lookout* Charlie Hall.

Ollie shows two apples to Stan and tells him once they are thrown over the wall, they will become a signal for a fellow con's confederates to get them out. The warden (Tiny Sandford) comes over to demand the apple from Ollie while Stan hides his—in his mouth. Later, the warden kicks Stan, and the apple is swallowed whole. Indignantly, the warden throws Ollie's apple over the wall.

Opening title: "**Neither Mr. Laurel nor Mr. Hardy had any thoughts of doing wrong. As a matter of fact, they had no thoughts of any kind.**"

A patrol wagon has brought the boys to prison from a raid, a raid they assure the warden they were only watching.

At once a rope ladder is thrown into the yard from outside, and the curious warden climbs it. At the top he looks over and the two thugs on the other side, seeing him, let go of the ladder, spilling the warden below.

By accident, Stan and Ollie are locked outside the prison. Stan knocks sternly on the gate trying to get back in. Ollie pulls him away, and as they run off, the warden blasts them with a shotgun. Properly chastened, the boys are brought back to their destiny.

121

During their labors, Stan's pick gets caught in Ollie's coat.

On discovering that Stan's pick is smaller than his, Ollie indignantly makes a switch.

Ollie's troubles grow.

Chow time—and no place for the boys. One of the prisoners points to the warden's choice table and says, "Why, there's your table over there."

Gratified, the boys walk over and sit at the warden's table. He in turn comes over and regards them with vast interest.

Stan, after loosening the top of the pepper shaker and extracting some, sets the shaker down without tightening the top. Ollie pours all the pepper into his soup, and then dumps the soup unwittingly all over the warden's shoes. The warden chases the boys away.

At the cook's tent, they ask for food, and the cook (Dick Sutherland) tells them that the more wood they cut, the more food they get.

Stan, in his zeal, attacks a large tree but only succeeds in destroying part of Ollie's coat.

Ollie attacks the tree vigorously, and as he does so the camera pans up to the top of the tree where a guard sits on a lookout platform, snoring comfortably. The tree inexorably falls on the cook tent, the guard yelling for help as he descends.

The governor (James Finlayson) and two haughty ladies (Ellinor Van Der Veer and Retta Palmer) come to the camp on a surprise visit. Stan and Ollie bid bashful hellos.

Stan's pick gets caught in Ollie's coat again, and Ollie grabs the pick, throwing it angrily out of sight. The pick lands in the radiator of the governor's car.

Fearful they'll get life for this new offense, they listen to a prisoner's suggestion: "I'll tell you how to stop that leak. Put some rice in the radiator." Ollie is pleased with what seems to be an eminently sensible idea. They take rice from the cook tent and implement the idea.

The governor and his ladies get into their car. The rice begins to swell up and proliferate. The warden, suspecting the source of this difficulty, takes the offensive against Stan with the spewing rice. Stan throws rice at the warden, who returns it. Stan ducks, the governor receives it in the face. He hurls some in return, and bit by bit, person by person, the rice fight becomes orgiastic in scope. The prisoners look on in delighted satisfaction.

The warden and the governor plan to speed off and get the militia. Their car backs into the end of a paint truck, and from the rear seat of their car arise Stan and Ollie, resplendent in white paint.

120 minutes; 11,669 feet / Sound by Movietone: "All Singing, Talking, Dancing" / Filmed largely in black and white, with isolated Technicolor sequences that have now hyped out of existence / Released November 23, 1929, by M-G-M / Produced by Harry Rapf for M-G-M / Production managed by Joe Cohn / Directed by Charles F. Riesner / Direction assistance by Lionel Barrymore, Jack Cummings, Sandy Roth, and Al Shenberg / Photographed by Maximilian Fabian, John M. Nickolaus, John Arnold, and Irving G. Ries / Edited by William S. Gray and Cameron K. Wood / Dialogue by Al Hoasberg and Robert E. Hopkins / Skit by Joe Farnham / Settings by Cedric Gibbons and Richard Day / Costumes by David Cox / Dances and ensembles by Sammy Lee, assisted by George Cunningham / Sound by Douglas Shearer / Sound recording assistance by Russell Franks, William Clark, Wesley Miller, and A.T. Taylor / Orchestra and musical arrangement supervised by Arthur Lange / Musical score arranged by Arthur Lange, Ernest Klapholtz, and Ray Heindorf / Music by Gus Edwards / Lyrics by Joe Goodwin / Interpolations by Nacio Herb Brown, Arthur Freed, David Snell, Jesse Greer, Ray Klages, Martin Broones, Fred Fisher, and Andy Rice.

Masters of ceremonies Jack Benny, Conrad Nagel / *Announcing the program* The Misses Mawby: Angela Mawby, Claudine Mawby, Claudette Mawby / *"Gotta Feelin' for You" song and dance specialty* Joan Crawford / *Supporting Miss Crawford* The Rounders, The Biltmore Quartet / *"You Were Meant for Me" act* Anita Page / *Bungling magicians skit* Stan Laurel, Oliver Hardy / *"Tommy Atkins on Parade"* Marion Davies / *"The Dance of the Sea" Egyptian novelty* Buster Keaton / *Daring adagio number* The Natacha Nattova Company / *"Romeo and Juliet" balcony sequence in Technicolor* Norma Shearer, John Gilbert / *Director appearing in above skit* Lionel Barrymore / *Chorus girl* Ann Dvorak / *Comedy songs throughout* Cliff (Ukulele Ike) Edwards / *"Pearl Ballet" number* Beth Laemmle / *Performing as themselves in miscellaneous songs, dances, comedy skits, tableaux, "blackouts," and other specialty acts* Gwen Lee, William Haines, Nils Asther, Bessie Love, Myrtle McLaughlin, Marie Dressler, Nacio Herb Brown, Polly Moran, The Brox Sisters, George K. Arthur, Karl Dane, Gus Edwards, Ernest Belcher's Dancing Tots / *"Orange Blossom Time" Technicolor finale* Charles King / *Dance ensemble in Technicolor* The Albertina Rasch Ballet. (Working titles: *M-G-M Revue of Revues*, then *Hollywood Revue*.) (Academy Award nomination for "Best Picture, 1928-1929." Incredible.)

This is a Metro-Goldwyn-Mayer star-scrambled grab bag featuring the studio's leading players in a mélange of mostly tedious turns. Jack Benny is the master of ceremonies and he is able to relieve the general dullness only twice during the film's 82 minutes by bringing us a dance number by Joan Crawford, and later, Laurel and Hardy in their nonfunctional magic act. Their tricks fail, one after the other, in an amusing variety of ways.

As Benny introduces another act, the curtain opens revealing Stan and Ollie in tails and derbies, backs to the audience, still hastily preparing their magic props on a table. Realizing they must begin, Ollie tips his hat to Benny, but as Stan does the same, a dove flutters out of his derby. One trick ruined. Ollie's annoyance at his assistant's blunder overrides stage decorum, and angry words escalate to pokes, jabs, and a shove into a bowl of eggs. Ollie wipes his hands on Stan's coat and tosses the bowl of eggs offstage. The egg trick gone.

Card routines and sleight-of-hand tricks follow—all spectacularly unconvincing—but one could never tell that from Ollie's beaming euphoria and grandiose gestures. Stan brings a huge cake on stage and, after handing it to Ollie, clears the table for it. In so doing Stan brushes everything to the floor—on which lies, in ominous wait, a banana peel from a previously ruined trick. Inevitably Ollie skids on it and half-somersaults into the giant cake. He emerges to say sheepishly, "I faw down—and go *plop!*" With this, he heaves the cake offstage, and as Stan and Ollie exit stage left, waving daintily, Jack Benny comes on stage right bespattered with the cake.

The Laurel and Hardy skit lasts eight minutes, and although very enjoyable (particularly because of Ollie's elegant pantomime), the act suffers from uninspired camera work. The boys must play to a single immobile camera that is bolted to one spot on the stage.

LAUREL AND HARDY MAGICIANS

ANGORA LOVE

■ ■ ■ **1929**

Laurel and Hardy Series / Two reels / Silent, but with synchronized music and sound effects, sound on disc only / Released December 14, 1929, by M-G-M / Produced by Hal Roach / Directed by Lewis R. Foster / Photographed by George Stevens / Edited by Richard Currier / Titles by H.M. Walker / Story by Leo McCarey.

Stan Laurel Himself / *Oliver Hardy* Himself / *Landlord* Edgar Kennedy / *Neighbor* Charlie Hall / *Officer* Harry Bernard / *Mr. Caribeau* Charley Young. *Note:* George Stevens is pictured in publicity stills as a theatre box-office clerk; whether a gag or an actual appearance, it does not appear in the final release print.

(Remade as *Laughing Gravy* two years later, and reworked into *The Chimp* three years later. Represents the last nontalking Laurel and Hardy film made and released; it was produced immediately before *Unaccustomed as We Are* but was held out of release until the end of the year.)

Opening title: "**The dramatic story of a goat—a strong dramatic story.**"

A goat breaks away from his tether at a pet shop and finds immediate if inexplicable comradeship with Stan and Ollie. Ollie has just condemned Stan for his profligacy in spending their last dime for pastry with a hole in it. Stan feeds the goat, over Ollie's objections—"Goats are bad luck." The pet shop owner reports a goatnapping to the police.

In attempting to flee the goat, Ollie falls into a mud puddle at the street corner. Two nights later. A title tells us, "They lost the goat once —but it caught up with them in St. Paul." The goat follows them into their boarding-house unbeknownst to their vicious landlord.

To relieve his fatigue, Ollie picks up what he believes to be his foot and flexes it comfortingly. Stan enjoys it hugely, and Ollie does also —until he realizes whose foot he has.

The goat eats some of the wallpaper, and in repairing the wall, Stan hammers at it, rousing the landlord to consciousness and indignation. The boys hide the goat under the bed. The landlord pounds on their door, the boys open it, and the landlord yells, "I want you guys to know this is a respectable hotel!" As he says this, a girl and a sailor pass in the background. The landlord retires, and the goat starts eating again.

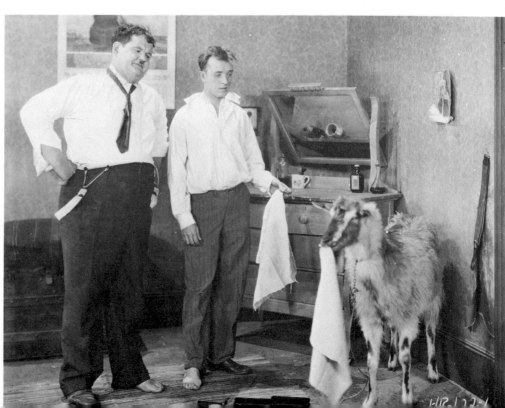

To account for the noise from the room, Ollie resorts to delicate employment of his exercise machine. Stan regards him rather as he would a waltzing octopus, and the landlord (Edgar Kennedy), after incredulous surveillance, leaves.

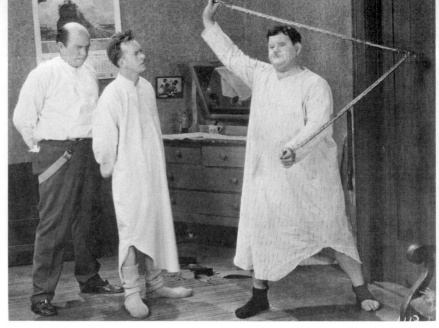

The goat's natural odor seems unnatural in the confined atmosphere. Ollie orders Stan to give him a bath, "an' if he don't smell any better, you'll both get out!" The water spills over, dripping down into the landlord's apartment. Ollie falls into the tub with the goat.

Edgar reappears and the boys try to get the goat under the bed again. Edgar goes to call the police.

Edgar returns and throws water on Ollie. A water fight follows—between Stan, Ollie, Edgar, and another boarder (Charlie Hall) in round-robin fashion. A policeman comes in to arrest Edgar as the man who stole the goat, and leads them both away. When Ollie says wearily, "I hope I never see a goat again as long as I live!," three kids—the goat's progeny —come out from under the bed. Stan wonders "Won't her husband be surprised?"

NIGHT OWLS

1930

Laurel and Hardy Series / Two reels / Sound / Released January 4, 1930, by M-G-M / Produced by Hal Roach / Directed by James Parrott / Photographed by George Stevens / Edited by Richard Currier / Story by Leo McCarey / Story edited by H.M. Walker / Sound by Elmer R. Raguse / Introductory musical compositions by Marvin Hatley and Harry von Tilzer.

Stan Laurel Himself / Oliver Hardy Himself / Bungling Officer Kennedy Edgar Kennedy / Meadows, the butler James Finlayson / Surly police chief Anders Randolph / Officers Harry Bernard, Charles McMurphy, Baldwin Cooke / Part cut from final release print: Officer Charles McAvoy. (At least four foreign-language versions were made, each expanded to four reels in length: Ladrones [Spanish], as well as French, Italian, and German versions.)

The neighborhood cop (Edgar Kennedy) rages inwardly against the world. The chief of police has told him that if there are any more robberies on his beat and no arrests, Edgar is through, finished. As he looks at two vagabonds in the park, an idea presents itself.

He wakes up Stan and Ollie, suggesting a frame-up beneficial to them all: the boys will rob the police chief's house, Kennedy will arrest them and glory will be his; as for the boys, Edgar will "fix it," a somewhat vague phrase. Since the alternative presented to them is the rock pile, the boys agree.

Later, Edgar shows them the alley behind the chief's house. Ollie falls over the garbage cans, causing a terrific ruckus that the chief hears as he prepares for bed. "It's the garbage men, sir," his valet assures him. After much difficulty and a giant rip in Ollie's pants, the boys attain the chief's back wall—and come crashing down in the flower bed. They pretend they are cats, meowing extravagantly, thus relieving the chief's suspicions again. The valet throws slippers at the "cats," hitting them smartly. Stan returns a slipper—in the valet's face. The valet throws back a heavy shoe that connects sharply with Stan's head. Stan prepares a brick for riposte but Ollie throws it away, back over the wall. The brick hits Edgar who is waiting in the alley, knocking him out.

Stan gets in the house through an open window, accidentally setting fire to the curtain. He throws a brimming fishbowl over it, most of which hits Ollie who is just outside. Ollie starts to climb in the window; Stan inadvertently lowers the window on Ollie's fingers. Ollie orders Stan to go around and open the front door.

Stan opens the front door, comes out, looks around, and the door slams shut, locking itself. Taking the burglar tools furnished him, Stan looks for another window, finds one open, enters, and crashes over a little table. (Hardy's is a posed presence in the still; in the film he is still trying to jimmy the first window.) Stan goes to the front door again.

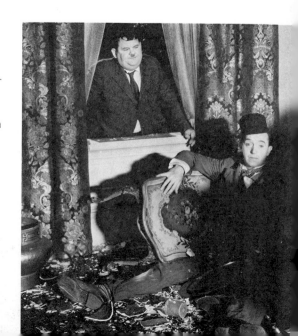

He summons Ollie. They seem to be locked out again but Stan simply walks back in. Not seeing this, Ollie starts to pry open the front door; Stan at an open window motions for him to enter the house. Ollie comes into the house. Stan leaves through the window, goes to the front door, and tries to open it. It is locked but Stan knocks loudly. The valet comes to the landing of the stairway; Stan rings the doorbell; the valet gets frightened and falls downstairs, discharging his gun in the process. Ollie runs out the front door very frightened, and, together with Stan, hides around the corner. The valet comes out of the front door, looks around, goes back in. Stan finds yet another window open, enters, goes to the window nearest Ollie, opens it and hands him a hammer.

Now both are inside. Stan finds a musical jug that plays a lively tune when picked up. Ollie shushes him vigorously.

Ollie starts putting silverware into a bag. Frightened, Stan turns around suddenly, causing Ollie to drop a handful of the utensils. Ollie orders him to find something to tie the bag with; Stan tears the bellpull off the wall causing the valet's bell to jingle loudly.

(These two stills have nothing whatever to do with the rest of the film. The boys never meet the police chief, played by Anders Randolph. Such stills served the purpose of intriguing the small fry as they examined them in the display panels outside the theatre of a Saturday mornin

The film actually ends with Ollie accidentally starting a player piano that bursts into "Under the Anheuser Busch." The police chief shouts to his valet (James Finlayson) to quit playing at this time of night and to call the police! Edgar, out back, regains consciousness and comes into the house as the boys try to stop the piano. Edgar finds the bag of silverware and the police chief accuses *him* of being the neighborhood burglar. Stan and Ollie flee out back, and in helping Ollie over the wall, Stan pulls out the seat of his pants, again. Stan falls down from the wall and is jackknifed into a garbage can. Ollie falls off the wall and, as Stan starts hopping away in his garbage can, Ollie throws tin cans at him.

BLOTTO

Laurel and Hardy Series / Two reels / Sound / Released February 8, 1930, by M-G-M / Produced by Hal Roach / Directed by James Parrott / Photographed by George Stevens / Edited by Richard Currier / Dialogue by H.M. Walker / Story by Leo McCarey / Sound by Elmer R. Raguse / Incidental music track added by film editor William Ziegler for a 1937 reissue, with compositions by Le Roy Shield and Marvin Hatley.

Stan Laurel Himself / Oliver Hardy Himself / Waiters Stanley (Tiny) Sandford, Baldwin Cooke / Moustachioed cabdriver Charlie Hall / Melancholy singer at the Rainbow Club Frank Holliday / Phone-booth gawker Dick Gilbert / Extra in night-club scenes Jack Hill. (At least two foreign-language versions were made: La vida nocturna [Spanish] with Linda Loredo [as Mrs. Laurel] added to the cast; and either La Nouba or Une Nuit extravagante [French], with Georgette Rhodes [as Mrs. Laurel] added to the cast.)

(The stills for Blotto used here are taken from the French version, and Mrs. Laurel is played by Georgette Rhodes, a French actress. Hence Anita Garvin does not appear. All the supporting players in these stills, however, are American players who appeared in the original version.)

Stan, anxious to get out of the house, pleads that he needs fresh air. Mrs. Laurel gives him plenty.

Mrs. Laurel fidgets at his fidgetiness.

Ollie makes a number of attempts to reach his chum by telephone but each time Stan, believing his wife will be suspicious of any conversation with the roistering Ollie, hangs up. Finally, Ollie gets through.

But Mrs. Laurel is omnipresent. Ollie introduces himself and, incredibly, Mrs. Laurel responds graciously, hands the phone to Stan, and says, "Why didn't you tell me it was Mr. Hardy? I don't care to listen to your conversation. I'll go into the kitchen." She goes at once to the bedroom and picks up the telephone extension to listen. Stan says he simply can't find an excuse to get out tonight; Ollie advises him to send himself an "important business" telegram. "Great!," Stan says. "She's so dumb she'll never know the difference." Ollie says he has a table reserved for the opening of the new Rainbow Club. Because this is the Prohibition era, Ollie asks anxiously if Stan knows where to get a bottle. Stan says yes, his wife has been saving one. The boys arrange to meet outside the Laurel house in 15 minutes. Mrs. Laurel hurries to the kitchen, empties her liquor bottle, and fills it full of tea, spices, various condiments, and hot sauce, then returns the bottle to the cupboard.

131

Stan makes out his telegram, goes out a window, puts the telegram against his porch light, rings the doorbell, jumps back through the window. Mrs. Laurel says she thinks someone's at the door. Stan opens the door and carries on a conversation with the imaginary messenger. Inside, he expresses regret that he is being called away on "important business." While his wife gets his hat, he finds the liquor bottle and hides it under his coat.

Sweetly, his wife urges him not to stay out too late.

Ollie beamingly contemplates what promises to be the principal source of their evening's pleasure.

The head waiter at the Rainbow Club (Tiny Sandford) escorts the pair of big-time spenders to their table, but their minds are not on the menus.

They are concerned with their bottle, and after the waiter (Baldwin Cooke) brings ice and glasses, Stan takes a corkscrew from Ollie and tries to open the bottle. The cork makes a loud squeaky noise, arousing the curiosity of other patrons.

Finally Stan pulls the cork, knocking the table over in the process. The head waiter glowers as he puts down the seltzer water. Ollie hides the liquor on the floor. Surreptitiously, Ollie fills his glass from the bottle but even the seltzer he splashes on cannot do much good. "Oh! Whew!" After another drink, Ollie says, "You can certain tell good liquor when you taste it." Stan takes his drink, eye-blinks in reaction, and agrees with Ollie.

As they drink apace, the Spanish dancer seems to epitomize the wild grace of the awfully good time they are convinced they're having. Meanwhile, Mrs. Laurel drops into a sporting goods store to buy a double-barreled shotgun and ammunition.

A singer (Frank Holliday) renders "The Curse of an Aching Heart" with searching pathos. The boys are overwhelmed. At the triumphant finish Stan offers the man a drink. He spits it out in revulsion.

The "liquor" continues to affect Stan: he puts the empty ice tray on his head and assumes monarchical posture. Ollie is delighted.

The waiter removes the tray from Stan's head, twists Stan's ear, and raps his fingers with the tray. Ollie snatches the waiter's shirtfront and throws it away, then Stan tears a mustard plaster from the waiter's chest.

Stan begins what seems to be a laughing jag. Ollie is puzzled. Stan explains. "Wait 'til my wife finds out we drank her liquor!"

Stan does not see Mrs. Laurel slip into a booth at one side of the club, where she sits with a package, staring intently. But Ollie sees her, picks up the bottle, and laughs as she comes over. He urges Stan to tell her what has happened, and roaring with laughter, Stan explains that they drank her liquor. Frigidly, she tells them that it was nothing but cold tea.

The boys react with instant sobriety, and Mrs. Laurel opens the package to reveal a shotgun. The boys flee the nightclub, pile into a cab, and tell the driver (Charlie Hall) to drive them anywhere. Mrs. Laurel fires both barrels, the taxi falls completely apart and its occupants roll out into the street.

133

BRATS

Laurel and Hardy Series / Two reels / Sound /
Released March 22, 1930, by M-G-M / Produced by Hal Roach / Directed by James Parrott / Photographed by George Stevens /
Edited by Richard Currier / Dialogue by H.M.
Walker / Titles edited by Nat Hoffberg / Story
by Leo McCarey and Hal E. Roach / Sound by
Elmer R. Raguse / Compositions used in incidental music scoring on the original track
(most surviving prints carry the reissue background music) by Leslie-Donaldson-Skinner;
Rayaf-Waller-Sisson; Mary Litt; Hackforth;
Selver-Mitchell-Pollack; and Marvin Hatley.

Stan Laurel Himself / *His son* Stan Laurel /
Oliver Hardy Himself / *His son* Oliver Hardy.
(At least three foreign-language versions were
made: *Glückliche Kindheit* [German], *Les
bons petits diables* [French], and Spanish.)

1930

Opening title: "**Mr. Laurel and Mr. Hardy
remained at home to take care of the children—
Their wives had gone out to target practice.**"

Mr. Laurel and Mr. Hardy are playing checkers, and Mr. Laurel is doing an undue amount of checking.

While, on the other side of the room, their progeny, Stan and Oliver, play with the equivalent of their daddies' heads. They are creating a rumpus, and when Mr. Hardy tells them to play quietly, Mr. Laurel adds, "if you must make a noise, make it quietly."

Stan and Oliver, in attempting to decide who will be "it," take down a long-necked vase from the mantel (on which inexplicably rests a photo of Jean Harlow), which they use in hand-over-hand fashion to determine the loser. They both lose by dropping the vase.

Stan and Oliver are sent to bed. Oliver chases Stan who climbs on top of the dresser. In following, Oliver opens up the drawers to reach the top and when close to it crashes through the drawers. Mr. Laurel and Mr. Hardy run upstairs. "Oh—if you brats don't get to bed," says Mr. Hardy, "I'll break your necks." Mr. Laurel chastises his partner, adjuring him to kindness. "Remember the old adage," he tells Mr. Hardy, "you can lead a horse to water but a pencil must be lead." Mr. Hardy decides he is right. Satisfied—after promising a nickle to the boy who gets ready for bed first—Mr. Hardy goes downstairs—on his back—after stepping on a misplaced skate.

The daddies prepare to play pool. Mr. Laurel offers a marshmallow to Mr. Hardy, who puts it on the table edge. After making a shot, Mr. Hardy absentmindedly picks up the pool chalk close by and puts it in his mouth. Mr. Laurel, not to be outdone, picks up the marshmallow and tries to chalk his cue with it.

After freeing his cue from Mr. Hardy's coat where it has stuck, Mr. Laurel, in drawing back to shoot, breaks the cabinet's glass door. Mr. Hardy grabs the offending cue and in so doing shatters the other glass door.

Stan and Oliver hear a mouse squeaking near the bed. Oliver looks for the offender, Stan cocks his air gun in preparation, and the mouse runs up over Oliver's back. Stan fires, hitting Oliver full in the rear.

135

To help assuage the pain, Stan beckons Oliver into the bathroom where he perches on the bathtub. Stan's sock is caught under the stool, and in pulling it away, the stool upsets and Oliver falls into the tub, accidentally turning on the shower.

Climbing out of the tub, Oliver slips on a cake of soap and crashes down forcefully, causing plaster to rain down on the pool table. The fathers start to run upstairs; Mr. Hardy trips over the upturned checkers table.

Stan and Oliver decide to settle their differences with boxing gloves.

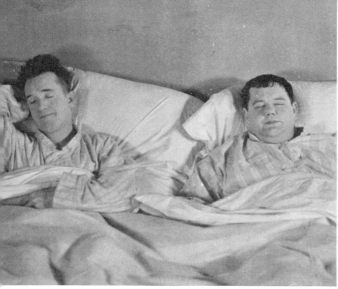

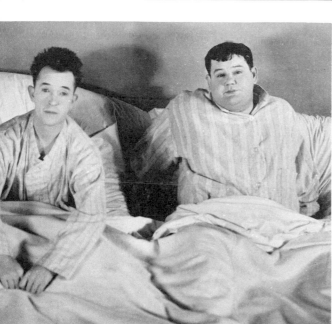

The youngsters, hearing their daddies rush upstairs, hop into bed and pretend to be sleeping. The boys look at Mr. Hardy as he asks plaintively, "Why is it when your mother's home, you always go to sleep?" "Mama always sings us to sleep," says Oliver. Mr. Hardy sings them a lullaby, gets them to sleep, and Mr. Laurel joins loudly in the lullaby, waking the boys up.

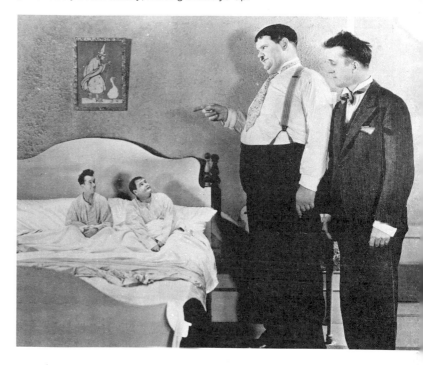

Mr. Hardy finally gets the boys to sleep, and in tiptoeing away from the bed, Mr. Laurel steps on the bulb of a horn, the honk arousing the boys again. They ask for a drink of water, and Mr. Hardy asks, "If I give you a drink of water, will you go to sleep?" Yes. Mr. Laurel starts to leave for the bathroom but Mr. Hardy stops him and goes first. "You might spill it," he explains. Mr. Hardy opens the bathroom door and a backed-up deluge of water pours in, flooding the bedroom and washing Mr. Laurel and Mr. Hardy into the corner.

Production Sidelights

A deleted sequence, occurring after the pool-table cloth has been ripped. With liquid glue Stan tries to repair the table — and to patch Ollie's clothing.

BELOW ZERO

▪▪▪   **1930**

Laurel and Hardy Series / Two reels; 1,220 feet / Sound / Released April 26, 1930, by M-G-M / Produced by Hal Roach / Directed by James Parrott / Photographed by George Stevens / Edited by Richard Currier / Dialogue by H.M. Walker / Titles edited by Nat Hoffberg / Story by Leo McCarey / Sound by Elmer R. Raguse / Compositions used in incidental music scoring by William Axt, Maud Nugent, Lawler, Marvin Hatley, Rayaf and Weller, and Sam Grossman.

Stan Laurel *Himself* / Oliver Hardy *Himself* / *Street cleaner who is "one of the lower element"* Charlie Hall / *The officer* Frank Holliday / *Crook* Leo Willis / *Pete, the proprietor of Pete's for Eats* Stanley (Tiny) Sandford / *Woman at window* Kay Deslys / *Amazonian woman who smashes instruments* Blanche Payson / *Bits as ladies leaving buildings* Lyle Tayo, Retta Palmer / *Man at window* Baldwin Cooke / *"Blind" man* Robert (Bobby) Burns / *The bozo who couldn't pay his check* Robert (Bobby) Burns / *Busboy* Jack Hill / *Grubby extras in restaurant* Charley Sullivan, Charles McMurphy, Bob O'Conor. (At least two foreign-language versions were made: *Tiemba y Titubea* [Spanish] with Bob O'Conor [as the officer] added to the cast; and also a German version.)

Opening title: **"The freezing winter of '29 will long be remembered—Mr. Hardy's nose was so blue, Mr. Laurel shot it for a jay-bird."**

Street musicians Stan and Ollie have been playing for two hours in the bitter cold outside this building without raising a nickle from the people leaving it. Even their favorite tune, "In the Good Old Summer Time," seems to make no impression. "I think we'd better find another spot," says Ollie, and as he leaves he discovers a sign on the building, which until now has been unwittingly covered by Stan: Deaf and Dumb Institute.

Removing their bass viol and organ to another site, they commence playing cheerfully until a lady opens her window and calls down, "Mr. Whiteman . . . about how much money do you boys average a street?" Ollie says it is 50 cents, and the lady throws down some money. "There's a dollar," she says. "Move down a couple of streets." After similar disheartening encounters, they set up again and play resolutely. A "blind" man (Bobby Burns) enters, spots a coin on the sidewalk right in front of them, and appropriates it.

A formidable lady with a pail (Blanche Payson) receives a snowball intended for Stan by a man in a window. Ollie has prepared a snowball for return to the man but when Blanche appears, she regards Stan as the culprit and washes his face with snow. Stan throws the woman's pail in the street, Ollie laughs and Blanche breaks his bass viol over his head. Stan hastily folds up his organ but Blanche throws it out in the street, and a truck runs over it.

To show their gratitude, the boys insist the cop join them for a meal. The cop takes them to a nice place he knows and introduces them to Pete, the headwaiter (Tiny Sandford). At Ollie's suggestion, they all order steak, Ollie adding that he would also like a parfait. "Put one on my steak, too," directs Stan. After Ollie cancels the parfaits, he orders a small demitasse; Stan orders one also, "in a big cup," he specifies. Ollie, appalled at seeing Stan peeling an olive on his fork, dips a large piece of celery in the sugar bowl and eats it comfortingly.

Their bad luck seems to end. They find a very fat wallet in the snow. But a menacing thug (Leo Willis) spots them and follows them as they rush fearfully away. The boys run around a corner . . .

. . . and crash into a policeman (Frank Holliday). They confide their fears to the officer who chases the thug off.

Tho three enjoy their succulent steaks. During the meal they shrink back as five brutal waiters throw out a man who couldn't pay his check. When their check comes, Ollie insists on paying the officer's. As Stan pulls out the wallet, he recognizes the officer's picture in it and realizes just whose money they have found.

The cop sees his wallet, calls them a couple of cheap pick–pockets, and threatens them with ten years. But he gets a better idea. He pays for his part of the check, leaving Stan and Ollie to the mercies of the headwaiter.

The boys are pitched outside, with Stan deposited in the rain barrel.

Ollie looks into the barrel but can't find any water. "Where's the water?," he asks Stan.

"I drank it!," says Stan —and, tipped out of the barrel, verifies his statement.

Production Sidelight

As this still shows, there was to be another sequence with the blind man, in which Ollie, in turnabout situation, finds the *blind man's* money and is forced by the cop to give it back.

(no rating—film currently unavailable for screening)

The Rogue Song

115 minutes; 9,723 feet—
Sound by Movietone
Filmed in two-color Technicolor
Released May 10, 1930, by M-G-M
Produced by Lionel Barrymore for M-G-M
Directed by Lionel Barrymore
Direction assistance by Charles Dorian
Laurel and Hardy scenes directed by Hal Roach
Photographed by Percy Hilburn, and C. Edgar Schoenbaum
Edited by Margaret Booth
Original story by Frances Marion and John Colton
Suggested by Wells Root

Based on the 1912 London opera *Gypsy Love, A New Musical Play in Three Acts,* by Franz Lehar, A. M. Willner and Robert Bodansky
Art direction by Cedric Gibbons
Gowns by Adrian
Sound by Douglas Shearer and Paul Neal
Ballet music arranged by Dmitri Tiomkin
Songs by Herbert Stothart, Clifford Grey, and Franz Lehar

Yegor . . . . Lawrence Tibbett
Princess Vera . . . . Catherine Dale Owen
Countess Tatiana . . . . Judith Voselli
Princess Alexandra . . . . Nance O'Neil
Nadja . . . . Florence Lake

Ossman . . . . Lionel Belmore
Prince Serge . . . . Ullrich Haupt
Petrovna . . . . Kate Price
Hassan . . . . Wallace McDonald
Count Peter . . . . Burr McIntosh
Azamat . . . . James Bradbury, Jr.
Frolov . . . . H. A. Morgan
Yegor's mother . . . . Elsa Alsen
Murza-Bek . . . . Oliver Hardy
Ali-Bek . . . . Stan Laurel
Dancers . . . . The Albertina Rasch Ballet
Guard . . . . Harry Bernard
(Working title: *The Rogue's Song.*)
(Academy Award nomination: Lawrence Tibbett for "Best Actor 1929-1930.")

This M-G-M film is purely a display case for the singing of the company's newest star at the time, the Metropolitan Opera baritone, Lawrence Tibbett. To guarantee the success of the film in foreign markets, Laurel and Hardy were borrowed briefly from Hal Roach to add a few touches of comedy. The essential plot concerns Tibbett in the role of a charming bandit-rogue, whose charming habit of breaking into charming song quite overcharms a charming Russian princess, played by Catharine Dale Owen.

Tibbett's henchmen, Stan and Ollie, are just along for the ride. Their contribution to the film . . .

. . . is not extensive. They are the archetypal comedy sidekicks with precious few opportunities for sidekicking. In their first appearance they ride up to an inn with Tibbett and his men; Tibbett tells Ollie to care for the horses, goes in. Ollie explains his boss's instruction, "He always talks to me like that. That's for the benefit of the other men. I was with his father before him. In fact, I saved his father's life once. There were lions—mountain lions—four of them. Was I afraid? No. I just finished polishing my saber—" Ollie pulls out his dagger, "—not wishing to dirty it!—" Stan joins in Ollie's oft-told punch line: "—I slapped them to death!" After Tibbett leaves the inn, Ollie shows Stan how to close the inn door properly—thereby causing a mound of snow from the roof to crash down on Ollie. Ollie has difficulty mounting his horse, and Stan suggests that he get on a conveniently nearby barrel. Thanking him, Ollie adds, "At last you have shown some intelligence." Ollie gets on the barrel and crashes through into its watery contents.

When the bandits stop again, Stan catches his foot in Ollie's coat pocket while dismounting. In trying to remove it, Ollie rips his coat.

As the boys wait for Tibbett, they become uneasily aware of a captain of guards looking suspiciously at them. Under questioning, Ollie denies knowing whose horse Stan is preparing to mount; he denies knowing Stan. The captain asks Stan whose horse it is. "What horse?," asks Stan. The captain asks Stan who he's with. "I'm with him!," Stan says proudly, pointing to Ollie.

"Arrest those men!," says the captain. But the boys quickly run away to freedom.

After a rousing Tibbett serenade to his princess, Stan and Ollie get a cheese vendor in something of a mess. They take their purchases to a table but the place is infested with flies—cheeseloving flies. Stan chases them carefully away and takes a big bite of the cheese. As he prepares to bite again, he hears a bee buzzing. Each time he prepares to bite, the bee sounds. Stan looks at his stomach, presses it—and the bee buzzes. "I think I swallowed a bee—or something!," Stan says, rising in horror. Ollie gets a long stick and in trying to hit the unseen bee accidentally whacks the boys' mule. The mule chases them away.

Stan and Ollie do not reappear in the film until 40 minutes later when Stan prepares to give Ollie a shave. Stan begins to apply lather to Ollie's face but Ollie warns him, "And don't dip your brush in the soup!" "I thought it was water," says Stan. Distracted by pretty girls walking by, Stan puts the shaving brush in Ollie's mouth. As Ollie removes the bristles from his teeth, Stan sharpens the razor on a rock, and drops the rock on Ollie's toe. Stan picks up the rock, Ollie pushes it angrily out of his hands and it drops on Ollie's toes again. To shave the back of Ollie's neck, Stan sits on a chicken crate. A chicken pecks Stan on the seat of his pants causing him to drop the razor down the back of Ollie's shirt. Stan reaches down for it—succeeding only in ripping Ollie's pants asunder. 143

That night a storm comes up and blows the bandits' tents away. Shelterless, the boys run into a cave. "I can't see a thing," Ollie says. "So can I," adds Stan. "Haven't you got a fur coat on?," asks Ollie. Stan denies it but Ollie persists: "Well, it feels like a fur coat." There comes the ravening growl of a bear and the boys run out into the night.

Tibbett is captured and the boys reconnoiter in a tree by the lake in the hope of helping their chief. Just as they overhear the false report that Tibbett is dead, the tree cracks, breaks, and dumps them in the lake.

Ollie tells a fellow bandit, Azamat (James Bradbury, Jr.), that their leader is dead. When asked if he had any last words, Ollie says solemnly, "His last words were: 'Oliver, I want *you* to carry on.'" Stan interjects, "He never—" Ollie shushes Stan, and, turning to his companions, says, "And if you boys don't mind, I'm your chief." Azamat and the others break into loud hilarity. Which is cue for Tibbett's voice to be heard singing their tribal theme, "The Rogue Song." The bandits are delighted to welcome their chief again. They join in his song:

Beyond the dawn, we belong—afar—
Where the frowning hills
guard us forever.

During this rousing chorus, Stan and Ollie resume their accustomed duties with the gang. They pick up shovels . . .

. . . Ollie judiciously selecting the smallest—and they walk down the line of horses, the shovels over their shoulders.

Production Sidelight

Note: No known print of *The Rogue Song* exists.

Studio lights "warm up" the film's most talked-about scene: the one in which Tibbett sings merrily away while being whipped.

HOG WILD

▮ ▮ ▮ ▮ **1930**

Laurel and Hardy Series / Two reels / Sound / Released May 31, 1930, by M-G-M / Produced by Hal Roach / Directed by James Parrott / Photographed by George Stevens / Edited by Richard Currier / Dialogue by H.M. Walker / Story by Leo McCarey / Sound by Elmer R. Raguse / Compositions used in incidental music scoring by Hal E. Roach, Alice K. Howlett, Marvin Hatley, and William Axt.

Stan Laurel Himself / *Oliver Hardy* Himself / *Mrs. Hardy* Fay Holderness / *Tillie, the housemaid* Dorothy Granger / *Streetcar conductor* Charles McMurphy. (Working title: *Hay Wire.*) (At least two foreign-language versions were made: *Pele Mele* [French], with Yola D'Avril [as Mrs. Hardy] added to the cast; and *Radio Mania* [Spanish], with Linda Loredo [as Mrs. Hardy] added to the cast. British title: *Aerial Antics.*)

Opening title: "**Amnesia! Mr. Hardy was beginning to forget things, but Mr. Laurel had no fear of losing his memory—As a matter of fact, Mr. Laurel never had a memory to lose.**"

Ollie is indignant when both his wife and their maid ignore his demands to help him find his hat. Then, catching sight of himself in the mirror, he realizes he is wearing it. Guiltily he stuffs it under his coat and shortly after pretends he has found it. His wife forces him to work on the radio, which hasn't functioned for three months because of his failure to fix the aerial.

Ollie mounts the ladder in the driveway, and as Stan sounds his horn nerve-rackingly, Ollie falls off.

Ollie tells Stan to turn the car around and back up into the driveway. Stan does so, turning off the motor, as Ollie stoops to pick up something. Stan retards the spark on the Ford's motor, it backfires and a flame shoots out of the exhaust pipe singeing Ollie's behind. Stan, after delaying interminably at a nearby fountain, brings back a pail of water and aims faultily, throwing it in Ollie's face. Stan throws the little water he has left on Ollie's pants, and Ollie reacts vigorously by hurling the pail at Stan.

The pail misses Stan and crashes into a window of the Hardy house. Mrs. Hardy (Fay Holderness) glares out.

Mrs. Hardy crowns her husband with a skillet.

The boys place a tabletop and a ladder on the rear seat of Stan's car. They climb up the ladder, Stan sustaining his balance by hanging on to Ollie's suspender strap, which gives way, precipitating Stan back into the car.

Ollie gets on the roof carrying poles, wire, and tools. Stan slips and clings to his pal who doesn't enjoy the sensation.

Stan puts a pole down near Ollie and carries another one to the roof's far end. Not seeing it, Ollie slips on the pole and tumbles down the roof into his little garden fountain below. Stan is bewildered. "What did you go down for?," he asks.

Energetic work by Stan on an aerial wire again causes Ollie to roll off the roof into the fountain. Climbing back up, Ollie insures future safety by tying a rope around himself, with the other end attached to the chimney. In trying to affix the aerial wire to the pole he has set up, Stan gets on Ollie's back. A cleat that Ollie had nailed to the roof as another safety device gives way, and both Stan and Ollie roll off the roof. We see a large splash of water at roof level: the boys attained the fountain together.

They also pulled the chimney with them Mrs. Hardy opens the window and yells out, "Will you stop *playing!*"

Ollie passes the aerial wire into the house to Stan. Not knowing where to connect it, Stan touches it to both the battery-binding posts causing sparks to fly up the wire to Ollie who . . .

148 . . . falls down the chimney hole. Mrs. Hardy suggests he give up the job but Ollie refuses adamantly.

Ollie mounts the ladder again, behind him Stan accidentally steps on the gas, and off the Ford goes. Hanging on to the ladder with one hand and the steering wheel with the other, Stan drives down the boulevard, missing cars, just clearing a viaduct.

Ollie's ladder rests briefly on the top level of a sight-seeing bus and he has presence of mind enough to tip his hat to the passengers. Ollie falls off the ladder; his wife runs up to comfort him, or so it seems, because she is weeping. Not so. "I'm not crying over you," she says. "The man came and took the radio away!" They get in the Ford with Stan who tries to start the car, which has stalled on the streetcar tracks. Next we see a cop and two ladies on the street corner covering their eyes to hide the sight of some debilitating horror. We hear a terrific crash, then behold the Ford sandwiched between two streetcars. The motorman of one (Charles McMurphy) shouts for them to get out of the way. Stan signals with his left hand and drives the car straight ahead.

149

THE LAUREL & HARDY MURDER CASE

⬛⬛⬛⬛ 1930

Laurel and Hardy Series / Three reels / Sound / Released September 6, 1930, by M-G-M / Produced by Hal Roach / Directed by James Parrott / Photographed by George Stevens and Walter Lundin / Edited by Richard Currier / Dialogue by H.M. Walker / Sound by Elmer R. Raguse / Introductory musical compositions by William Axt, Marvin Hatley, and Nathaniel Shilkret.

Stan Laurel Himself / *Oliver* Hardy Himself / *Police chief* Fred Kelsey / *Officer* Stanley (Tiny) Sandford / *Guileful transvestite* Del Henderson / *Nervous man by the window* Robert (Bobby) Burns / *Outraged young lady* Dorothy Granger / *Menacing butler in league with Del* Frank Austin / *Elderly couple* Lon Poff, Rosa Gore / *Detective* Stanley Blystone / *Well-dressed theatre patron* Art Rowlands / *Stunt double for Stan Laurel* Ham Kinsey / *Stunt double for Oliver Hardy* Cy Slocum. (Working title: *The Rap.*)

(At least three foreign-language versions were made, each of which incorporated reworked scenes from *Berth Marks: Der Spuk um Mitternacht* [German], with Otto Fries [as the conductor] added to the cast; *Noche de Duendes* [Spanish], with Bob [Mazooka] O'Conor [as the conductor] added to the cast; and *La Maison de la peur* or *Feu mon oncle* [French], with Jean de Briac [as the detective] added to the cast. Each foreign-language version also featured Clara Guiol as a passenger.)

Opening title: "**Mr. Laurel and Mr. Hardy decided that they needed a rest—They had been out of work since 1921.**"

Fishing in the best style—on the ocean pier, at leisure—but principally at leisure. Ollie has made a virtually full-time vocation of sleeping.

Stan catches a fish, unhooks it, and places it behind his sleeping pal. Hearing an unseemly flapping, Ollie wakes, removes the fish from under his posterior, and throws it back in the water. Stan rebaits his hook, swings the line dramatically; the hook catches Ollie's derby and drops it in the water.

After his hat has been salvaged, Ollie notices a vagrant newspaper nearby. In astonishment, he reads: "Legal Notice! Will the heirs of the $3,000,000 estate of the late Ebeneezer Laurel be at the Laurel Mansion, Dover Road, at 8 o'clock tonight for the reading of the will. L.A.H." Stan doesn't remember any of his relatives or where he was born ("I was too young to remember"). He vaguely recalls an uncle—who fell through a trapdoor and broke his neck. It seems he was on a gallows. Painfully, Stan reads the notice and is astounded. "$3,000,000! Is that as much as 1,000?," he asks. "Why man alive," says Ollie enthusiastically, "it's twice as much!"

Meanwhile the other Laurel relatives foregather at Ebeneezer's mansion. So, too, do a number of detectives. It seems that Ebeneezer did not die a natural death and the possible heirs must remain in the mansion until the mystery is solved.

The least prepossessing of the potential heirs appears in the middle of a downpour. It is a good night for a murder mystery.

A mysterious-looking butler (Frank Austin) admits the two hopefuls.

After a blithe self-introduction by Ollie, Stan shakes hands with the butler. Ollie hits Stan on the arm with the newspaper in deep disapproval of this social gaffe.

The chief detective (Fred Kelsey) tells them no one leaves the house until the mystery is unraveled. "Garçon!," he says to the butler, "show them to a room."

The butler points out where Ebeneezer's body was secreted in a cupboard—in the very room the boys are to spend the night.

After being frightened several times, principally by themselves, a hand comes slowly around the door. It is the butler, asking if everything is all right.

After traditional frights, including a wandering black cat, lightning flashes, a portrait mistaken for a ghost, a night scream, and all the paraphernalia of a mystery plot, Ollie says he has had enough—he is going to find out what it's all about.

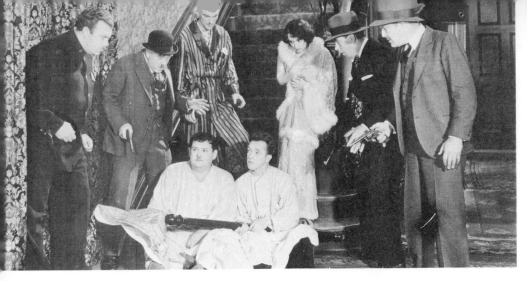

A lamp hung with a white dust cover is connected to a rope that Stan finds and uses for a belt. The ghostly object follows him without cease, and the boys panic and fall down the stairs—before the astonished gaze of an officer (Tiny Sandford), the chief detective, several of the heirs (Art Rowland and Dorothy Granger), and two detectives (unknown, and Stanley Blystone).

Everyone is ordered back to bed, but once in it, the boys find a bat. The bat takes a tour of the room.

A number of the heirs vanish from sight through the device of a disappearing chair. Stan and Ollie aren't caught that way: the murderer comes to them directly. It is one of the heirs, a sweet old lady.

But the sweet old lady turns out to be a nasty middle-aged man (Del Henderson). Ollie struggles with him, and during the battle there is a dissolve to a shot of Stan and Ollie back on the dock, struggling with each other—in a dream. They roll back and forth, and crash down into the water.

Production Sidelights

These stills show the high points of a deleted scene in which the boys journey by train to get the inheritance. The Pullman scenes are derivative of *Berth Marks,* made the year before.

ANOTHER FINE MESS

1930

Laurel and Hardy Series / Three reels / Sound / Released November 29, 1930, by M-G-M / Produced by Hal Roach / Directed by James Parrott / Photographed by George Stevens / Edited by Richard Currier / Dialogue by H.M. Walker / Story based on a sketch written by Arthur J. Jefferson (Stan Laurel's father) entitled *Home from the Honeymoon* / Sound by Elmer R. Raguse / All compositions used in incidental music scoring by Le Roy Shield.

Stan Laurel Himself / *Oliver Hardy* Himself / *Lady Plumtree* Thelma Todd / *Colonel Wilburforce Buckshot* James Finlayson / *Meadows, the real butler* Eddie Dunn / *Lord Leopold Ambrose Plumtree* Charles Gerrard / *The real maid* Gertrude Sutton / *Officers* Harry Bernard, Bill Knight, Bob Mimford / *Bicycle rider* Robert (Bobby) Burns / *One-half of the bicycle-riding goat* Joe Mole. (At least one foreign-language version was made, *De Bote en Boto* [Spanish].)

Opening title: "**Mr. Laurel and Mr. Hardy have many ups and downs — Mr. Hardy takes charge of the upping, and Mr. Laurel does most of the downing.**"

We read a newspaper ad: "For rent. Palatial residence. Completely furnished with maid and butler service. The owner, Colonel Wilburforce Buckshot, who is leaving for a hunting trip in South Africa, desires to rent his residence to reliable tenant. The right party can have immediate possession. To see this property, apply to 1558 Poinsettia Ave., Beverly Hills."

We also see Colonel Buckshot (James Finlayson), at departure time, leaving everything in care of his butler and maid. After Fin goes, the butler says, "South Africa has my sympathy!" Nearby, Stan and Ollie are running away from a policeman; it seems that when told to move on, Stan tipped his hat and said, "Yes, ma'am."

The boys find refuge in a cellar but when they slam it shut, the hook outside falls into place, locking them in. The cop cannot find them.

When the cop leaves, Ollie suggests they go up the stairs and depart.

The boys overhear the butler (Eddie Dunn) and the maid (Gertrude Sutton) making plans to go away for the weekend. The colonel will never know because he is not slated to return for another six months. They leave, and the boys try to go also but their policeman nemesis is still about the grounds. A town car pulls up and a fashionably dressed lady and gentleman walk up to the house and ring the bell. They have come to rent the place. Ollie tells Stan to rush upstairs, put on the butler's uniform, and come to the door with the information that Colonel Buckshot is not at home.

Stan does so, but before he is aware of what has happened, the man, Lord Leopold Ambrose Plumtree (Charles Gerrard), and Lady Plumtree (Thelma Todd) have gone inside to look the house over. Baffled, Stan calls upstairs to Ollie, "Colonel Buckshot!" Entering into the subterfuge, Ollie puts on the colonel's smoking jacket, and with florid cordiality greets the visitors, "Good-morning. Many, many, many good-mornings." The Plumtrees have just returned from their honeymoon, his lordship explains, and they would like to rent the place and move in immediately. "Besides the butler, you have maid service?," asks Thelma, and when Ollie verifies this, she asks to see the maid. "Oh, Hives," says Ollie turning to Stan, "will you call Agnes?" Ever agreeable, Stan yells, "OH, AGNES!" Ollie gets Stan aside and explains that in order to get out of this mess, Stan must play both Hives and Agnes.

153

After playing the scales from the bass on up, and hitting a chord that causes the piano top to fall on Lord Plumtree's hand, Ollie hears a whistle. He excuses himself, and finds Stan, in long underwear at the top of the stairs, holding a pair of corsets. Stan is ordered to put them on, and Ollie rejoins his aristocratic friends. When Lord Plumtree asks to be taken to the billiard room, the baffled Ollie takes him vaguely along unknown corridors, pointing out various paintings—"Physic at the Well" is one of them—and one that Ollie describes as "a gondola going through the Panama Canal in Venice."

On their way to the elusive billiard room, the men meet "Agnes," slightly askew. When Lord Plumtree asks if she is related to the butler, Ollie says they are twins—one born in Detroit, the other in Miami. Lord Plumtree says he doesn't quite understand. "That's all right," says Ollie. "Neither do they."

"Agnes" goes on to be interviewed by Thelma, and explains, among other things, that "she" has been at this job half a year—"to be exact, three months." And when asked how many maids the colonel keeps, "Agnes" replies, "Oh, he never tells me his private affairs." Thelma is greatly taken with this cheery domestic and hugs "her" warmly. Meanwhile, Ollie speculates aloud about just what he did with the billiard room. "That's quite all right, old fellow," says Lord Plumtree, "I never play anyway."

Thelma tells her beloved "Plummie" that this dear girl has consented to stay on with them. Ollie doesn't quite follow this. Plummie asks what the rent is, and Ollie asks if $20 a month would be too much. On being told this is practically giving it away, Ollie says he picked it up for practically nothing himself. Upon Plummie's asking if he has any horses, Ollie says they have all been shipped to the Kentucky plantation, and when asked what part of Kentucky he comes from, he says, "Omaha." "Agnes" is surprised: "I thought Omaha was in Wisconsin."

While a simplistic financial transaction is being computed, Colonel Buckshot returns and is met at the door by "Agnes," who asks him if he'd like to see Colonel Buckshot. "Why, nothing would suit me better," says Fin. When Ollie is summoned, he cannot understand why Stan keeps waving and pointing. Finally, Ollie recognizes both the portrait and the person of the man he has so briefly been. Ollie hastily pushes Fin out on the porch, and the boys flee to the Buckshot trophy room. Fin chases Plummie out of the house with a revolver. Three cops come into the house and Fin tells them that burglars ran into his trophy room.

The police break down the doors and find a grotesque animal seated on a chest. (In the film, Stan and Ollie remain hidden under the animal skin.) The animal rises, brays loudly, and runs out of the house as Fin and the cops fall over. Fin pursues "it" with bow and arrow but the boys evade him, knocking down two cyclists on a tandem, taking over the bicycle themselves. The animal follows streetcar tracks into a tunnel, into which the three pursuing cops shoot. A streetcar comes through the tunnel; the policemen step back but the streetcar takes their uniforms with it, leaving them in their underwear. When they emerge from the tunnel, the animal skin as well as the bicycle are now rent asunder, and the man in the front part of the skin is pedaling behind the other.

BE BIG

☐☐☐ 1931

The worldly bellboy (Charlie Hall) looks on dubiously as Mrs. Hardy (Isabelle Keith) and Mrs. Laurel (Anita Garvin) say good-bye.

Laurel and Hardy Series / Three reels (American release) / Sound / Released February 7, 1931, by M-G-M / Produced by Hal Roach / Directed by James Parrott / Photographed by Art Lloyd / Edited by Richard Currier / Dialogue by H.M. Walker / Sound by Elmer R. Raguse / Compositions used in incidental music scoring by Le Roy Shield, Ring-Hager, Frederic Van Norman, Mel Kaufman, Jessie Deppen, and Marvin Hatley.

Stan Laurel Himself / *Oliver Hardy* Himself / *Mrs. Laurel* Anita Garvin / *Mrs. Hardy* Isabelle Keith / *Bellboy* Charlie Hall / *Cookie, a fellow lodge member* Baldwin Cooke / *Passersby at railway station* Jack Hill, Ham Kinsey / *Cabdriver* Chet Brandenberg. (Working title: *The Chiselers.*) (At least three foreign-language versions were made, each of which appended an expanded version of *Laughing Gravy*, and was directed by that film's director, James W. Horne: *Les Carotttiers* [French], with Jean de Briac [as the fellow lodge member] added to the cast; *Los Calaveras* or *El Canelo* [Spanish], with Linda Loredo [as Mrs. Hardy] added to the cast; and a German version.)

Opening title: **"Mr. Hardy is a man of great care, caution, and discretion—Mr. Laurel is married too."**

The Laurels and the Hardys have been busy packing for a trip to Atlantic City. Stan has had to pack only one item to satisfy his holiday requirements.

When the ladies depart, Ollie jubilantly removes the towel from his head and explains to Stan why they must remain behind. Suddenly Mrs. Hardy is heard coming back; Ollie shouts out, "The towel!," and Stan grabs it, wraps it around his own head, and sinks into a chair, exhausted. Ollie puts his wife's white fur around his head and resumes invalidhood. Mrs. Hardy comes in to say she has forgotten her fur; Stan hands her the towel. Ollie explains to his "ducky lover" that the fur reminded him of her.

Just before departure, one of the members of Stan's and Ollie's club calls to say that a surprise stag party is being given in their honor tonight. Ollie says they can't make it, and in response to heavy pleading, says, "That's final. When a Hardy makes his mind up, it's as firm as the rock of Gibraltar." The man from the club persists, whispering details of the specially planned floor show, adding, "Remember the old saying: 'No man is bigger than the excuses he can make to his wife. So don't forget. Be big. Get me? BE BIG!" Ollie decides to be big. Draping a towel dolorously over his head, he fakes illness, insisting that Mrs. Hardy and Mrs. Laurel go on the trip alone.

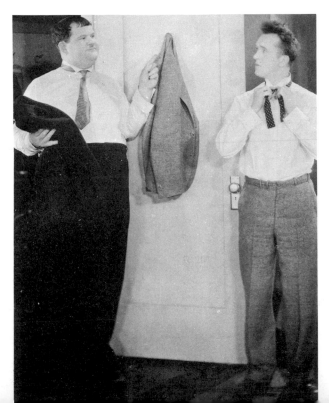

In preparing to put on their club uniforms, taking off their street clothes gets to be a problem for Ollie. Each time he turns to hang one of his garments on his clothes hook, Stan anticipates him by hanging there a garment of his own. Stan doesn't notice that each time this happens, Ollie throws the offending garment into the closet. When Ollie finally hangs his own coat on the hook, it falls off onto the floor.

Meanwhile the wives arrive at the railroad station to find that they are just in time to be too late. This evening's last train for Atlantic City has gone.

In full fig for the club party—except for Ollie's boots. The reason is elemental and typical: Stan is wearing Ollie's footgear.

Ollie tries to remove his boot with a bootjack; Stan tries to help by pounding the heel of the boot into the jack. The boot and the jack become permanently joined until Ollie, trying to pull them apart, somersaults backward and breaks the jack. Stan persists in trying to help Ollie get the boot off. The next attempt wrecks the chair Ollie is sitting in.

After further painful contortions, Ollie pleads with his pal, "Let's concentrate and use our brains . . . Remember the old adage, 'A task slowly done is surely done.' Do you understand?" "Sure," says Stan. "A cool head never won fair lady."

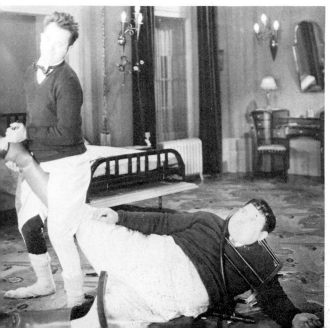

Ollie gets down on the floor to give Stan the best leverage to seize the boot. For an anchor, Ollie grabs the radiator, which burns his fingers. Next, he holds the curtains and brings them down over his head. The struggle continues as Stan gets up on the bed to find a better vantage point, but the bed folds up in the wall, enclosing him. Ollie pulls frantically on the bedcord and the bed comes down, crushing him to the floor.

157

In demonstrating on Stan's person how easy it is to pull off a boot, Ollie is outstandingly successful: his backward tug propels him through the door into the bathroom.

The Hardy sweater expands, falling down over his ankles. They try to wring it out. "What could be worse?," asks Ollie.

They learn very shortly. The wives return to see Stan in his convivial garb.

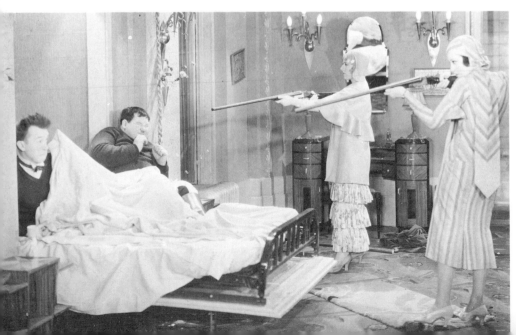

Stan shuts the door in their faces and runs crying to Ollie, who is in bed. Stan dives into the bed, asking, "What'll we do?" "Be big!," says Ollie. The bellboy admits the ladies, Ollie pulls the bedcord frantically and the bed folds up in the wall. The wives enter the bedroom, calling for their spouses. Stan's head appears at the top of the bed, and he shushes them, explaining that Ollie is asleep. (The still is slightly different from the action.) Mrs. Hardy grabs a nearby shotgun and says she'll wake him up. Both ladies aim their guns—and we next see the apartment's exterior. Suddenly a huge opening appears in the wall, and the bed comes flying out in an effusion of bricks, dust, feathers, and smoke.

CHICKENS COME HOME

1931

Laurel and Hardy Series / Three reels / Sound / Released February 21, 1931, by M-G-M / Produced by Hal Roach / Directed by James W. Horne / Photographed by Art Lloyd and Jack Stevens / Edited by Richard Currier / Dialogue by H.M. Walker / Sound by Elmer R. Raguse / Compositions used in incidental music scoring by Le Roy Shield, Marvin Hatley, and Alice K. Howlett.

Stan Laurel Himself / *Oliver Hardy* Himself / *Ollie's old flame* Mae Busch / *Winsome Mrs. Hardy* Thelma Todd / *Ollie's double-dealing butler* James Finlayson / *Dinner guest* Frank Holliday / *Mrs. Laurel* Elizabeth Forrester/Norma Drew / *Busybody gossip friend of Mrs. Laurel* Patsy O'Byrne / *The judge* Charles French / *The judge's wife* Gertrude Pedlar / *Dinner servant* Frank Rice / *Passerby outside apartment* Gordon Douglas / *Elevator operator* Ham Kinsey / *Office employee* Ham Kinsey / *Office clerks* Baldwin Cooke, Dorothy Layton. (Literal remake of *Love 'Em and Weep*, four years earlier.) (At least one foreign-language version was made: *Politiquerias* [Spanish], with Linda Loredo [as Mrs. Hardy], Carmen Granada [as Ollie's old flame], Ellinor Van Der Veer [as a dinner guest], Rina de Lignoco [as Mrs. Laurel], Pedro Regas [as an office worker], and Vera Zouroff and Benito Fernandez [as dinner party guests] added to the cast.)

Opening title: "**Every man has a past—with some little 'indiscretion' he would like to bury—Mr. Laurel and Mr. Hardy have 30 or 40 they would like to cremate.**"

Ollie, tycoon and candidate for mayor, has been wreathed in the incense of his own cigar smoke, contemplating his new status in society's top echelon and awaiting the arrival of Stan, his general manager. A knock on the door. Ollie goes to open it when Stan swings it open, smack into his boss's face. Stan's flyswatter indicates where he has been—in the sample room of their fertilizer plant. Stan sits down to take dictation for a Hardy campaign speech. Unexpectedly there is a commotion in the outer office.

The commotion is a sultry girl friend (Mae Busch) from Ollie's past, come to cash in on his present affluence. She has a photo of Ollie carrying her, in bathing suit, astride his shoulders. "You can't bluff me," Ollie says. "That was in my gilded youth. My primrose days—before I was married." Ollie sends Stan out of the office. Mae sits flauntingly on Ollie's lap; he accidentally rests his elbow on his buzzer button, causing Stan to open the door and all the office force to look in.

Ollie hastily agrees to meet Mae at seven this evening to make a settlement. Mrs. Hardy (Thelma Todd) comes to visit hubby, and Mae is put in abeyance. (In the film she is put in a closet.) In the rush, Mae has dropped her white fur and Ollie hastily stuffs it under his coat. Mrs. Hardy brings news that she is giving a dinner party tonight at seven for all the people who have helped his campaign. Thelma spots the white fur, and her husband, in hearty confusion, offers it to her, saying, "Merry Christmas, sweetheart." She points out that it's only July, but Ollie says a vital part of his election platform is the need to do Christmas shopping early.

Mae leaves after Mrs. Hardy, snarling that Ollie had better be visiting her at seven. Meanwhile, Mrs. Laurel is entertaining a gossipy friend who advises her that it is folly to trust any man. Ollie phones to say that Stan must work with him tonight on the campaign; Mrs. Laurel says that if Stan isn't home for dinner tonight, she'll break his arm. Ollie tells Stan his wife is perfectly content to have him out this evening.

That night Stan appears with tributes from Ollie, which Mae disdainfully hurls to the floor. She forces Stan to give her Ollie's home phone number . . .

. . . and she assures her old chum that if he doesn't come over instanter, she will join his little party. He says he'll be over as soon as he can get away.

Ollie realizes that the butler (James Finlayson) has overheard every word. He passes a bill to Fin, and both laugh appreciatively.

Stan tries to say something but Mae shuts him up. After she turns away, Stan realizes that the framed photograph on the table is the one that compromises Ollie, he stuffs it under his overcoat.

Trying to get out of the house during the dinner party. Ollie hides the cigars under his coat and insists he must go out and buy some for his chief guest, the judge. Fin appears at once with a new box on a tray. Ollie takes them, kicks Fin in the leg, and puts a bank note on the tray. They laugh appreciatively. Ollie gives the cigars to the judge, and when the phone rings, rushes over, spilling all the cigars under his coat. Thelma answers; it is Mae demanding Ollie. Stan grabs the phone from Mae and tells Ollie to hurry over. Flustered, Ollie explains to the suspicious Thelma that it was just an old schoolmate: "We used to room together." The judge asks Ollie to sing for them. Thelma grimly hands him a song sheet titled, "You May Be Fast, But Your Mama's Gonna Slow You Down."

Stan is under siege from the turbulent Mae.

After finishing his song, Ollie rushes toward the ringing telephone, bumps Fin, spilling his loaded tray. Ollie hands him another bill and they laugh appreciatively. Stan is on the telephone, pleading for aid. Ollie tells everyone it's a wrong number whereupon Thelma socks him on the chin and leaves.

To the prim and thrilled horror of Mrs. Laurel's gossipy friend (Patsy O' Byrne), the battle between Mae and Stan extends out into the hall. Patsy declares she'll tell his wife. (The elevator operator is Ham Kinsey, for many years Stan's friend and stand-in at the Hal Roach Studios.)

Stan backs into an open window and falls down through the awning over the building's entrance. Mae announces she is going to Hardy's.

But Stan takes her car key and she searches him in some depth. Patsy looks on in delighted anticipation, chanting again, "I'll tell your wife!" When Stan tries to stop her, she shrinks back haughtily and says, "Don't touch me, you Bluebeard!," and flees. Mae finds the key and roars off after her car smacks a lamppost, which drops a light globe on Stan's head. Patsy has gone on to Mrs. Laurel's with her news. Mrs. Laurel picks up a large hatchet.

Apprehensively Ollie begins the first line of his new rendition, "Somebody's coming to my house . . . " His nervousness increases as the song progresses. A horn honk is heard, and Ollie tells Fin to say he's not at home. Fin does so . . .

... but Mae will have none of it. She comes in and Ollie quickly says to the guests, "Meet Mr. and Mrs. Laurel." Thelma greets Mae graciously, and Stan in taking off his coat lets the incriminating photo fall to the floor. A guest puts it upright on a table. As the guests leave, Ollie puts the photograph under a couch cushion.

Ollie tells Mae to get out or he'll shoot her and kill himself. She faints. Thelma comes in and Ollie explains that Mrs. Laurel has just fainted. The Hardys place Mae on the couch, and Stan picks up a cushion for her head—thereby revealing the photograph. Ollie hastily sits on it. Thelma goes to arrange a guest room for the Laurels to spend the night.

The boys contrive to get Mae out before Thelma returns. Stan puts Mae on Ollie's back, placing Mae's coat over her shoulders, letting it hide Ollie. (The same device used in *Sugar Daddies,* 1927.) Stan guides her out, and Thelma, returning, marvels at Mrs. Laurel's grotesque bulkiness. They reach the door—on the other side of which is Mrs. Laurel, impatiently ringing the bell. The boys become worried by that unrelenting ringing, turn hurriedly, and start for the living room. Ollie falls, dropping Mae and Stan to the floor with him. Thelma opens the front door, and when the real Mrs. Laurel introduces herself, Thelma quite understands. Meanwhile Mae is now astride Stan's back with Ollie as the escort. They go to the door; Stan falls, spilling Mae. Ollie runs off into the night, followed by Stan, followed in turn by his hatchet-wielding wife.

A Laurel & Hardy Cameo Appearance

the stolen jools

1931

Special promotional short presented by National Variety Artists (a company union of the Albee Theatre chain), by arrangement and cooperation with Chesterfield cigarettes, to raise funds for the relief work of the N.V.A. tuberculosis sanitarium at Saranac Lake, New York (which is today the Will Rogers Memorial Hospital for Respiratory Diseases). Two reels / Sound / Released April 1931 by Paramount and National Screen Service (although it is grouped together with the Masquers Club shorts for domestic release, *The Stolen Jools* is not a part of that series) / Produced by Pat Casey with the cooperation of the studios to which the various stars were under contract, supervised by E.K. Nadel / Directed by William McGann.

In this literally star-packed short virtually no featured player is on screen for more than a minute. The detective (Eddie Kane), who hears by phone that Norma Shearer's jewels have been stolen, tells the caller, "I'll get right over with two of my best men." We then see Kane in the back seat of a Ford Model T driven by Ollie, accompanied on the front seat by Stan who is fiddling with the car's controls. Siren screaming, the car pulls up before Miss Shearer's house, where the Our Gang kids are discovered, chattering and munching ice-cream cones. The kids, seeing Stan and Ollie in cop uniform, run away.

Ollie parks the car fastidiously. Stan pulls at another of the car's levers, and the Model T collapses in a heap. Kane thanks the boys and asks where they'll be if he needs them. "Right here," says Ollie in deep disgust. Then, still holding the steering wheel, he turns to Stan and complains, "I *told* you not to make that last payment."

In order of appearance, "When Came the Dawn": *Police station sergeant* Wallace Beery / *Keystone Kops* Buster Keaton, Jack Hill, Allen Jenkins, J. Farrell McDonald / *Initial thieves* Edward G. Robinson, George E. Stone / *Detective* Eddie Kane / *Two of inspector Kane's best men* Stan Laurel, Oliver Hardy / *Our Gang, eating ice cream at Norma Shearer's home* Allen (Farina) Hoskins, Matthew (Stymie) Beard, Norman (Chubby) Chaney, Mary Ann Jackson, Shirley Jean Rickert, Dorothy (Echo) De Borba, Bobby (Wheezer) Hutchins, Pete the pup / *Norma Shearer's housekeeper* Polly Moran / *Victim of the jewel robbery* Norma Shearer / *Cigarette-smoking friend of Miss Shearer* Hedda Hopper / *Couple sharing indoors tête-à-tête* Joan Crawford, William Haines / *Amorous lady on porch swing* Dorothy Lee / *Uniformed servicemen* Edmund Lowe, Victor McLaglen / *Swedish waiter* El Brendel / *Hotel desk clerks* Charlie Murray, George Sidney / *Lady singing in bathtub, Room 807* Winnie Lightner / *Clerk selling Chesterfields behind counter* Fifi D'Orsay / *Cisco Kid characterization* Warner Baxter / *Lady in the hallway* Irene Dunne / *Drugstore patrons doing "Rio Rita" routine* Bert Wheeler, Robert Woolsey / *Exiting at stage door* Richard Dix / *Actress in scene* Claudia Dell / *Director* Lowell Sherman / *Newspaper reporter ("No")* Eugene Pallette / *Newspaper reporter ("Yes")* Stu Erwin / *Newspaper reporter ("Maybe")* Richard (Skeets) Gallagher / *Editor* Gary Cooper / *Reporter who covered the Screen Stars Annual Ball* Wynne Gibson / *Other reporter* Charles (Buddy) Rogers / *French detective friend of Rogers* Maurice Chevalier / *With Loretta Young under the tree* Douglas Fairbanks, Jr. / *"Everybody Knows Her"* Loretta Young / *Reluctant to identify himself* Richard Barthelmess / *Louise Fazenda* Charles Butterworth / *Couple having confab* Bebe Daniels, Ben Lyon / *Reading poetry* Barbara Stanwyck / *Reading paper* Frank Fay / *Couple working in a movie scene* Jack Oakie, Fay Wray / *Man with beard* Joe E. Brown / *Projectionist (with teeth, without beard)* George (later, Gabby) Hayes / *Midget about to bury the reel of film* Little Billy / *Solves the mystery* Mitzi Green. *Note:* Bert Lytell served as the curtain-speech pitchman for the charity appeal. (British title: *The Slippery Pearls,* 1932.)

LAUGHING GRAVY ▄▄▄ 1931

Laurel and Hardy Series / Two reels (American release) / Sound / Released April 4, 1931, by M-G-M / Produced by Hal Roach / Directed by James W. Horne / Photographed by Art Lloyd / Edited by Richard Currier / Dialogue by H.M. Walker / Compositions used in incidental music scoring by Le Roy Shield and Marvin Hatley.

Stan Laurel Himself / *Oliver Hardy* Himself / *The bristling landlord* Charlie Hall / *Officer* Harry Bernard / *Drunk* Charles Dorety / *Laughing Gravy* Himself. (Working title: *True Blue.*) (At least three foreign-language versions were made, each of which tacked on additional footage and incorporated *Be Big: Les Carotliers* [French], with Harry Bernard's role deleted; *Los Calaveras* or *El Canelo* [Spanish], with Linda Loredo [as Mrs. Hardy] added to the cast; and a German version.)

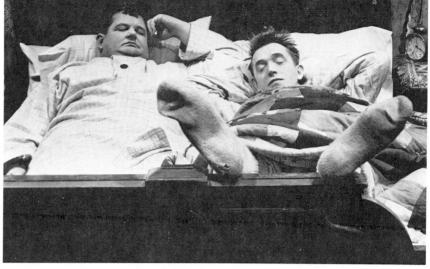

Opening title: "**Mr. Laurel and Mr. Hardy stuck together through thick and thin—one pocketbook between them—always empty.**"

Serene—except for Stan's hiccups, which threaten to rock the bed. The hiccups awaken their dog Laughing Gravy, who begins to bark. Ollie tells Stan to keep quiet: "If the landlord finds out we've got a dog here, he'll throw us out."

Ollie gets out of bed to calm the dog, and on returning, jumps into bed. It falls to pieces and Laughing Gravy barks joyously.

Their landlord (Charlie Hall), sleeping below, is awakened by plaster falling on his head. He demands to know where the dog is, and Ollie replies loftily, "My friend, Mr. Laurel, has the hiccups." The door of the cabinet where they have hidden the dog opens, and Charlie says, "Aha! You know my rules about dogs—I'm going to throw him out." And he does—into the snow. Stan plans to go out and rescue him but Ollie will trust only his own intelligence in such an enterprise. He goes downstairs after Laughing Gravy, and gets locked out. From their window, Stan drops knotted bed sheets down and pulls the dog up. Pleased to have his pet again, Stan fondles him, quite forgetting Ollie in the freezing weather below. Ollie whistles up; Charlie's lights go on. Ollie gets behind a bush and barks like a dog. Charlie hurls a potted plant at him and makes the connection. Stan throws the knotted sheets out again and hauls Ollie up—almost. The sheets unknot and Ollie lands in a barrel of ice water.

Stan opens the front door and Ollie walks in, clothes and spirit frozen stiff.

Going to bed, Ollie jumps in eagerly, and once more it crashes to the floor, waking Charlie. Stan hides Laughing Gravy in the chimney as Charlie prepares to break down their door by hurling himself at it. However, Stan opens the door at just that moment, and Charlie runs headlong through the room into the kitchen where numerous pots and pans break his fall. He orders the boys out "first thing in the morning."

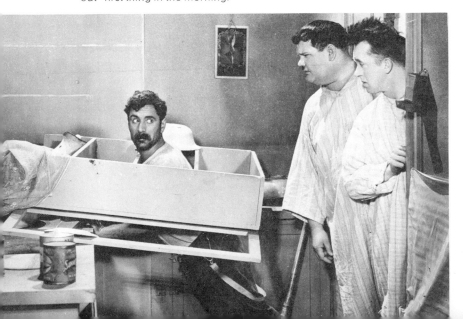

Stan follows Laughing Gravy up the chimney to the snow-covered roof and holds him as Ollie stands up out of their window to reach the dog. The window slams shut and Ollie asks Stan to pull him up on the roof.

Several times Ollie slides down through the icy snow to the very edge of the roof. Stan descends to their room with the dog by going down the chimney. Ollie tries to get down the same way but breaks the chimney in the process, causing bricks to cascade down off the roof onto Charlie's inquiring head as he leans out of his window. Charlie is knocked out.

Ollie gets stuck in the chimney until Stan pulls him down in a flurry of bricks. "Now look at us," says Ollie, "we'll have to take a bath before we go to bed." It is agreed that Laughing Gravy will be washed first.

In preparing their rather primitive ablutions, Stan places a cake of soap near the tub, amply convenient for Ollie to step on, introducing him to the tub before his turn. When they ultimately get around to washing Laughing Gravy, a knock is heard at the door. The dog is hidden in the buffet, and Ollie puts Stan's head under water and begins washing. "Come in!," Ollie says, and a drunk momentarily looks in, and walks out, incredulous.

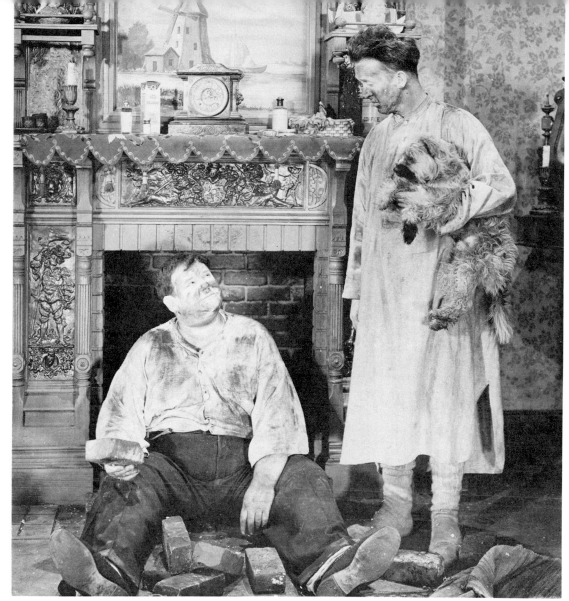

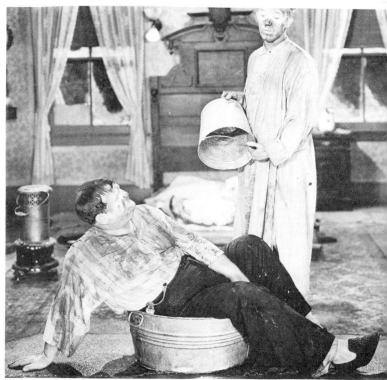

Charlie revives and catches the boys washing the dog; with gun in hand, Charlie orders them out of the house in 15 minutes. The boys and their little pal are preparing to depart, when a policeman arrives and puts a quarantine sign on the boardinghouse door, stipulating that no one can leave the premises for two months. "This is more than I can stand," Charlie says soberly, and he leaves the scene. Shortly after, several shots are heard, and the three men solemnly doff their hats.

Production Sidelights

Stills from the French version of the film showing material never released in America. Stan is left an inheritance, and he prepares to leave his pal in a scene gently satirizing the two-friends-departing-in-bravely-mournful-style Hollywood cliché.

Our Wife

■ ■ ■   **1931**

Laurel and Hardy Series / Two reels / Sound / Released May 16, 1931, by M-G-M / Produced by Hal Roach / Directed by James W. Horne / Photographed by Art Lloyd / Edited by Richard Currier / Dialogue by H.M. Walker / Sound by Elmer R. Raguse / Compositions used in incidental music scoring by Le Roy Shield and Marvin Hatley.

Stan Laurel Himself / *Oliver Hardy* Himself / *Dulcy, the bride* Jean (Babe) London / *The father of the bride* James Finlayson / *William Gladding, justice of the peace* Ben Turpin / *Finlayson's butler* Charley Rogers / *Turpin's wife* Blanche Payson.

Stan sets the table for the wedding feast, carries the large stack of plates left over back into the kitchen. The door swings, hitting him in the back and the plates crash down. Then, in flicking flies off the cake, Stan gets icing all over Ollie's new hat. Meanwhile, Ollie's fiancée is devastated because her father, after seeing Ollie's photograph, sternly forbids the marriage.

Opening title: "**Mr. Hardy was making big preparations to get married—Mr. Laurel was taking a bath, too.**"

Ollie gazes fondly at the photograph of his intended, dear Dulcy (Jean "Babe" London). He practices his "I do," sprays his throat with an atomizer, and gaily hums the Wedding March.

Deciding to do a good turn, Stan gets rid of the flies on the wedding cake by spraying it thoroughly with insecticide.

The telephone rings. It is Dulcy. Ollie excuses himself for a moment to see if there are any eavesdroppers. Satisfied they are alone, he returns to the phone to learn that Dulcy's father has refused to let her marry her "Dimple Darling." Bravely casting gloom aside, Ollie tells his "Ducky Lover" that they will elope at midnight.

Finding Stan listening in, Ollie tells him that now he must help by renting a closed car and meeting them at Dulcy's home tonight.

This must be done on the "qui-vee-vee," Ollie tells Stan: a private car must be rented so they can drive themselves. Stan, beaming, agrees to help.

Ollie goes into his bedroom humming the Wedding March, reaches for his atomizer but picks up the insecticide instead. Merrily, he sprays his throat—and finds it afire. Rushing to the kitchen, he sucks on ice that Stan chips off for him.

A piece of ice falls on the floor and shortly after, Ollie slips on it, diving into the living room, crashing into the table, and burying his face in the wedding cake.

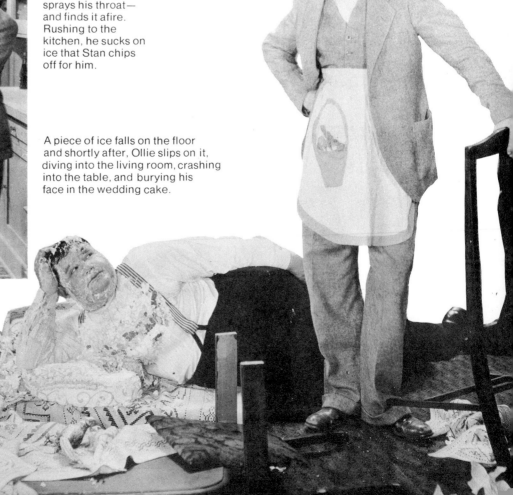

That night Ollie calls up to Dulcy from beneath her window, telling her that Stan is on the way with the rented limousine. Stan shows up, but unable to comprehend the essential meaning of the word *elopement,* rings the front doorbell of Dulcy's house. Stan tells the butler (Charley Rogers) that he'd like to see Mr. Hardy. In the bushes, Ollie groans. "Hardy?," asks the butler.

"Yes," says Stan. "He's going to elope with Dulcy." "Elope?," the butler asks in horror, swiftly closing the door. Ollie tells Dulcy they have been discovered; the butler goes upstairs to tell Dulcy's dad that "there's a fellow at the door announcing an elopement."

As he holds the ladder for Ollie, Stan realizes he has caught his foot under the bottom of it. He pulls out his foot, twisting the ladder, and Ollie and the ladder crash through a window.

Dulcy throws down her suitcase, and it lands on Ollie's head. The bag flies open and the boys try to retrieve all the clothing, together with an alarm clock that begins to ring violently. Dulcy, meanwhile, has tricked her father, locking him in her room.

She runs down the stairs and into Ollie's arms. A smiling Stan throws rice and an old shoe, which hits Ollie smartly on the neck. "Not yet!," Ollie tells him. Dulcy's dad threatens them from above. The wedding party runs for the rented car, which turns out to be a baby Austin, looking as if it might just accommodate Stan alone. Incredibly, but happily, the three of them get in, baggage and all . . .

. . . and arrive at the home of the justice of the peace (Ben Turpin) and his wife (Blanche Payson).

Ben mumbles unintelligibly through most of the ceremony. Finally, he says, "NOW! Do you take this woman to be your lawful wedded wife?" "Who, me?," asks Stan. "Not you," says Ollie, "he means me." "Well, he's looking at me," says Stan. Ollie says "I do," and, in turn, so does Dulcy. After Ben says, "I pronounce you man and wife," he walks over to Stan, shakes his hand, and says, "Congratulations, my boy. You married the sweetest little girl in all the world." Next, Ben turns and says, "With your permission, I'll kiss the bride." Ben walks to Ollie and gives him a resounding smack.

Stan begins to cry, and Ollie in great indignation walks from the scene.

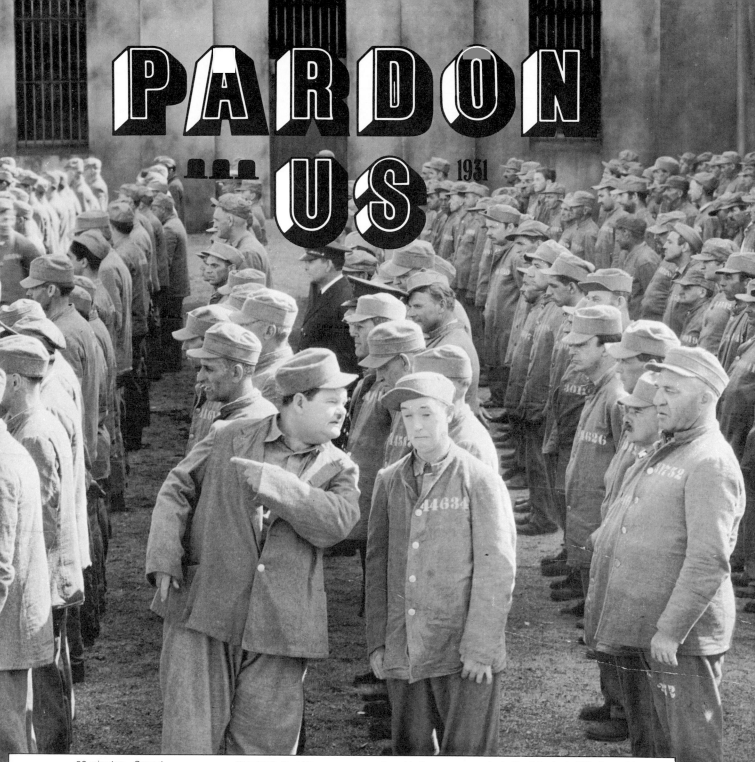

PARDON US 1931

56 minutes—Sound
Released August 15, 1931, by M-G-M
Produced by Hal Roach
Directed by James Parrott
Photographed by George Stevens
Edited by Richard Currier
Dialogue by H. M. Walker
Sound by Elmer R. Raguse

Compositions used in incidental music scoring by Le Roy Shield, Edward Kilenyi, Arthur J. Lamb, H. W. Petrie, Will Marion Cook, Irving Berlin, Cole and Johnston, Abe Olman, M. Ewing, Frederic Van Norman, L.E. de Francesco, J. S. Zamecnik, Freita Shaw, and Marvin Hatley.

Stan Laurel . . . . Himself
Oliver Hardy . . . . Himself
"The Tiger," a wily convict . . . . . . Walter Long
Schoolteacher . . . . James Finlayson

Warden's daughter . . . . June Marlowe
Dental Assistant, "All right, Rosebud" . . . . Charlie Hall
Deliveryman . . . . Charlie Hall
Prison guards . . . . Sam Lufkin, Silas D. Wilcox, George Miller
The warden . . . . Wilfred Lucas
Officer in classroom . . . . Frank Holliday
Warren, the desk sergeant . . . . Harry Bernard
Officer Le Roy Shields . . . . Stanley J. (Tiny) Sandford
Prone dental patient . . Robert (Bobby) Burns
Dental patient in waiting room . . Frank Austin
Dentist . . . . Otto Fries
Pals of "The Tiger" . . . . Robert Kortman, Leo Willis
Convict who can't add . . . . Jerry Mandy
Insurgent convicts . . . . Bobby Dunn, Eddie Dunn, Baldwin Cooke, Charles Dorety, Dick Gilbert, Will Stanton,

Jack Herrick, Jack Hill, Gene Morgan, Charles A. Bachman, John (Blackie) Whiteford, Charley Rogers
Typist at desk . . . . Gordon Douglas
Prisoner marching in formation next to Hardy, right after The Boys' recapture . James Parrott
Prisoner marching (as above) in front of Hardy . . . . Hal Roach
Plantation overseer on horseback . . . . Eddie Baker
Cotton pickers . . The Etude Ethiopian Chorus
Belle . . . . Bloodhound
Parts cut from final release print:
Boys fishing by stream . . . . Bobby Mallon, Buddy MacDonald

(Working titles: *The Rap* and then, *Their First Mistake.*)

(A burlesque on Frances Marion's *The Big House*, made the previous year by M-G-M, with Chester Morris and Wallace Beery.)

Opening title: "Mr. Hardy is a man of wonderful ideas—so is Mr. Laurel—as long as he doesn't try to think."

Stan and Ollie are in harmony with the laws of the land when making tasty home brew; they are in discord with those laws when they sell the amount they can't drink. Stan sold a bottle of beer to a policeman ("I thought he was a streetcar conductor"), and now they are being embraced by the state penal system.

Stan has a bad tooth that occasionally forces him to emit a buzzing raspy sound—a Bronx cheer or raspberry. The desk sergeant (Harry Bernard) is treated to it; he doesn't care for it. "Huh! A couple of beer barons, eh?," barks the sergeant. The boys are ordered to divest.

In handing over their personal possessions, Ollie gives up an alarm watch that doesn't always work well. It starts to ring on the sergeant's desk and Ollie turns it off. Later, Ollie grabs it furtively and returns it to his pocket. As the boys are being led out the door to their cell, it rings again and Ollie returns it to the desk with what he considers ingratiating good humor.

The august warden (Wilfred Lucas) utters a line never spoken before or since by any warden in the history of penology. Looking at the boys, he shakes his head and says sadly, "My, my! And still they come!" He tells them, as the guard (Tiny Sandford) looks on intently, that their future here is up to them. "If you are good prisoners, everything will be OK. If you are not, if you break the rules, then it will be just PLAIN HELL ON EARTH! Now, do you understand?" "Yes, sir," says Stan, emitting the tooth-razz. The warden tries to control his temper, pounds on the desk, orders them to be sent to Cell 14, adding, "Get them out of here before I lose my temper." After they go, the warden—with delicious improbability—paces the floor, muttering, "The idea, talking to a warden like that!"

A rough convict in a cell the boys are passing says "Hello, squirt!" to Stan. Stan, again involuntarily, goes into the tooth-razz. The guard directs the boys to Cell 14—home base of the rough convict.

The rough convict is an old Laurel and Hardy nemesis, tough guy Walter Long, known in these precincts as The Tiger. Again Walter addresses Stan as "squirt"; again Stan gives the tooth-razz, although, as always, he puts a finger to his lips too late to prevent it. Walter comes over menacingly to Stan and says, "Put 'er there!" They shake hands and Walter laughs. "You're the first guy that ever had the nerve to raspberry The Tiger. I like a guy that does that." Ollie, listening intently, walks confidently over to Walter who asks what they're in for. "We're a couple of beer barons," says Ollie, concluding with a very loud raspberry. Walter crashes him.

The prison schoolroom. After chanting "Good-morning, dear teacher" to their rather overattired instructor (James Finlayson), the pupils sing " . . . good-morning, dear playmates . . . " to each other, bowing formally. In catechizing his charges, Fin asks Stan what a blizzard is; he replies, "A blizzard is the inside of a buzzard." At another point Fin asks Ollie to spell *needle*. Ollie spells, *"n-e-i-d-l-e."* "There's no *i* in needle," explains Fin. "Then it's a rotten needle!," says Stan. Another convict is asked to define a comet. He explains that it is a star with a tail on it; Stan can illustrate that: "Rin-Tin-Tin!," he says.

During a paper-wad shooting session, Ollie accidentally hits Fin with an ink-soaked wad. The boys are now consigned to solitary confinement for several months. Just before he enters his long stretch of oblivion, Stan asks the guard if he's got the time.

When the boys get out of confinement, they encounter The Tiger in the yard. This is the day Walter plans to escape, and he does, sweeping the boys along with him. Walter is eventually caught but the boys seem to have vanished, a guard explains to the warden. The warden says not to worry "about those two babes in the woods. Use the bloodhounds."

Stan and Ollie have escaped to the cotton fields where they put on blackface for protective coloring. "They'll never recognize us in 100 years," says Ollie. "For once in your life you've hit upon a good idea." Their only worry about a giveaway is Stan's razzing tooth but Stan has seen to that. "I vulcanized it," he explains. "I just put some chewing gum in there and it don't buzz anymore." In a diverting episode, Stan and Ollie join the chorus of cotton pickers—Ollie singing "Lazy Moon" in a charming tenor and Stan doing an eccentric slide dance of quiet and graceful inanity.

Later, the boys are picking cotton in the field when the warden's car approaches. The car stalls, and the warden's daughter (June Marlowe) asks the boys if they can lend a hand. They cooperate happily, but as they begin to work on the motor they recognize the warden and try to efface themselves. Stan touches a wire with a wrench, causing an explosion but, after some struggle, they seem close to success. It remains, however, for the warden's daughter to discover the trouble—the car is out of gas. The warden thanks them heartily, and in saying good-bye Stan absentmindedly takes the vulcanizing chewing gum out of his mouth. The consequent tooth-razz makes Ollie realize the holiday is over. Resigned, he starts to wipe the blacking off his face.

The boys find innocent amusement principally by sitting near the wall in the prison yard. Stan's loose tooth almost gets him in trouble with a guard who insists on . . .

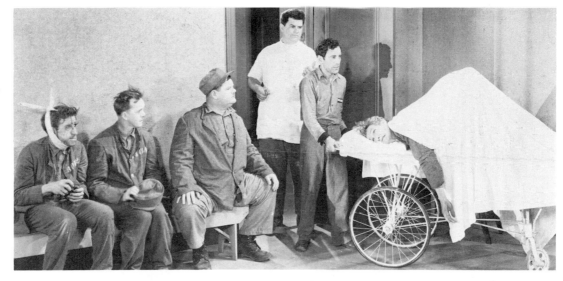

. . . a visit to the prison dentist (Otto Fries), who does not seem to have a gentle touch. A dental assistant (Charlie Hall) wheels out a patient who has just finished a session.

The problem of Stan's razzing tooth is explained to Charlie who tells him to sit down. Ollie patiently tells his pal that there's nothing to be afraid of: "Why, you won't even feel it." "You won't feel it," agrees Stan, "but what about me?" Ollie relaxes happily in the neighboring dental chair, saying, "Why, they could pull every tooth in my head and I wouldn't feel it."

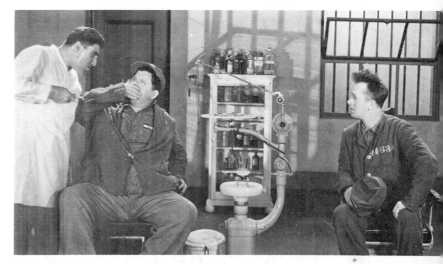

At which point, the dentist enters and without a word goes swiftly to Ollie and energetically extracts his tooth. (This is a still of the actor who played the dentist's role for the French version of *Pardon Us.* See note.) When Ollie protests, the dentist asks if he didn't get the right tooth. The right tooth, Ollie admits sadly, but the wrong man. The dentist goes to work on the right man but this time he gets the wrong tooth. Stan's razz remains intact.

175

The boys threaten a hunger strike but succumb to an invitation. A guard assures them a great turkey dinner awaits in the dining hall. The boys go down in anticipation and sit down in frustration. They learn once more why it is called a *mess* hall. All is as before . . .

. . . except for the guns The Tiger has had smuggled in for a break. Weapons are passed under the tables from convict to convict. Unknowing, Stan receives a machine gun, frightens Ollie and himself with it, and fires off shots into the ceiling.

The break begins prematurely.
Convicts fight the guards . . .

... guards fight the convicts ...

... and The Tiger is in the forefront.

Most of the convicts mill about aimlessly, trying to get in the prison door, away from the guards firing in the gatehouse.

Stan and Ollie are also scrambling for the door. It is locked but they finally get inside.

The Tiger rages at them for firing the shots in the mess hall, thereby tipping off the guards before the plotters were ready. A convict with a bunch of keys rushes in happily, giving them to Walter who takes them exultantly, unthinkingly handing his machine gun over to Stan. Stan, again badly frightened by this formidable instrument, fires it wildly in all directions. He and Ollie dance about in a panic as the machine gun seems to become uncontrollably alive. There is a lull, and Walter with his gang approaches the boys menacingly. Ollie takes the gun away from Stan, admonishing him to be careful, and the gun starts to spurt bullets again. After a lull, the convicts approach the boys threateningly; Ollie hands the gun back to Stan—and it starts to spew again.

177

The mutinous convicts are terrorized by the peripatetic machine gun. Suddenly the state militia bursts in through the gate, and the outbreak is at an end.

Stan and Ollie receive pardons for firing the warning shots that, the warden says, "saved us from a disaster of *cataclysmic* dimensions." The boys nod agreeably, then look at each other in astonishment; this is becoming hard to follow. The warden charges them to begin life anew. "Let this episode here," he continues, "be just a *hiatus* to be obliterated from your memory." A who to be what?, the boys ask mentally. The warden adds that if there is anything he can do to help them start where they left off, to call on him at any time. Ollie says they'll start all over again. "We certainly will," says Stan. Then, turning to the warden, he asks, "Can we take your order for a couple of cases?" Stan's tooth goes into a razzing spasm, and the boys run out of the office.

Note: Pardon Us was filmed in four other languages, French, Spanish, Italian, and German, using four separate supporting casts. Laurel and Hardy, both monolingual, wrote their lines on a blackboard, out of camera range, in their own phonetic approximations of the sounds spoken to them by a language coach. *Pardon Us* was the only feature done in this fashion. Ten shorts were similarly produced before the practice was abandoned.

Production Sidelights

This is a deleted sequence that features the boys' participation in the prison's fire department. Here Stan misconnects the hose, giving Ollie the benefit of all the good water.

A deleted sequence of Stan and Ollie rescuing the warden's daughter from the top floor of a burning building.

A still from the French version of *Pardon Us,* which verifies that, just for a fleeting moment in history, Laurel and Hardy were teamed with Boris Karloff.

A deleted scene with three separate sets of supporting players for the German, Italian, and French versions of the film, here portraying the governor of the state and the prison warden. The sequence concerns the convict known as The Tiger who gives Stan and Ollie a bomb— gift-wrapped—for the warden. The warden likes cigarettes, The Tiger says, and this package of them will delight him. Seeing the warden and the governor strolling the prison yard, the boys walk over and Ollie presents the token of his esteem. The governor says that this shows a "marvelous spirit"; the warden, very touched, says, "I shall not forget this in a hurry." Indeed, he will mention the boys favorably in his weekly report.

The boys go back to the Tiger, who asks what the warden said. Stan brags, "He says he's going to give us a great big report." There is the sound of a loud explosion. The camera cuts to a large cloud of smoke, and when it clears away, we see a huge hole blown out of the prison wall. The warden steps out of the hole, his clothing torn to shreds, still holding the

piece of string from the package in his hands.

COME CLEAN

1931

Laurel and Hardy Series / Two reels / Sound / Released September 19, 1931, by M-G-M / Produced by Hal Roach / Directed by James W. Horne / Photographed by Art Lloyd / Edited by Richard Currier / Dialogue by H.M. Walker / Sound by Elmer R. Raguse / Compositions used in incidental music scoring by Le Roy Shield, John Philip Sousa, and Marvin Hatley.

Stan Laurel Himself / *Oliver Hardy* Himself / *Mrs. Hardy* Gertrude Astor / *Mrs. Laurel* Linda Loredo / *Kate, floozy wanted by the police* Mae Busch / *Soda jerk* Charlie Hall / *Detective* Eddie Baker / *Doorman* Stanley (Tiny) Sandford / *Desk clerk* Gordon Douglas. Part cut from final release print: *Officer* Harry Bernard. (Remade as *Brooklyn Orchid* eleven years later by Hal Roach, with William Bendix, Joe Sawyer, and Marjorie Woodworth starring in this Roach streamliner.)

Opening title. "**Mr. Hardy holds that every husband should tell his wife the whole truth—Mr. Laurel is crazy too.**"

The Hardys are secure in their little love nest, cozy because they are deliciously alone. "What a relief not to be bothered with those Laurels tonight," says Mrs. Hardy (Gertrude Astor). As they are congratulating each other, the Laurels appear in the hallway outside. The Hardys try to pretend they're not at home, but the door's viewing panel slowly opens.

Instantly the atmosphere becomes excessively cordial. Mrs. Laurel (Linda Loredo) is overwhelmed by such graciousness. In asking the Laurels what they'd like, an answer is quickly forthcoming from Stan— ice cream. "We haven't got any ice cream," Ollie says. "Well, you could *get* some ice cream," Stan tells him.

In three separate attempts to get out of the kitchen Ollie is smacked on the face by the swinging door as others enter. His last attempt ends with the water cooler dominating him. Mrs. Hardy orders him to go out and get the ice cream. Stan says never mind, he doesn't think he wants any. "You'll have ice cream," Ollie says, "if it's the last thing I do."

At the soda fountain, Stan discovers that the clerk (Charlie Hall) doesn't seem to have what he fancies— chocolate. Among the other flavors Charlie is out of is an exotic one Stan asks for— moustachio. Stan asks Charlie what other flavors he is out of, and the reply is " . . . orange, gooseberry— and chocolate." Stan is particularly upset because of the chocolate. Ollie asks for a quart of anything handy. Stan idly picks up the soda straw holder, turns it upside down and when the straws fall out, attempts to reorder them.

181

On the way home, the boys are treated to
a bit of drama. Sitting on a bridge is a
jaded lady (Mae Busch) who shouts,
"Good-bye, old world—I'm leavin' yuh
flat." She jumps, and when Stan asks
Ollie why she's committing suicide, Ollie
doesn't know; but he gets on the railing,
pretends to dive, and Stan pushes him
in. On a boat landing beneath, Stan hauls
Mae in. Ollie calls for help and Stan
throws him a rope. Then Stan throws
him a life preserver and an anchor.

Ultimately everyone is safe but Mae is not happy with the
arrangement. "Well," she says sardonically, "now that you've
saved me, you can take care of me." They try to leave her but
she threatens to scream and accuse them of murder.

Back at the apartment house, when they seem to be leaving
her, she screams exquisitely.

They think they've given her the slip.

Ollie stashes Mae in his bedroom; she makes herself at home in Mrs. Hardy's
negligee. She turns on the radio, and for a cover-up the boys bang on pans in time
to the music. The ladies don't get it. "Just playing," says Ollie. The ladies retire
to the living room.

Ollie tells Stan to entertain the wives. Mae takes Mrs. Hardy's coat; Ollie protests but then says she can have it if only she'll go.

The boys are feeling secure when she leaves, but Mae goes down the elevator and runs into a detective who has been on her trail. She runs back into the Hardy bedroom and turns on the radio. The boys leave their ladies, run out, and push Mae into the hall; the wives come out into the hall, the boys get Mae back into the bedroom. Stan takes her into the Hardy bathroom, locks the door, and turns on the bath tap.

When the wives ask Ollie why Stan is taking a bath, he explains that Stan couldn't wait for Saturday. Mrs. Laurel demands that Stan let her in; the detective appears and demands that Stan let *him* in. Stan gets into the tub and begins taking a bath with his clothes on while Mae hovers in the corner.

The detective (Eddie Baker) breaks through the door. Mrs. Laurel asks Stan what he's doing in there. "I was looking for the soap," he says. Ollie blames Stan for bringing Mae into the apartment. "Come over to the station," the detective says to Stan, "there's a $1,000 reward waiting for you." The detective takes Mae away.

Jealously, Ollie asks Stan what he will do with his $1,000. "I'm going to buy a $1,000 worth of *chocolate* ice cream" is the reply. Disappointed, Ollie pulls the bath plug, the water gurgles, and Mrs. Laurel comes back in. She looks at the bathtub and asks,"Where's Stanley?" "He's gone to the beach," says Ollie.

Production Sidelight

A deleted segment. In the film we see the boys on their way to buy ice cream; now we see what the film failed to show—the ultimate disposal of it—all over Ollie's face.

ONE GOOD TURN

🎩🎩🎩 **1931**

Laurel and Hardy Series / Two reels / Sound / Released October 31, 1931, by M-G-M / Produced by Hal Roach / Directed by James W. Horne / Photographed by Art Lloyd / Edited by Richard Currier / Dialogue by H.M. Walker / Sound by Elmer R. Raguse / Compositions used in incidental music scoring by Le Roy Shield and Marvin Hatley.

Stan Laurel Himself / *Oliver Hardy* Himself / *Old lady* Mary Carr / *The drunk* Billy Gilbert / *Community players* Lyle Tayo, Dorothy Granger, Snub Pollard, Gordon Douglas / *Extras at street auction* Dick Gilbert, George Miller, Baldwin Cooke, Ham Kinsey, Retta Palmer, William Gillespie, Charley Young.

Opening title: "Seeing America: Mr. Laurel and Mr. Hardy have cast off all financial worries—Total assets: one Ford, model 1911, one tent, model 1861. One union suit, two shirts, and three socks."

Stan the soup maker. (In the film he tastes it alone—to Ollie's distraction. Note the tattoo on the Hardy forearm, a vagary of his youth, which he afterward tended to hide.)

Ollie the laundryman. Stan encourages their campfire by fanning it with his hat; he turns, stumbles over a rope, and the tent falls on the fire, flaming up furiously. Stan takes a tin cup from their supplies and wades through the stream to a pump on the other side, fills the cup, wades back, and throws it on the fire.

After several of these expeditions, Ollie takes some notice. "You haven't got another cup, have you?," asks Stan. When Ollie asks what for, Stan says, "The tent's on fire." It cremates itself neatly.

"Well," says Ollie, "our earthly possessions are slowly getting less and less. No place to sleep and no food. What could be worse?" Ollie decides they shall actually have to beg for food.

Not very far away, a charming old lady is rehearsing a scene with a few friends for this year's community play. They declare her acting superb, particularly in a scene showing her being confronted by a heartless villain.

Ollie decides to ask for food at the pleasant house
—the home of the charming old lady.

They enter the gate, and at the door Stan wipes
his feet so vigorously on the doormat that it flies
up and hits Ollie full on the nose. Ollie knocks,
a window blind goes up suddenly with a
fearful rattle...

...and the boys run off the porch—Ollie
diving through a pile of tin cans. The
charming old lady (Mary Carr) comes to
investigate. Ollie introduces himself
and friend as victims of the Depression
who haven't tasted food for three whole
days. "Yes, ma'am," affirms Stan,
"yesterday, today, and tomorrow." She
says she will give them a meal, and Ollie
asks if there is some work they can do for
her. Stan suggests Ollie chop some wood
—an idea the lady calls splendid.
"Splendid it shall be," says Ollie. But
alone in the woodshed, Ollie is not happy
about the task, and he tells Stan to cut
since *he* suggested it. "You once told
me your father was in the lumber
business." Stan admits this, but he
explains it was only in a small way: "...
he used to sell toothpicks." In cutting the
wood, Stan axes a log that spins up and
crashes down—inevitably on Ollie's head.

The old lady serves them their reward.
Having done so, she retires to the other
room and knits. The doorbell rings, she
answers, and one of the community
players (James Finlayson) enters and
begins at once to rehearse the scene
they worked on this morning. He
threatens to foreclose if the mortgage
money is not forthcoming...

Ollie gathers a crowd around their Ford and announces that he and his pal are on an errand of mercy: offering their car to the highest bidder to raise $100 to save a poor old lady from being thrown out in the streets.

...and the boys listen intently, believing every word of it. She goes to her sewing basket to get the money, and as rehearsed, screams that she has been robbed. "Christine Demendville, I have you in my clutches," Fin snarls, laughing with ripe villainy. She pleads for a little more time to pay the $100, and Fin gives her until three o'clock. "What will I do?," sobs the old lady.

What indeed, ponder the boys. They decide to sneak out and raise the $100.

A genial drunk (Billy Gilbert) announces he'll gladly help. He mistakenly puts a pocketbook into Stan's coat and announces he will bid $100. A man asks Stan for the time and he replies, "One twenty-five." "SOLD!," booms Ollie, "for 125."

Despondent on learning the outcome of the auction, Ollie finds the pocketbook in Stan's coat, and accuses him of robbing the old lady. "To think for all these years I've been fostering a common thief, a viper in my bosom," says Ollie. "You Judas! You— you—!!" "STOP!," yells Stan. "Don't call *me* a you you." Ollie and Stan struggle, wrecking their car in the process.

Ollie finally gets Stan back to the old lady's place and tells her his onetime friend has a confession to make. The old lady laughs when she hears the story and tells them that no money has been stolen, they were just rehearsing a play for the community theatre.

Ollie laughs but Stan displays his indignation in several ways. Ollie runs into the woodshed and Stan waits outside with an ax, exhorting him to come out. Stan chops the woodshed down.

Ollie emerges untriumphant. Stan axes a log that sails up and falls—conk— on his own head. He cries and Ollie loosens himself from the fallen roof.

Production Sidelight

A candid shot of the boys and Mary Carr during a take of the "victims of the Depression" scene. Cameraman Art Lloyd is in the foreground.

187

Beau Hunks

Opening title: **"Love comes: Mr. Hardy is at last conscious of the grand passion— Mr. Laurel isn't even conscious of the Grand Canyon."**

Laurel and Hardy Series / Four reels / Sound / Released December 12, 1931, by M-G-M / Produced by Hal Roach / Directed by James W. Horne / Photographed by Art Lloyd and Jack Stevens / Edited by Richard Currier / Dialogue by H.M. Walker / Sound by Elmer R. Raguse / Compositions used in incidental music scoring by Le Roy Shield, Herbert Ingraham, Riesenfeld, and Marvin Hatley.

Stan Laurel Himself / *Oliver Hardy* Himself / *The cheerful commandant* Charles Middleton / *New recruit Number "Thirteen"* Charlie Hall / *Legionnaire officer* Stanley (Tiny) Sandford / *Captain Schultz* Harry Schultz / *Legionnaire at Fort Arid* Gordon Douglas / *Menacing Riffian* Sam Lufkin / *Riffians* Marvin Hatley, Jack Hill / *New recruits* Jack Hill, Leo Willis, Bob Kortman, Baldwin Cooke, Dick Gilbert, Oscar Morgan, Ham Kinsey / *Commander at Fort Arid* Broderick O'Farrell / *Abdul Kasim K'Horne* (gag credit line for the film's director, who appears in the closing scenes as, in Hardy's words, "The Chief of the Riff-Raff") James Horne / Gag billing at the end of the film's credit list 3,897 Arabs, 1944 Riffians, 4 Native Swede Guilders. *Note:* Portrait photo of Jean Harlow (". . . You vampire") is used. (At least two special foreign-language versions were released, each of which incorporated *Helpmates: Les deux legionnaires* [French], and a Spanish version. Research has not disclosed whether separate versions were shot, or whether the foreign-language versions were simply edited together and dubbed from American release negatives. Released in certain European areas as *Beau Chumps*.)

Ollie is singing "I love you, I love you, I love you"— and Stan finds the mush pretty sloppy. Ollie reveals he is going to be married. "Who to?," asks Stan. "Why, a woman of course," Ollie says. "Did you ever hear of anybody marrying a man?" "Sure," says Stan. "My sister." Ollie's ladylove is, from all accounts, a nonpareil: "well read, traveled all over the world, loved by everyone." This is the perfect moment for a messenger to bring a letter from her, and because Ollie can't find his glasses, he listens as Stan reads the remarkable missive aloud: "My dear, darling, precious Oliver. As I sit writing this note to you, with your picture in front of me, I have decided that all is over between us, for I love another. Your onetime sweetheart, Jean." Ollie is crushed, especially by the addendum Stan reads: "B.S. It's best we never see each other again—Jeanie Weenie." Ollie asks what "B.S." means; "Big Sucker, I guess," says Stan. We see a picture of the girl. (Jean Harlow, who had appeared in Laurel and Hardy films three years earlier.)

Ollie crashes into a piano and it is no contest. But what has he to do with such mundane matters? As he says to Stan, "We are going where we can forget." "What d'ya mean, *we've* got to forget?," Stan asks with some justification. "None of your business" is the firm reply. "Come on and let's go."

They go to the burning deserts of Africa as recruits for the Foreign Legion. Their hard-nosed colonel (Charles Middleton) is nothing if not candid: "Well, you certainly are a sorry-looking pair." "We're not sorry," says Ollie. "No, sir," adds Stan, "we're just discouraged." When the colonel asks them why they joined up, Stan can't remember. "You forgot what you came here to forget?," asks the colonel. "Well, we'll see that you don't forget what you're here for."

Unable to get a private room—it's evidently not the custom here—the boys are reduced to sharing the barracks with others. In very short order, the boys find three comrades—each mooning over a photograph. The photographs are signed, respectively: "Yours always—Jean," "Forever yours—Jean," and "Yours always—Jean." One of the soldiers sobs out, "You didn't ought to have done it, baby." Manifestly, Jean has lived up to her reputation as a world traveler. That settles it for Ollie.

The boys come into the colonel's office to (in Ollie's words) "rectify a small mistake." They've decided to leave because they found out in time that the woman wasn't worth it. Bitingly, the colonel tells them they are going to stay with this "army of forgotten souls," which men join "to forget and be forgotten . . . and to laugh at it all." The colonel laughs feverishly as he declaims the sad story of these gallant few. We see a close-up of a photograph in the office. It is of a certain young lady, and the inscription reads, "Yours till Niagara Falls—Jean."

The colonel has ordered that all the recruits be taken through their paces. Eight hours later, the boys are resting where available. They straggle . . .

. . . and struggle not to straggle. Meanwhile, news has come that the Riffs are preparing to make an attack on a Legion outpost, Fort Arid. The colonel tells the captain to take every available man to the fort—no matter how tired they are. Concerning their fatigue, Stan puts it best: "I feel just like Jeanie Weenie . . . like I've traveled all over the world."

The legionnaires are drummed up into line—with one inevitable exception who can't seem to find the line.

189

Stan also couldn't seem to find his trousers this morning. When Ollie asks Stan what he did with his pack equipment, Stan says, "I wrapped it up in yours." "Why, you can't do that," sputters Ollie, sadly aware from the weight on his shoulders that Stan most emphatically did.

Sandstorm, and the men go Indian file, holding onto the bayonet of the man before. Stan falls, the bayonet of the man in front of him breaks, and Stan gets up, still holding the unattached bayonet, and circles endlessly. Ollie follows, holding Stan's bayonet.

Meanwhile at Fort Arid, the fort commander refuses to surrender despite impossible odds against him. They are doomed, he says, unless help arrives. "Why don't they come?" Suddenly, outside the wall, Ollie can be heard counting out a march cadence ending with "Company, *halt!*" Relief at last. The beleaguered legionnaires throw open the huge gates to reveal—Stan and Ollie.

(The still is unlike the film's action.) The boys are not notably efficient guards. Stan gets his gun caught in Ollie's uniform, and the gun goes off. The Chief Riff takes this to be the signal from comrades who have been sent to scale the walls and open the gates. The Riffs attack.

The commandant tells the legionnaires to take hand grenades to the walls—and hold the gates at all costs. Ollie shows Stan how to operate a hand grenade; Stan pulls out the pin, then, panic-stricken, throws the grenade to Ollie, who hands it back. Stan throws it away, it bounces back, Ollie throws it over the gates where it explodes.

The boys prepare to take sacks of sand from the storeroom to bolster defenses when a ravening Riff starts to chase them. Ollie accidentally knocks over a keg of tacks, the barefooted Riff steps on them, yowls, howls, and falls to the floor. The boys go to the gates with tacks and throw them on the ground. The Riffs try to batter down the gates; Stan and Ollie open the gates. The Riffs rush in and fall victim to the tacks.

The boys hurl the tacks triumphantly.

The Legion is victorious and the dastardly leader of the Riffs (James W. Horne) is captured. "We've just captured the chief of the Riff Raffs," says Ollie to the captain (Broderick O'Farrell). "Yes, sir," says Stan, "he was trying to make a getaway on his dormitory." As the Chief Riff is being searched preparatory to being removed, Stan finds a photograph in his possession. The chief is in agony at the thought of its removal: "No, no, Sahib—not that—anything but--" The photograph is of a certain young lady, and it is signed, "To my Sheikie Weekie, from Jeanie Weenie."

Note: The actor cast for the Chief of the Riffs proved unsatisfactory in early rehearsals so director James W. Horne played the role. In the cast credits he listed himself as Abdul Kasim K'Horne.

1931
A Laurel & Hardy Cameo Appearance
ON THE LOOSE

Pitts-Todd Series / Two reels / Sound / Released December 26, 1931, by M-G-M / Produced by Hal Roach / Directed by Hal Roach / Photographed by Len Powers / Edited by Richard Currier / Dialogue by H.M. Walker / Story by Hal E. Roach / Compositions used in incidental music scoring by Le Roy Shield.

Thelma Todd Herself / *ZaSu Pitts* Herself / *British boyfriends* Claud Allister, John Loder / *Couturier* Billy Gilbert / *Would-be suitors* Stan Laurel, Oliver Hardy / *Shooting gallery attendant* Charlie Hall / *Fun house workers* Gordon Douglas, Jack Hill / *Boy* Buddy MacDonald / *Bully* Otto Fries.

Stan and Babe have only a surprise walk-on in this Thelma Todd-ZaSu Pitts two-reeler.

The girls are increasingly bored with Coney Island, the only place their various dates ever seem to take them. But things begin to look up when they meet two charming Englishmen (John Loder and Claud Allister) who come up with the inspired idea to take them, one Saturday afternoon, to "a frightfully original place"—Coney Island. The girls hide their disappointment because of the Britishers' gallantry. After diverting episodes at various attractions…

…they wind up in the rotating barrel. (Prostrate: John Loder, Otto's girl friend; striving to keep balance: ZaSu, Claud Allister, Otto Fries, and Thelma.) Otto and his girl are strangers to the foursome but she keeps winding up accidentally in Claud's arms. Otto menacingly tells Claud to keep his hands off his girl but he tells him one time too many. Thelma belts Otto resoundingly.

The next Saturday, ZaSu and Thelma are home alone, and amply prepared to be alone. The bell rings and at the door appear Stan and Ollie. The boys suggest that it just might be fun to go to Coney Island. The girls grab their large collection of Kewpie dolls and kindred Coney Island memorabilia and hurl them at the boys, who run away—Stan crying, Ollie yelling.

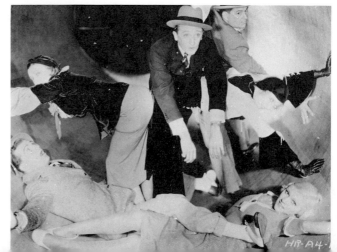

Helpmates

1932

Laurel and Hardy Series / Two reels / Sound / Released January 23, 1932, by M-G-M. / Produced by Hal Roach / Directed by James Parrott / Photographed by Art Lloyd / Edited by Richard Currier / Dialogue by H.M. Walker / Compositions used in incidental music scoring by Le Roy Shield and Marvin Hatley.

Stan Laurel Himself / *Oliver Hardy* Himself / *Congenial Mrs. Hardy* Blanche Payson / *Neighbor watering his lawn who does a "108" fall* Robert (Bobby) Burns / *Messenger boy* Robert Callahan.

Opening title: "**When the cat's away— the mice start looking up telephone numbers.**"

While his wife is visiting her mother in Chicago, Ollie has had the chance (in his words) to "pull a wild party," and this hung over morning he regards himself in the mirror, and says, "Now aren't you ashamed of yourself? A man with your supposed intelligence, acting like an empty-headed idiot." A telegram arrives from Mrs. Hardy saying she will be home at noon that day, and Ollie—needing help to clean up the debris-distressed house—phones his pal. Ollie: "Why weren't you at the party last night?" Stan: "I couldn't make it. I was bitten by a dog." Ollie: "I can't understand you. Spell it." Stan: "A dog bit me. B-l-*it* me. Bit me." Ollie: "Where?" Stan: *pulls up his sleeve and puts the telephone to the injured area.* Stan explains that he was taken to the hospital last night because he might have, in his word, "hydrophosphates," but Ollie impatiently interrupts, asking him to come over and help.

On Stan's arrival, Ollie explains his predicament with, "Look at this house!" Stan asks him what's the matter with it, and Ollie fumes, "What's the matter with it? You never met my wife, did you?" "Yes," says Stan, "I never did." Ollie explains that first they'll have a nice breakfast and then "…we'll put our shoulder to the wheel, grab the bull by the horns, and put our best foot forward."

In doing just that, Ollie falls over a misplaced carpet sweeper.

Stan tackles the dirty dishes as Ollie finishes dressing, putting on an impeccable Panama hat. Coming out of his bedroom, he goes into the living room, steps on the same carpet sweeper, and is precipitated forthwith into the kitchen, crashing into a vast pile of dishes.

As Ollie is ordering Stan to clean up the mess, the stovepipe falls in a great whoosh of soot. Stan blows it off Ollie's Panama into Ollie's face.

Ollie glares at the essential perpetrator of these misdeeds; Stan, typically, ponders with vague eyes why these misfortunes should come all of a heap.

While washing up, Ollie picks up a cake of soap that, upon application, proves to be a chunk of butter. He demands a towel; Stan promptly springs to the cupboard, opens it and a large can of flour cascades down on Ollie.

Ollie puts on clean clothes and in the process loses a collar button.

Stan asks where Ollie keeps his handkerchiefs and, told they are in the top bureau drawer, opens it, finds what he wants, walks away. Ollie rises from his collar button search—right into the drawer.

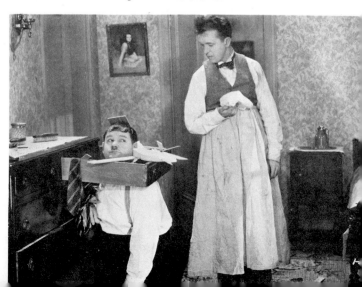

Trying to get rid of water from a plugged-up sink, Stan asks Ollio what he should do with it. Ollie tells him to use his own judgment —a perilous suggestion at best. Just as Stan throws the water out of the open window, it drops shut and the water splashes back forcefully into Ollie's face. Ollie pushes Stan down, and he lands with foot in bucket.

Ollie goes outside, puts a stick up under the sash to prop it open, explaining, "That's the way to do it." Knocking a flowerpot off the windowsill, he bends down to pick it up, and as he rises, Stan throws another basin of dishwater out of the window on Ollie, drenching his suit thoroughly.

As Ollie leans exasperatedly on the sill, Stan asks brightly, "How about some breakfast?" Ollie hurls the flowerpot at Stan but it misses, hitting the man next door. Ollie asks, "Do you realize this is the only suit I've got left? It's enough to make a man burst out crying." He points out that his wife is due home at noon, causing Stan to declare indignantly, "Say, what do you think I am—Cinderella? If I had any sense, I'd walk out on you." Ollie says, "Well, it's a good thing you *haven't* any sense." "It certainly *is!,*" says Stan, who then ponders his own statement for a long moment.

Ollie hands his pants to Stan and demands they be wrung out while he dries the coat. Stan runs the pants through a wringer that empties into a tub of water. Ollie grabs the pants, hangs them in front of the open oven, turns on the gas, searches for a match, cannot immediately find one.

After he lights the stove, the ensuing explosion throws him crashing through the door. Stan enters through the shattered frame.

Mrs. Hardy phones to say she's at the station, and Ollie agitatedly tells Stan to get the suit from its drying rack in the kitchen.

Investigation reveals that the suit is also a victim of the explosion. Ollie tells Stan to clean up the place quickly while he investigates a possibility he has just thought of.

Shortly after, Ollie appears resplendent in his lodge uniform, thus baffling Stan. Stan: "You're not going like that, are you?" Ollie: "Certainly, why?" Stan: "Well, you haven't got a horse!" The phone rings again and Ollie tells Stan to get cleaned up and out of the house: "I'll see you tonight." Ollie leaves the house, and Stan, trying to create a homey touch for Mrs. Hardy's arrival, attempts to light several logs in the fireplace. Realizing finally that a single match won't do the job, he douses the logs liberally with kerosine, and takes a match from his pocket. Fade-out.

Some minutes later, Ollie returns with a black eye and his beautiful ceremonial sword considerably bent. He opens the door of his house, sees Stan hosing down the roofless interior, and promptly crashes through the floor.

Ollie asks Stan what happened. Stan blubbers, "Well, I wanted to build a nice fire to make it comfortable for you!" Ollie, at a loss for words, ponders life's inequities as Stan adds, "Well, I guess there's nothing else I can do." Ollie: "I guess not." Stan: "Well, I'll be seeing you." Ollie: "Hey— would you mind closing the door? I'd like to be *alone*." Stan leaves, and it starts raining. Ollie, seated in the only chair left in the household, carefully removes a piece of lint from his pants.

195

ANY OLD PORT

∎∎∎   1932

Laurel and Hardy Series / Two reels / Sound / Released March 5, 1932, by M-G-M / Produced by Hal Roach / Directed by James W. Horne / Photographed by Art Lloyd / Edited by Richard Currier / Dialogue by H.M. Walker / Sound by Elmer R. Raguse / Compositions used in incidental music scoring by Le Roy Shield and Marvin Hatley.

Stan Laurel Himself / *Oliver Hardy* Himself / *Mugsie Long, proprietor of Ye Mariner's Rest* Walter Long / *Fleeing bride-to-be* Diane Duval/Jacqueline Wells/Julie Bishop / *Boxing promoter* Harry Bernard / *Stan's second* Charlie Hall / *The diffident justice of the peace* Robert (Bobby) Burns / *Referee* Sam Lufkin / *Long's second* Dick Gilbert / *Police chief* Eddie Baker / *Drunken wagerer at ringside* Will Stanton / *Spectators at match* Jack Hill, Baldwin Cooke, Ed Brandenberg / *Parts cut from final release print: Shipmates* Stanley (Tiny) Sandford, James Finlayson.

Opening title: "**In port—Mr. Laurel and Mr. Hardy were just home from a whaling voyage—Mr. Hardy shipped as head harpooner; Mr. Laurel went along as bait.**"

At the seedy fleabag called Ye Mariner's Rest, proprietor Mugsie Long is assuring his pretty slavey that she is going to marry him, like it or not.

Mugsie (Walter Long) faces two potential roomers. Stan explains that they would like a room with "southern explosion," and Ollie grandly asks for a floor plan of the hotel. They do not find either of these amenities, and in registering, much ink is spilled and Stan signs his usual emphatic *X*. Disgustedly throwing them their key, Mugsie growls, "Upstairs, third door on the left."

As the boys play pool, the slavey (Jacqueline Wells) runs to them for protection from Mugsie. Ollie asks him loftily, "Don't you think you're overstepping your bounds?" Mugsie chases the girl, locks her in a room, and calls the justice of the peace to come over at once and perform the wedding ceremony. The boys bounce billiard balls off Mugsie's skull but their only effect is to sting him into chasing them out of the hotel.

But the girl's screams deter them, and in the presence of the justice of the peace (Robert "Bobby" Burns), Stan takes the key out of the girl's door.

They wrestle for the key, rolling out of the room...

... into the dining room where they effectively isolate Mugsie. But in his wrath he smashes the table ...

...and the scuffling continues out to the dock area where Stan throws the key in the water. Mugsie follows it in.

Ravenously hungry, the boys go to a lunch-wagon counter where they encounter a pal of Ollie's (Harry Bernard) who asks Ollie how he's doing. "Oh, just as usual," says Ollie wearily, looking meaningfully at Stan. The pal says he is running a boxing tournament and if Ollie wants to go a few rounds, he'll get $50. The boys ask for something in advance, the pal asks how much, and Stan replies, "About $60." They arrange to meet at the stadium that evening. Ollie orders a sumptuous meal, countermanding Stan's similar order, telling him, "You've got to fight tonight." Stan cries.

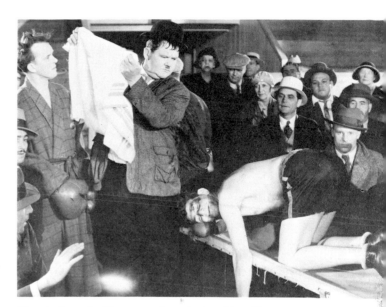

The stadium. As Stan goes down to ringside with Ollie, a battered battler is brought by on a stretcher. Quick!y Ollie throws a towel over Stan's head so he won't see the carnage.

Getting into the ring, Stan takes a typical pratfall. His opponent turns out to be Mugsie who, thirsting for revenge and a quick knockout, loads his gloves with weighty nuts and bolts.

197

The spectacularly unmatched contestants engage —and disengage.

Told by his trainer to stay close in every clinch, Stan does that with a vengeance. They each lose a glove, and Stan unwittingly puts on Mugsie's loaded mitt. Frightened, Mugsie tries to pull the lethal glove off Stan but it hits him in backlash, knocks him out, and Stan wins. Stan observes Ollie giving money to a ringside drunk. Ollie admits he is paying off a bet, and he explains to Stan: "Why, I bet on you to lose and you double-crossed me!" Stan goes to hit Ollie but the glove accidentally hits a cop. The boys run off with alacrity.

Production Sidelights

Any Old Port was originally a three-reeler. The following stills indicate the general nature of the deleted material.

Counting their money at voyage's end, the point at which the film originally began.

Tiny Sandford, James Finlayson, and (alas!) the ostrich were all cut from the film.

One can imagine what vitriolic Walter Long would have said about parking that ostrich there. Note the lobster escutcheon on his hotel wall, a totally congruent ambience because the crustacean and Walter both have a tough shell and a mean bite.

THE MUSIC BOX ■■■ 1932

Laurel and Hardy Series / Three reels / Sound / Released April 16, 1932, by M-G-M / Produced by Hal Roach / Directed by James Parrott / Photographed by Walter Lundin and Len Powers / Edited by Richard Currier / Dialogue by H.M. Walker / Sound by James Greene / Compositions used in incidental music scoring by Le Roy Shield, Francis Scott Key, Marvin Hatley and Harry Graham.

Stan Laurel Himself / *Oliver Hardy* Himself / *Professor Theodore von Schwarzenhoffen, M.D., A.D., D.D.S., F.L.D., F.F.F., und F.* Billy Gilbert / *Piano salesman* William Gillespie / *Postman* Charlie Hall / *Billy Gilbert's wife* Gladys Gale / *Wizened officer* Sam Lufkin / *Haughty nursemaid* Lilyan Irene / *Playing piano just off camera* Marvin Hatley / *Horse* Susie. (Academy Award winner for "Best Live Action Comedy Short Subject of the Year, 1931-1932.")

Opening title: "**Mr. Laurel and Mr. Hardy decided to reorganize and resupervise their entire financial structure—so they took the $3.80 and went into business.**"

A lady has bought a surprise birthday present for her husband—a player piano—and the boys are delivering it with the help of their bored chum, Suzie.

They ask the postman (Charlie Hall) where 1127 Walnut Avenue might be found. "That's the house up there," he says, "right on top of the stoop." The stoop is a formidable rise of terraced steps. (These are the same steps used in *Hats Off*. Now, five years later, the surrounding neighborhood has been considerably built up.)

With his usual air of competent superiority, Ollie insists on taking over. "Just a moment," he says. "This requires a little thought. Now ease it down on my back."

He gets down on his knees, Suzie looks back at him and moves ahead quickly for a little divertissement, causing the piano to fall smash-crash on Ollie's back.

Stan lifts; Ollie scrambles out from under.

They get the piano box part of the way up, and a maid (Lilyan Irene) with a buggy tries to get past them. Ollie gallantly assures her he'll help but the box gets literally out of hand and goes jingling down to the bottom of the stairs. The boys run down, and as the maid reaches the street she laughs and says, "Of all the dumb *things!*" As she bends over to fix the buggy blanket, Stan cannot resist kicking her; she turns, hits Stan on the chin, and when Ollie laughs heartily, she smashes a baby bottle over his head. The boys start upstairs again. The maid reappears on the scene with a policeman to whom she confides, " . . . he kicked me . . . right in the middle of my daily duties."

The cop shouts up to the boys, "Com'ere!" Ollie sends Stan down but the cop doesn't want him: "I want that other monkey." Stan duly relays the information in those words. Ollie, standing in front of the box, is startled to see it move; it chases him down the stairs, finally passing over his prostrate body. The policeman chastises Ollie with a kick and a "Now let that be a lesson to you." The cop walks off, and when Stan asks Ollie if he's going to stand for that, Ollie blusters into belligerency that fades into embarrassment when the cop returns. The cop kicks him again: "Now let that be *another* lesson to you." Indignantly, Stan asks the officer, "Say listen, don't you think you're bounding over your steps?" The policeman turns threateningly to him and Ollie tie-twiddles ingratiatingly, saying, "Why, ah—he means, ah, overstepping your *bounds.*" The cop takes Stan's hat off, bops him on the head, saying, "Now let that be a lesson to *you!,*" and follows up with a blow in the stomach.

The boys have gotten the box halfway up when a distinguished-looking gentleman (Billy Gilbert) appears. He testily asks these "two numskulls" when they are going to take the box out of his way. Ollie very reasonably asks why he doesn't walk around. Billy's incredulity is boundless: "What? Walk around? Me? Professor Theodore von Schwarzenhoffen, M.D., A.D., D.D.S., F.L.D., F.F.F. und F. should walk *around*?" He demands they get out of the way, Stan knocks his top hat off, and it bounces saucily down the steps to the street, where a truck runs over it. "Very lovely," says the gentleman heavily. "*I'll have you arrested for this!* I'll have you thrown in jail. I'm Professor . . . ," and he snorts off down the steps.

The boys finally reach the top, but they also mount the stairs leading to the garden pool, into which Ollie falls.

They push the box to the proper door, and when relaxing their hold, the piano goes along the walk, turns at the stairway, and starts down. Ollie catches up with it at the midway landing and holds onto it firmly, even though it picks up speed and drags him, prostrate behind it, to the very bottom. Stan comes down after him.

We are spared further anxieties by a title: **"That afternoon…"**

They again have the box at the top of the stairs when the postman confronts them. "Did you fellows carry that piano all the way up these stairs?" Stan nods, gaspingly. "You didn't have to do that," Charlie tells them. "Do you see that road down there? All you had to do was to drive around that road to the top here. Whew!" He shakes his head in disbelief. Ollie asks Stan feelingly why they didn't think of that before. So now nothing to be done but carry the box— "Heave *ho!* Heave *ho!*"—down the steps again.

Minutes later, Suzie has driven them up the winding road, and because no one answers the bell at the house, they decide to pull the box up into an open balcony window. They are not a whit surprised that the block and tackle they hitch to the fragile awning frame works perfectly and hauls the heavy box upward with consummate ease.

After an extended hat mixup, Ollie gets the worst end of the moving arrangements as they take the box down the staircase in the house. They come to a window at the landing, out of which Ollie falls into the pool. In exasperation he throws his water-filled derby at Stan, who, in duplicating the gesture, tumbles over into the pool.

Back where they started—almost.

Stan gets the box onto the balcony and unhooks the block and tackle, which falls with a resounding crash on Ollie's head.

Ollie, standing on the ladder, falls forward, hitting the door, which opens at once. He walks into the house, steps on a radio—exploding all the tubes—and walks up the stairs. He hears Stan call him, walks back down, goes outside, and asks what Stan wants. Stan says that somebody's home: he just heard them coming up the steps inside.

They get the box in the living room, Stan trying to extract the piano with his hammer. Ollie decides to get it out but as he moves forward the box opens and a rush of water almost engulfs him. As Ollie takes off his hat, Stan dips his handkerchief in the great pool of water. Looking around for a place of deposit, Stan sees Ollie's hat held opening upward, and wrings his handkerchief in it. Ollie steps on a nail, getting his shoe stuck on a board, pulls on it—and the sole comes off. Trying to find an electric outlet to plug in the player piano cord, Stan climbs up on the box, unscrews a chandelier globe, fumbles, and the globe explodes on Ollie's head.

Stan falls to the floor, pulling the chandelier and ceiling debris with him. Ollie takes the plug from Stan, puts it in a wall socket where it explodes. But it works: Ollie turns on the piano, which swings into a medley of patriotic songs. The boys do a knee-slapping, fast-stepping, eccentric minuet in time to the music.

Billy reappears—anguished, aghast, appalled. This is his house, he howls. "What are *you* doing here?" When they say they just delivered his piano, he goes into a vituperative tirade on how he hates and detests pianos. Promising to "take care" of the boys, he rushes out, comes back with an ax, and smashes the piano resoundingly. The piano begins to play "The Star Spangled Banner," and the three spring into rigid salutes.

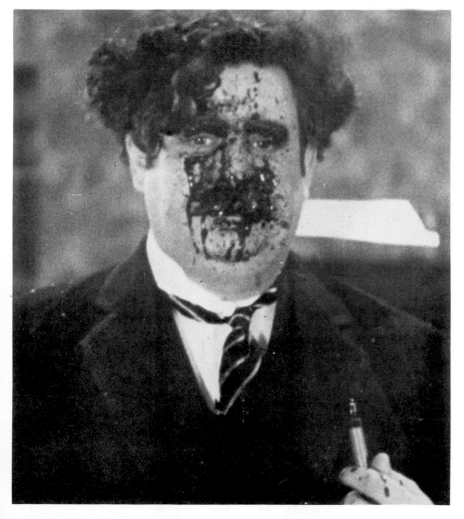

Billy turns off the piano and lays to with a will. As he shouts "I hate pianos," his wife appears at the door, shocked at his savagery. Billy explains to her that "these two blundering idiots delivered a piano here by mistake." She explains it's not a mistake: the piano was a birthday surprise for him. As she sobs on his shoulders, he declares that he wouldn't have had this happen for $1,000,000. "I thought you said you hated pianos," she says. "What?," says Billy. "Me hate pianos? Why, I'm *nuts* about them...gentlemen, what can I do to show you how sorry I am?" Ollie asks him to sign a delivery receipt and Billy accepts it and a pen from Stan.

Billy opens the pen and ink sprays over his face. He takes his shotgun and drives the boys from the house.

THE CHIMP

1932

Opening title: "Mr. Hardy's aesthetic nature thrilled at the beauties of circus life— Mr. Laurel never got any further than the monkey cage."

Laurel and Hardy Series / Three reels / Sound / Released May 21, 1932, by M-G-M / Produced by Hal Roach / Directed by James Parrott / Photographed by Walter Lundin / Edited by Richard Currier / Dialogue by H.M. Walker / Sound by Elmer R. Raguse / Compositions used in incidental music scoring by Le Roy Shield, Walt Eufel, Marvin Hatley, Rosas, John Philip Sousa, and John N. Klohr.

Stan Laurel Himself / *Oliver Hardy* Himself / *Joe, the jealous landlord* Billy Gilbert / *Ringmaster* James Finlayson / *Destructo, the Cannonball King* Stanley (Tiny) Sandford / *The Chimp* Charles Gamora / *Most of the audience* Jack Hill / *Tenant* Robert (Bobby) Burns / *Owner of Colonel Finn's Big Show* George Miller / *Laid-off performers* Baldwin Cooke, Dorothy Layton, Belle Hare / *Ethel, the landlord's wife* Martha Sleeper. *Note:* A photo of Dorothy Granger is used as Ethel, the landlord's wife.

In his chosen calling as half of a two-man horse, Ollie has decided, after various physical indignities, that he will never again play the rear end. Stan doesn't agree: "You look better in that end than I do."

The ever florid ringmaster (James Finlayson) has his artistes take a bow. There are more people in the circus company than in the stands. Fin announces the next act: Destructo the Cannon Ball King.

After ruining Destructo's first trick by accidentally bouncing a cannon ball on Ollie's back and crushing a tower stand, the boys now attempt to prepare the catch. setup for the second trick—the cannon

Destructo, blindfolded, will catch the cannon ball that Ollie has dropped into the cannon. Stan lights the fuse.

With delicate strength, Ollie packs the powder in. Stan pours in more powder. Ollie asks for still more. Ollie even pours in more himself, from his cupped hand, like a chef adding the final dusting of fresh pepper to the salad. The fuse burns down—explosions!—and the entire tent collapses.

Fade-in on the circus manager talking to the performers. He explains that, after seven weeks of rain and no business, he is flat broke. When the performers protest that they have not been paid, the manager says that he will split up the show among them—each performer will receive a valuable part of the show in lieu of salary, and all items will be chosen by lot.

Ollie "wins" Ethel the Human Chimpanzee (Charles Gamora)—as she is billed—"She reads, writes, plays the piano, and milks a cow." Stan gets the flea circus. Ethel takes quite a shine to Stan.

A title reads: "The night was dark—they usually are." The penniless trio is looking for a room.

Sotto voce, Ollie explains that tomorrow they'll sell Ethel—and be on Easy Street. Ethel is severely suspicious.

They decide to get a room at Billy Gilbert's boardinghouse. Inside, Billy is confiding to a friend that he fears his wife is chasing around again. If she is—"well, I wouldn't be responsible for my actions."

The boys explain that they'd like their friend to stay with them but Billy is warmly negative. Ethel can't understand; after all, in her smart tutu, she is clearly soignée and should be acceptable anywhere. But the boys take the room without her. They go back outside and ponder. In order to sneak Ethel in, they go to the garage, Ollie puts on Ethel's clothes, she puts on Ollie's. "Now you sneak her upstairs quietly," Ollie explains to Stan, "and throw my clothes out the window." The plan succeeds up to the moment when the clothes are being thrown down to him. His trousers get caught on a projection of the house, and in trying to free it, both Ethel and Stan fall down on top of Ollie. They put Ethel in a box and go upstairs to bed.

A title reads: "3:00 o'clock—If nothing happens, it will eventually be 3:30." Ethel gets out of her box and climbs up the rainspout to the boys' room, and gets in bed with Ollie. (The still differs from the film's action; Stan is by himself in the other bed.) Ollie grouses about his companion's fidgetiness and failure to cut his toenails. When he realizes Ethel is in with him, Ollie forces her to sleep in the closet. Later, Ethel takes Ollie's cover off and keeps it for her own comfort. Ollie has to get in with Stan but they both must move to Ollie's bed—Stan's bed has been preempted by the flea circus.

Meanwhile, downstairs, Billy is looking yearningly at his wife's picture, which is signed, "Lovingly your wife, Ethel." A man in one of the rooms puts on a phonograph record and Ethel, perhaps inspired by her tutu, comes out of the closet, puts on a hat, and begins to dance around the boys' room. Caught up in the sheer madness of the dance, Ethel takes Stan by the arm and leads him into her euphoria. Ollie sits up in bed and asks loudly, "Ethel! Will you stop that and come to bed?" In his room below, Billy overhears and glances up murderously. "Ethel," Ollie says. "Will you let him alone?," Stan pleads, "Ethel! Will you stop it and go to bed?" Billy takes a gun and comes to the door of the boys' room. "If that fatheaded landlord finds she's in here, he'll throw us all out," says Ollie.

Billy threatens to kick the door down. "I know she's in there!" The boys put Ethel in Ollie's bed and cover her up; then they get in Stan's bed, fleas and all. Billy shoots the door open and demands to know where she is. He sees the figure covered up in the other bed, stands over it, and addresses it in solemn tones, "You deceitful trifler, you…you, the bearer of my name…the mother of my children."

As his rhetoric reaches its highest flight—"You know that I've loved you. Loved you more than life itself!"—Billy's wife (Martha Sleeper) comes in and stands there, astounded. Billy sees her, Ethel the chimp sits up in bed, and Mrs. Gilbert screams. Billy orders the chimp out. "But you said you loved her," Ollie protests. Ethel the chimp finds Billy's revolver on the bed and begins firing at random; everyone exits en masse.

Production Sidelights

Stills of deleted footage. The boys looked rather good as a horse act—and they were even more inefficient roustabouts than extant footage indicates.

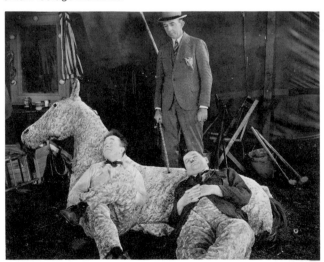

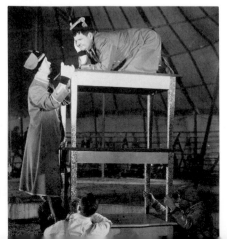

COUNTY HOSPITAL

■ ■ ■   1932

Laurel and Hardy Series / Two reels / Sound / Released June 25, 1932, by M-G-M / Produced by Hal Roach / Directed by James Parrott / Photographed by Art Lloyd / Edited by Bert Jordan and Richard Currier / Dialogue by H.M. Walker / Sound by James Greene / Compositions used in incidental music scoring by Le Roy Shield, and Marvin Hatley.

Stan Laurel Himself / *Oliver Hardy* Himself / *Doctor* Billy Gilbert / *Officer* Sam Lufkin / *Orderlies* Baldwin Cooke, Ham Kinsey / *Head nurse* May Wallace / *Hospital visitor* Frank Holliday / *Nurses* Lilyan Irene, Belle Hare, Dorothy Layton / *Daffy Englishman who is all aflutter* William Austin.

Opening title: "**Mr. Hardy fell on his leg, and was laid up for two months. Mr. Laurel fell on his head—and hadn't felt better in years.**"

Stan tries to obey the warning sign but his car won't obey him.

He is visiting Ollie—Stan tells him in serene candor—because he didn't have anything else to do. Ollie is also not overjoyed with Stan's gift—hard-boiled eggs and nuts. Ollie complains that he can't eat those things. "Why didn't you bring me a box of candy?" "They cost too much," Stan says, also pointing out that Ollie didn't pay him for the last box he bought.

Stan starts to eat the eggs. One of them rolls into Ollie's water pitcher, and in extricating it, Stan gets Ollie and the bed thoroughly wet. The doctor (Billy Gilbert) comes in, and asks, "And how is my little patient today?" Billy tells the little patient he'll be here a couple of months and Ollie is delighted. This is the first time in his life he's had such a wonderful rest. Stan is cracking nuts—with his teeth. He looks down on the floor at the weight that holds Ollie's foot suspended in the air. Stan puts a nut on the windowsill, picks up the weight, and Ollie's foot crashes down on Billy's head.

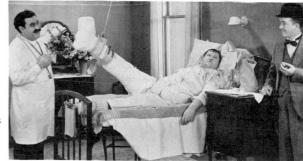

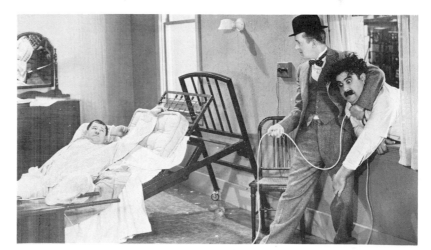

Billy, in taking the weight away from Stan, lurches out the window (it's the **top** floor) and is suspended out the window, hanging onto the weight for dear **life**. Ollie yells for help to get his leg back in traction, and when Stan goes to help him, Billy slides farther down the outside of the building. This continues in a seesaw sequence—Stan helping first one, then the other—until Stan finally gets Billy back inside the window. A nurse coming in to help sets a hypodermic needle on a chair. As Billy is pulled through the window, his trousers are torn, embarrassing him greatly. He tells Ollie to get his clothes on and leave the hospital at once.

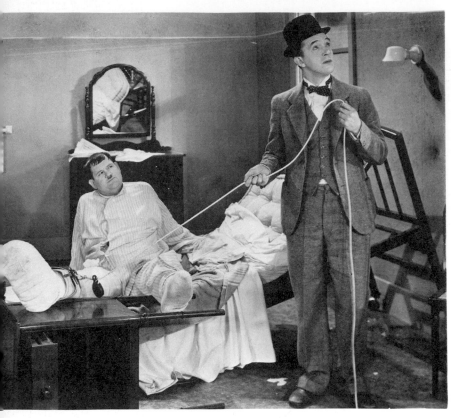

"You had nothing else to do, so you thought you'd come around and see me," Ollie tells Stan. "Here I was, for the first time in my life, having a nice peaceful time and you had to come and spoil it. Get my clothes."

In helping Ollie get dressed, Stan is told to cut the leg from the trousers to accommodate the cast.

Ollie puts on the trousers, discovers the wrong leg has been cut off.

Hardy's roommate, a jolly Englishman (William Austin), admits that he is "all aflutter" because he's going home. He puts on his clothing only to discover it's Ollie's. Stan sits down on the hypodermic needle. The nurse removes the needle and later, as she hands it to the head nurse for a refill, that lady points out that Stan will sleep for a month.

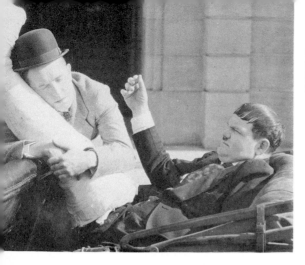

Stan begins his dozing directly he gets Ollie in the car...

...and sinks more fully into lethargy.

Ollie tries to nudge him awake as they drive along.

They narrowly miss cars and trucks—finally smashing up between two streetcars.

A policeman orders them to get it out of the way. Their car bent nearly double, they drive around and around...

...and around and around and around.

"SCRAM!"

1932

Laurel and Hardy Series / Two reels / Sound / Released September 10, 1932, by M-G-M / Produced by Hal Roach / Directed by Raymond McCarey / Photographed by Art Lloyd / Edited by Richard Currier / Dialogue by H.M. Walker / Sound by James Greene / Compositions used in incidental music scoring by Le Roy Shield, Marvin Hatley, Ring-Hager, Warren-Green, and J.S. Zamecnik.

Stan Laurel Himself / *Oliver Hardy* Himself / *The cavalier drunk* Arthur Housman / *The sneering Judge Beaumont* Rychard Cramer / *Judge's wife, playful Mrs. Beaumont* Vivien Oakland / *Officers* Sam Lufkin, Charles McMurphy / *Court reporter* Baldwin Cooke / *Other defendant awaiting trial* Charles Dorety.

When Stan and Ollie are called up before a hard-nosed judge (Rychard Cramer) on a vagrancy charge, he asks them how they plead. Ollie: "Not guilty, your highness." Judge: "On what grounds?" Stan: "We weren't on the grounds. We were sleeping on a park bench." The judge snarls that he would soak them 180 days if the jail wasn't full and gives them one hour to get out of town. Stan asks if that means they can go back and sleep on the park bench, prompting the judge to say grimly, "Scram, or I'll *build* a jail *for* you." The boys scram to the street where, in the driving rain, they encounter a roistering drunk who has dropped his car keys down a sidewalk grating. After they help him to retrieve them, he invites them to spend the night at his home.

The drunk (Arthur Housman), badly in need of support, arrives at his home.

But he cannot find his door key, and Ollie, after asking permission to make the search, goes through the drunk's pockets. Determined to help, Stan looks through *Ollie's* pockets.

Ollie tells Stan, "Lean him up against something and help me try to get in the window."

They proceed...

...but the going is fraught with mischance...

...causing a loud crash as Ollie tumbles in over some plants.

Meanwhile the drunk has fallen against the front door, which—unlocked all the time—opens. He enters the house; the boys come out of the house, look for him, are locked out as the door slams shut. They ring the bell. The drunk answers, carrying a jug of gin. He tells them to go upstairs to his room: "You palsies go up and make yourselves comfy." While the boys mount the stairs, the drunk pours the gin into a pitcher, placing it on a tray with glasses, and carries them upstairs. Confronted by the butler, the drunk realizes he is in the wrong house, and leaves via a noisy fall down the stairs. The aroused lady of the house is told by the butler that the intruder was a drunken man who came to the wrong house. "It's a good thing my husband isn't here," says the lady. "He'd probably kill me. He detests people who drink."

The boys luxuriate in what they think is their drunken pal's bedroom. Attired in "his" pajamas, they smoke "his" cigars and Ollie squirts on a dash of "his" cologne.

They look for their pal, encounter the lady of the house (Vivien Oakland) who faints at sight of them. They revive her with the gin (thinking it to be water); she comes to and asks them who they are. They explain that as friends of her husband they helped him out of a little difficulty and they undressed because they were all wet. "Did my husband get wet, too?," she asks. "Wet?," says Stan, "why he's soaked."

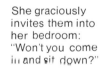

She graciously invites them into her bedroom: "Won't you come in and sit down?"

During pleasant chitchat, the lady, provoked by the gin, begins to laugh, the boys joining the laughter companionably. She asks Ollie to dance but he doesn't want to. "Come on," she says, "I want to dance," and begins to pull him up. "If you don't want to dance," she giggles, "we'll *wrestle*." She jumps on Ollie happily, loudly demanding another drink. On her promise to remain quiet, Stan goes out to get her a drink of the "water."

As Stan pours the drink, the master of the house returns. It is the judge, who recognizes his own pajamas, and in them a vagrant he ordered out of town.

211

The judge's wife is given her drink and leaves the shores of sobriety even further behind. Outside, the judge smells the pitcher.

Stan, the wife, and Ollie relapse into another, more stimulating laughing jag.

The judge advances grimly into the bedroom. As the celebrants dissolve into laughter...

... they one by one recognize the judge. The boys jump up and run— right into a wall. They back up against it as the judge advances with baleful eye. Stan sees a light switch, clicks it, and, in the darkness that persists to the end, the sound of mayhem reigns unchecked.

PACK UP YOUR ... TROUBLES
1932

68 minutes—Sound
Released September 17, 1932, by M-G-M

Produced by Hal Roach

Directed by George Marshall
and Raymond McCarey*

Photographed by Art Lloyd

Edited by Richard Currier

Dialogue by H. M. Walker

Sound by James Greene

Compositions used in incidental
music scoring by Le Roy Shield
and Marvin Hatley

Stan Laurel . . . . Himself
Oliver Hardy . . . . Himself
Recruiting sergeant . . . . Tom Kennedy
Eddie, the silly groom . . . . Grady Sutton
The Boys' buddy,
Eddie Smith . . . . Donald Dillaway
Eddie's baby . . . . Jacquie Lyn
Woman who delivers Nan's letter to
Eddie . . . . Mary Carr
Mr. Hathaway, nearly nervous father of the
bride (part originally slated for Frank
Brownlee) . . . . Billy Gilbert
The groom's father . . . . . . C. Montague Shaw

The bride . . . . Muriel Evans
The general . . . . James Finlayson
Butlers . . . . Al Hallet, Bill O'Brien
Mrs. MacTavish, baby-sitter. . . . Mary Gordon
Saunders, the bank guard . . . . Lew Kelly
Irascible drill sergeant . . . . . . Frank Brownlee
Pierre, the army post cook . . George Marshall
Rogers, the butler with a cold in his
nose . . . . Charley Rogers
Parkins, the butler . . . . Frank Rice
Police officers . . . . . James C. Morton,
Gene Morgan, James Mason
Passerby . . . . Charles Dorety
Officers in the Eastside Welfare
Association . . . Charles Middleton, Nora Cecil
New recruit . . . . Jack Hill
Pedestrian at end . . . . Jack Hill
Man who delivers telegram . . . . . Ham Kinsey
Doughboy . . . . Ham Kinsey
Bridesmaid . . . . Dorothy Layton
Crowd extra . . . . Charley Young
Doughboys . . . . Marvin Hatley,
Ben Hendricks, Jr., Pat Harmon, Bud
Fine, Frank S. Hagney, Bob (Mazooka)
O'Conor, Pete Gordon, Baldwin Cooke

Drill soldier . . . . Henry Hall
Unperturbed society matron at the
wedding . . . . Ellinor Van Der Veer
Man near dumb waiter . . . . Charlie Hall
Detective . . . . Robert Emmett Homans
Street extras at end . . . . George Miller,
Chet Brandenberg

Bank president, and Jacquie's
grandfather, Mr. Smith . . . . . . Richard Tucker
Uncle Jack, the child-and-
wife-beating lout . . . . Rychard Cramer

Parts cut from all reissue prints due to the unpleasant wife-and-child-beating scenes:

Uncle Jack's wife Annie . . . . . . Adele Watson
Jerry, grubby friend of
Cramer . . . . Dick Gilbert

Note: Anita Louise was loaned by RKO "to por-
tray the leading female role" in *Pack Up Your
Troubles,* but, for whatever reasons, was sub-
sequently written out of the production.

*Inexplicably, Leo McCarey's brother Ray is
given codirector's credit on this picture. He
was one of the chief gag writers for *Pack Up
Your Troubles,* but in fact the film's only director was George Marshall.

Opening title: "**April 1917—when the scratch of a pen on Capitol Hill caused crowns to rattle.**"

Here we see our heroes facing up to the fact of national emergency. Ollie: "Well, looks like we're in it. Gee, I wish I could go!" Stan: "Go where?" Ollie: "Why, to war!" Stan: "Why can't ya go?" Ollie: "There you are. I knew you'd take that selfish attitude. I'd go in a minute if it wasn't for my flat feet!"

A forthright recruiting sergeant (Tom Kennedy) confronts "a couple of good prospects" whose lack of enthusiasm stings him to say, "Just as I thought—a couple of crummy, no-good slackers." Ollie explains deferentially that they are incapacitated; Stan confirms this by adding, "There's been a lot of it going around lately."

A highly tentative approach to army life.

The title card preceding this scene reads: "It didn't take Uncle Sam long to whip this raw material into a real fighting machine." The drill sergeant (Frank Brownlee) is not searching for an appropriate Shakespearean quotation but if he were, it would be "Confusion now hath made his masterpiece!"

A crack drill team passes smartly by, and the squad gawks in wonder. "Why don't you have *us* do like that?," Ollie asks the numbed sergeant.

On KP, the boys encounter their buddy Eddie Smith (Donald Dillaway), who inquires, "What've you two eggs been up to now?" What they are up to is simple, in all senses of the word. When they are ordered to take out the garbage, they inquire politely of the cook where they should take it. He tells them with heavy sarcasm, "To the *general*, of course." They proceed to carry out orders, as good soldiers should.

The general (James Finlayson) has been blaming his orderly for the unusual odor on the premises. Now he uncovers the cause: two fragrant GI cans and two bewildered perpetrators.

Languishing in the guardhouse, the boys are confronted by the cook (George Marshall, who also directed the film). Witheringly, the cook says, "So ya told on me, huh? OK, ya snitchers, some day I'm gonna catch up with you guys again. And when I do, I'm gonna have my *knife.*"

Preceding this scene, the title card has proclaimed, "Somewhere in nowhere, the cannons boomed all day and the cooties boomed all night." Concerned about the lack of amenities, Ollie asks, "Don't you think it's about time we had some fresh water?" Stan replies, "That's not water, it's coffee!"

By a typical Laurel-and-Hardy convolution of order, the boys find themselves in a tank. The tank in its ramblings accumulates some barbed wire, straddles an enemy trench and gathers up a whole brigade of Boche. (Including, right foreground, Dave O'Brien, later famous as the star of the Pete Smith Series.)

Their pal, Eddie Smith, having fallen in battle, the boys assume the care of his motherless child (Jacquie Lyn) and take on themselves the responsibility of finding the girl's grandparents. They have a clue: the people are named Smith.

In their search for the Smiths, Stan and Ollie are not always accurate. They believe they have discovered the correct Smith in a man just about to be married. When they announce they have his youngster, the irate father of the bride (Billy Gilbert) throttles the innocent groom (Grady. Sutton).

Stan is exhausted from his trip to the cough-drop factory at Poughkeepsie. It was there he learned that neither of the Smith Brothers is the girl's grandfather. Stan's evening duty is to read the little girl her bedtime story but tonight she takes over and satisfactorily sends him off to beddy-bye land. Ollie is irritated at this alteration in housekeeping protocol.

As part of a pattern of harassment, a grim-jawed officer from a local welfare association (Charles Middleton) queries the boys about the little girl. Now a cliché of humor, but uttered in this film for the first time, Ollie asks him, "How much would you charge me to haunt a house?"

Desperate for money to flee the officer and to continue their search, the boys try to raise a loan on their business— a lunch wagon. The bank president (Richard Tucker) assures them that he would have to be unconscious to lend them money on *that* business. The statue of Shakespeare falls off its pedestal, knocking him out, and the boys feel quite justified in taking the money.

They get their funds from the inner sanctum.

In order to get the baby-sitter (Mary Gordon) out of the way for their hasty departure, Ollie tells her, "I just heard a rumor your house is on fire." It is also at this point that Stan locks himself in the closet, and his frantic knocking is mistaken for the police demanding entry. When Ollie asks him, "Why didn't you tell me it was you?," Stan replies, "It was so dark I didn't think you would hear me."

Apprehended by the police, the culprits look distinctly unculpritlike. Three babes in the alley.

It looks like the end, and virtually is. All that remains is for them to be identified by the bank president.

The bank president's name is, of all things, Smith, and he is, ineluctably, Eddie's father. The baby is reunited with her grandparents and the boys are invited to dinner—where they are told they can pack up their troubles from now on.

And so the fates pursue. The Smith's cook turns out to be their old army nemesis. He gloats grindingly, "Well, if it ain't the snitchers —and I've got my knife." Exeunt, running.

The First Tour...

Arriving in England, July 23, 1932. From left: Myrtle and Babe Hardy, Stan between his dad, Arthur J. Jefferson, and his stepmother.

Babe and a bobby, on the Thames Embankment, London, July 24, 1932.

Arrival at Gare Saint-Lazare, Paris, 1932.

Their First Mistake

🎩🎩🎩   1932

Laurel and Hardy Series / Two reels / Sound / Released November 5, 1932, by M-G-M / Produced by Hal Roach / Directed by George Marshall / Edited by Richard Currier / Compositions used in incidental music scoring by Marvin Hatley and Le Roy Shield.

Stan Laurel Himself / *Oliver Hardy* Himself / *Mrs. Arabella Hardy* Mae Busch / *Process server* Billy Gilbert / *Neighbor* George Marshall. *(Their First Mistake was a working title for Pardon Us.)*

Opening title: **"Mr. Hardy was married — Mr. Laurel was also unhappy."**

Mrs. Hardy (Mae Busch) is giving Ollie a hard time for the wasted hours he spends with his worthless friend Stan. As they talk, the phone rings. It is Stan to tell his pal that he has a couple of tickets for the Cement Workers' Bazaar tonight. "We might win a prize," Stan enthuses. "They're going to give away a steam shovel." Ollie thanks his caller, pointedly calling him "Mr. Jones," and, after hanging up, identifies the caller as Mr. Jones, his new boss, who wants Ollie to attend a big business meeting tonight. Mae is enraptured at the thought of Ollie's getting someplace at last.

Shortly after, Stan enters to explain that it was he on the phone. He retreats quickly to the hall as marital storm clouds gather and listens attentively to the Hardys as they battle in word...

...and deed.

220

It takes two to keep Mae out when she is on the warpath. Before she slams out of the house, she tells Ollie that if he goes out with Stan again, she is through.

Ollie explains the cause of Mae's disaffection. He tells Stan, "She says that I think more of you than I do of her!" "Well, you do, don't you?," asks Stan. Ollie says they won't go into that. Stan says he knows what the whole trouble is—the Hardys need a baby in the house, someone to keep Mae occupied so the boys can go out together. Ollie thinks that a pretty good idea and he admits Stan is right.

"You bet your life I'm right," Stan says. "You know, I'm not as dumb as you look." Ollie decides to adopt a baby.

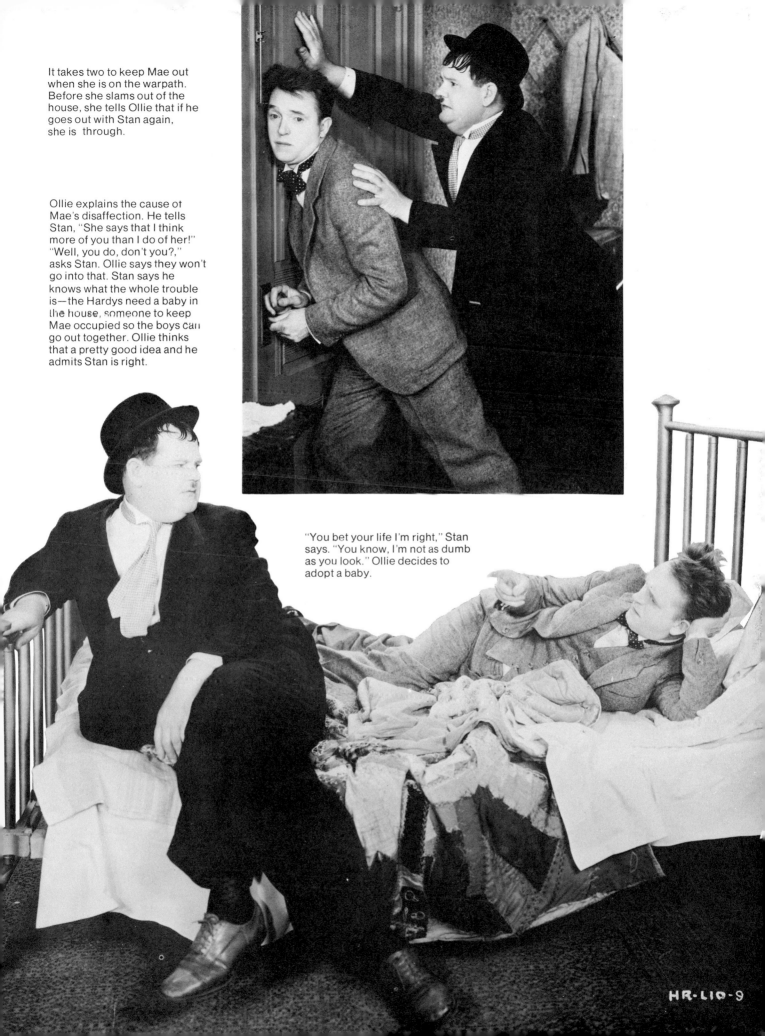

HR-L10-9

Stan hands out cigars on behalf of the now parent. (The man with the cigar is George Marshall, the director of the film.) Ollie can hardly wait to show the baby to Mae.

But Mae isn't at home and doesn't seem likely to be. The process server (Billy Gilbert) delivers a divorce summons to Ollie and an alienation of affections summons to Stan. Stan proposes to leave the situation entirely and at once, but Ollie reminds him that he is very much responsible for the child. Stan asks what he has to do with it, and Ollie replies, "What have you got to do with it? Why, you were the one that wanted me to have the baby and now that you've gotten me into this trouble, you want to walk out and leave me flat!" But Stan doesn't "want to get mixed up in this thing." He points out, "I have my future, my career to think of." Ollie forces him to stay—and fix some milk. The baby begins to cry stridently.

After preparing the milk, Stan discovers, upon taste-testing, that he rather enjoys the stuff. The boys finally get the baby to sleep. Stan switches off the lights, then strikes a match to look at the switch. When Ollie asks him why he struck the match, Stan says, "I wanted to see if the switch was off." Ollie tells him to get the floor lamp, "I don't want you striking matches all night long." Stan brings the lamp over; Ollie trips on the cord and crashes into the kitchen, getting up moments later with a mousetrap on his nose. "You woke the baby up," Stan says accusingly.

The lamp cord catches Ollie as he comes back and he stumbles, crashing through the door. The baby howls on. Ollie tells Stan to put the lamp "over there," but Stan says it won't reach. "You gotta pull the plug out of the socket," Ollie says, pulling the lamp cord. The socket comes loose from the wall, hitting Ollie in the face.

The phone rings as the baby screams. Ollie shouts into the phone, "How do you expect us to keep this baby quiet with you ringing the phone?" The phone comes loose from the wall. Stan finally gets the baby to sleep. Cautioned that if he makes a noise he must make it quietly, Stan puts cotton in his ears on the theory that if he makes a noise he won't be able to hear it.

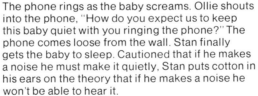

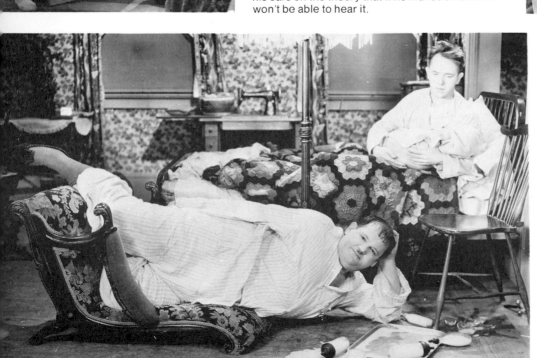

Needing an electrical outlet for their lamp, Stan plugs into the socket of the flashing electric ROOMS sign on their building. The light in their room now goes on and off, on and off, frightening Stan badly. Ollie, fixing the baby's bottle in the kitchen, returns during an off phase of the light, trips, and winds up sprawling on the floor with a rubber nipple stuck to his nose. Sometime later, Stan, Ollie, and the baby have all gone to bed. The baby cries and Ollie drowsily feeds it, not noticing that it is the sleeping Stan who is consuming the milk so quickly. Finally realizing this, Ollie grabs the bottle from Stan, the milk spills out over the bed, and Ollie jumps up out of bed in exasperation.

TOWED IN A HOLE

1932

Laurel and Hardy Series / Two reels / Sound /
Released December 31, 1932, by M-G-M /
Produced by Hal Roach / Directed by George
Marshall / Photographed by Art Lloyd / Edited
by Richard Currier / Sound by James Greene
/ Compositions used in incidental music scor-
ing by Le Roy Shield and Marvin Hatley.

Stan Laurel Himself / *Oliver Hardy* Himself /
Junkyard owner Billy Gilbert.

The sign on the truck reads:
LAUREL AND HARDY—FRESH FISH—
Crabs a Specialty. "Fresh fish!,"
sings Ollie. "Caught in the ocean
this *morning.*"

Stan's fish horn is an emphatic and happy countermelody to Ollie's chanted call—even when the horn flats razzingly once in a while. "For the first time in our lives we're a success," says Ollie. "A nice little fish business, and making money." Stan says that they could make a lot more money: "...if we caught our own fish, we wouldn't have to pay for it, then whoever we sold it to, it would be clear profit." Impressed, Ollie says, "Tell me that again." "Well," Stan says as his thought processes slowly strangle his rhetoric to inanition, "if—if you caught a fish and whoever you sold it to, they wouldn't have to pay for it—then the—profits would—would go to the fish. If—er—if you—." He seeks relief by blowing the fish horn. Ollie knows exactly what he means: eliminate the middleman. It's a $1,000,000 idea, he announces.

At Joe's Junkyard ("Anything from a Needle to a Battleship") the boys buy an old boat that they propose to fix up and use as their new fishing craft. To discover any leaks, they must fill the boat with water, Ollie says; and Stan, handing the hose into the craft, inevitably soaks his pal several different ways. After the boat is filled, Stan so informs Ollie, and Ollie—hard at work painting the rudder—orders him to scrub the deck. On deck, Stan sees the rudder bar and pushes it. The rudder knocks Ollie over, his hand going into a can of paint. Ollie pushes the rudder back; Stan, seeing the rudder bar out of "place," pushes it back again. The rudder knocks Ollie over, the contents of the paint can besmearing him. Later Stan asks, "What'd you put that stuff on your face for?"

In a tit-for-tat sequence in which they pour buckets of water over each other, Stan picks up the ultimate water weapon, the hose. "Now, wait a minute," Ollie says. "Isn't this silly?... Here we are, two grown men, acting like a couple of children. Why, we ought to be ashamed of ourselves, throwing water at one another." The matter of airing their maturity terminated, the conversation continues with: "Well, you started it." "No, I didn't." "Yes, you did." "Well, I didn't." "You certainly did." And Stan cries. Shortly after, Ollie explains that this is why "we never get any place. Let's put our brains together so that we can forge ahead. Remember, united we stand; divided we fall." They fall—or rather Ollie does—on a cake of soap left on deck. Once more he flies over the side of the boat into the paint.

To stop the leak, Ollie starts to hammer a sheet of tin over the hole. (Stan is not in the action as depicted in this still.) Stan is on deck scrubbing the anchor and chain. When finished, he puts it on top of the cabin, where it falls down into the boat. Stan, holding the chain, follows the anchor down below...

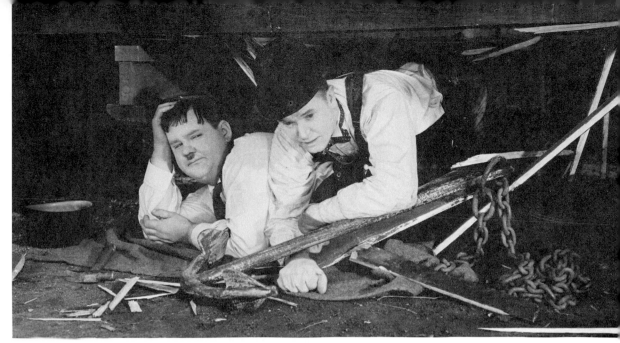

...where it crashes through the hull onto the hapless Hardy. Fade-in to Ollie painting the mast. Stan, a black eye prominent, has been imprisoned below where he plays ticktacktoe, managing to cheat himself slyly and emerge a proud winner. Bored, Stan finds a saw, and after eliciting musical notes by hitting it with a nail...

...comes up on deck—pushing Ollie into the fresh paint—to announce that he just got a good idea. Justifiably alarmed at this, Ollie says, "I don't want to hear it. Now, you get back in there, and don't come out again until I call you." Going down into the cabin, Stan gets his head caught between the mast and the bulkhead. He tries every way to get loose but has to resort to sawing the mast. Meanwhile, Ollie has mounted a ladder so he can paint the very top of the mast. He hears a curious persistent sawing sound, leading in time to an even more interesting sound—a mast splintering in half.

Ollie crashes down in a well-fashioned mud puddle. (The still is inaccurate: Stan is not in the puddle at any time in the film.)

The boat has finally been painted and repaired. Ollie fastens a rope from their car to the boat's prow. To keep him out of mischief, Stan is placed on the running board of a junked car with his hands tied around a barrel.

Ollie's look defies Stan to get them in further trouble. Stan now has two black eyes. Ollie relents, unties the rope, and puts Stan in the car preparatory to their driving the boat away. They don't get far because the rear wheels of the car spin around in the dirt. The boat is too heavy to haul. Ollie tries to move the boat. Stan suggests that he put the sail up. Another good idea, but Ollie tries it anyway. Wind fills the unfurled sail and the boat begins to move. Indeed it moves so smartly that it crashes into the car. Boat *and* car then crash through some fences, both winding up together as a huge pile of first-class wreckage.

Stan blows the fish horn and smiles with the look of "Well, *this* we've got anyway." Ollie chases him out of sight.

Note: George Marshall, the director of *Towed in a Hole,* said recently, "We had a wonderful ending all prepared for the picture: in putting up the sail, the boat was supposed to get totally out of hand, to be blown down the highway, passing cars right and left. Stan would be throwing out the anchor and catching it on fire hydrants, and so forth. But the studio wouldn't let us go beyond a certain footage so that last bit was never filmed. Would have been marvelous though."

TWICE TWO

1933

Laurel and Hardy Series / Two reels; 1,866 feet / Sound / Released February 25, 1933, by M-G-M / Produced by Hal Roach / Directed by James Parrott / Photographed by Art Lloyd / Edited by Bert Jordan / Sound by James Greene / Compositions used in incidental music scoring by Marvin Hatley and Le Roy Shield.

Stan Laurel Himself / Mrs. Hardy Stan Laurel / Oliver Hardy Himself / Mrs. Laurel Oliver Hardy / Soda jerk Baldwin Cooke / Delivery boy Charlie Hall / Passerby outside store Ham Kinsey / Voice-over for Mrs. Hardy Carol Tevis / Voice-over for Mrs. Laurel Mae Wallace. (The duplicate identity gimmick also formed the basis of Brats, three years earlier, and Our Relations, three years later.)

We are at (as the sign on the door tells us) the office of OLIVER HARDY, M.D., Brain Specialist. ASSOCIATE ADVISOR, Mr. Laurel. It is exactly a year ago that Stan married Ollie's sister and Ollie married Stan's. Ollie wants to take the girls out tonight and celebrate. For all his exalted title, Ollie is the total office force as well. Ollie is indignant at Stan's listening in on his conversations, even when they are with Stan's sister. But Ollie does this himself under the same circumstances. To spite him, Stan pours water in the mouthpiece at the switchboard, blows hard, and Ollie gets a shower of it from his office phone.

Mrs. Hardy (Stan) and Mrs. Laurel (Babe). (Laurel and Hardy play dual roles: sisters to themselves and wives to each other.) Mrs. Laurel is adamant about not going out tonight. She is cooking dinner for all of them—and there is a special surprise awaiting Ollie.

To get back at Stan, Ollie blows ink into the receiver of his phone; it promptly sprays back at him from the mouthpiece. Stan conveys the message about the evening's plans, adding, "She's got a surprise for you." "What else did she say?," asks Ollie. "She told me not to tell you that she had the surprise." Ollie tells Stan *not* to tell him. "I won't," says Stan. "I can keep a secret."

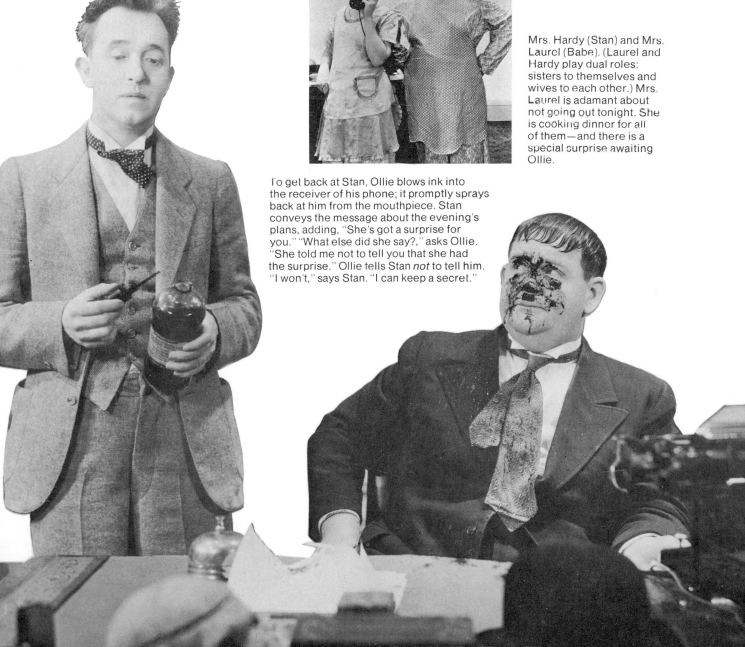

The big cake promised for tonight's affair accidentally winds up on Mrs. Laurel's head as the ladies are preparing the table. They send out to the bakery for another one. Ollie's pants get ripped asunder when he opens the door, and the flowers are caught in the door and beheaded.

Mrs. Laurel asks Stan if he has any money. He hands over some bills and 15 cents in silver; she keeps the bills and tells him to go down to the corner and buy 15 cents worth of strawberry ice cream. (In 1933 15 cents was not an insignificant amount of money.)

While Stan is at the store, the celebrants are at their soup. Mrs. Laurel is *noisily* at her soup. Mrs. Hardy complains, Mrs. Laurel explains that it's her asthma. At the corner store, Stan asks for strawberry ice cream and is told they have none. He calls home and is directed to get tutti-frutti. The clerk says they haven't any. Stan calls again and is ordered to get chocolate. The clerk says they haven't any. Stan calls again and this time is told to get vanilla— *anything*. Stan asks the clerk for vanilla and is told they haven't any. "We don't sell ice cream here," the clerk explains tardily. "Next door." Stan returns home without any ice cream. "I spent the 15 cents callin' you up." (The blessed days when phone calls were a nickel apiece.)

After trying a variety of ways to get his napkin satisfactorily hitched to himself, Stan succeeds. A piece of bread he picks up gets implicated in the process and he does succeed in buttering his hand rather neatly. Mrs. Laurel and Mrs. Hardy natter back and forth, until they actually begin to throw things. Mrs. Laurel tells Stan, "Get that dame out of my house before I go nuts!" " 'Tisn't your house," challenges Mrs. Hardy. " 'Tis my house." " 'Tisn't!" And so on, to another snapping session between the ladies, which is terminated by Ollie telling his wife that they'll go somewhere and eat in peace.

"Come, Ollie dear. Let's go to the Ambassador where we can get something *good* to eat." The ladies have at it again until there is a knock at the door.

The delivery boy (Charlie Hall) says that this cake is for Mrs. Laurel: "Will you please see that she gets it?" "I certainly will," says Mrs. Hardy, and delivers it right in Mrs. Laurel's face. The Hardys depart.

Me and My Pal

Ollie is preparing for the happiest day of his life. As he eats his breakfast, the radio interrupts itself with "a very important news flash. Mr. Oliver Norvell Hardy is to be married today at high noon to the only daughter of that well-known oil magnate, Mr. Peter Cucumber. The wedding is to be held at the bride's home and will be one of the highlights of the social season." Ollie listens with increasing pleasure to the account of how he began as an elevator boy and worked his way to the top. He is not particularly delighted, however, to hear the next bit of commentary. "Mr. Stan Laurel, who has been the lifelong friend, adviser, and severest critic, who guided Mr. Hardy to the pinnacle of success, is to be best man." The best man arrives with the couple's railroad tickets and ring—and a wedding present: a jigsaw puzzle.

Laurel and Hardy Series / Two reels / Sound / Released April 22, 1933, by M-G-M / Produced by Hal Roach / Directed by Charles Rogers and Lloyd French / Photographed by Art Lloyd / Edited by Bert Jordan / Sound by James Greene / Compositions used in incidental music scoring by Le Roy Shield, Wagner, and Marvin Hatley.

Stan Laurel Himself / Oliver Hardy Himself / Mr. Peter Cucumber James Finlayson / Officer James C. Morton / Smart-aleck cab-driver Eddie Dunn / Delivery boy Charlie Hall / Telegram messenger Bobby Dunn / Brides-maids Carroll Borland, Mary Kornman / Officers at end of film Charles McMurphy, Eddie Baker / Bride Marion Bardell / Usher at wedding Charley Young / Hives, the butler Walter Plinge.

Stan suggests it's the perfect gift for one about to be married. "You won't be goin' out much at nights and I thought it'd be something for us to play with." "My playing days are over," announces Ollie. "My time is too valuable to waste on such childish falgadash."

Ollie, preparing to leave, sits down for a moment to help his pal.

230

The cab they have ordered arrives, and Ollie receives his inevitable door-nose-smash. Mounting the cab, they wait for the driver who is in Ollie's house picking up the traveling bags. The wait lengthens. Stan is sent in to get the driver when the meter reads $4.75.

Ollie goes in to get Stan *and* the driver (Eddie Dunn); he tells the driver they must be going. "OK, fatty," says the driver. "I'll be with you in just a minute." The driver is looking for a piece with "a little more straight edge."

A policeman (James C. Morton) comes in to give the driver a parking ticket. The bride's father, Mr. Cucumber (James Finlayson), phones to tell Ollie he's late. Engrossed with the puzzle, Ollie tells Stan to tell Fin, "I left ten minutes ago." Stan tells Fin, "He's right here and he told me to tell you that we just left—ten minutes ago." The policeman scolds Ollie for wasting his time on the puzzle; then the policeman idly picks up a piece of the puzzle and wonders where it should go.

The boys are finally set to leave when Stan finds a piece of the puzzle in his pocket. He returns it to the house. After a time, Ollie again goes to get him. At the bride's house there is a stir when some flowers arrive— a large wreath with a ribbon marked IN MEMORY. It is not a mistake, the delivery man insists. "Mr. Laurel picked it out himself." Fin orders the car, takes the wreath, saying, "I may have some use for this."

231

Back at Ollie's house, a telegram boy (Bobby Dunn) delivers a wire. Stan takes it and, distracted by the puzzle, puts the telegram in his pocket.

The puzzle takes shape. Gradually it is all together, except for one piece, and that piece is missing. Fin, frothingly irate, arrives to carry away his laggard son-in-law-to-be; but the policeman insists that everybody must be searched for the elusive puzzle piece.

A brouhaha ensues among all the puzzle fans—participant against participant—until a police car is summoned to quell the riot. The puzzle is swept headlong to the floor. In the midst of it all, Stan remembers the telegram. It is for Ollie from his brokers advising: "CAN SELL YOUR GREAT INTERNATIONAL HORSECOLLAR STOCK AT 2,000,000 PROFIT. ADVISE IMMEDIATELY." Ollie grabs the telephone, when suddenly the radio sounds off: "Another news flash. After a sensational rise today in the stock market, the Great International Horsecollar Corporation took a tremendous crash and failed. This will mean the loss of millions to its investors. More good news later." "Don't worry," Stan tells his pal. "Prosperity's just around the corner." Stan finds the missing piece of the puzzle on the floor; he gets back down on the floor and begins to reassemble the puzzle. Ollie drives Stan out of his sight and returns to kick the puzzle around the room.

The Devil's Brother
(Fra Diavolo)

1933

90 minutes — Sound	Stanlio . . . . Stan Laurel	Man who owns the bull . . . . John Qualen
Released May 5, 1933, by M-G-M	Ollio . . . . Oliver Hardy	Village children . . . . Edith Fellows
Produced by Hal Roach	Fra Diavolo . . . . Dennis King	Jackie Taylor
Codirected by Hal Roach and Charles Rogers	Lady Pamela Rocberg . . . . Thelma Todd	Tavern patrons . . . . Rolfe Sedan
Lord Rocberg . . . . James Finlayson	Kay Deslys
Photographed by Art Lloyd and Hap Depew	Matteo . . . . Henry Armetta	Leo White
Lieutenant . . . . Lane Chandler	Lillian Moore
Edited by Bert Jordan and William Terhune	Lorenzo . . . . Arthur Pierson	Walter Shumway
Zerlina . . . . Lucille Browne	Louise Carver
Based on the 1830 comic opera *Fra Diavolo* by Daniel F. Auber, with Laurel and Hardy in the reshaped parts of Giacomo and Beppo	Village minister . . . . George Miller	Francesco . . . . Matt McHugh
Tremulous woodchopper . . . . . . Stanley (Tiny) Sandford	Bandit . . . . Harry Bernard
Imbiber at the Tavern de Cucu Harry Bernard
Cunning old woodchopper . James C. Morton	
Adaptation by Jeanie MacPherson	Fra Diavolo's mistress . . . . Nina Quartaro	Parts cut from final release print:
		Alessandro (though credit erroneously
Sound by James Greene	Brigands . . . . Jack Hill	remains in title-card billing) . . . . Wilfred Lucas
Music by Auber	Dick Gilbert	Second woodchopper . . . . Carl Harbaugh
Musical direction by Le Roy Shield	Arthur Stone	(Reissued as *Bogus Bandits*, and *The Virtuous Tramps*.)

233

Opening title: "In the early eighteenth century, Northern Italy was terrorized by bandits. Boldest among the robber-chieftains was Fra Diavolo (The Devil's Brother), who masqueraded as the elegant Marquis de San Marco in order to mingle with the rich. Great lords lost their gold to him—great ladies their hearts."

In his camp Diavolo (Dennis King) enchants one of his ladies (Nina Quartaro) who is strenuously willing to be enchanted. His followers are more interested in knowing if he has found them quarry to apprehend. Diavolo tells them, in flashback, that he...

...has met the lusciously beautiful Lady Pamela Rocberg (Thelma Todd) and her wealthy and bumbling husband, ripe for cuckolding. In the Rocberg coach Diavolo beguiles her with song while hubby dozes. Lady Pamela reveals that she has insured the safety of her jewels from thieves by hiding them in the fruitcake. She indiscreetly mentions the 5,000 francs her husband has also hidden elsewhere. Flashback ended, Diavolo tells his gang, "As a marquis, I'll hold up tradition; you hold up the coach."

Stanlio's and Ollio's life savings have given them ultimate security—from everything but bandits in mountain passes. The bandits dash off, and Ollio looks after them dejectedly, pondering the incalculable loss. Stanlio, however, is philosophical. "Come easy, go easy," he says. "That's my motto." Ollio is intrigued by Stanlio's suggestion that they need not start all over again at the bottom. Why not start at the top by becoming bandits? Stanlio is not crystalline clear how they shall go about this, but he concludes triumphantly, "It's the law of conversation. As you cast your bread on the water, so shall you reap!" Ollio tells him in congratulatory tone, "That's *very well* thought out."

They are resident in the forest, full-fledged robber fledglings. They hold up a woodcutter whose tale of personal woe causes the boys to weep and give him what money they have left. As they leave, they turn to see the woodcutter carefully adding their mite to a fat bag of gold.

Warned to have a care of Diavolo, the boys prepare their next robbery carefully. "Stand and deliver!," Ollio says imperiously to their next victim. "Tell him who you are," Stanlio advises. "That ought to scare him." Ollio begins to sing the ringing Fra Diavolo theme that always identifies the great rogue, but he forgets the words—and Diavolo himself completes the refrain, scaring the boys out of what is left of their wits.

Diavolo's crew joins him and he confronts his would-be imitators: "First you steal my name, then you try to rob me...."

235

"…Hanging's too good for you!" Taking pity on the weeping Stanlio, Diavolo says he will let him go if he does a competent job of hanging Ollio.

Diavolo looks at the jewels obtained from the coach, but he knows he must follow the Rocbergs in order to get the rest of their fortune.

Stanlio tries to be as gentle as possible in hanging his pal and politely inquires of him if, after the execution, Ollio has a preference for being buried or stuffed. Stanlio carefully explains to his incredulous chum that it would be nice to have Ollio in the living room permanently. The rope branch breaks, Stanlio pleads for another chance. Diavolo resolves to use them as his menservants in a plan to fleece the Rocbergs. Diavolo explains his present guise as the Marquis de San Marco to the boys, and orders the gang to clean Stanlio and Ollio by currycombing.

The Tavern del Cucu. The coach has arrived with Lord and Lady Rocberg.

Lorenzo (Arthur Pierson), Captain of the Carabiniers, is distraught because his poverty is forcing his love, Zerlina (Lucille Browne), to marry another—at her father's insistence. But if the reward money will assure captured, the reward money will assure Lorenzo and Zerlina of sufficient dowry. Meanwhile, Lady Pamela tells her husband that their money is still sewn into her petticoat.

The two lackeys prove to be unstable conveyors of their master's sedan chair. The innkeeper rushes out to assure the Marquis that he can have any room in the inn.

"Any room but ours!," haughtily sniffs Lord Rocberg (James Finlayson). "I would rather sleep in the barn," gallantly avows the Marquis, "rather than discommode you."

Flirting with some serving wenches, Stanlio waves his kerchief and a bull takes up the invitation, wrecking the sedan chair. The bull's owner comes over and asks indignantly what the boys are trying to do to his animal.

237

Ollio reads the sign to Stanlio and tells him that if they capture Diavolo, they have another fortune in their grasp.

Lord Rocberg, painfully suspicious of his wife's yearning for the Marquis, trickily arranges for an assignation between the two younger folk but the forged note suggesting it miscarries. Rocberg hides in Diavolo's room to await his wife...

...but Diavolo meets the lady unexpectedly elsewhere and admires both her beauty and her bauble.

Rocberg, waiting in Diavolo's room, is seized by the boys in the belief he is the bandit. Rocberg is haled outside, Stanlio looks up and discovers Diavolo on the balcony above. Stanlio and Ollio run into the barn, pursued by Diavolo with a drawn knife. The boys flee even to the depths of a well, but Diavolo captures them, securing their loyalty by threatening to cut Ollio's gizzard.

HR-F3-89

The affairs of state are too oppressive, Diavolo tells the landlord (Henry Armetta). Might he have some sleeping powders? The landlord leaves to get them.

Meanwhile, the boys sit on a nearby bench, and for relaxation Stanlio plays his little game of kneesie-earsie-nosie. As Ollio watches in astonishment, Stanlio slaps his knees, crosses his arms, pulls his nose with his left hand while he simultaneously pulls his left ear with his right hand. He again slaps his knees and reverses the pulls, doing all this with casual grace. Ollio attempts it and comes a cropper. The landlord, sent to find the boys, discovers them at their little game, and for the rest of the film is frustratingly committed to learning the kneesie-earsie-nosie.

Stanlio and Ollio are sent with a doctored drink to waft Lord Rocberg to dreamland. Rocberg, considering the source, refuses the drink, and Stanlio consumes it on the grounds that he is apprehensive about its spilling.

Diavolo tells the boys to await his signal, a burst of song, out in the courtyard. Stanlio begins to doze off.

In the courtyard
Stanlio cannot
hold up. The signal
comes and Diavolo
orders them upstairs.

Despite Stanlio's
increasing
lassitude, the
boys find a way to
get up to the balcony.

Leaving the boys hidden and on guard in Zerlina's room, Diavolo searches
Lady Pamela's room for the money. A soldier chorus returning to the inn arouses
Zerlina who leaves her room, and Stanlio falls into her bed asleep. Lorenzo
climbs to Zerlina's room, Diavolo observing him carefully.

In the morning Zerlina is to
be married to her rich and
unwelcome suitor; her
father, the landlord,
encounters the boys in the
yard doing the finger-wiggle,
another of Stanlio's games
that he plays with an ease
infuriating to all would-be
imitators. Both hands are
clasped palms down, fingers
interlocked, with one center
digit sticking out above, and
the other center digit
below. Stanlio's game is
to do this quickly, wiggling
the center fingers frantically
but rhythmically. Frustrated
at this, the landlord tells
Stanlio, "What I wish you, I
could not say!" He sends
the boys to the cellar for wine.

Lady Pamela has been robbed of her jeweled medallion. Diavolo plays his game: he accuses Lorenzo of climbing up the tavern wall the evening before. Lorenzo admits this, but he is willing to be searched. The medallion is conveniently found in his cloak, he protests his innocence and Diavolo silkily says that love will make people do strange things. Lady Pamela will not press charges. Diavolo is asked if he ever encountered Fra Diavolo. He says he has, and sings one of Diavolo's songs, which puts Lord Rocberg (and at least a part of the audience) to sleep.

The boys, meanwhile, dutifully enter the wine cellar. (The look of apprehension is purely for the benefit of the still photographer.)

As usual, help from Stanlio is total encumbrance: he singes Ollio's rear handily. It is decided that a chain of wine-pouring will best serve their task: Ollio to draw a full flagon, passing it to Stanlio, duly receiving an empty one from him—Stanlio to pour the full flagon into a large pitcher. The pitcher is gradually filled and Stanlio is desperate for another source of deposit. It does not occur to him to tell Ollio that the big pitcher is full. Stanlio carefully pours the wine down his own throat, smacking his lips spectacularly at each consummation. In time, Ollio confronts him: "Why, you're spiffed!"

Diavolo, realizing by now that Lady Pamela has secreted the money on her person, tells her he would love to see her wearing the dress from the night before. She agrees, retiring behind a screen.

At the wedding celebration Stanlio develops a laughing jag that Ollio finds irresistible. In the course of it they inadvertently reveal to Lorenzo the true identity of the Marquis de San Marco. Lorenzo has the inn surrounded. In the interim Diavolo has found Lady Pamela's petticoat with its sewn-in money; he hides it inside his shirt. He triumphantly sings the Fra Diavolo theme, terrifying all in the inn...

...save Lorenzo, who engages him in a frenzied duel.

The boys attempt to flee, and in hurdling the counter, Stanlio grabs a small keg. He falls into the middle of the duel and Diavolo's sword becomes stuck in the keg. Diavolo is apprehended.

Diavolo gives up part of the jewelry while still retaining the money. The young lovers are anxious for Rocberg to provide the reward money for Diavolo's capture, but Rocberg says he does not carry large amounts. Diavolo, holding the stolen money, graciously provides it, thrilling the lovers. Diavolo throws Lady Pamela's petticoat over Rocberg's head, and Rocberg prepares to confront her with this ample evidence of her indiscretion.

The three bandits prepare to face the firing squad. Stanlio has only one final request: he would like to blow his nose. He uses his red handkerchief again; two bulls come roaring out of the stable, all the soldiers scatter. Diavolo takes a horse and flees. Stanlio and Ollio, on top of the roof, fall on the back of a bull and ride off madly into the final credits.

THE MIDNIGHT PATROL

1933

Laurel and Hardy Series / Two reels / Sound / Released August 3, 1933, by M-G-M / Produced by Hal Roach / Directed by Lloyd French / Photographed by Art Lloyd / Edited by Bert Jordan / Compositions used in incidental music scoring by Marvin Hatley and Le Roy Shield.

Stan Laurel Himself / *Oliver Hardy* Himself / *Spare-tire thief* Robert Kortman / *His partner* Charlie Hall / *Safecracker* Walter Plinge / *Visitor by cell door* Harry Bernard / *Surly Police Chief Ramsbottom* Frank Brownlee / *Officers* James C. Morton, Stanley (Tiny) Sandford, Edgar Dearing / *Sergeant* Eddie Dunn / *The police radio dispatcher* Billy Bletcher. (Working title: *Calling Car Thirteen*.)

Officers Laurel and Hardy in their radio patrol car have just stopped at a police call box, from which they intently remove their lunch; and Stan accidentally cuts the phone cord in the process. As they eat, the radio operator gives their number: "Calling Car 13…Look out, boys. Somebody's stealing your spare tire. That is all." Two thieves run back to their own car and Stan assures them that if they come back again, he'll arrest them. "Oh, is that *so?*," minces the effeminate member of the thieving pair. Stan throws a brick at them and they return the favor. The radio voice intrudes to tell Stan and Ollie of a man breaking into a house nearby.

Ollie didn't get the address of the break-in, so he drives to the call box to phone headquarters. Finding the cut cord, he tells Stan to find another phone. Stan spots a nearby jewelry store and enters while a burglar (Walter Plinge) is polishing off the safe. Stan apologizes for the intrusion—"It's a good thing you came back to open your store"—and asks if he may use the phone. The burglar is most gracious and Stan calls headquarters to find the address of the break-in. Stan asks the burglar if he's lost the combination, and hearing that he has, stays and tries to help open the safe.

An impatient Ollie comes in, catches the burglar at his little game and brusquely writes him a ticket, telling him he'll have to appear at court on Tuesday. The burglar says he can't appear Tuesday because he is having his hair cut. Wednesday? The burglar consults his datebook and notes a Wednesday engagement at the lower vault of the National Bank and a Thursday visit to a pal in Sing Sing. He *can* however, make it on Monday. Stan and Ollie squabble with each other about their availability that day, and the burglar interrupts impatiently. "Make up your minds one way or the other," he tells them, "or we'll call the whole thing off!" Ollie apologetically suggests a week from Tuesday, and this is mutually and politely agreed upon. The burglar asks one more favor: will they push his stalled car? They do, but Ollie discovers in time that it is *their* car. Just for that, he tells the burglar, he will have to appear *tomorrow*.

244

The boys drive away in their car (from which the tires have been stripped) to the home where a break-in is reported imminent. They see a prowler go into the cellar and follow him. They do not realize the prowler is the owner of the house, locked out.

The boys can't find a satisfactory way into the house...

...so they try the front door. Ollie prevents Stan from ringing the bell. "There's no use wasting any more time," Ollie says. "We'll break in the door and surprise him." At Stan's suggestion, they move back ten paces to get a good flying start. On the ninth step backward, Ollie falls into a fishpond. Next, they decide to use a garden bench as a battering ram, and in swinging it back to get good leverage, Ollie is catapulted into the pond.

Ollie asks a favor of Stan: "Let me do this my way once." They grasp the bench and run with it, crashing smartly through the door. They fall onto the stairs inside, smash through them, and fall into the basement— Ollie dropping into a sauerkraut barrel.

As they sprawl among the sauerkraut, the owner of the house comes down the stairs with shotgun cocked. He falls down the hole in the stairway, and the gun goes off.

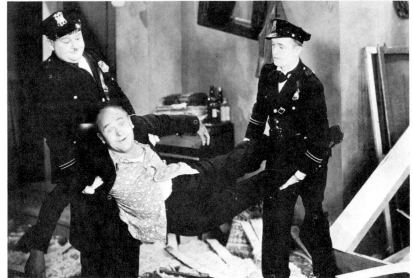

Stan struggles with the man and Ollie hits him over the head with a bottle. The boys haul the owner (Frank Brownlee) off to the police station for robbing a house without a license.

At the station, the policemen salute the owner—Chief Ramsbottom, their superior. Ollie apologizes: "We only started this morning"; but Ramsbottom takes a revolver and fires two shots after the boys as they flee. The policemen all solemnly remove their hats, and Ramsbottom says, "Send for the coroner!"

BUSY BODIES

▪▪▪ 1933

Laurel and Hardy Series / Two reels / Sound / Released October 7, 1933, by M-G-M / Produced by Hal Roach / Directed by Lloyd French / Photographed by Art Lloyd / Edited by Bert Jordan / Sound by James Greene / Compositions used in incidental music scoring by Le Roy Shield, Marvin Hatley, and Alice K. Howlett.

Stan Laurel Himself / *Oliver Hardy* Himself / *Leering foreman* Stanley (Tiny) Sandford / *Double-crossed pal* Charlie Hall / *Another worker* Jack Hill / *Shoveler* Dick Gilbert / *Man with coat* Charley Young.

Stan and Ollie feel euphoric this lovely morning because, in Ollie's words, "It's great to have a good job to go to." At the sawmill where they are employed, Stan hammers a nail in the wall as a peg for his coat, not knowing that the nail has penetrated a water pipe behind the wall. Bossily, Ollie stops Stan from hanging up his coat, hanging up his instead. As he turns away, the nail comes out and water spurts all over his head.

Ollie, unable to get a window frame to move either up or down, asks Stan's help—an inevitable prelude to disaster. Stan forces the frame closed, and as it snaps into position, Ollie's fingers are caught at the top and bottom of the window. After ponderously examining a blueprint of Boulder Dam, Stan feels qualified to help Ollie out of his predicament.

The exertion causes the frame to crash against a man (Charlie Hall) they almost ran over on their way to work this morning. Charlie takes a liking to Stan, however. "You've got a kind face," he tells him.

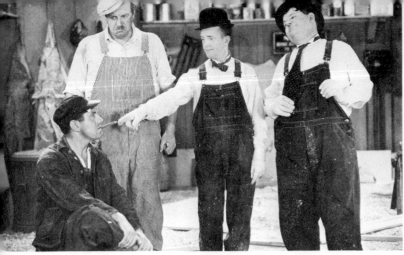

Gratified, Stan gives Charlie a cigar, which he begins to smoke. When the foreman comes by, Stan points to a nearby No Smoking sign, then to Charlie. The foreman takes the vituperative Charlie away as he sputters threats of revenge.

Stan accidentally planes off the seat of Ollie's trousers and tries to glue the piece back on. Ollie bends a saw and lets it hit Stan, who, in turn, takes the brush from a glue pot and sticks it on Ollie's chin.

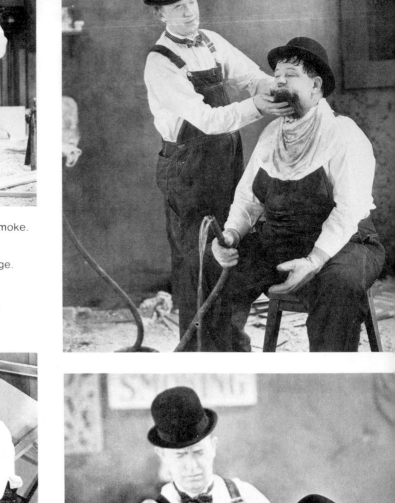

After other indignities heaped on his pal, Stan takes pity on him and tries to pull the brush off, and for the most part succeeds—with the help of a vise, a pair of tin snips, and a newly sharpened plane.

Ollie is accidentally knocked into a sawdust flue, gets caught at the top of it where paddles spank him emphatically, and he is ultimately propelled halfway out the end, where he becomes stuck. Stan gallantly mounts a ladder and brings Ollie his hat. "You dropped this," he points out. "Thank you," Ollie says. Stan tries to pull Ollie out of the flue by his ears, but a workman drops a barrel of shellac into the flue and it comes down to engulf Ollie. But the boys persist…

…and together with the ladder, they crash into a small shed, smashing it to pieces. Their foreman (Tiny Sandford) is in the wreckage. (An instructive example here of how the still cameraman made a more striking photograph. In the film, the *foreman* comes up out of the door, as the boys stand by. For still purposes, the reversal of the action is more interesting.) The boys get into their Model T Ford. The barrel caught in the flue pipe spins out and crashes over Tiny's head. The boys drive off in their car, which is now aimed at a huge band saw. The saw slices the Ford precisely down the middle, leaving Stan and Ollie on either side.

A Laurel & Hardy Cameo Appearance
WILD POSES

1933

Our Gang Series / Two reels / Sound / Released October 28, 1933, by M-G-M / Produced by Robert F. McGowan for Hal Roach / Directed by Robert F. McGowan / Photographed by Francis Corby / Edited by William Terhune / Sound by Harry Baker.

Hal Roach's Rascals George (Spanky) McFarland, Matthew (Stymie) Beard, Tommy Bond, George (Darby) Billings, Jerry Tucker / *Otto Phocus, the prissy portrait photographer* Franklin Pangborn / *Emerson, Spanky's father* Emerson Treacy / *Gay, Spanky's mother* Gay Seabrook / *Cute babies, whom the photograph salesman describes as "two of the most beautiful gorgeous photographic subjects I have ever seen in my life"* Stan Laurel, Oliver Hardy / *Part cut from final release print: New Hal Roach Gangster* George Stevens, Jr.

Spanky's folks take him to be photographed by a dithery photographer, Otto Phocus (Franklin Pangborn), and the burden of the story is Spanky's various forms of resistance to the whole idea.

Stan and Ollie, having played their own children three years earlier in *Brats,* were well disposed for this single medium shot that lasted only 20 seconds. Dressed as babies in nightgowns and bonnets, they fight over a milk bottle. Stan grins into the camera, scratching his head, and Ollie looks into the camera, waving. The giant chair and wall in the scene were left from the huge oversized set used in *Brats.* The photograph salesman in the film describes the boys—not quite accurately—as "two of the most beautiful, gorgeous photographic subjects I have ever seen in my life."

249

DIRTY WORK

1933

Laurel and Hardy Series / Two reels / Sound / Released November 25, 1933, by M-G-M / Produced by Hal Roach / Directed by Lloyd French / Photographed by Kenneth Peach / Edited by Bert Jordan / Sound by William B. Delaplain / Introductory musical compositions by Marvin Hatley and Le Roy Shield.

Stan Laurel Himself / *Oliver Hardy* Himself / *Professor Noodle, the mad scientist* Lucien Littlefield / *Jessup, the butler* Sam Adams / *Monkey* Jiggs.

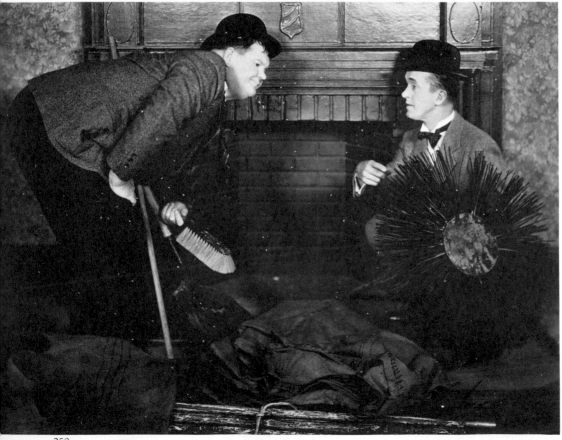

Chimney sweeps Stan and Ollie have come to do a job of work at the home of eccentric Professor Noodle—a gentleman convinced that he has found "the greatest scientific discovery of the age— rejuvenation." With his formula, he is able to make any living thing retrogress to infancy.

The boys, in typical fashion, are not doing the very best job in the world. They have developed a pet phrase: whenever one insults or hurts the other, the injured party says stonily, "I have *nothing* to say."

Ollie asks the rather odd butler (Sam Adams) how to get on the roof. He replies, "The…er…skylight…uh…is in the closet at the top of the stairs. You'll know which is the closet, it has a door on it." "Ohhh!," says Ollie. Stan pushes a broom up the chimney as Ollie looks down it, and receives the broom in his face. Stan pushes up a broom extension; Ollie pulls up the extension and Stan with it, then drops them both down the chimney. Because there is no adequate broom extension for this job, Stan borrows a shotgun and shoots a broom extension up the chimney. The broom zooms up in a cloud of soot, up and up, until it gets itself a duck, which drops down the chimney to Stan. Walking up to the roof, Stan opens the door suddenly as Ollie is bending over, knocking him…

…down below into the greenhouse, partially wrecking it. (Stan is not in this scene, despite the still.)

Stan lets Ollie back in the house and asks if he is hurt. "I have *nothing* to say!," Ollie tells him.

251

Ollie again goes to the roof and, in guiding the extension broom through the chimney, falls down into the fireplace. The boys start to clean up the soot, shoveling it into a sack Ollie is holding. But he is holding it tight against himself, inadvertently opening his pants at the belt—into which Stan pours the soot.

Professor Noodle (Lucien Littlefield) tells the boys they will be "the first to witness the greatest scientific discovery of the age." He brings them to a tank in which swims a duckling the professor has retrogressed from duckdom. After the youth formula is put into the tank, the water bubbles, smoke swirls up and gradually clears—and an egg comes to the surface. The professor now plans demonstration with a human. He searches for his semimad butler, to be used as the subject of the experiment, leaving Stan and Ollie alone in the lab. Experimentally, Ollie puts a fish in the tank and pours in the youth formula. Stan warns Ollie not to pour in too much. Ollie falls in the tank accidentally. Bubbles and smoke arise as Stan looks down into the tank. Then a chimpanzee, wearing Ollie's hat, emerges from the tank and sits next to Stan. "Ollie," Stan asks, "don't you know me? Won't you speak to me?" "I have *nothing* to say," the chimp says, in orotund Hardy tones. Stan cries.

HR-L16-11

68 minutes—Sound
Released December 29, 1933, by M-G-M
Produced by Hal Roach
Directed by William A. Seiter
Associate direction by Lloyd French
Photographed by Kenneth Peach
Edited by Bert Jordan
Titles edited by Nat Hoffberg
Story by Frank Craven
Continuity by Byron Morgan
Dance direction by Dave Bennett
Sound by Harry Baker
Compositions used in incidental music
scoring by Marvin Hatley, William Axt,
George M. Cohan, O'Donnell-Heath,
Marquardt, and Le Roy Shield

Stan Laurel . . . . Himself
Oliver Hardy . . . . Himself

Charley Chase . . . . Himself
Mrs. Lottie Chase Hardy . . . . Mae Busch
Mrs. Betty Laurel . . . Dorothy Christie/Christy
Dr. Horace Meddick,
veterinary . . . . Lucien Littlefield
Exalted/Exhausted Ruler . . . . John Elliott
Sons of the Desert coterie . . . Charley Young,
John Merton, William Gillespie, Charles
McAvoy, Robert (Bobby) Burns, Al
Thompson, Eddie Baker, Jimmy Aub-
rey, Chet Brandenberg, Don Brodie

Assistant Exhausted Ruler . Philo McCullough
Lead hula dancer. . . . . Charita
Bartender . . . . Harry Bernard
Police officer. . . . . Harry Bernard
Waiters. . . . . Sam Lufkin,
Ernie Alexander, Charlie Hall
Man who introduces steamship
official. . . . . Baldwin Cooke
Extra at the Sons convention . Baldwin Cooke

Brawny speakeasy
managers. . . . Stanley Blystone, Max Wagner
Doorman . . . . Pat Harmon
Singer at Sons convention . . . . Ty Parvis
Crowd extra during steamship radiogram scene
. . . Blade Stanhope Conway/Bob Cummings
Sons Oasis "13" crowd dress
extras . . . The Hollywood American Legion Post
People parading in the newsreel
footage . . . . The Santa Monica Lodge of Elks
Voice-over as Mr. Ruttledge . . . . Billy Gilbert
Parts cut from final release print:
Character identifications
unknown . . . . Nina Quartaro,
Lillian Moore, Brooks Benedict.
(Working title: *Fraternally Yours.*)
(Released throughout Europe, variously, as
Sons of the Legion, Convention City, and *Fra-
ternally Yours.*)
(One of the ten top-grossing films of 1934, as
designated by the trade magazines *Film Daily*
and *The Motion Picture Herald.*)

The Exalted Ruler of that splendid social fraternity, the Sons of the Desert, is exhorting all the members at a special meeting to "meet the situation with determination!" At this solemn moment, two latecomers arrive and walk gingerly, and noisily, to their seats down front.

Stan moves his chair closer to his pal who gets his hand stuck, yelling sharply. The Exalted Ruler looks at them stonily, then goes on to declare that every man in the group must do his part. "There must be no weaklings in our midst...The weak must be helped by the strong!" Ollie looks significantly at Stan. The Exalted Ruler, with rising fervor, declares that "this, the oldest lodge in the great order of the Sons of the Desert must be represented 100 percent in our annual convention at Chicago next week!" He tells them to prepare for their oath, an oath that once taken "has never been broken by any man down through the centuries of time."

All the members rise to take a solemn oath committing themselves to attend the Chicago convention (Stan falters a bit), and in answer to the question, "Do you all solemnly swear...," the group thunders, "I do!!" "Me too," says Stan. Later he admits he was reluctant to take the oath because his wife might not let him go. Ollie points out that since Stan has taken the oath, his wife will have to let him go. "That's what I'm worrying about," says Stan. "The Exhausted Ruler said that if...you took an oath, it would have to be broken for...generations and...centuries of...hundreds of years and my wife would let..." "Do you have to ask your wife everything?," Ollie asks scornfully. "Well, if I didn't ask her," Stan says, "I wouldn't know what she wanted me to do." Pityingly, Ollie advises Stan to pattern his life after his. "I go places...and *then* tell my wife. Every man should be the king in his own castle!"

But there is indication that the Hardy castle is ruled by a rather formidable queen—Mrs. Hardy (Mae Busch). Ollie asks his "sugar" if Stan can come in and wait until Betty Laurel returns from duck hunting.

Making himself right at home, Stan helps himself to an apple. It doesn't occur to him that there is anything unusual about it until Ollie points out that it is made of wax— ornamental fruit. "That's the third apple I've missed this week," says Mae. At Stan's instigation, the subject of Ollie's going to the convention is brought up and Mae forcibly informs him that he is not going to Chicago—he is going to the mountains with her. Ollie tries to reason with her but in a rising tirade she informs him that he has no chance of going to Chicago, and she crowns her argument by breaking a vase over his head.

In order to get to the convention, the boys have arranged for Ollie to fake a nervous breakdown. Stan has fixed it for a doctor to come in and prescribe a Honolulu trip for the Hardy nerves. Mae pours hot water for Ollie's nerve-racked feet, and in short order Stan loses the aspirin he is holding; he hunts avidly for it, accidentally propelling both Mae and himself into the tub. Stan carries the tub out to the kitchen, bumps into Mae, knocking her down. Mae throws the tub at Stan...

...but misses. Just then the doctor arrives but there is something unusual about him. "Why did you get a veterinarian?," asks Ollie. "Well," says Stan, "I didn't think his religion would make any difference." The good doctor suspects Ollie's may be a case of "Canus Delirous," and in administering a pill to the afflicted one, taps him on the nose and says, "Sit up. Sit up. Open your mouth." The doctor recommends the Honolulu trip but, as anticipated, this forbids Mae's presence because she is a very bad sailor. Ollie insists that Stan must go with him but Stan reveals that his wife said he could go to Chicago, and he plans to do so. Frustrated, Ollie says that under the circumstances he will not go to Honolulu. "Oh, yes, you are," Mae tells him. "You're going to Honolulu if you have to go alone!" "Well," says Ollie, indicating Stan, "if I have to go to Honolulu alone, *he's* going with me!"

In Chicago, a few of the Sons have discovered the ultimate in gags: placing a wallet on the floor and giving those who pick it up a warm welcome.

The prime mover among the kidders is a hearty type from Texas (Charley Chase), who boasts that not even in California do they grow flowers "that smell like this."

Ollie smells it and gets a squirt of water in the smeller. "That's a darb, isn't it, boy?," chortles Charley.

Charley ebulliently insists on a round of champagne, and the waiters (Sam Lufkin and Charlie Hall) oblige.

As a tenor (Ty Parvis) and a hula dancer (Charita) render the bouncy song "Honolulu Baby," Ollie is delighted because he and Stan have killed several birds with one stone: they're seeing as much here as they would in Honolulu; they've had a swell time; and nobody's the wiser. But fate closes in. On their way home the news is released that the ship the boys were reputedly on during their return from Hawaii has sunk. Mae and Betty Laurel go down to the steamship company to learn the details.

Meanwhile the boys come home, liberally Hawaiianized. The cabby comes around to reach for the door but Stan opens it smartly, knocking him to the ground. Stan puts his suitcase down and the cabby falls over it. "Here you are, old man," Ollie tells him, "just keep the change."

Ollie sings "Honolulu Baby" joyously as Stan rings his own bell. (The Laurels and the Hardys live next door to each other, a providential arrangement for this plot.) Once inside, they read the newspaper story of their supposed ship's demise. Panic-stricken, they look and see their wives getting out of a cab.

The boys hide in the Hardy attic. "Oh, I have the strangest feeling," Mae tells Betty Laurel, "I feel as if they were hovering right over me."

Ollie proposes that they fix themselves a nice bed where they'll be just as comfortable as two peas in a pod. "To catch a Hardy," says Ollie proudly, "they've got to get up very early in the morning." "What time?," asks Stan. "Oh, about half past—" says Ollie, then catching himself up, retorts scornfully, "What *time!*"

Mae and Betty (Dorothy Christy) relax at the movies as they wait for the rescue ship to come in. Suddenly they find themselves staring unbelievingly at newsreel footage of the Sons of the Desert conclave. There, skipping down a Chicago street during the convention parade, they see Stan and Ollie having the time of their lives.

Stan congratulates Ollie: "I've certainly got to hand it to you." "For what?," Ollie asks. Stan replies, "Well, for the meticulous care with which you have executed your finely formulated machinations in extricating us from this devastating dilemma." Ollie stares piteously at the camera. A storm commences but the boys feel secure in the attic. "We're just like two peas in a pot," says Stan. "Not pot," Ollie corrects him. "Pod-*duh.*" "Pod-*duh*," says Stan. A vagrant lightning flash suddenly touches the rope holding up their improvised bed and it crashes to the floor.

The ladies determine to investigate...

...but the boys flee to the roof...

...where they are all prepared to go exactly nowhere. It begins to rain. Stan wants to go down and confess all to the girls but Ollie says, "If you go downstairs and spill the beans, I'll tell Betty that I caught you smoking a cigarette!" Horrified, Stan gives in, and, indeed, comes up with an idea of sorts: "We'll climb down the garage and we'll change our clothes in the drainpipe; then we'll go to a hotel and we'll be just as comfortable as two peas in a pod-*duh!*"

They both go down the drainpipe—into a full rain barrel—and are confronted by a cop (Harry Bernard) who extracts their addresses from them by dealing primarily with Stan.

The boys unravel their alibis. It seems a terrible storm came up ("we floundered in a typhoid!," explains Stan), and they both dived overboard just as the boat was going down for the third time. Mae, in a voice of steel, informs them that the rescue ship with the survivors aboard does not get in until tomorrow. Stan explains that it must have got there after they left—and *they* left, Ollie and he, by *ship-hiking*. Mae grimly tells Betty that Stan, whatever Betty's hopes, is no different from the rest of mankind: "They're both like two peas in a pod." "Pod-*duh!*," Stan corrects her.

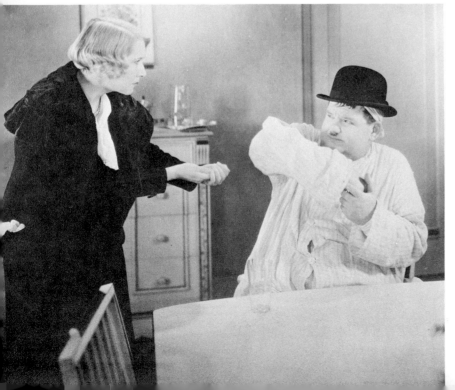

But Ollie insists their story is true. "Why, it's too farfetched *not* to be the truth. Isn't it, Stanley?" "It's imposterous!," affirms Stan. Betty cooingly convinces Stan to tell the truth, which he does, tearfully. The Laurels leave and Mae confronts her mate. Ollie tips his hat to her and asks winsomely, "How about you and me goin' to the mountains?" Mae runs out to the kitchen and begins to pull dishes out of the cupboard, stacking them up in the sink. "You're not movin' out tonight, are you, sugar?," Ollie asks.

Betty mixes Stan a drink and says, "See, Stanley? Honesty is the best policy."

Stan agrees—as the sound of a battle royal is heard next door.

Ollie armors himself against the continuing assault. After it subsides, the doorbell rings and Stan enters to ask what Mae said. "Never mind what she said," Ollie tells him. "What did Betty say?" "Betty said honesty was the best politics," Stan replies. "Look!" He puffs at a cigarette and goes out singing "Honolulu Baby" as Ollie vengefully hurls a pot at him.

OLIVER THE EIGHTH

Laurel and Hardy Series / Two reels / Sound / Released January 13, 1934, by M-G-M / Produced by Hal Roach / Directed by Lloyd French / Photographed by Art Lloyd / Edited by Bert Jordan / Sound by William B. Delaplain / Compositions used in incidental music scoring by Le Roy Shield and Ray Henderson.

Stan Laurel Himself / *Oliver Hardy* Himself / *Eccentric widow at Box 204J* Mae Busch / *Jitters, the butler* Jack Barty / Part cut from final release print: *Laundryman* Charlie Hall. (Title is probably a play on the previous year's Alexander Korda film, *The Private Life of Henry VIII*, and was in fact released in Great Britain as *The Private Life of Oliver the Eighth.*)

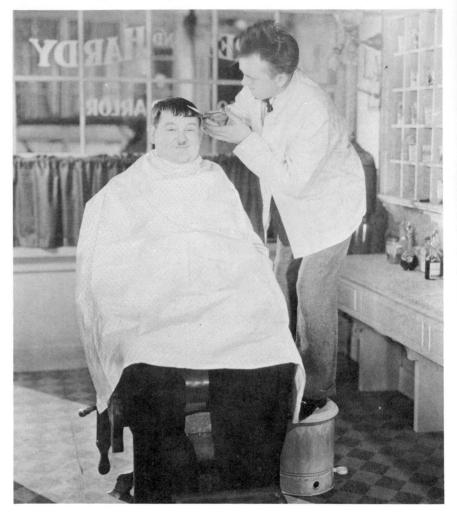

Stan and Ollie are barbers but they always have their eyes on the main chance. They part company, however, on the subject of who they would marry for money. Ollie proudly insists he would never marry an ugly lady for her fortune. Stan, however, has no doubts. "Well, after all, beauty's only skin-deep. I'd take some of the money and I'd have her face lifted; then I could settle down and I... I wouldn't have to scrape chins anymore ...I wouldn't have to work hard anymore. Er..." "Tell me that again," says Ollie. Stan does, in his own wonderful fashion: "Er...if beauty was only knee... skin-deep, I could take some of the money and I could have her skinned and ...then she'd be able to look at the clock without havin' to work hard anymore; then we could settle down .. and I could scrape her chin and congenial...if...if I didn't have to work hard anymore." "That's a *good* idea," says Ollie.

What got the boys off on this tangent is an ad in the Personals Column of the newspaper: a widow with a large fortune wishes to communicate with a congenial young man. Object—matrimony. The boys both decide to write her—and may the best man win.

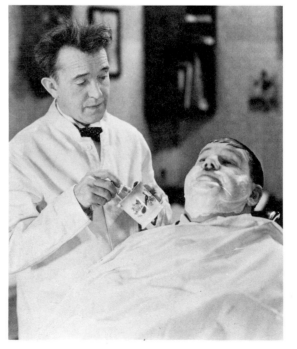

Confident that he is unarguably the best man, Ollie takes Stan's letter and does not mail it. The Hardy philosophy is, essentially: I am bigger,

therefore I am better. He settles back for a comfortable shave, which he regards as his proprietary due. Ollie's letter is delivered to the widow (Mae Busch), who exults fiendishly on seeing the name Oliver. Her butler asks, "Another Oliver? Is he to share the same fate as the other seven Olivers?" "And why not?," the widow sneers. "It was an Oliver who first came into my life and double-crossed me—left me on the eve of my wedding, and I've sworn to take revenge on every Oliver that crosses my path." "Strange," the butler ponders ponderously, "that on the eve of every wedding, you walk in your sleep—and in the morning a body is found with its throat cut!"

Ollie appears at Mae's but is discomforted by the appearance of Stan who, as partner, wants *his* half. As for the barbershop, Stan sold it—for a beautiful gold brick, and some nuts.

Ollie wonders about Mae's butler Jitters—a man with the uningratiating habit of playing solitaire without cards. Mae says Jitters is crazy but dangerous only if one fails to humor him. Mae picks an imaginary spot off Ollie's tie.

Mae cuts Ollie's tie in half, throws both the tie end and the scissors over her shoulder. The butler blows a bugle to announce dinner.

The butler (Jack Barty) serves an imaginary dinner. Mae and Ollie toast each other with imaginary water. Stan can't imagine anything, including the fact that he is present.

Later, the butler in speaking of Mae tells the boys confidentially, "Don't believe a word she says. Ha! She's the one that's crazy—not me. Did you ever have your throat cut?" "No," says Ollie. "Well," the butler says, "you're going to...When you're asleep tonight, she's going to come into your room and cut your throat, the same as she did to seven other Olivers."

The boys prepare to leave but Mae forestalls them. She makes sure all the doors are locked—and Stan and Ollie consigned to the guest chamber where, says Mae to them, "I hope you have a nice *long sleep!*"

Mae bids a strong good-bye. "Good-bye —Oliver the *Eighth!*" The butler blows "Taps" expressively.

The butler bids them good-bye personally—and locks them in.

The boys find a shotgun. Ollie asks if it's loaded; Stan finds out by shooting through the seat of Ollie's pajamas. Meantime, Mae asks the butler if the knife is good and sharp. It is.

Stan has been ordered to stay awake on the first shift of guard duty. Ollie awakens him a few minutes later, but Stan defends himself: "Well, I couldn't help it. I was dreamin' I was awake and then I woke up and found myself asleep!"

In readying the gun, Stan dispenses a shell that flies out and arouses Ollie. Ollie ties a string around the gold brick, puts the brick on the chandelier, ties the string around a candle on the dresser. He pulls a drawer out of the dresser, ties a string around it and explains that as the flame gets near the string, Stan must move the string down. If he doesn't, the string will burn and the brick will hit him—all this to insure wakefulness.

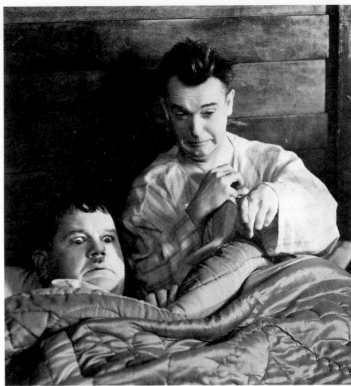

Stan sees a man's hand holding onto the foot of the bed. He shoots it; it is Ollie's foot. In short order, the flame burns the string and the brick falls on Ollie's head. Mae is heard approaching, sharpening her knife. Stan runs into the closet, looking for the shotgun. Mae poises the knife above Ollie's throat...

...and it has all been Ollie's very bad dream in the soft recesses of the barber chair.

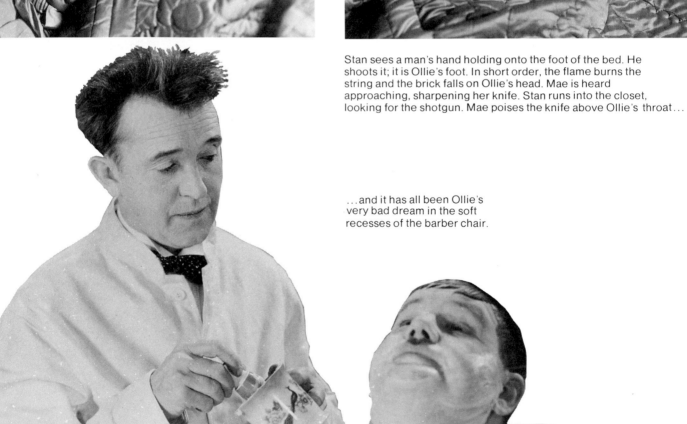

Hollywood Party   ▮▮▮   1934

68 minutes—Sound

Filmed in black and white, but with one Technocolor sequence

Released June 1, 1934, by M-G-M

Produced by Harry Rapf and Howard Dietz for M-G-M

Directed by Richard Boleslawski, Allan Dwan, and Roy Rowland (uncredited)

Photographed by James Wong Howe

"Red-Hot Chocolate Soldiers" animated cartoon sequence in Technicolor by courtesy of Walt Disney Productions, Ltd.

Edited by George Boemler

Original screenplay by Howard Dietz and Arthur Kober

Art direction by Fredric Hope

Interior direction by Edwin B. Willis

Costumes by Adrian

Dance numbers arranged by Seymour Felix, George Hale, and David Gould

Music and lyrics by Richard Rodgers and Lorenz Hart; Walter Donaldson and Gus Kahn; Nacio Herb Brown and Arthur Freed

Stan Laurel	Himself
Oliver Hardy	Himself
Jimmy Durante	Himself
Schnarzan the shouting conqueror	Jimmy Durante
Mrs. Jean Durante	Herself
Lupe Velez	Herself
Jaguar woman	Lupe Velez
Ted Healy	Himself
and his Stooges:	
Moe Howard	Himself
Jerry (Curly) Howard	Himself
Larry Fine	Himself
Frances Williams	Herself
Robert Young	Himself
Harvey Clemp	Charles Butterworth
Henrietta Clemp	Polly Moran
Beavers, the doorman	Tom Kennedy
Charley	Ben Bard
Knapp, Schnarzan's manager	Richard Carle
Liondora, the rival star	George Givot
Bob	Eddie Quillan
Baron Munchausen, the intrepid explorer	Jack Pearl
Linda, the Klemp's niece	June Clyde
Cabdriver	Leonid Kinskey
Bartender	Tom Herbert
Paul Revere, in flashback	Tom London
Theatre manager	Jed Prouty
Singers	Arthur Jarrett, Harry Barris, The Shirley Ross Quartet
Buddy Goldfard, Liondora's manager	Edwin Maxwell
Scientific pedants	Rychard Cramer, Clarence Wilson, Nora Cecil
Holding the door for the scientific gentlemen	Baldwin Cooke
Opening scenes dress extra	Bess Flowers
Seated at the table during bidding	Muriel Evans
Butlers	Sidney Bracy, Arthur Treacher
Show girl	Irene Hervey
Party guest	Frank Austin
Theatre patron	Ray Cooke
Servant at the party	Ernie Alexander
Voice-over for Mickey Mouse	Walt Disney
Voice-over for the Big Bad Wolf	Billy Bletcher

(The animated cartoon characters appear on screen together with and at the same time as human actors.)

Schnarzan, mighty jungle-film star, polo player, and dilettante sculptor (Jimmy Durante) is warned by his manager that his pictures are flopping because the public knows that all his lions are anemic. Explorer Baron Munchausen (Jack Pearl) is on his way from Africa with a fresh batch of lions that Schnarzan covets but a rival jungle-film star, Liondora (George Givot), plots the theft of the animals.

Schnarzan throws a party for the Baron, and in the course of the festivities many Hollywood personalities appear and do little but walk around and pretend to be themselves. The real owners of the lions show up in the persons of Stan and Ollie. Their brief appearance toward the end of the film consists primarily of a sequence with peppery Lupe Velez. The New York *Herald Tribune*, appreciatively reviewing this bit, describes it: "Miss Velez...kicks off her dainty golden slipper. After a spirited debate, Mr. Laurel wins the right from Mr. Hardy to return the lady's footwear, whereupon she throws it at him. Mr. Hardy then impulsively takes off his own slipper and is about to crack her over the head with it when his companion interferes. At which Miss Velez, seated at a bar upon which a bowl of eggs is handy, deftly breaks an egg in two, and pours the contents into the shoe held by the amazed Mr. Hardy. This naturally leads to the breaking of more eggs in the bowl in a fierce battle for supremacy."
This is followed by Stan and Ollie accidentally loosing a lion on the party; a stampede to the exits ensues, followed by the mighty Schnarzan vanquishing the big cat. However, Schnarzan has lost his new lions to a rich Oklahoman (Charles Butterworth) who has purchased them by connivance with Liondora. Schnarzan tells the Oklahoman's wife (Polly Moran) that if she'll sell him the lions, she can play opposite him in a picture. The deal is made.

Arriving at the party, the boys are met with great deference by the footmen—and with a rather more prosaic greeting from the butler (Tom Kennedy). "Whadda ya want?," he asks. The boys explain that Baron Munchausen bought some lions from them and they have been all over town trying to cash the check he gave them.

The check is made out for "50,000 tiddlywinks," the Baron having explained that a tiddlywink is worth a dollar and a half in his country. "That is," says Ollie, "at the present rate of exchange." The butler slams the door on them. Ollie rings the bell again...

...and the butler opens the door, demanding to know who rang. "I did!," says Ollie. The butler boffs him on the head, and slams the door again. But the boys contrive to lock the butler out.

Inside, they yell loudly for the Baron.

Stan whistles, and Ollie admonishes him not to be rude. Ollie asks a man nearby if he has seen Baron Munchausen. "Oh, yes! Many times!," says the man appreciatively.

At the bar, Lupe Velez demands service but the bartender tells her Mr. Durante has ordered that she is to have nothing to drink. Lupe throws a tantrum, and as the boys walk up, she tells them sternly, "You keep out of this! So you wanna fight me, eh?"

The reciprocal egg-breaking sequence commences; and ends with Stan putting an egg on Lupe's barstool and Ollie telling her, "Sit down, I want to talk to you." Lupe tells him to "make it snappy," and sits on the egg. Ollie laughs, Stan joins in. Lupe laughs, then starts to chase the boys...

...who run into the butler. The lions break loose and confusion roars unchecked.

Production Sidelights

Playing checkers on the set.

A prop fish makes an awfully good prop.

"Extra" added attractions.

Babe selecting his favorites, Agua Caliente racetrack, Mexico, 1934.

269

Going Bye-Bye!

■ ■ ■   **1934**

Laurel and Hardy Series / Two reels / Sound /
Released June 23, 1934, by M-G-M / Produced
by Hal Roach / Directed by Charles Rogers
/ Photographed by Francis Corby / Edited by
Bert Jordan / Sound by Harry Baker / Intro-
ductory musical composition by Le Roy Shield.

Stan Laurel Himself / *Oliver Hardy* Himself /
Butch Long Walter Long / *Long's vamp girl
friend* Mae Busch / *Man who offers friendly
advice* Sam Lufkin / *Judge* Harry Dunkinson /
Courtroom dress extras Ellinor Van Der Veer,
Baldwin Cooke, Fred Holmes, Jack (Tiny) Lipson, Lester Dorr, Charles Dorety. (Working
title: *On Their Way Out.*)

The judge congratulates two virtuous gentlemen on behalf of the state for having furnished the court with evidence used to bring a notorious criminal to justice. The criminal is sentenced to life imprisonment but Stan asks, with some surprise, "Aren't you going to hang him?"

Butch, the criminal (Walter Long), shouts, "You rats! I'll get even with you if it's the last thing I ever do!…and when I *do* get out, I'll break off your legs and I'll wrap 'em around your necks!"

Butch almost breaks loose, and the courtroom spectators trample over Ollie and Stan.

A bystander (Sam Lufkin) tells them Butch has the memory of an elephant.

Ollie mimics Stan's expression in the courtroom when he asked, "Aren't you going to hang him?" Deciding that getting out of town will be a politic thing to do, the boys prepare to advertise for a companion to help drive and share expenses. Stan will put the ad in the paper.

Stan can't read their ad because he is wearing Ollie's glasses. Ollie reads it instead. It ends with the stimulating afterthought: "P.S. Those not interested, do not answer." Ollie approves sarcastically.

While packing, they decide they might need milk. Stan takes a can of it from the shelf, and in so doing, a razor blade is knocked off into a clothes brush. The phone rings and Stan answers. It's for Ollie. Stan lets the receiver dangle and hands the can of milk to Ollie. Ollie puts the can to his ear and says hello. Wondering at the bad connection, he sees the receiver hanging from the phone. Dropping the milk, he takes proper control of the phone to utter one of the classic lines in all film comedy, "Er—excuse me, please. My ear is full of milk." He quickly tells Stan to brush off the Hardy coat. Stan does so, with interesting results. Meanwhile, Butch Long has escaped. He flees to the apartment of his girl friend (Mae Busch), who is busily packing when he appears. He has an account to settle, he tells her, "A couple of mugs opened their traps too wide." Doorbell. Panicky, Mae hides Butch in a trunk in her bedroom.

The boys bring flowers for their potential traveling companion. Mae asks nervously if the boys could make room for a friend of hers who is awfully anxious to leave town. "The more the merrier," chuckles Ollie. Stan explains they must leave soon because a certain fellow has promised—if he ever catches up with them—that their legs will be broken and tied around their necks.

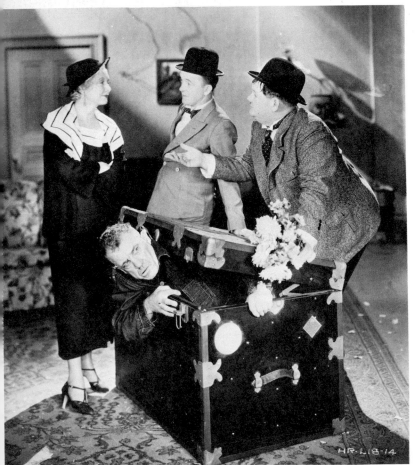

(This action does not occur in the film; very much a posed still, it nonetheless encapsulates the trouble abrewing.) In the film's action, Mae has lost the key to her trunk, depriving Butch of the chance to come out and meet her new friends.

The boys will help. Stan energetically applies a brace and bit to give Mae's friend some air. Butch suggests the boys get a blowtorch and melt the lock off. The flame shoots against the side of the trunk and Butch's clothes catch fire. The boys force a water hose into the trunk and blast away. Butch blubbers inside.

The trunk breaks open, and Butch yells, "I told you I'd get you!"

(Not in the film. The last shot is of Stan and Ollie on the divan with legs twisted around their necks and Butch, in custody, exultantly telling them he *said* he'd get them. Ollie tells Stan, "Well, here's another fine mess you've gotten me into!" Stan cries, saying, "Well, I couldn't help it…")

273

THEM THAR HILLS

■■■ 1934

Laurel and Hardy Series / Two reels / Sound / Released July 21, 1934, by M-G-M / Produced by Hal Roach / Directed by Charles Rogers / Photographed by Art Lloyd / Edited by Bert Jordan / Sound by James Greene / Compositions used in incidental music scoring by Hill, Le Roy Shield, and Marvin Hatley.

Stan Laurel Himself / *Oliver Hardy* Himself / *Doctor* Billy Gilbert / *Sullen motorist who runs out of gas* Charlie Hall / *Hall's wife* Mae Busch / *Moonshiners* Bobby Dunn, Sam Lufkin, Dick Alexander / *Officers* Eddie Baker, Baldwin Cooke, Robert (Bobby) Burns. (Antecedent for *Tit for Tat*, half a year later.)

Ollie has the gout. Too much high living, the doctor tells him. "Maybe we better move down to the basement," says Stan.

"Go out into the country," the doctor (Billy Gilbert) says. "Get away from all this wild life. Remember, you can't burn the candle at both ends. Take a trip up into the mountains. Drink plenty of water— and *lots* of it."

Stan suggests they rent a house trailer to hook onto the back of their car. Stan prepares to carry him down to the car, but Ollie's suspenders catch on a table...

...and the boys are snapped back through the bathroom doorway into a full tub.

Stan sits on the bath stool and hands a towel to Ollie. Ollie hits him with a long-handled bath brush. Stan cries.

Up in the mountains, at an old shack, moonshiners and federal agents are shooting at each other. Deciding to run, the moonshiners dump their liquor in the well, and are finally caught and taken away. Minutes later, the boys arrive and are particularly elated to find the well. "It's just what the doctor ordered," says Ollie.

When Stan asks what they'll have for dinner, Ollie suggests a plate of beans and a pot of steaming hot coffee. "Swell!," says Stan with admiring enthusiasm. "You sure know how to plan a meal!" Stan is deputized to fix the coffee. In so doing he is struck by the unusual color of the well water. "It's the iron in it," says Ollie. "That's the way all mountain water tastes. That's why the doctor said to drink plenty of it." Stan tastes it. "It tickles," he says. They sing "The Old Spinning Wheel" in lively fashion.

On a nearby mountain road two tourists (Mae Busch and Charlie Hall) are walking along in unhappy frame of mind. They are out of gas. Mae sees the boys' trailer and decides to investigate the possibility of borrowing some fuel. They are courteously received and Charlie borrows the gas. The thirsty Mae asks for water, and is much struck by its deliciousness. "It's the iron in it," says Ollie. Mae asks Charlie if he wants some. No. "OK, baby," she says, winking, "you don't know what you're missin'."

Mae decides to wait with the boys while Charlie takes the gas to their car. The water tastes better and better. They sing "There's an old spinning wheel in the parlor—*PUM PUM!*" Charlie drives up to the trailer and is puzzled by the hilarity coming therefrom. He walks in to find his wife in a considerably stimulated condition and tries to haul her away. She goes, with merry reluctance. Charlie asks what the boys mean by getting his wife drunk?

Now begins a sequence in which the three heap mutual indignities on each other. Charlie hits Ollie; Stan puts butter on Charlie's head; Charlie pushes Stan's head in the pail; Stan cuts a wad of hair from Charlie's head and affixes it to Charlie's chin with molasses. Ollie laughs and Stan takes a moist plunger and presses it against Charlie's forehead. Stan cuts Charlie's belt, forcing him to use natural suspenders. Ollie pours molasses over Charlie's head; Stan takes up a pillow, from which Ollie takes feathers to throw on Charlie. Charlie detaches the boys' trailer from their car; the boys roll out on the ground. Charlie pours the kerosine from a lamp on Ollie, asks Stan for a match, Stan obliges. Ollie is ignited.

Ollie stamps around, clothes afire. "Why don't you jump in the well?," asks Stan. "The water'll put it out!" Ollie thanks him and jumps in. Ollie is exploded from the well and comes down in sad repose.

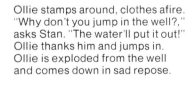

BABES in TOYLAND

79 minutes—Sound
Released November 30, 1934, by M-G-M
Produced by Hal Roach
Directed by Charles Rogers and Gus Meins
Photographed by Art Lloyd
and Francis Corby
Edited by William Terhune
and Bert Jordan
Screenplay by Nick Grinde
and Frank Butler
Adapted from the musical comedy
by Victor Herbert
Book and lyrics by Glen MacDonough
Sound by Elmer R. Raguse
Music direction by Harry Jackson
Music composed by Victor Herbert
and Glen MacDonough; and Ann Ronell
and Frank Churchill

Stannie Dum	Stan Laurel
Ollie Dee	Oliver Hardy
Little Bo-Peep	Charlotte Henry
Tom-Tom	Felix Knight
Evil Silas Barnaby	Harry Kleinbach/Henry Brandon
Little Boy Blue	Johnny Downs
Curly Locks	Jean Darling
Mary Quite Contrary	Marie Wilson
Mother Goose	Virginia Karns
Widow Peep	Florence Roberts
The Toy Maker	William Burress
Santa Claus	Ferdinand Munier
Justice of the peace	Frank Austin
Candle Snuffer	Gus Leonard
Barnaby's minion	John George
Schoolchildren	Scotty Beckett, Marianne Edwards, Tommy Bupp, Georgie Billings, Jerry Tucker, Jackie Taylor, Dickie Jones
Little Miss Muffett	Alice Dahl
Cat and the Fiddle	Pete Gordon
Tom Thumb	Sumner Getchell
Chief of police	Billy Bletcher
Two of the Three Little Pigs:	
Jiggs	Payne Johnson
Elmer	Angelo Rossitto
Fisherman	Charley Rogers
Queen of Hearts	Alice Moore
Mother Hubbard	Alice Cooke
Old King Cole	Kewpie Morgan
Duckers	Stanley (Tiny) Sandford, Eddie Baker
King's guards	Dick Alexander, Richard Powell
Town crier	Scott Mattraw
Balloon man	Fred Holmes
Demon Bogeymen	Jack Raymond, Eddie Borden
Toyland townspeople	Sam Lufkin, Jack Hill, Baldwin Cooke, Charlie Hall.

(Reissued as *Revenge Is Sweet, March of the Toys*, and *March of the Wooden Soldiers*.)

(Laurel and Hardy's roles in *Babes in Toyland* were originally conceived by Hal Roach as Simple Simon and the Pie Man; parts they did "play," in turn, in a 1938 Walt Disney cartoon, *Mother Goose Goes Hollywood*, which was nominated for an Academy Award.)

Mother Goose emerges from her good book, singing "Toyland," as the pages flutter over and Toyland's inhabitants are seen. One page coming to life is captioned, "Stannie Dum and Ollie Dee loved to sleep as you can see." Riding the air between their respective exhalations is a feather, which Stannie finally swallows, causing him to laugh in his sleep.

The nasty Silas Barnaby (Henry Brandon) approaches Mother Peep about the mortgage due distressingly soon, then inquires about Bo-Peep's whereabouts. Appropriately finding her with her sheep, Barnaby presents the lovely girl (Charlotte Henry) with a bouquet, saying, "Good-morning, my pretty little butterfly. Just a fragrant token of my devotion." He proposes marriage; she rejects his rather clammy hand.

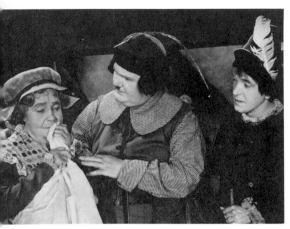

Stannie and Ollie (who live upstairs in the shoe) come below to find Mother Peep (Florence Roberts) distraught. She says Barnaby's hold on the mortgage means eviction for them all. Ollie insists she take the boys' life savings, and when she protests, he says, "Tut-tut-tut-ta-*rut*. One good turn deserves another." Stannie brings in their money box, but it contains only a $1.48 I.O.U. from Stannie who took the money . . .

. . . for an urgent necessity. "I needed a new peewee," he explains. "I lost three of them playing with Little Jack Horner." Ollie tells Mother Peep he'll ask the Toy Maker for help. Crossing his fingers, Ollie boasts he and the Toy Maker are just like *that*. "Which are you?," asks Stannie.

If his money is going to be expended on peewees, Ollie wants to learn all about them. Stannie shows him how to hit the little wooden peewee with the stick. Ollie's performance is less than brilliant.

278

At the toy factory, the Toy Maker (William Burress) tells the boys they are late for work. Stannie urges Ollie to speak to the Toy Maker about Mother Peep's plight . . .

. . . but the Toy Maker is not in a receptive frame of mind after Stannie accidentally releases a little locomotive, which knocks a can of paint onto their boss.

Bo-Peep, once again, has lost her sheep, but her devoted swain, Tom-Tom (Felix Knight), comforts her with a song, "Don't Cry, Bo-Peep."

Tom-Tom gently pinions her in the stocks so he can steal a kiss. The townspeople sneak up behind and revel in Tom-Tom's announcement of his engagement to Bo-Peep.

Celebration follows, with special high-jinks from a cat (Pete Gordon), a fiddle, and Mickey Mouse (played by a monkey).

At the toy factory Santa Claus (Ferdinand Munier) comes in to see all the new playthings. The Toy Maker displays one of the new soldiers Santa ordered. But Santa says there is a great mistake: he ordered 600 soldiers one foot high. Unfortunately Stannie took the order, and the result has been 100 soldiers six feet high. Stannie and Ollie are fired...

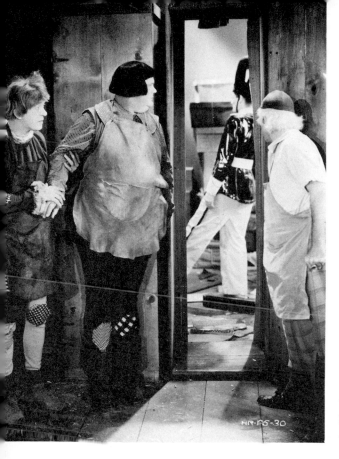

...and as they try to put the big toy soldier back in the box, it runs amok...

...destroying most of the toy factory. Stannie asks Ollie if he isn't going to ask the Toy Maker about the money. The boys are thrown out.

Meanwhile, Barnaby again proposes, but Mother Peep is confident Stannie and Ollie will save the day. The boys enter, dejected. Stannie says Ollie made a bit of a mistake: he and the Toy Maker are *not* like *that.* Ollie reaches into Barnaby's pocket for the mortgage but finds only a very efficient mousetrap —prompting Barnaby to say, "Big bait catches big rat."

Barnaby leaves, and Stannie says, "I'd like to put on this shoe and kick him right in the pants." Barnaby hits Stannie on the head, and as the nasty man leaves, Stannie conks him with a peewee.

The plan is for Stannie to take Ollie in a big box to
Barnaby's house, offering it as a Christmas present. This
will allow Ollie to steal the mortgage when Barnaby
sleeps. As Stannie moves the box across the street, he
says to his pal that they are almost there. "So far, so
good," says Ollie. "It wasn't so far," says Stannie. "We
just came across the street." Stannie gives the Christmas
box to Barnaby who is understandably baffled to receive
it in the middle of July. "Well, we always do our Christmas
shopping early" is the explanation. Stannie agrees with
Barnaby's compliment that this is awfully nice of him.

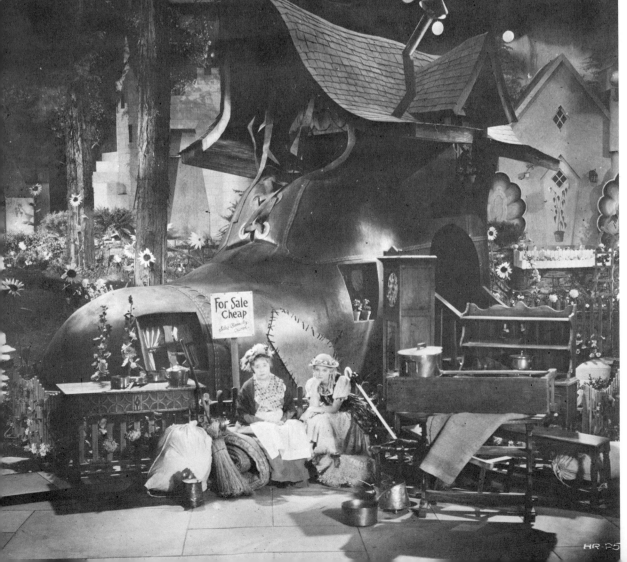

All is going famously
until Stannie says
good-night to
Barnaby, following
it up with "Good-night,
Ollie!" The reply from
the box is prompt:
"Good-night,
Stannie!" The plot
collapses. (Victor
Herbert's song, "I
Can't Do the Sum,"
is not sung in the
film but is invariably
used as leitmotif for
Stannie and Ollie.)

Mother Peep has
been dispossessed.

The boys have been found guilty of burglary, and after a stay in the stocks, they are to be dunked and exiled to Bogeyland forever. As they sit in the stocks, Ollie looks at Stannie and says witheringly, "Good-*night*, Ollie!"

After Stannie kindly holds his watch to keep it from immersion, Ollie is dunked...

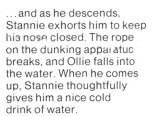

...and as he descends, Stannie exhorts him to keep his nose closed. The rope on the dunking apparatus breaks, and Ollie falls into the water. When he comes up, Stannie thoughtfully gives him a nice cold drink of water.

Bo-Peep rushes in and says to stop it all. She will marry Barnaby. Stannie and Ollie are freed by Old King Cole (Kewpie Morgan), and Stannie rejoices that he will not be dunked. "Oh, no?," says Ollie, pushing his pal into the water. "Ollie," says Stannie, "here's your watch!"

Bo-Peep is being readied for the wedding; Ollie is to be best man. He looks at Stannie and says, "If you hadn't said 'Good-night, Ollie,' this wouldn't have happened."

Mother Peep goes to reason with Barnaby but Ollie doesn't believe it will do any good. "You're right, Ollie," Stannie says, "you can't turn blood into a stone...her talking to Barnaby is just a matter of pouring one ear into another and coming out the other side." Ollie says to Bo-Peep, "Why, you know, Stannie is so upset—he's not even going to the wedding." Turning to his pal, Ollie asks, "You are upset, aren't you?" "Upset?," Stannie says tearfully. "I'm *housebroken!*"

After the justice of the peace (Frank Austin) pronounces the pair man and wife, Ollie asks Barnaby if he hasn't forgotten something. Barnaby gives over the mortgage and Ollie tears it up. The bridegroom lifts the veil to kiss his lady—who turns out to be Stannie. Barnaby asks the meaning of this. "Big bait," Ollie says comfortingly, "catches big rat." Barnaby rushes off, shouting that the king shall hear of this. Ollie tells Stannie good-bye: he must stay here with Barnaby. "I don't want to stay here with him," says Stannie. Ollie asks why and Stannie replies, "I don't *love* him."

Tom-Tom tells Bo-Peep they will have no more trouble because he is going to take her away with him—the cue for the song, "Castles in Spain."

Spoiling for revenge, Barnaby decides to pignap one of the Three Little Pigs— Elmer.

Barnaby tells his henchman (John George) to take the cat, the fiddle, and some sausage to Tom-Tom's house and plant them there. The sausage is to be conclusive evidence that Tom-Tom not only did the pignapping but thoroughly disposed of his victim.

Tom-Tom, accused of the crime, cannot refute the evidence, and is banished to Bogeyland.

Stannie and Ollie are told to guard the trial exhibits—the pig sausage being the key evidence. Stannie takes a bite of it and says, "It doesn't taste like pig sausage to me—it tastes like pork!" Ollie takes a bite and says, "Why, that's neither pig nor pork. That's beef. I smell a rat."

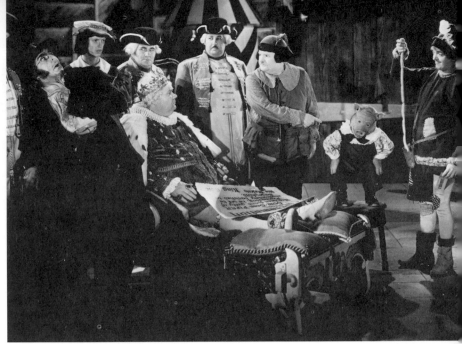

Ollie says to Old King Cole, "Mr. Majesty, Tom-Tom is innocent. We found little Elmer in Barnaby's cellar." Barnaby rushes off, with the entire town after him. The king offers 50,000 guineas for his apprehension—dead or alive. Stannie asks the king, "Can't you make up your mind how you want him?"

Bo-Peep follows Tom-Tom to Bogeyland's fearful precincts.

Bone-weary, she sinks on the ground, and Tom-Tom sings her an enchanting lullaby, "Go to Sleep, Slumber Deep."

The boys have chased Barnaby to the back of his house where he whisks down his well and, there, through a secret door into Bogeyland. Stannie and Ollie wait patiently at the top of the well for Barnaby to reappear. After a considerable wait, Stannie yells down, "Ya better come up, dead or alive!" Ollie asks reasonably, "How can he come up dead when he's alive?" "Well," says Stannie, "let's drop a rock on him. Then we'll make him dead when he's alive." "Now you're talkin'," says Ollie, and drops the rock down the well. "Look out!," Stannie yells below, to Ollie's great disgust. Ollie orders Stannie down to see if Barnaby has been hit. Stannie demurs. "I thought you and he were just like *that*," says Ollie. "Well, that was before we were *married,*" says Stannie.

So both the boys go down the well, enter Bogeyland, find the young lovers and capture Barnaby. But they look around and see the Bogeymen coming at them in full force.

They run for their lives, going through the secret door into the well—and freedom.

287

In the meantime Barnaby has taken the Bogeymen with him on another route. "I'll get them," he shouts, "if I have to destroy all of Toyland!" Back in Toyland the populace greets Stannie and Ollie jubilantly, congratulating them on rescuing Bo-Peep and Tom-Tom. The boys are asked to describe the Bogeymen, and as they begin to do so...

... Barnaby and his pitiless crew stream through the gates of Toyland and chaos is triumphant. The Bogeymen begin to ravage Toyland.

Two Bogeymen chase the boys into the toy factory where they find darts to throw at their pursuers.

Ollie has the inspired idea of attacking the Bogeymen by using the darts as Stannie's peewees. Stannie shoots them out with unerring accuracy. Mickey Mouse climbs in a toy blimp and throws torpedoes down on the invaders. When the boys run out of darts, they go back into the toy factory—where they remember the oversized toy soldiers...

...who, after being triggered into action by a button on their backs, march through Toyland...

...and rout the Bogeymen.

As the Bogeymen are chased out, Ollie says, "Let's get
the cannon and give them a parting shot." They prime the
cannon, load it with darts, aim it at the Bogeymen, and
fire. But the cannon turns around and blasts the full load
of darts into Ollie's posterior. Stannie begins to pull them
out, one by one.

Production Sidelights

The camera on a crane with Gus Meins, codirector, in the chair behind the cameraman. The "Don't Cry, Bo-Peep," number.

Virginia Karns (Mother Goose) with her makeup kit, as Stan and Babe watch. Opposite them is Kewpie Morgan (Old King Cole).

In the background, the Three Little Pigs' masks; on the hangers at right, the body costumes for the Pigs (played by midgets). The actors here are Alice Moore (Queen of Hearts); Charley Rogers (Simple Simon, also codirector of the film); Felix Knight (Tom-Tom); Charlotte Henry (Bo-Peep); and Henry Brandon (Barnaby).

Wide-eyed at being set free in Mother Goose Land, the Our Gang kids visit the set.

Codirector Gus Meins sitting between Babe and Stan, with Henry Brandon, Florence Roberts, and Charlotte Henry.

THE LIVE GHOST

🎩🎩🎩   1934

Laurel and Hardy Series / Two reels / Sound /
Released December 8, 1934, by M-G-M / Produced by Hal Roach / Directed by Charles
Rogers / Photographed by Art Lloyd / Edited
by Louis MacManus / Compositions used in
incidental music scoring by Marvin Hatley,
Irving Berlin, Arthur Kay, and Le Roy Shield.

Stan Laurel Himself / *Oliver Hardy* Himself /
Captain Walter Long / *Waterfront vamp* Mae
Busch / *Drunken sailor in the title role* Arthur
Housman / *Bartender* Harry Bernard / *Shang-
haied sailors* Pete Gordon, Leo Willis, Charlie
Hall, Charlie Sullivan, Jack (Tiny) Lipson, Sam
Lufkin, Dick Gilbert, Baldwin Cooke, Arthur
Rowlands, Hubert Diltz, Bill Moore, John
Power.

Short of crew, the tough and rough captain (Walter Long) of a putative ghost ship
enters a waterfront dive to recruit. He is jeeringly rejected by all hands. The captain
sees Stan and Ollie fishing on the dock and asks if they are working. They are indeed
—fish cleaners at the local market. The captain tells them a real job is available,
sailing with him. "We don't like the ocean," Ollie says. "I heard the ocean is infatuated
with sharks," Stan explains. "He means *infuriated,*" Ollie says loftily. The captain
offers them easy money: shanghaiing sailors at a dollar a head. Agreed.

At the dive, the plan is set: Stan is to go
in, get someone to chase him out, and
Ollie will clunk the victim as he exits
with a big frying pan.

Inside, Stan sits with a couple of
toughs (Charlie Hall and Leo Willis), who
listen to his intriguing offer. Holding
an egg, Stan says, "I'll bet you a dollar
you can't put it in your mouth without
breaking it." Leo takes him up, Stan hits
him under the chin, the egg collapses.
Leo chases Stan out the door where Ollie
stands waiting with the frying pan. The
captain hauls the unconscious Leo off
to the ship, dumping him in the hold.
After a series of these encounters, Ollie
says to Stan, "I'd better go this time.
They know you by now. And lay it on
heavy," handing the pan to Stan. Inside,
Ollie sits down with Charlie Hall, who
is now amply privy to the egg trick.
Pretending disbelief that the trick can
be done, Charlie says he'll do it if Ollie
does it first. Ollie inserts the egg in his
own mouth and Charlie hits him under
the chin; Charlie opens his mouth wide
in laughter, Ollie inserts an egg therein
and follows through.

Ollie runs out of the dive pursued by Charlie; the swinging door knocks the waiting Stan down. Charlie chases Ollie around and around the porch post; Stan rises, tries to hit Charlie but knocks out Ollie instead. Stan succeeds in knocking Charlie out, and in unwitting continuation of his frenzy bounces the captain on the head to absolutely no effect. The captain efficiently knocks Stan out.

In the hold Stan and Ollie have joined their victims.

The captain tells the resentful crew that Stan and Ollie must not be touched until they are off ship at the next port. A sailor says that they will get even with the boys for bringing them on this ghost ship. The word *ghost* sends the captain into a paroxysm of anger. If he hears the word *ghost* again, he says, he will take the offender's head and twist it around so that when he is walking north he'll be looking south.

Ten ports later, Stan and Ollie have never left ship because they know that ashore they are fair game for the vengeful crew. The crew drunk (played, inevitably, by Arthur Housman) is making plans to go ashore but the captain tells Stan and Ollie to watch him and keep him aboard.

The boys "check" each other while the drunk prepares to sneak ashore. He puts a suitcase in his bunk, throws a blanket over it, then leaves ship. The boys go into the cabin to retire. Stan finds a gun, shows it to Ollie who tries to take it away from him. The gun goes off, the bullet hits the suitcase and it sags—like a newly made corpse. Terrified, Stan and Ollie decide to throw "him" overboard. They go to get a sack from the hold. Meanwhile, on shore, the drunk has fallen into some whitewash, which turns him into a rather credible ghost. He returns to the ship, throws the suitcase from his bunk, and gets under the blanket himself.

In the clammy darkness of the hold Stan asks Ollie if he thinks the drunk went to heaven. After replying regretfully that he thinks the man went to the other place, Ollie asks Stan to get some coal. Stan is wide-eyed at the idea that one must take one's own fuel to the other place but Ollie explains that they must use the coal to weight the sack. On return to the cabin, they put the sleeping drunk into the sack...

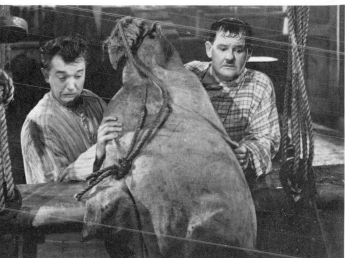

...and throw him overboard. Meanwhile the captain has met a dockside floozy (Mae Busch) at a bistro, and asks, quite seriously, what a nice doll like her is doing "in a place like this." She says she was married to a sailor who deserted her, and if she ever finds him, she'll break him in two. The members of the crew decide to return to the ship and wreak vengeance on the boys for shanghaiing them.

The boys go to bed and, in closing the cabin door, Stan sees the drunk climbing back on the ship. Terrified, Stan tells Ollie he's seen a ghost, and Ollie instructs him not to let the captain hear that word. Ollie says he'll look around; Stan goes out the other way. The drunk enters the cabin and gets up in the boys' bunk; Ollie returns, saying there is nothing to fear. He explains this to Stan who is looking at him from outside the cabin window. The drunk sits up, says a cheerful "Hi!," and Ollie skitters away in horror. The drunk gets on deck, meets the crew advancing to confront Stan and Ollie—and the crew all jump overboard at the spectral sight. The captain, bringing Mae on board for who knows what purpose, meets Stan and Ollie jumping about excitedly and asks what's going on.

The drunk walks up and Mae, recognizing him as her husband, attacks him with her umbrella, worrying him off the ship. Ollie explains to the captain that they saw a ghost. Upon hearing the fateful word, the captain grabs Ollie, and when Stan admits he also has seen a ghost, the captain gets to work on him as well. The last shot is of the boys—heads turned permanently 180 degrees—and Ollie saying to his pal, "Well here's another nice mess you've gotten me into."

TIT FOR TAT

■ ■ ■   1935

(This is the only Laurel and Hardy sequel, the denouement to *Them Thar Hills*.)

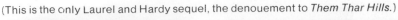

Laurel and Hardy Series / Two reels / Sound / Released January 5, 1935, by M-G-M / Produced by Hal Roach / Directed by Charles Rogers / Photographed by Art Lloyd / Edited by Bert Jordan / Sound by William Randall / Compositions used in incidental music scoring by Le Roy Shield and Marvin Hatley.

Stan Laurel Himself / *Oliver Hardy* Himself / *Proprietor, Hall's Groceries* Charlie Hall / *Hall's wife* Mae Busch / *Officer* James C. Morton / *Thorough shoplifter* Bobby Dunn / *Shopper* Baldwin Cooke / *Passersby* Jack Hill, Pete Gordon, Elsie MacKaye, Dick Gilbert, Lester Dorr, Viola Richard. *Note:* According to one source, Frank Tashlin contributed gags to this film, as well as *The Fixer Uppers* and *Thicker Than Water.* (Academy Award nomination for "Best Live-Action Short Subject" of the year.) (Sequel to *Them Thar Hills*, made half a year earlier.)

The boys have opened an electrical supplies shop. Courtesy is their byword. A policeman who has just wished them great success is standing out front on the sidewalk service elevator. He gets a sudden ride in the air. The propelling force is Stan, coming up from the basement to get light globes for their electric sign. Ollie apologizes to the officer, explaining that his partner is not quite over his nervous breakdown. Stan is ordered to get a ladder and put the globes up in the sign while Ollie goes over and pays his respects to their new neighbor, Mr. Hall. Stan decides to join Ollie. As they walk over to Hall's grocery, a little man enters the boys' shop despite the Will Be Back Soon sign they have put up.

Stan and Ollie introduce themselves as partners in the new electrical shop next door. Stan whispers to Ollie that this is the man they met in the trailer, the one whose wife asked for a drink of water. Mae starts to hum "The Old Spinning Wheel." "*Pum pum!,*" adds Stan. Charlie recognizes them as he would a case of cholera morbus. Airily, Ollie says, "Henceforth, we'll neither nod, nor speak. Come, Stanley." As the boys return to their store, the little man they saw walking in their shop now walks out— with a waffle iron.

Ollie will put in the light globes. He tells Stan to get some more. Stan goes down in the basement for them and returns again via the sidewalk elevator. The elevator pushes Ollie on the ladder...

...high up to the Hall's window ledge. "What you doin' up there?," Stan asks Ollie. "I'm waiting for a streetcar" is the measured reply. Mae has previously gone upstairs, where she is now surprised to find an old friend. "I'm in a slight predicament," Ollie tells her. "Would it be asking too much if I used your stairway?" She says it would be a pleasure. Stan, meanwhile, goes into his store, turns on the switch for their display sign, and all the light globes in it explode.

Charlie reacts with frigid suspicion as Ollie comes down from the Hall apartment with Mrs. Hall. "I've never been in a position like that before," Ollie says to Mae. "Well, it's certainly been a pleasure to see you again." Mae's cordiality—"Oh, it's my pleasure!"—is not shared by Charlie. As Ollie returns to his store, the mysterious little man enters the Laurel and Hardy shop again. Ollie takes a bucket of light globes from Stan and starts up the ladder. Charlie bustles over to demand what the secret is between Ollie and Mae. "I have nothing to say," says Ollie in the tone of Louis XIV to a footman suffering from halitosis.

The little man (Bobby Dunn) leaves the electric shop cheerfully, carrying a lamp and clock. He says, "How do you do?" most pleasantly, and the boys are intrigued and rather interested. Charlie tells Ollie that if he ever looks at Mae again, he'll hit him so hard that *Stan* will feel it. Charlie returns to his shop; Ollie plans to go after him to demand an apology for treading maliciously on a Hardy's reputation. "You're right, Ollie," Stan says. "He who filters your good name steals trash!" The boys go over to Charlie's, where Ollie demands an apology; Charlie hits him on the head with a wooden spoon. "Ohhhh!," Ollie says, "I shall take this up with my barrister!"

Ollie presses a cash register release key and the drawer flies open, smacking Charlie. Ollie defiantly takes one of Charlie's marshmallows and leaves. "Come, Stanley." Charlie follows them into their shop and, in reprisal for Ollie's scorning laugh, catches the Hardy nose in a curling iron. "Come on," says Ollie, putting up their Will Be Back Soon sign. As they leave for Charlie's, the little man reenters their store. At Charlie's, Ollie takes a spoonful of cottage cheese and flicks it in Charlie's face. The boys take marshmallows and eat them spiritedly as they leave. "Tit for tat!," says Ollie. Charlie takes alum and sprinkles it over the marshmallows. As the boys walk back to their store, the little man is just going out with a lamp and a small electric stove. "How do you do?," he says. "How do you do?," Ollie says. Charlie follows the boys to their shop, takes a display of dollar watches, puts them in a malted milk shaker, and starts the machine. He leaves, Ollie pours the remains of the watches on the counter. Once more the boys leave their shop, hanging up their sign. The little man enters with a wheelbarrow.

At Charlie's store, Stan opens the cash register and Ollie pours a bottle of honey in it.

Charlie takes Ollie's hat to the meat slicer and neatly cuts off the crown. Together the boys lift a large can of lard and push it down over Charlie's head. They lift off the can; the lard remains in a gelid, glutinous blob on his head. The boys take some marshmallows and leave.

The little man is wheeling a washing machine from their shop as they enter. "How do you do?"

The alum takes effect; the boys spray it out of their mouths with a seltzer bottle.

Charlie enters their shop, pushes the boys' ceiling light fixtures into a series of collisions—one smacking the next smacking the next smacking the next—until the last one breaks through their plate-glass window. "Now will you stop?," asks Charlie. The boys follow Charlie back to his place, and as Ollie is explaining that he will give him one more chance to apologize, Charlie sprays them with cottage cheese.

The boys pour a case of eggs over him.

The policeman (James C. Morton) asks if all this hasn't gone far enough. Ollie explains his demand for an apology; Mae confirms Ollie's innocence, despite Stan's explanation to the cop that Ollie was up in Mae's room waiting for a streetcar. Charlie finally shakes hands but warns that it must not happen again. The boys return to their store to see—"How do you do?"—the little man putting a table lamp into a large van loaded with electrical appliances. The policeman puts one of Charlie's marshmallows in his mouth, and as he tells the gathering crowd to disperse, he wonders why his mouth succumbs to a gigantic pucker.

The Fixer Uppers

1935

Laurel and Hardy Series / Two reels / Sound / Released February 9, 1935, by M-G-M / Produced by Hal Roach / Directed by Charles Rogers / Photographed by Art Lloyd / Edited by Bert Jordan / Sound by James Greene / Compositions used in incidental music scoring by Le Roy Shield and Marvin Hatley.

Stan Laurel Himself / *Oliver Hardy* Himself / *Middleton's wife* Mae Busch / *Pierre Gustave* Charles Middleton / *The drunk* Arthur Housman / *Passerby in hall* Bobby Dunn / *Bartender* Noah Young / *Officers* Dick Gilbert, Jack Hill, James C. Morton / *Waiter* Bob (Mazooka) O'Conor.

Christmas card salesmen Stan and Ollie advertise their wares by reading them aloud *con amore.* One of their first customers this day is a melancholy drunk who is much affected by one of their cards, addressed to Mom: "Merry Christmas, mother. Merry Christmas, ma. Hi, mommy, mommy—and a hot cha cha!" The boys next come to the apartment of Mrs. Pierre Gustave (Mae Busch), a deeply distraught lady. They read her "one of Stanley's tenderest," perfect for a husband: "A Merry Christmas, husband—Happy New Year's nigh. I wish you Easter Greetings—Hooray for the Fourth of July!" But Mae sobs that she is not interested. The boys discover her trouble: her husband neglects her, and she feels the need to make him recognize the fact.

Stan suggests the way out of the difficulty is to make her husband jealous. Mae seizes on the idea and promises the boys $50 if they can accomplish it.

Mae explains: "If my husband saw you kissing me like he kissed me the first time we met, I'm sure *that* would make him jealous." She demonstrates on Stan. Ollie watches in exasperation as the kiss grows longer and longer and longer and longer. At the conclusion of it, Stan drops. "That's all you have to do," Mae says, and faints on the divan.

Mae's husband, Pierre Gustave (Charles Middleton), enters. Seeing him, Mae quickly sweeps into a kiss with Ollie. Pierre slaps Ollie with his glove, hands him his card. Mae protests that this gentleman means nothing to her but Pierre is adamant. Pierre explains that giving the card means that "at 12 o'clock tonight, here in this room, we will meet in mortal combat—a duel to the death." Ollie is not cheered to hear from Mae that Pierre is the best shot in all Paris. "Why, it'll be premeditated murder! They'll hang you for it!" "What do I care?," asks Pierre. "I have nothing to live for." He tells Ollie to come tonight "...or I'll track you to the end of the world."

At the Café des Artistes Ollie is very despondent but Stan provides the silver lining by calling Pierre's threat to track Ollie to the ends of the world pure baloney. "He doesn't know where we live. He hasn't got the address." Ollie tells Stan, "Now, why didn't you think of that before instead of letting me worry all the time? Selfish!"

Stan tells Ollie to call Pierre and "tell him you won't be there. He might have something else to do." Ollie calls, tells Pierre off—"you cheap little brush pusher." Stan adds *his* insult: "Say, listen, if you had a face like mine, you'd punch me right in the nose and I'm just the fella that can do it!"

Their first customer of the day, the genial drunk (Arthur Housman), has been refused service by the barkeeper. The drunk asks the boys to buy drinks for him on the side. He will not only foot the bill for all the drinks but will buy every Christmas card they've got.

At 11 o'clock that night, two officers carry the drink-bemused Stan and Ollie to the address of the card found on them—Pierre's. They are deposited on Mae's bed. Mae and Pierre discover them, and when Pierre asks what he is doing there, Ollie says, "Well, you told me to be here at 12 o'clock." Mae swears to Pierre that she was unaware of Ollie's presence but Pierre insists on the duel. They are to stand back to back, take six paces, and at a given signal, turn and fire.

Mae tells the boys that she has put blanks in the guns. When Pierre fires, Ollie is to pretend death, and somehow she'll help him escape.

Ollie receives his dueling pistol; Stan receives a pistol to sound the signal.

"Vive la France!," says Ollie.

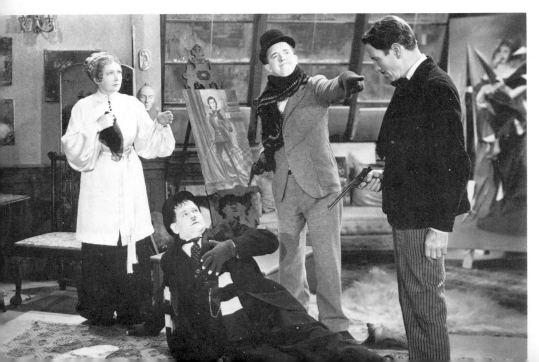

Ollie is "shot," falls yelling to the ground, and pretends it's all over. Pierre's plan to dispose of the body is simple: he'll cut Ollie up into little pieces. Ollie gets up and crashes through the door, and the boys run down the stairway, Pierre shooting after them. Later, Stan knocks on a garbage can to tell the hiding Ollie that Pierre is gone...But Ollie has been carried away by a garbage wagon.

Thicker Than Water

1935

Laurel and Hardy Series / Two reels / Sound / Released March 16, 1935, by M-G-M / Produced by Hal Roach / Directed by James W. Horne / Photographed by Art Lloyd / Edited by Ray Snyder / Story by Stan Laurel / Compositions used in incidental music scoring by Le Roy Shield and Marvin Hatley.

Stan Laurel Himself / Oliver Hardy Himself / Mrs. Daphne Hardy Daphne Pollard / Auction operator James Finlayson / Auctioneer Harry Dowon / Bank tellers Ed Brandenberg, Charlie Hall / Nurse Goodall Grace Goodall / Nurse Dorr Flowers / Dress extra at auction Lester Dorr / Auction bidder Gladys Gale / Dr, F.D. Allen Allen Cavan / Visitor at hospital Baldwin Cooke.

Mrs. Hardy (Daphne Pollard) demands of her husband and their boarder why they are going to the ball game. When Ollie says, " . . . we businessmen have to relax sometime," she points out an interesting form of relaxation that she now declares mandatory for him—washing the dishes. Ollie insists Stan remain and do the drying.

The dishes get cleaner and the boys get weaker. After Ollie washes and rinses the dishes, Stan wipes them and puts them right back in the pan, and Ollie washes them again. Finally catching on, Ollie directs Stan to put the wiped dishes in a nice, dry place. Stan puts them on a functioning gas burner, and later, when Ollie picks them up to put away...

...he burns his little patties.

A dour gentleman (James Finlayson) has come to collect the payment on the furniture. Mrs. Hardy insists it was paid yesterday because she gave it to her husband for that purpose. Ollie agrees, saying he gave the money to Stan to pay the furniture bill for them. Stan says he gave the money back to Ollie. This surprises Ollie but Stan says he gave the money to Ollie for room and board. Mrs. Hardy asks incredulously, "Do you mean to say that the money he gave to you that you gave to him that he gave to me was the same money that I gave to him to pay *him*?" Stan replies, "Well, if that was the money that you gave to him to give to me to pay to him, it must have been the money that I gave him to give to you to pay my rent." Mrs. Hardy gives Fin an apology and $37. Fin goes out muttering, "He gave it to you and you gave it to him and who gave it to what. Why, you're all *nuts!*"

Stan has suggested the Hardys draw out their $300 savings to pay off the total furniture bill—thus relieving them of interest payments. Mrs. Hardy coldly rejects the idea but, left alone with Stan, Ollie thinks the idea brilliant. He draws the $300 from the bank.

Moments later, they walk by an auction room displaying an intriguing sign. It is hard to resist such a bargain; they go in and sit down.

A lady (Gladys Gale), who is bidding on a beautiful antique clock, has run the bid up to $230 when she realizes her money is at home. She asks Ollie to keep bidding on the clock while she rushes back to get the money and *not* to let anyone else get the clock "under any consideration." Moreover, she will pay him well for his trouble. Ollie says, "My dear madam, being a true Southerner, chivalry is my middle name, to say nothing of the hospitality." Ollie bids against one man, then against another persistent bidder, who turns out to be Stan. Horrified, Ollie asks why his pal is bidding against him. "Well, you're bidding against *me*," says Stan, and he goes on until Ollie clamps his mouth shut.

Ollie's final bid is $290. The auction store owner (Fin) and the auctioneer (Harry Bowen) demand that Ollie pay up and take the antique clock with him. Meanwhile, Mrs. Hardy, in trying to alter the joint bank account so she alone can withdraw money, learns from the bank that all the Hardy money has been taken out.

The boys carry the clock across the street but Stan is fatigued, and he suggests putting it down for a moment.

And it only takes a moment for a truck to come along and run over it.

And it only takes a moment for $290 to reduce itself to approximately the worth of a three-cent stamp.

Unspilling spilled milk may not be rewarding but there is a certain macabre fascination about it. Meantime, at the auction office, Mrs. Hardy asks Fin if her husband has come in to pay for their furniture. "He did not," Fin tells her. "He bought himself a grandfather's clock."

Ollie has resolved to keep this little episode to himself. Mrs. Hardy storms in, asking for the $290 clock. Ollie laughs at the ridiculousness of such an idea.

"Where's that clock?," she asks Stan. "I don't know" is the reply. "He said he was going to keep it in the dark." Infuriated, she beans Ollie with a skillet. The next scene is at the hospital where Stan is giving blood for his badly battered pal. However, the transfusion process goes awry; and Ollie gets most of Stan's blood, Stan gets most of Ollie's. When Ollie recovers, days later, he has inherited Stan's mannerisms and vice versa. "Here's another fine mess you've gotten me into," Stan tells Ollie, who cries in reply. Stan bids a courtly good-bye to the nurse, twiddling his tie at her—and imperiously orders

BONNIE SCOTLAND

1935

80 minutes—Sound
Released August 23, 1935, by M-G-M
Produced by Hal Roach
Directed by James W. Horne
Photographed by Art Lloyd
and Walter Lundin
Edited by Bert Jordan
Screenplay by Frank Butler
and Jefferson Moffitt
Technical advice by Colonel W. E. Wynn
Sound by Elmer R. Raguse
Compositions used in incidental music
scoring by Le Roy Shield
and Marvin Hatley

Stanley McLaurel . . . . Stan Laurel
Oliver Hardy. . . . . Himself
Lady Violet Ormsby . . . . Anne Grey
Mr. Miggs, the attorney . . . . . David Torrence
Lorna McLaurel. . . . . June Vlasek/June Lang
Alan Douglas . . . . William Janney
Butler . . . . James Mack
Sergeant Major. . . . . James Finlayson
Mrs. Bickerdike, the innkeeper. Mary Gordon
"It's Mae West". . . . . May Beatty
Milly, Lady Vi's maid . . . . Daphne Pollard
Postman . . . . James May
Hotel lobby extra . . . . Jack Hill
Part of the new draft . . . . Jack Hill
Native henchman . . . . Jack Hill
Schoolteacher . . . . Kathryn Sheldon
Storekeeper . . . . Minerva Urecal
Housekeepers Margaret Mann, Claire Verdera
The miscreant Khan Mir Jutra . Maurice Black
Colonel Gregor McGregor,
D.S.C. Vernon Steele
Highlander Quartet. . . . . Noah Young,
Dan Maxwell, David Clyde, James Bur-
tis
Military policeman . . . . Brandon Hurst
Scotch sergeant. . . . . Olaf Hytten
Soldier with accordion . . . . Marvin Hatley
General Fletcher of the
Highlanders . . . . Claude King
Scotch village street extras
. . . . Bill Moore, Art Rowlands
Groom . . . . Frank Benson
Gamekeeper . . . . Gunnis Davis
Blacksmith. . . . . Lionel Belmore
Blacksmith's helper. . . . . Dick Wessell

Insurgent native
henchmen. . . . . Charlie Hall,
Bob (Mazooka) O'Conor, Leo Willis,
Sam Lufkin, Bobby Dunn

Man handing out flyers for the
Twiddle Tweed Co. . . . . Bobby Dunn

Hindus. . . . . Carlos J. de Valdez,
Lal Chand Mehra, Anthony Francis,
Raizada Devinder Nath Bali

Gossiping women. . . . . Phyllis Barry,
Belle Daube, Elizabeth Wilbur

English military officers . Colin Kenny,
Pat Somerset, Jack Deery, Colonel
McDonnell, Clive Morgan, Major Harris,
Jay Belasco

Jhan Mir Jutra's dancing
girls Carlotta Monti/"Mrs." W.C. Fields,
Hona Hoy, Vaino Hassan, Julia Halia,
Shura Shermet

Walla, the Hindu servant. . . . . . Gurdial Singh

Hindu musicians . . . . Eddie Dass,
Bogwhan Singh, Otto Frisco, Abdullah
Hassan

Bit men . . . . Ted Oliver,
Murdock MacQuarrie, John Power,
Barlowe Borland

Bit women . . . Frances Morris, Mary McLaren
John Sutherland's Scotch Pipers Themselves

(Working titles: *McLaurel and McHardy*, and
Laurel and Hardy in India. Reissued as *Heroes
of the Regiment*.)

(Burlesque on Gary Cooper's *Lives of a Bengal Lancer*, 1935. Each feature employed the
same technical adviser.)

307

Scotland. Lawyer Miggs (David Torrence) looks on disapprovingly as Lorna McLaurel (June Lang) graciously accepts the tribute of Alan Douglas (William Janney), Miggs's clerk. Minutes later, Miggs reads aloud to a number of those concerned the last will and testament of the late Angus Ian McLaurel. The first of the heirs cited is absent, an American grandson, Stanley McLaurel . . .

. . . who this very moment is walking down a Scottish lane with a friend.

They ask the innkeeper (Mary Gordon) if she can give them a room and a bath. The room, yes, but, sternly: " . . . you'll have to take the bath yourself."

Ollie trips over his portmanteau on the way upstairs.

Stan, expecting to be the sole heir, is thrilled to learn that he will receive two of his grandfather's most cherished possessions, a snuffbox and a pair of bagpipes. He is not thrilled to learn that this is all. Lorna gets most of the estate, but she must go to India where her guardian is, with his regiment.

Making the best of it, Ollie partakes of the snuff, sneezes, sneezes, falls over the bridge into a stream, sneezes and sneezes all the water away.

Stan is helping Ollie dry out his pants.

They philosophize on their situation. Ollie is disturbed that Stan talked him into agreeing to a jailbreak back home. They had only a week of their sentence left to serve, and now they can never go back to that warm, comfortable jail. Another worry is that the innkeeper is becoming impatient for the rent.

Triumphantly Stan shows Ollie what he has gotten in trade for their overcoats.

To cook it, they will use the bedspring as a grill, setting a candle beneath.

In the cooking, it has shrunk a bit. The rest just "schrizzled," says Stan. "Well, I'm glad you didn't bring a sardine," observes Ollie.

Ollie has fallen down, relapses onto the bed as the innkeeper comes in to discover all the bother and upset. During this, the candle is still burning beneath the bed. It finally reaches Ollie's rear, and he erupts. The innkeeper throws them out as they are, Ollie pantsless, keeping the baggage as security.

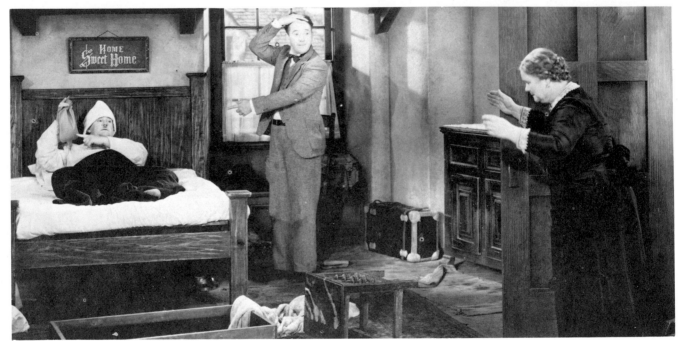

Receiving a tailor's handbill that promises a new suit on 30 days' free trial, the boys accidentally go to an army recruiting office on the floor below the tailor's shop. Ollie explains, "We've come to accept your offer." "Yeah, we'd like to get measured right away," confirms Stan. They sign the papers; the major tells they they're in the army and orders the sergeant to take them away to get a suit of clothes they'll be proud of.

The sergeant orders them along peremptorily.

They ask Lawyer Miggs to forward any mail to their new address—Pellore, India. *Just* where Lorna McLaurel has gone, observes Mr. Miggs.

Alan, who has forced himself to stay away from Lorna because of her fortune, now decides love cannot be denied. He, too, will join the boys' regiment and go to Pellore.

The regiment disembarks, and their sergeant (James Finlayson) has never seen a more suspicious-looking vanguard for any body of fighting men.

The barracks. Stan and Ollie have not exactly endeared themselves to Fin by asking, with much sincerity, where they can get the key for their room.

Stan finds that, when cleaning his gun, blowing on the barrel produces an interesting quasi-musical effect.

Sotto voce, Ollie scathingly refers to Fin as "old leatherpuss," and Stan calls out to that worthy, "Sergeant Leatherpuss!" Fin asks Stan who told him the name was Leatherpuss; Stan explains without guile, and Ollie shrinks away from the baleful Finlayson stare.

General Fletcher (Claude King) toasts the engagement of Lorna to Colonel Gregor McGregor (Vernon Steele). Alan, who is nearby, observes this and is horrified to find he's too late. He tries to rush in but is prevented and sent to jail for a few hours.

Alan asks the boys to give Lorna a note.

Stan asks Colonel McGregor where they can find Lorna, and in short order the note is in his hands.

Irritated at Stan's stupidity, Ollie kicks an officer, blaming it on Stan.

The officer orders Ollie to take the offender to Sergeant Finlayson at once.

Colonel McGregor gallantly decides that the note must reach Lorna in any case. Ecstatic when she receives it, Lorna hurries to the rendezvous Alan set up, but is horrified when he rudely condemns her for succumbing to the fripperies of her new life. Alan leaves, not knowing that every letter he sent Lorna in recent months has been intercepted by a scheming friend of the girl, McGregor's sister.

Congenitally unable to keep in step, Stan marches resolutely forward. Soldiers nearest him get into *his* step, and one by one the entire company changes step. Stan pantomimes to Fin, marching alongside, to get into proper step. Fin conforms.

Stan shows Ollie one of his infuriatingly simple tricks—simple for Stan to do, infuriating for Ollie when he cannot perform them. As he blows on his finger like a pipe, Stan slowly levitates his headgear by pressing it against the wall. Ollie can't figure it out.

Fin has told the boys to police the area. While the regimental band plays "One Hundred Pipers," Stan and Ollie improvise a little dance with broom and stick.

Ollie, seeing the cold Finlayson stare, skips away.

Stan, not knowing Ollie is gone, grabs Fin as partner.

Stan, dashing off, with Fin in pursuit, gracefully leaps over the horse trough. Fin doesn't quite make it. The boys salute respectfully, march off into a cell, lock it, throw the key away—and exuberantly finish their dance.

The rascally Mir Jutra plans to lead a native uprising against the regiment's headquarters at Fort Rannu. In order to allay suspicion, Mir Jutra has invited Colonel McGregor and his aides to luncheon at the palace. Once there, Mir Jutra will blow the gates of Fort Rannu and the insurrection will begin. McGregor, however, uncovers the plot and will welcome the natives at the fort when they attack. Meanwhile, to forestall Mir Jutra's suspicions, he has Fin scout up volunteers who will wear officers' uniforms and go to the palace luncheon. Alan bravely volunteers for the dangerous mission; Stan and Ollie go because Fin asks them if they'd like to have a nice lunch.

Mir Jutra (Maurice Black) asks "Colonel McGregor" to join him in a water pipe of friendship. Ollie does so enthusiastically—followed by Stan who exhales where he should have inhaled.

The signal has been given that the British "officers" are with Mir Jutra. The gates of Fort Rannu are blown up and natives swarm through the opening only to be apprehended by the waiting Colonel McGregor and his men.

Inside Mir Jutra's palace, the banqueters banquet.

After the festivities, Mir Jutra tells them tauntingly that Fort Rannu is no more—and, shortly, *they* shall be no more. The boys are politely presented with the means of blowing out their brains. Stan cries but is led behind a screen to shoot himself. He bids a plaintive farewell to Ollie, telling him there'll be no trouble recognizing him in heaven: "I'll keep me hat on." He goes behind the screen. There is a shot, and the screen is pulled away—to reveal Stan cringing. He missed.

Just as the natives are about to jump the soldiers, a large chandelier crashes down, and the boys run out. The natives chase them but Stan and Ollie find some beehives, which they throw at their oppressors. Bees reign supreme, and even a column of soldiers sent to relieve the volunteer heroes falls prey to the tiny scourges.

Production Sidelights

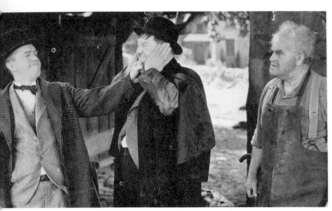

These pictures are all that remain of a deleted scene in which the boys enter the shop of a blacksmith (Lionel Belmore) and get into difficulties that include Ollie singeing his hand on a red-hot horseshoe and, later, falling into a tub of water.

Bonnie Scotland, as these remnants of two deleted scenes show, is a partial pastiche of *Lives of a Bengal Lancer,* released just a few months before. In this still the *Bengal Lancers* scene in which Gary Cooper makes a native talk by threatening to put him in a pigskin is adumbrated.

Stan's playing and the snake weaving over Ollie's shoulder are clear imitations of the *Bengal Lancers* scene in which a jovial Franchot Tone plays a native flute, thus stimulating a snake to come out of the masonry.

The actual shooting of the Stan-flute/Ollie-snake scene. Note the proximity of the still photographer to the cinematographer.

Scots-born and bred Jimmy Finlayson, flying in from New York, being appropriately greeted by Stan and pipers, Glendale Airport, California, 1935. "Fin" wore a moustache only in the films.

The Scottish village set was beautifully detailed and authentic.

Production shot of the troops arriving in India.

Director James W. Horne speaks to Stan and Babe between shots on the lawyer's office set.

The Roach recording unit following the regimental band.

Posed—but charmingly so—on the set.

The Bohemian Girl

1936

70 minutes—Sound
Released February 14, 1936, by M-G-M
Produced by Hal Roach
Production managed by L. A. French
Directed by James W. Horne
and Charles Rogers
Photographed by Art Lloyd
and Francis Corby
Edited by Bert Jordan and Louis McManus
Comedy version of the 1843 opera
by Michael W. Balfe
Book by Alfred Bunn
Art direction by Arthur I. Royce
and William L. Stevens
Sound by Elmer R. Raguse
Musical direction by Nathaniel Shilkret
Additional music compositions by
Nathaniel Shilkret and Robert Shayon

Stan Laurel	Himself
Oliver Hardy	Himself
Gypsy queen's daughter	Thelma Todd
Arline as an adult	Jacqueline Wells/Julie Bishop
Arline as a child	Darla Hood
Captain Finn	James Finlayson
The fishwife, Mrs. Hardy	Mae Busch
Devilshoof	Antonio Moreno
The drunk	Harry Bowen
Gypsy queen	Zeffie Tilbury
Count Arnheim	William P. Carlton
Town crier	Harry Bernard
Salinas, attendant to the Gypsy queen	Mitchell Lewis
Maid and governess	Antoinette Lees/Andrea Leeds
Arnheim's mother	Margaret Mann
Gypsy kid	Harold Switzer
Constable	James C. Morton
Foppish nobleman	Eddie Borden
Shopkeeper	Sam Lufkin
Guard in torture chamber	Sam Lufkin
Pickpocket victim	Sam Lufkin
Waiter at the tavern	Bob O'Conor
Cross-eyed bartender	Bobby Dunn
Gypsy lyric tenor	Felix Knight
Brutes in torture chamber	Dick Gilbert Leo Willis
Soldiers	Jack Hill, Arthur Rowlands, Lane Chandler, Baldwin Cooke, Lee Phelps
Bit men	Bill Madsen, Frank Darien
Gypsy vagabonds	Sammy Brooks, Howard Hickman, Edward Earle, Alice Cooke, Tony Campenero, Jerry Breslin, Eddy Chandler, Rita Dunn
Voice-over for Gypsy offering congratulations	Charlie Hall
Talking myna bird	Yogi
Dog	Laughing Gravy

Gypsy caravans encircle a merry group of merrymakers making merry. The Gypsy Queen's daughter (Thelma Todd*) sings the "true song of the Gypsies." The Queen of the Gypsies has deliberately encamped here on the land of her great enemy, Count Arnheim, with the purpose of sending her thieves into the village to steal and rob as best they may.

Two of her less efficient thieves are working at probably the height of their capacity—peeling potatoes. Stan throws a potato in the pot, splashing Ollie lavishly.

Yogi, the Talking Myna Bird laughs immoderately at this, and Ollie tries to splash Stan with disastrous results.

Another of Ollie's disastrous results is his marriage. His willful wife (Mae Busch), yearning for someone big, strong, and brave, has found him in Devilshoof (Antonio Moreno). Stan finds them kissing, reports this to Ollie who doesn't believe it until he sees it. And even then he explains to Stan that Mae and Devilshoof are just having a little innocent fun: "You must understand that a man, to be married, must be broad-minded."

---

* This, alas, is the last screen appearance of Thelma Todd before her tragic death. Much loved on the Roach lot, her loss was keenly felt by Laurel and Hardy.

In the village nearby, the town crier intones, "Nine o'clock, and all is well!" Stan stops him and asks, "Could you tell us the time?" "Certainly," the crier says, "hold my bell." As he looks at his watch, Stan steals his purse as well as the clapper from his bell.

Later, Stan shows Ollie his purse-snatching technique: telling the victim, "Your eyes are the windows of your soul and to know all I must touch them"; closing the victim's eyes with a finger from each hand, then switching to forked fingers from one hand against the eyes, and using the other hand to lift the victim's purse.

Ollie tries it on a man (Sam Lufkin) but fares poorly. When he closes the victim's eyes, he simply jabs them, getting a good poke in return. Stan tries the technique on Ollie; takes his purse, Ollie tries it on himself, finds his purse gone. Stan tries it on himself, pokes himself in the eyes. Ollie slaps him, takes the purse away, and chases him.

Satisfied he now knows the procedure, Ollie approaches an effete gentleman (Eddie Borden) and begins the "windows of your soul" palaver. But Ollie fails to recognize the difference between the gentleman's eyes and his lorgnette, and as he holds his fingers up against the glass, he gleefully divests the gentleman of all his wealth. The gentleman looks on, astounded, as Ollie robs him, while prattling on with the story of Little Red Riding Hood. Stan leaves. The gentleman levels a gun at Ollie, demanding back all that he took. Stan comes back shortly with an officer (James Morton) who has seen the gentleman level his gun at Ollie. "Give this man back his valuables," the officer tells the effete one. "I saw the whole thing with my own eyes." Ollie makes a windfall . . . including the gentleman's jewelry, cane, and lorgnette—and pistol.

The boys celebrate at a nearby tavern, and to settle a dispute over ownership of the newly got coins, they play "Fingers." Ollie explains that if Stan puts out the same number of fingers he does on a simultaneous call, he wins; if he doesn't, he loses. Stan cheats by keeping his hand below table level and bringing it up with the number needed to win. Ollie finally catches on to this, grabs the offending hand to "freeze" it—when Stan slowly brings up the *other* hand with the winning number.

But Stan has more diverting finger play to offer. He bends back the first two joints of his left index finger, and in their place fits the top joint of his right thumb. Ollie is fascinated by what appears to be a finger fashioned at will.

In roaming the palace grounds, Devilshoof is captured and flogged. Count Arnheim has ordered the Gypsies to be on their way.

Count Arnheim (William P. Carlton) shows his beloved daughter Arline (Darla Hood) the medallion that belonged to her great-great-grandfather who founded the house of Arnheim. She asks to wear it but he cautions her not to lose it because it is very precious to him. Later, as Arline's pet rabbit runs away, she opens the palace gate and skips after it.

Mae nurses Devilshoof after his flogging. "Curse you, Count Arnheim!," she says in her finest cursing vein. "For every stroke you have given my beloved, may you suffer a year of woe!"

Mae looks out of her wagon and sees Arline on the road, searching for her rabbit.

Mae gently abducts Arline and dresses her as a Gypsy. Devilshoof asks Mae how she is going to account for Arline to her husband. "He'll believe anything I tell him," Mae says.

He does indeed. When Mae brings Arline home, Ollie demands to know who she is. "If you must know," Mae says, "she's yours!" "Mine? Well, why didn't you tell me before?" Mae is to the point: "I didn't want her to know who her father was 'til she was old enough to stand the shock." When Ollie introduces his new daughter to Stan—pointing out that he became a father "just a minute ago"—Stan says, "Blow me down with an anchovy." Stan tells Arline, "I hope you will grow up to be as good a mother as your father."

Meanwhile, Devilshoof, feeling the call of the open road, plans to leave the Gypsy band. As the persuasive strain of "You'll Remember Me" (sung by Felix Knight) tears at her emotions, Mae insists that Devilshoof take her with him. He explains that he is penniless, " . . . if only we had some money . . . some jewels." Mae sees in Stan the way to get the needed traveling funds.

323

Mae comes to Stan at the butter churn ("I'm making a malted milk," he says) and she tells him, "I'm going to be very, very nice to you." When asked if she will be nice to Oliver too, she says she is planning a big surprise for him. Ollie comes in nearby and watches them closely. Mae wants Stan to go into the wagon, get her clothes, and also hand her all the money and jewels Ollie has.

She tells Stan to be careful. "Don't worry," Stan assures her, "I can gyp that Gypsy anytime." She embraces Stan gratefully. Ollie quickly gets in the van, puts his money bag in a sock, hangs the sock out the window, and dives into bed feigning sleep. Stan looks under Ollie's pillow, ultimately working himself under the pillow to the point where Ollie has to jump down from the bunk. Meanwhile, Mae sees the sock hanging from the window, takes it, and goes off. Ollie asks Stan what he's looking for under the pillow. "Got a match?," Stan asks. Ollie chastises him verbally for his actions, reducing Stan to tears. Ollie explains he hid not only his own valuables but Stan's as well. He reaches for the sock but finds a note from Mae announcing her departure and the fact that he is not Arline's father.

Arline begins her good-night prayer, "Now I lay me down to sleep, I pray the Lord my soul to keep. If—what's next?" Ollie hasn't a clue what's next, but Stan whispers to him, and Ollie concludes for her, "*If* at first you don't succeed, try, try again."

Twelve years later. The Gypsies again encamp in Count Arnheim's woods.

The boys, now sleeping in the trailer, are awakened by Arline calling them cheerily for breakfast.

As Ollie is about to eat, Arline (Jacqueline Wells) tells "Daddy" and Stan of her wonderful dream. A perfectly functional cue for one of Michael Balfe's most beautiful songs, "I Dreamt I Dwelt in Marble Halls."

The song's burden is that riches and greatness were all hers—"but I also dreamt, which charmed me most, that you loved me still the same." And she embraces Ollie. Ollie resumes his breakfast and finds it gone. He asks Stan why he ate it all. "I didn't want it to get cold," he explains. "I didn't know how long she was going to dream."

In getting things in order, Stan notices that the wine they have been preparing is "fuzzling." He is told to bottle it. Ollie is going off to his zither lesson, and he tells his pal not to get into any mischief. Stan really doesn't try to—but—every shoemaker to his last. In siphoning the wine from the barrel to the bottles, he neglects an elementary step in the sequence. When one bottle is full, instead of crimping the hose shut as he prepares the next empty bottle, he sticks the flowing hose in his mouth. It seems to him, on the whole, the only sensible place to put it during corking and uncorking procedures. Gradually, languorously, he reaches pleasant benumbment, the wine literally coming out of his ears. (This is a quieter reworking of the flagon-drinking gag in *The Devil's Brother* of 1933. Both are pantomimic masterpieces.)

Arline, on her way to shop in the village, wanders into the grounds of Count Arnheim's castle, faint memories stirring. The count can be heard singing "But Memory Is the Only Friend That Grief Can Call Its Own."

Considered just another "thieving Gypsy," Arline is apprehended and thrown into the dungeon in the castle. Ollie witnesses her seizure from afar. The count is told about her and he orders that, woman or not, she shall be lashed.

Ollie wakes the hiccuping Stan to tell him of Arline's capture and of the need to rescue her. Stan staggers to his feet. "You're guzzled," Ollie says. "Oh, poof! Nothing of the kind." They go to help her.

They try to sneak into the castle but Stan's hiccups are like clarions in the night. They manage to reach Arline's cell, and Stan immediately takes a file and gets to work on the cell window. Ollie quiets him and he starts filing Ollie's nose. The captain of the guard (James Finlayson), hearing the noise, walks up to the boys aghast, surveys them with a lantern. Stan, half-blind anyway, turns, sees the lantern, takes it from Fin and holds it while Ollie tries to get in. Seeing the keys on Fin's belt, Stan takes them, opens the cell door. Ollie, seeing Fin, reacts, and the boys run into the cell, closing the door. Stan puts on Arline's coat. Fin hurls Ollie back into the cell, hustles Stan out with a "Now, my proud beauty, your time has come." Fin hurries the cloaked figure to the whipping post, and in the struggle Stan pokes Fin in the eye, then in the other eye. "Oh, my good eye!," shouts Fin. (This was an "in" joke at the studio: for years Fin's best comic reaction or "take" was a forward thrust of the head, the squint of one eye, and the wide opening of the other, lifting the eyebrow high.)

But the three are handily seized; the boys are sent to the torture chamber, and Arline is removed to the whipping post...

...where she is prepared for lashing. Fin's gleeful villainy is exuberant to the point of intoxication.

Fin grabs the medallion from Arline's neck and hurls it to the ground. Count Arnheim, looking on, recognizes both the medallion and a birthmark on Arline's shoulder. "Arline, my child," he says, with the joyous emphasis of one uttering the final exultant words of a fairy tale.

But two complications remain: Ollie has been placed on the rack to be stretched; Stan has been placed in a cage to be pressed. Just a shade too late Arline pleads with the count, who releases them. The last shot of the film shows Fin on guard at an arch as an elongated Ollie and a diminutive Stan waddle by.

A Laurel & Hardy Cameo Appearance

ON THE WRONG TREK

1936

Charley Chase Series / Two reels / Sound / Released April 18, 1936, by M-G-M / Produced by Hal Roach / Directed by Charles Parrott/ Charley Chase, and Harold Law / Photographed by Art Lloyd / Photographic effects by Roy Seawright / Edited by William Ziegler / Sound by William B. Delaplain.

Charley Chase Himself / *Mrs. Chase* Rosina Lawrence / *Charley's mother-in-law* Bonita Weber / *Office workers* Gertrude Sutton, Jack Egan, Frances Morris / *Highway Patrol officers* Charles McAvoy, Eddie Parker, Bob (Mazooka) O'Conor / *Mixed-up hitchhikers* Stan Laurel, Oliver Hardy / *Roadside holdup men* Bud Jamison, Leo Willis, Bob Kortman, Harry Wilson / *New district manager* Clarence H. Wilson / *His wife* May Wallace / *California border officer* Harry Bowen / *Bums* Harry Bernard, Dick Gilbert, Robert (Bobby) Burns, Charlie Sullivan, Joe Bordeaux, Jack Hill, Lester Dorr.

In this Charley Chase short the hero is telling (by way of flashback) details of the dreadful vacation he just had with his pert wife and bossy mother-in-law. Hard luck rides them all the way and we share these various encounters, one of which is with a pair among the many hitchhikers the trio meet as they drive along. The mother-in-law wants to pick them up, saying, "Those two

fellows over there. They have kind faces." The camera pans slowly along the roadside to reveal a shabby Stan and Ollie thumbing their way—in opposite directions.

Ollie, realizing Stan is undermining their combined efforts, slaps the offender's hand down. Charley doesn't share his mother-in-law's benevolence. "Look like a couple of horse thieves to me!," he says of Stan and Ollie, then tops his remark by mimicking Stan's foolish grin and hair-scratching gesture.

Charlie, his wife (Rosina Lawrence), and mother-in-law (Bonita Weber), robbed of their clothing and out of gas, are reduced to hitchhiking.

OUR RELATIONS

74 minutes—Sound
Released October 30, 1936, by M-G-M
Produced by Stan Laurel for Hal Roach
Supervised by L. A. French

Directed by Harry Lachman
Photographed by Rudolph Mate
Photographic effects by Roy Seawright
Edited by Bert Jordan
Suggested by the short story,
"The Money Box,"
by William Wymark Jacobs
Screenplay by Richard Connell
and Felix Adler
Adaptation by Charles Rogers
and Jack Jevne
Sound by William Randall
Musical score and direction
by Le Roy Shield
Settings by Arthur I. Royce
and William L. Stevens

Stan Laurel . . . . Himself
Alfie Laurel . . . . Stan Laurel
Oliver Hardy . . . . Himself
Bert Hardy . . . . Oliver Hardy
Captain of the S.S. Periwinkle . . Sidney Toler

Joe Groagan, waiter . . . . Alan Hale, Sr.
Mrs. Daphne Hardy . . . . Daphne Pollard
Mrs. Betty Laurel . . . . Betty Healy
Alice, the beer garden girl . . . . Iris Adrian
Lily, the other café girl . . . . Lona Andre
Finn, the chief engineer . . . . James Finlayson
Inebriated stroller . . . . Arthur Housman
Other drunk . . . . Jim Kilganon
Pawnshop extra . . . . Charlie Hall
Officers . . . . Harry Bernard
Harry Arras
Charles A. Bachman
Harry Neilman
First mate . . . . John Kelly
Seamen . . . . Art Rowlands
Harry Wilson
Bartenders . . . . Baldwin Cooke
Nick Copland
James C. Morton
Lee Phelps
Café manager . . . . George Jimenez
Cabdriver . . . . Bob Wilbur
Doorman . . . . Jim Pierce
Mrs. Addlequist . . . . Ruth Warren
Finn's friend Snuffy . . . . Walter Taylor
Tuffy . . . . Constantine Romanoff
Waiter . . . . Alex Pollard

Grubby wharf toughs . . . . Joe Bordeaux
Stanley (Tiny) Sandford*
Billy Engle
Bob O'Conor
Messenger boy . . . . Bobby Dunn
Gangsters . . . . Ralf Harolde
Noel Madison
Judge Polk . . . . Del Henderson
Bailiff . . . . Fred Holmes

Bits and dress extras in Denker's Beer
Garden and Pirate Nightclub
scenes . . . . Bob Finlayson,
Alex Finlayson, Foxy Hall, Jay Eaton,
Jack Hill, Rita Dunn, Alice Cooke, Ed
Brandenberg, Jack Egan, Bunny Bron-
son, Marvel Andre, Dick Gilbert, Jack
Cooper, Jerry Breslin, Bill Madsen,
Ernie Alexander, Tony Campenero,
Polly Chase, Jay Belasco, Gertrude
Astor, Buddy Messinger, Gertie Mes-
singer Sharpe, David Sharpe, Rose
Langdon, Johnny Arthur, Kay McCoy,
Mrs. Jack W. Burns, Rheba Campbell,
Margo Sage, Ed Parker, Leo Sulkey,
Marvin Hatley, Sam Lufkin, Barney
O'Toole, Ray Cooke, Art Miles, Crete
Sipple, Dick French, Rosemary Theby

Stunt double for Stan Laurel . . . . Ham Kinsey
Stunt double for Oliver Hardy . . . . Cy Slocum

*Working in last of his 23 films with Laurel
and Hardy.

The Laurels and the Hardys at high tea as the cups are passed in a merry round robin. Stan and Ollie simultaneously congratulate Mrs. Hardy (Daphne Pollard) for her tea brewing, which causes them to touch each other on the nose and clasp their little fingers, whereupon Stan says "Shakespeare!," and Ollie, "Longfellow!" Throughout the film this is their little ceremonial to acknowledge, beamishly, the accident of their speaking in unison. Mrs. Hardy and Mrs. Laurel (Betty Healy) must prepare to leave for a bridge party.

A messenger delivers a letter to Ollie from his mother, and just as he is about to read it, Stan crunches down noisily on a crisp celery stalk. Ollie takes it from him and commences reading but his glasses fall into the jam. Ollie orders Stan to clean them off, and Stan obligingly pours boiling water over them in a bowl. The glasses break. "My eyes are getting worse every day," Ollie sighs. "This letter's just a blur. Hurry up!" Stan hands him the glass frames. "Thank you," says Ollie as he puts them on. "Now—*that's* better!"

Ollie's mother says that in cleaning the attic, she came across a picture of Ollie and Stan, and their brothers, Bert and Alf . . .

. . . an intriguing brace of twins. Stan takes Ollie's glasses to look at the picture, but even with this visual aid cannot be certain who is who. Ollie asks for his glasses, and Stan first considerately cleans them by running a napkin through the rims, breathing heavily on them before he polishes. Ollie feels for the lens of the glasses, saying disgustedly, "No wonder I couldn't tell which was you. Here, you read it." Stan reads Mom Hardy's letter, which says, "I forgot to tell you that after you and Stan left home, your twin brothers, Alf and Bert, turned out to be bad lads and ran away to sea, and I did hear they joined a mutiny on board one night and they both got hanged . . . Let this be a lesson to you. Mother." Igniting the photograph, Ollie says it is best to burn their past—because their wives would hate to know the boys have "low-down brothers like that."

eaving for the bridge party, Mrs. Hardy is kissed by Ollie, and
tan, who is fleetingly under the impression that his wife's
iend, Mrs. Addlequist, is his spouse, kisses her. Mrs. Laurel is
ot amused.

t the same time, aboard the S.S. *Periwinkle*, Alf Laurel and
ert Hardy are pursuing their aquatic destiny. They have been
pending their substance through the years. Ruefully, they
ealize that if Finn, the chief engineer (James Finlayson), had
aved their money for them as he has been urging, they would
ow (in Alf's phrase) be "sitting on the fat of the land." Finn
alks the boys into giving him their current pay—$74—which he
roposes to run up into a million for them. However, for
npending shore leave, Finn gives them money for a little fling
-50 cents apiece. Bert cannily asks a receipt of Finn for
heir money. Agreeably surprised at this businesslike
fficiency, Finn makes out an I.O.U. for the $74, which he asks
he boys to sign. They do so, and, knowing their own profligacy,
olicit Finn not to give them their money. He earnestly assures
hem he will not.

lf and Bert are called in by the captain (Sidney Toler) to take
n important package and deliver it to him later at Denker's
eer Garden. (The monkey was added by the still photographer
ecause of the close Laurel resemblance.)

At Denker's Groagan, the burly waiter (Alan
Hale), after bringing the boys a beer and two
nice, clean, unused straws (Alf's specifications),
marvels at the beautiful ring Bert—
unauthorized—finds in the captain's package.

331

The boys revel in their straitened luxury, and introduce themselves gallantly to two experienced harbor doxies, Lily (Lona Andre) and Alice (I is Adrian). Winningly, Bert says his mother's name was Alice, and when Alf denies this, Bert insists that Alice "was her second name on my father's side." After almost no urging at all, the girls order a tiny snack of lobster, steak, mock turtle soup, lyonnaise potatoes, broccoli hollandaise, a head of lettuce with Rocquefort dressing, demitasse and crepes suzette.

The boys need a private consultation to meet this emergency. They decide to make it more private by engaging a telephone booth. Realizing they must see Finn and get their money back, they plan to start saving on their next voyage. Alf says, "We can be millionaires anytime." A drunk (Arthur Housman) joins them in the phone booth when a call comes in from his wife, and after much threshing about . . .

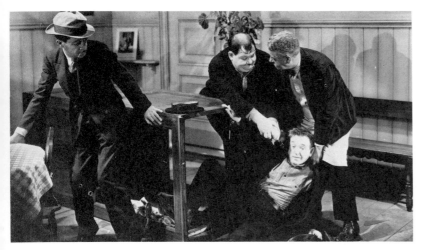

. . . the booth crashes to the floor, and Groagan adds the damage costs to Alf's and Bert's bill. The boys tell Alice and Lily that return to the ship is imperative so they can change clothes and come back to take the girls out on the town.

Groagan doubts their story, and the boys are compelled to leave the captain's ring for security.

Alf and Bert repair speedily to Finn's boardinghouse to get their money. He is adamantly uncooperative. The boys steal Finn's clothes, hoping to pawn them.

Bert tells Alf that his asking the pawnbroker if he has any secondhand ice-cream cones means that Alf must wait outsid Alf whiles away the time by blowing a French horn, going s far as to blow off Bert's hat as h comes out of the shop. Finn's clothes netted them a miserly $ but Bert is resolved not to be defeated. They come back, and Finn agrees to return their mon in exchange for his clothes' pav ticket. Finn tells the boys they must give him what they're now wearing—one outfit for Finn to don, the other to pay for the interest on the pawn ticket. The Finn can get his clothes from th pawnshop—clothes into which has sewn the boys' savings. Reluctantly, the boys disrobe.

Meanwhile Stan and Ollie have been waiting for their wives in front of—inevitably—Denker's Beer Garden. The girls show up, and Ollie reveals that Stan took him to see a Punch-and-Judy show that afternoon. Now ready for dinner, Mrs. Hardy suggests Denker's; Ollie says he knows a better place. They enter Denker's directly—where Alice and Lily look at the boys in amazement.

Groagan says to the boys, "Well, you got here at last, eh?" Stan can't understand how they got here at last. As he says, "We weren't coming in in the first place." The ladies order—Mrs. Laurel asking for a Welsh rarebit, which Stan carefully specifies must be "with cheese." Groagan says he knows what the boys are going to have. Mrs. Hardy wonders at these curious goings-on, and Stan and Ollie say in unison, "We never met him before in our lives." "Shakespeare!" "Longfellow!" Lily and Alice can endure it no longer; they indignantly come over to the table, and Alice says to Ollie, "I don't think much of your taste—ditching us for a couple of old frumps like these!"

Alice and Lily sit on the boys' laps. Stan and Ollie protest their innocence but Groagan confirms their previous appearance. The wives react in disgust and insist that the bill be paid and they be off. The boys pay their check—and Alf's and Bert's—whereupon Groagan gives them the captain's ring. Mrs. Hardy reacts in stung astonishment, telling Ollie he can see her lawyer in the morning. During this, Finn has wandered into Denker's, and in approaching the wives, inquires which is Alice and which is Lily. Finn identifies himself as an old pal of the boys, showing the wives a picture of himself, Alf, and Bert in bathing suits with three floozies. The wives stalk out.

Finn asks the boys to look through his fingers and, when they do, knocks their heads together so vehemently his toupee falls off. In slow, deliberate return, Ollie smears mustard on Finn's head and claps the toupee over it. Then the boys open Finn's mouth, insert the light bulb from the table lamp, and Ollie hits Finn on the jaw. There is a glass-crunching sound, and smoke pours out of Finn's mouth. Stan puts an open lamp socket on Finn's nose, Ollie turns on the switch, Stan removes the lamp. Finn holds his burned member tenderly.

Stan fills Finn's hat with beer and plops it back on his head. Groagan sets the Welsh rarebit down, and Finn seasons it —for heaving at Stan, who runs. Finn throws—and it smacks the burly bartender.

333

Finn is evicted
as an unruly
customer.

Ollie resolves that to teach their wives a lesson, the boys will stay out all night, not going home "until they come to us and apologize." Stan is pleased at this, adding, "We'll give them enough rope so we can hang ourselves." They confide these plans to the drunk who says he is in the doghouse too, and that they all should make a night of it. In unison, the boys say, "All for one and one for all!" "Shakespeare!" "Longfellow!"

Back at the boardinghouse Alf sees the only way out of their predicament is to take Groagan to the ship, let the captain pay the bill, and then repay him next voyage. But they can't go out in the streets unappareled—unless, as Alf suggests, they dress up like "those guys in Singapore . . . that look like Eskimos . . . the guys that walk around with rugs." In other words, cover up in bed quilts. Bert is dubious but says, "You've got to be right *once* in your life." While they are preparing to leave, the captain goes to Denker's and learns the fate of his ring.

Alf and Bert return to Denker's—where Groagan throws them out heartily after they accuse him of stealing the ring.

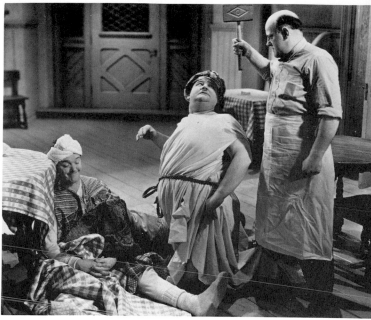

The boys return to conk Groagan over the head in order to get their ring. The bartender (James C. Morton) reciprocates by knocking out Alf and—in due time—Bert. The police come to haul the boys off to the paddy wagon, and as they do so, Mrs. Addlequist, the bridge-playing pal of Mrs. Laurel and Mrs. Hardy, stands by aghast, watching. This choice bit of gossip is quickly relayed to the wives, who go down to the police station to argue for the boys' release with a judge they know, a fellow lodge member of Stan's and Ollie's. Reunion is effected, and as the ladies hold out their arms to their errant boys, Bert kisses Mrs. Laurel and Alf kisses Mrs. Hardy. The judge advises the boys to stay out of beer gardens: "Go to a high-class place." Mrs. Hardy quickly takes this up, saying they'll do just that—have a good time, and if the boys promise never to get into any more trouble, "we'll forget all that's happened." Mystified, Alf and Bert agree.

Meanwhile, at the exclusive Pirate Club, Stan, Ollie, and the drunk are celebrating. Ollie says their wives are probably at home crying their eyes out, which is the appropriate moment . . . for Bert and Alf to enter the club with Mrs. Laurel and Mrs. Hardy.

The drunk, accidentally seeing Bert and Alf, faces Stan and Ollie and says, "Say now, you four guys stay away from me." Meanwhile, at a nearby table, Alice and Lily encounter Alf and Bert following the older ladies. Bert tells the tarts that they will join them "as soon as we get rid of these two old battle-axes." Mrs. Hardy is not pleased at this or at Bert's introduction of Alice and Lily as "the two girls we met this afternoon."

Mrs. Hardy shoves Bert into a chair as Alf covers his pal's head with a tureen. She swings a bottle at Bert, hits the tureen, and starts to swing at Alf. Bert puts the tureen on Alf's head, Mrs. Hardy swiftly hits Bert on his unguarded noggin. Mrs. Hardy picks up a nearby birthday cake, with Alf's help, and crashes it down on Bert. The wives exit in renewed dudgeon.

As Stan and Ollie continue their celebration, the captain approaches and indignantly demands his ring. Ollie defies him and the captain knocks him over. The drunk pulls off the captain's shirt, and Stan ignites the hair on the captain's chest. Ollie tells Stan to get the manager. After Stan goes, Alf—looking for a temporarily absent Bert—approaches Ollie who asks him where the manager is. Ollie takes the ring from his pocket and slips it into Alf's. Two crooks watch this transaction with interest. The captain returns to chase Alf, and in so doing, collides with a waiter bearing a pastry tray. The captain is duly marked.

Stan and the manager come to Ollie at the bar, and the captain confronts Stan. Ollie accuses the captain of trying to rob them, and the drunk tries to prevent the captain from hurting his buddies.

Waiters bear the struggling captain off. Ollie asks Stan for the ring but Stan denies receiving it. Ollie is indignant. One of the crooks (Ralf Harolde) insists to Stan that he saw Ollie slip the ring in his pocket.

The other crook (Noel Madison) asks Ollie if he can speak to him alone. Ollie puts both fingers in Stan's ears. The crook suggests they scare the ring *out* of Stan by pretending "we're a couple of tough guys" and fake taking Stan for a ride. Ollie removes his fingers and tells Stan that "these gentlemen have been kind enough to invite us for a nice ride." As they leave the club in the crooks' car (the drunk asks if he can be dropped off), a police car pulls up, spots the crooks leaving with their passengers, and follows, siren screaming. At this moment Bert leaves the club washroom, Alf approaches and asks his pal if he got rid of the captain. Bert is baffled, but on hearing that their irate boss is here, decides that the boys had best leave at once. In so doing, they meet Finn and two hired thugs. "If you think you can put mustard on my head and burn my nose and get away with it, you're crazy!," shouts Finn.

The boys flee . . . and are faced at one of the exits by a thug who follows them with Finn and the other thug . . . . . . up the ratlines . . . to the top beam . . .

. . . which cracks, splits in two, and drops Bert and Alf down to create some lively wreckage. 337

At the dock the crooks congratulate their driver on evading the cops, and invite the boys into their lair. Referring to the drunk, Stan says, "Say, what about our friend? You forgot to drop him off." "Oh, he's asleep," the crook says. "We'll do it later."

Inside, the crooks demand the ring, and the boys say in unison, "I haven't got the ring." "Shakespeare!," says Stan. "Not *now!*," replies Ollie. One of the crooks tells the boys their feet are going to be put in cement, and if they don't talk by the time it hardens, they'll be thrown off the dock. Ollie pleads with Stan to give up the ring; Stan cries, "You told me *you* had it!" The boys are set upright in round tubs, and concrete is poured over their feet. After it hardens, they are set on the edge of the dock and tormented by being rocked back and forth, closer and closer to the river's edge. After some spectacular rocking and crashing all over the dock area, they grab each other, roll over the edge and fall into the water.

The fleeing Bert and Alf run along the dock, open a warehouse door and dart inside. Stan's and Ollie's yells summon the police who proceed to hoist them out of the water with a hand derrick. The captain arrives on the scene, shouts down to the boys, demanding his ring—but Stan and Ollie know naught. The police continue hoisting them up. Inside the warehouse Alf discovers the ring in his pocket and wonders where it came from.

Alf and Bert come out, find the captain, and return his ring. The police, hoisting up Stan and Ollie, see Bert and Alf, yell in fright, and run away, dropping the handles of the winch. Stan and Ollie yell as they fall back in the water. Bert and Alf, realizing someone is in trouble, start to turn the winch handles, then see Stan and Ollie. They, too, yell, and let go of the handles. Once more Stan and Ollie fall back into the water. In short order the brothers are all united and the comedy of errors is explained. Ollie suggests they all go home and tell it to the wives. Twin walking with twin, Ollie tells Bert confidentially, "That Laurel is the dumbest thing I ever saw." "The other one, too!," says Bert. Ollie says, "Neither one of them can see any further than the end of their nose." Bert and Ollie walk off the end of the dock into the water, and as they splash to the surface, Stan and Alf look over the edge, shrugging their shoulders.

Production Sidelights

The genuine warmth between two perfectly functioning partners was probably never better revealed than in this informal shot.

Preparing for a low-angle shot—the scene in which Alf and Bert call up to Finn's window.

During the shooting the Laurel and Hardy Club of France sent the boys the world's largest postcard.

CARTE POSTALE

STAN LAUREL · OLIVER HARDY · CLUB

Du théâtre de l'Olympia de Paris, à l'occasion de la première grande réunion de la saison 1935-1936, les Membres du Club Laurel et Hardy de France se font une joie de transmettre à leurs patrons et amis l'assurance de leurs sentiments d'affectueuse admiration.

PARIS IX
Route de la MADELEINE

RF
FRANCE

M. M. Stan Laurel et Oliver Hardy
Studios Metro-Goldwyn-Mayer
Culver City
Californie
U.S.A.

Bouncing on the bar are Harry Lachman, the film's director, Stan, Babe, and Rudolph Mate.

The boys and Arthur Housman doing a scene at Denker's, with a lot of company.

341

A deleted shaving scene.

A traffic jam, updated from *Two Tars*, that was deleted.

WAY OUT WEST

1937

65 minutes—Sound
Released April 16, 1937, by M-G-M
Produced by Stan Laurel for Hal Roach
Directed by James W. Horne
Photographed by Art Lloyd and Walter Lundin
Special photographic effects by Roy Seawright
Edited by Bert Jordan
Original story by Jack Jevne and Charles Rogers
Screenplay by Charles Rogers, Felix Adler, and James Parrott
Art direction by Arthur I. Royce
Settings by William L. Stevens
Makeup by Jack Dawn
Sound by William Randall
Musical direction by Marvin Hatley

Compositions used in incidental music scoring by Marvin Hatley, Le Roy Shield, Van Alstyne, Leonard-Munson, J. L. Hill, Carroll-MacDonald, Nathaniel Shilkret, Irving Berlin, and Franz von Suppe

Stan Laurel . . . . Himself
Oliver Hardy . . . . Himself
Mickey Finn . . . . James Finlayson
Lola Marcel . . . . Sharon Lynne
Menacing sheriff . . . . Stanley Fields
Mary Roberts . . . . Rosina Lawrence
Anxious patron . . . . James Mason
Bartenders . . . . James C. Morton
                                        Frank Mills
                                        Dave Pepper
Molly, the sheriff's wife . . . . . . Vivien Oakland
Man eating at bar . . . . Harry Bernard
Cooks . . . . Mary Gordon
                                        May Wallace
Avalon Boys Quartet: . . . . Themselves
                                        Chill Wills
                                        Art Green
                                        Walter Trask
                                        Don Brookins

Worker at Mickey Finn's Palace . . . . Jack Hill
Baggageman for stagecoach line . Sam Lufkin
Bearded miner . . . . Tex Driscoll
Miner's wife, "Maw" . . . . Flora Finch
Janitor scrubbing floor . . . . Fred (Snowflake) Toones
The saloon chirp's raucous audience . . . . Bobby Dunn, John Ince, Fritzi Brunette, Frank Montgomery, Bill Wolf, Denver Dixon/Art Mix, Fred Cady, Eddie Borden, Helen Holmes, Ben Corbett, Buffalo Bill, Jr./Jay Wilsey, Cy Slocum
Cowboy extra . . . . Lester Dorr
Doubling for Stan Laurel . . . . Ham Kinsey
Doubling for Oliver Hardy . . . . Cy Slocum
Basso voice-over for Stan Laurel . . . Chill Wills
Mule . . . . Dinah

(Working titles: first, *Tonight's the Night,* then *In the Money.*)

(Academy Award nomination for "Music-Scoring.")

343

The social center of Brushwood Gulch: Mickey Finn's saloon, a roistering tavern under the steely-eyed control of its larcenously greedy owner, Mickey Finn (James Finlayson).

Mrs. Mickey Finn is the equally greedy Lola Marcel (Sharon Lynne), who spices up each evening for the patrons by fronting her dancing troupe and singing "Won't You Be My Lovey Dovey?"

Two desert rats *en trek*. Because the mule is slightly more intelligent than he is, Stan's guidance is a purely nominal one. In lordly fashion, befitting the sheer authority of his size, Ollie relaxes on their baggage as they ford the stream.

The mule unerringly heads for a large pothole in the creek, into which Ollie drops with alacrity, going in far over his head.

The first indication that their destination is near. Ollie is drying out in transit.

Having hitched a ride on a local stagecoach, the boys discomfit a haughty lady (Vivien Oakland) with their well-meant non sequiturs: "A lot of weather we've been having lately," Ollie says in a beguiling tone. She is not beguiled. "Only four more months to Christmas!," he adds archly. Her discomfort grows. "Do you believe in Santa Claus?," he asks beamingly. She does not beam back.

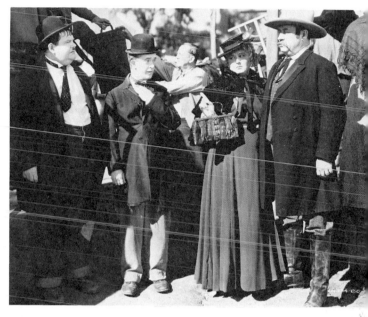

Distressingly, the haughty lady's husband turns out to be the hard-eyed sheriff of Brushwood Gulch (Stanley Fields), who, upon hearing of the boys' warm approaches to his wife, freezes them with a threat. He thunders, "Now, if you want to stay healthy, you better catch the next coach out of town." Ollie says they'd be glad to—just as soon as they've finished their business. The sheriff assures them that if they miss the next coach, they'll be riding out of town in a hearse.

Stan and Ollie set about their business. But first, made euphoric by a bunch of cowhands (the Avalon Boys Quartet) singing "At the Ball, That's All," Stan and Ollie provide counterpoint with an eccentric dance of easy elegance. 345

The boys hold the deed to a gold mine that a recently deceased friend has asked them to deliver to his daughter, Mary Roberts. Believing the girl to be a resident of Brushwood Gulch, Stan and Ollie plan to make a discreet investigation of the girl's whereabouts. As they make inquiries at the saloon, Finn asks Ollie why she is wanted. "Well, I'm sorry, sir," says Ollie, "we aren't supposed to discuss that with anyone but her." "Yes, you see it's private," says Stan. "Her father died and left her a gold mine. And we're not supposed to tell anybody but her." "Now that he's taken you into *our confidence*," says Ollie, glaring at Stan, "you might as well know the rest." He tells the rest, and Finn shivers with larcenous delight at his sudden thought that Lola can plausibly substitute herself for Mary and claim the deed. He gives the boys champagne and rushes upstairs to prepare Lola.

Finn takes the boys up to the pseudo-Mary Roberts, and Lola enacts with becoming bathos her sorrow at the news of "Daddy's" death. "Tell me, tell me about my dear, dear Daddy," Lola coos. "Is it true he's dead?" "Well, we hope he is," says Stan, —"they buried him!" "What did he die of?," she asks plaintively. "I think he died of a Tuesday," says Stan.

In a casual encounter, the boys meet the real Mary Roberts (Rosina Lawrence), a slavey-of-all-work in Finn's saloon. But before they can become aware of her identity, Finn sternly orders her back to work. After Finn's departure, the boys by chance encounter Mary again and she tells them her name.

Indicating the upstairs room where Lola lives (Stan can't see a thing), Ollie asks Mary just who that woman is. On learning Lola's true identity, the boys determine to retrieve the gold mine deed.

In a four-part roundelay of grabbing, snatching, losing, regaining, again losing, and once more regaining, Stan and Ollie battle with the Finns for the deed.

When Stan recovers the deed, Lola isolates him in her bedroom and makes the triumphant discovery that he is supremely ticklish.

Finn chortles
his triumph as his
spouse regains
the paper.

The boys are delighted by the timely
entrance of the sheriff, who un-delights
them by grimly pointing out that the
coach they were to leave on went ten
minutes ago. Stan and Ollie skip
helter-skelter ahead of his gunfire,
creating a mountainous cloud of their
own dust. Again they skitter across the
stream, and Ollie, with supreme talent
for disaster, plops into the same pothole
as before.

Reminding Stan of his boast that he'd
eat Ollie's hat if they didn't recover the
deed, Ollie offers his headpiece with
determination. Stan cries, eats a piece
of the derby apprehensively, and begins
to take increasing interest in the taste.
He tucks a napkin in his collar, salts the
hat, and proceeds to consume it with
gusto. The bewildered Ollie stops him,
orders him to get the Hardy clothing,
now quite dry. While Stan does so, Ollie
secretively takes a bite out of his derby,
chews hopefully, and spits it out
vehemently. The boys then prepare for
action, resolving to get the deed from
the Finns' bailiwick under cover of night.

They storm the saloon frontally but to no avail. They break open the lock of the guard gate; Ollie asks for support and Stan gets behind him and pushes. They crash through the unlocked front door, and run away in terror. Ollie indignantly asks Stan why he was pushed.

They reconnoiter in back of the saloon. How to get up to that second floor and the Finns' safe?

Ollie decides to climb up to an upper window with Stan's confidently inexpert help. Ollie gets up on the shed and promptly crashes through.

Using a block and tackle appended to the building, Stan hauls a trussed Ollie up toward the Finns' window. Things are proceeding splendidly and Ollie is virtually at his destination when Stan, preparing for a final lusty pull, yells up, "Wait a minute until I spit on me hands!" Ollie nods obligingly; Stan drops the rope, spits firmly on his hands, and Ollie goes plummeting down, his frame indenting the earth a foot.

Ollie regards his pal with his "Well—here we are again!" disgust.

He decides to chastise Stan by slapping him firmly on his extended palm with the rope end. Stan grimaces apprehensively before the blow and Ollie hits him resoundingly—on the head. Reacting to the pain with vigor, Stan rubs and blows on his hand to make it feel better.

Ollie peremptorily orders Stan to tie his end of the rope to Dinah the mule who can safely be counted on as propelling counterweight. Stan does so, and as Dinah, mounted by Stan, moves forward, Ollie moves upward. Now at high point, Ollie asks that the break-in tools be handed up to him. Stan obligingly gets off the mule with the tools, and Dinah, now outweighed by Hardy at the other end, whooshes up in the air to the second-floor balcony—and Hardy crashes down again this time into a storm-cellar door of the saloon.

Entering through the smashed door, they come up through a trapdoor opening—Ollie warning Stan to keep quiet. Stan accidentally lets the trapdoor crash down on Ollie, whose head protrudes through it. After a series of indignities to his noggin, all the result of Stan's trying to extricate him, the two gain entry to the house and alert Mary for flight when the deed is found

On their way through the darkened saloon, Stan inserts a coin into the slot machine and, hearing only a desultory trickle, proceeds upstairs. After he does so, the machine pays off ringingly, and Stan dashes down to collect the coins spilled all over the floor. At this point in the film, Stan again performs a standard bit of the white magic, which he can do under almost any condition: the igniting of his thumb. This both fascinates and irritates Ollie who has tried in vain to do it himself. He now essays it again and, to his frightened astonishment, his thumb does light up! He flails at it, putting it out in terror.

After a series of fruitless excursions downstairs to see what all the noise has been about, Finn literally uncovers his prey by discovering them hiding in the body of the piano. He lifts the lid, sees them huddled against the sounding board of the instrument. Vengefully, he plays some thundering arpeggios that pound the felt hammers against the boys' noses and stimulate the chaos that results in their falling to the ground, destroying the piano.

351

But the boys claim Finn's shotgun and order him upstairs to the safe. With the deed secure in their possession, they push Lola into her bedroom and tie Finn up to the ceiling light fixture in a diaper sling.

Preparing for departure, Ollie shows Mary the deed and they set off from the saloon.

What better way to secure Finn finally than in his own antiburglar gate?

The three reach the town outskirts. Now that their troubles are over, Ollie asks, where do they go from here? Back to the town where she was born— way down South, Mary says fervently. "Well, fan mah brow, I'm from the South!," Ollie says, proudly. "Well, shut mah mouth, I'm from the South, *too!*," says Stan. "The south of *what*, suh?," asks Ollie imperiously. "The south of London," says Stan. "London!," Ollie says scornfully, then comes up with the spirited idea that they'll *all* go down to Dixie. The three sing "We're Going to Go Way Down to Dixie" as they cross the stream where—inevitably—Ollie once more plunges into the pothole as Stan, Mary, and Dinah stroll blithely on.

70 minutes—Sound
Released May 21, 1937, by M-G-M
Produced by Hal Roach
Directed by Edward Sedgwick
Photographed by Norbert Brodine
and Art Lloyd
Photographic effects by Roy Seawright
Edited by William Terhune
Screenplay by Richard Flournoy,
Arthur Vernon Jones, and Thomas J. Dugan
Art direction by Arthur I. Royce
Settings by William L. Stevens
Dance direction by Eddie Court
Costumes by Ernest Schrapps
Makeup by Jack Dawn
Sound by William Randall
Musical score by Arthur Morton
and Marvin Hatley
Songs by R. Alexander Anderson,
Johnny Lange, Marvin Hatley,
and Fred Stryker

Stan Laurel	Himself
Oliver Hardy	Himself
Nellie Moore	Patsy Kelly
Joe Jenkins	Jack Haley
Rinaldo Lopez	Mischa Auer
Dagmar	Lyda Roberti
Cecilia Moore	Rosina Lawrence
Malheimer	Charles Halton
J. Aubrey Stone	Russell Hicks
Judge Pike	Spencer Charters
Sheriff	Sam Adams
Nightclub steward	Robert Gleckler
Lmia	Johnny Arthur
Ernie's bride	Joyce Compton
Laurel and Hardy's director	James Finlayson
Mexican tough guy	Walter Long
Bartender	James C. Morton
Pilots	Ralph Malone Blair Davies
Albert, the headwaiter	Eddie Kane
Studio guards	Charles A. Bachman, Charles McMurphy, Frank O'Connor
Unit assistants to Finlayson	Charlie Hall, Ray Cooke
Master of ceremonies	Cully Richards
Mexican hit with a chair	Sam Lufkin
Mr. McGregor	John Hyams
Mrs. McGregor	Leila McIntyre
Other judges	Otto Fries, Howard Brooks

Beauty contest winners:

Miss Gopher City	Margie Roanberg
Miss Centerville	Alino Moore
Miss Apple Valley	Mary Blackwell
Miss Mill Creek	Arline Abers
Eddie, in league with Russell Hicks	Brooks Benedict
Joe Jenkins' landlady	May Wallace
Oscar, the souse	Jack Norton
Oscar's wife	Wilma Cox
Hostess	Barbara Weeks
Bellboy	Edward Clayton
Announces bandits' arrival in scene	Bob (Mazooka) O'Conor
Street sweeper	Sid Saylor
Dress extra throughout	Jack Hill
Orchestra conductor	Jack Egan
Juicer	Charley Sullivan
Benny, the chauffeur	Eddie Hart
Old-timer	Si Jenks
Door greeter	Wilbur Mack
Undertaker	Murdock MacQuarrie
Undertaker's wife	Mary Gordon
Cashier	Al Williams, Jr.
Grip	Barney Carr
Nightclub singers	Felix Knight, Patricia Ka
Detective Nolan	James Burke
Playing harmonica off camera for Laurel and Hardy	Bob McClung

(Reissued as *Movie Struck.*)

PICK A STAR

1937

This feature-length musical starring Jack Haley, Rosina Lawrence, and Patsy Kelly uses Laurel and Hardy for "extra added attraction" purposes. Their scenes are not organically necessary to the film's structure. There are just two brief sequences.

In the first, film star Rinaldo Lopez (Mischa Auer) has brought two star-struck sisters (Patsy Kelly and Rosina Lawrence) to his studio to see movies being made. This moment shows Stan and Babe gently clowning while their old nemesis, James Finlayson (who plays the director of the first Laurel and Hardy sequence), looks on in typical dubiety. Fin directs…

…the arrival of two bandits at a Mexican cantina.

They are suave…

353

...and much feared as they swagger to the bar. There they encounter an old foe, Walter Long, with whom they engage in reciprocal bottle-smashing over each other's heads. After several turns of this, Fin yells "Cut!," and Patsy asks the director if he minds her going over to talk with the boys. "I wish you would," Fin says ambiguously. Patsy tells the boys admiringly that they certainly are able to take it, but Stan explains that the bottles are only breakaways that smash convincingly but inflict no injury. Babe asks the prop man for a bottle. It is brought, and Patsy is invited to hit them both. Unfortunately, it is a real bottle and both the boys are knocked out.

In the second sequence there is a vague tie-in to Rosina's preparation for a screen test. While her hairdresser works on her, a horn is heard, and the camera cuts to Stan playing. Babe says, "If you can't play a tune, put it down." Stan plays "Old Black Joe," then repeats the tune, making the tiny horn sound like a tuba. Babe throws the horn away, and it hits a mirror near Rosina, causing her to worry about the unlucky implication.

Stan takes a harmonica and plays "Reuben, Reuben." Competitively, Babe takes a tiny harmonica out of his pocket and plays "Listen to the Mocking Bird." "Top that!," he says to Stan. Stan plays the same tune with flourishes. Babe, putting the harmonica under his tongue, plays "Yankee Doodle," but then swallows the instrument. Stan prods his pal's stomach, and it sounds a chord. Manipulating with careful push-and-touch, Stan plays "Pop, Goes the Weasel!" brilliantly.

Production Sidelight

In a pleasant publicity shot for *Pick a Star* the featured cast is lined up: Charles Halton, Tom Dugan, Lyda Roberti, Mischa Auer, Rosina Lawrence, Jack Haley, Patsy Kelly, Stan, and Babe.

SWISS MISS

1938

72 minutes—Sound
Released May 20, 1938, by M-G-M

Produced by Hal Roach

Production managed by
Sidney S. Van Keuran

Directed by John G. Blystone,
and Hal Roach (uncredited)

Photographed by Norbert Brodine
and Art Lloyd

Photographic effects by Roy Seawright

Edited by Bert Jordan

Original story by Jean Negulesco,
Charles Rogers, and, uncredited, Stan Laurel and
Hal Roach (who is of Swiss descent)

Screenplay by James Parrott,
Felix Adler, and Charles Melson

Art direction by Charles D. Hall

Set decorations by William L. Stevens

Wardrobe by Ernest Schrapps

Dance direction by Val Raset

Sound by William Randall

Musical direction by Marvin Hatley

Music arranged by Arthur Morton

Compositions used in incidental music
scoring by Le Roy Shield, Phil Charig and
Arthur Quenzer, Nathaniel Shilkret,
Freedman-Slater, and Marvin Hatley

Stan Laurel	Himself
Oliver Hardy	Himself
Victor Albert	Walter Woolf King
Anna Hoepfel Albert	Della Lind/Grete Batzler
Franzelhuber	Adia Kuznetzoff
Village tradesman	Eddie Kane
His bickering wife	Anita Garvin
Flag thrower	Franz Hug
Edward Morton	Eric Blore
Anton Luigi	Ludovico Tomarchio
Bearded Swiss peasants	Sam Lufkin, Tex Driscoll
Emile, the cheese factory proprietor	Charles Judels
Joseph, the chauffeur	George Sorel
Organ-grinder	Harry Semels
Accordion player, with gorilla	Etherine Landucci
Gardeners	Gustav von Seyffertitz, Conrad Seideman
Yodeling, horn-blowing, and sideline music performers	Joseph Struder, Louis Struder, Otto Jehle, Fritz Wolfesberger

Astonished Swiss villagers	Bob O'Conor, Michael Mark
Enrico, the waiter	Jean de Briac
Man with mule-drawn cart	Agostino Borgato
Alpen Hotel waiters	Jacques Vanaire, James Carson, Ed Searpa
Driver of the ancient taxicab	Winstead (Doodles) Weaver
Bellboys at the Alpen Hotel	Hal Gerard, Nick Copeland, George Granlich, Earl Douglas, Alex Melesh, Jack Lubell, Eddie Brian, Eddie Johnson
Alpen Hotel atmosphere people	Baldwin Cooke*, Ed Brandenberg
Swiss dress extras for the Alpenfest	Jack Hill, Lester Dorr
Dancer	Val Raset
Stunt double for Stan Laurel	Ham Kinsey
Stunt double for Oliver Hardy	Cy Slocum
Gorilla	Charles Gamora
Mule	Dinah

(Working title: *Swiss Cheese.*)

*Working in last of his 30 films with Laurel and Hardy.

355

The scene is the Alpen Hotel, a charming hostelry high in the Swiss Alps. Speeding there from his home in Vienna is Victor Albert, great operatic composer, who is coming to find inspiration for a Tyrolean opera he conceives as his forthcoming masterpiece. To that end, every room in the hotel has been rented to keep him from distraction and the personnel fitted out in Tyrolean costumes. The manager, Anton Luigi (Ludovico Tomarchio), exhorts his staff to do their best, and he begins their preparations for the momentous visit by leading them in singing scales. Looking on approvingly is Edward (Eric Blore), Victor Albert's personal manager. (Victor Albert [Walter Woolf King] is not actually in this scene although included in the still.) He arrives…

…a few moments later, singing "Yo-Ho-Dee-O-Lay-Hee," a song based on the Swiss yodel. The hotel personnel, snappily lined up, know the song thoroughly.

Coinciding with Victor's arrival in town is that of two stupendously unsuccessful mousetrap salesmen.

They ask a housewife (Anita Garvin) if they can show her one of their latest mousetraps. The man of the house (Eddie Kane) says they don't want any. The lady says yes; her husband says no. They slap each other. Stan slaps the man, the man slaps Ollie, Ollie slaps the man—and the woman indignantly hits Ollie on the head with a frying pan. No sale—as the couple exits lovingly into the house.

Although it's a bit late in the game, Ollie asks Stan why he had the idea of coming all the way from America to sell mousetraps in Switzerland. Stan explains it easily: there should be more mice here than anywhere because they make more cheese here than anywhere. But they've been here for two weeks, haven't sold a mousetrap, and are flat broke. Stan has an answer for that. Go where the mice go to eat—a cheese factory. Sell mousetraps there. "Let me give that a little thought," says Ollie.

356

They go to Emil's Cheese Factory. Emil (Charles Judels) displays his wares for a gag never used in the film.

The boys explain to a very dubious Emil that they are making holes in his floor so the mouse has some place to get in. They cork the holes so the mouse can't get out, and they make a *number* of holes because a mouse never comes out of the same hole twice. In drilling through the floor, one of the bits drills into a gas pipe and the gas escapes upward. To see what the flow is, Stan lights a match, and the gas flames up like a torch. Stan covers the hole with his foot, the gas flames up under Ollie. Stan covers that hole with his foot, and the gas flames up in a new spot, again under Ollie. Gradually the boys cork up all the holes. The wily Emil, seeing a way to get rid of some worthless Bovanian francs he has, buys the boys' entire business for a 5,000-franc note. After they complete the transaction, in song, all the corks in the floor pop out in quick staccato.

Luxuriating after a splendid meal at the Alpen Hotel, the boys order dessert. Ollie has had his "mouth all set" for apple pie, and because none is available, he is considerably put out. Luigi has the waiter (Jean De Briac) summon the chef; and when that worthy comes, Ollie denounces him in lofty vein, calling him a jackass, and demanding to know why there is no apple pie. "I've had better chefs than you discharged for not having apple pie," says Ollie. Stan explains that Ollie had his face "all upset" for apple pie. Then, tired of it all, Ollie pays the bill with the 5,000-franc note. Luigi laughs heartily ("You Americans give always to me a sense of humor!"), and asks for real money. The money is good in Bovania but, as Luigi explains, there is no such place. Unable to pay, the boys are sent to the kitchen, where...

...the chef, Franzelhubor (Adia Kuznetzoff), with a sharkish smile, welcomes them. He is told they will work off their bill, and if they break any dishes, they work another day for each dish they break. The chef hands plates to them, then throws apples, which they try to catch, causing the plates to drop. The chef numbers their days on the blackboard.

"There *is* no better chef than me... By the time you leave this place," he says, "the gray hairs of your beard will be trailing on the kitchen floor."

Victor hears a sound he can't identify. Edward can—it's a cricket. Which is more than ample warrant for Victor to compose—on the spot, and with total ease—"The Cricket Song." Diners on the hotel terrace below join in as if rehearsed, and Victor's wife Anna pulls up in a cab before the hotel in time to sing the last chorus with charming fervor. Even Stan and Ollie, in the kitchen, do an impromptu dance to it, climaxed by Stan's opening a large cupboard from which hundreds of dishes spill down, smashing as they go.

Victor loves Anna (Della Lind) devotedly but he has come here especially so he can write a success on his own, unaided by her reputation as a great singer. He insists she go home until he has finished his music about "a simple, unsophisticated girl that a peasant could fall in love with." In response to her suggestion that she could play such a role, Victor hoots with laughter. Anna flounces out. She finds Stan's and Ollie's courtesy striking, and when they tell her their story of being forced to stay in the hotel because they couldn't pay the dinner bill, she says, "I'll take a double order of everything on the menu." When Stan and Ollie begin work as waiters, they go into the kitchen, get the dinners from the chef, and march out into the dining room. In so doing, they pass by the large blackboard on which the chef has marked down the extensive number of days they are due to remain. As Stan goes by, he quickly erases some of the chalk marks, whispers to Ollie, who erases some as he goes by. In and out, they do this several times until Ollie finds his entire backside is a superb eraser. As he wiggles the marks away contentedly, the chef finally catches on. The boys are forced to put down chalk marks until the chef tells them to stop—something he clearly has no disposition to do.

The boys are in the yard plucking chickens. Stan discovers that the little barrel under the St. Bernard's chin is full of brandy, put there for the humane purpose of succoring near-frozen travelers in the heavy snows. Ollie is called away by the chef, and Stan looks longingly at the brandy barrel. Attempts to woo the dog are fruitless...

...he can't even be bribed by a friendly handshake or a lump of sugar. The dog resists every pressure or blandishment. Angrily going back to chicken plucking, Stan throws the feathers high in the air. As they flutter down, they fall to the earth softly, gently, like—? Immediately Stan picks up a basket of the white feathers, throws them up furiously, lies down on the ground, and calls for help. "I'm freezing to death. Help, help, help . . . " The dog notices the soft white stuff falling and lays his head across Stan's body. Stan relieves him of the barrel. (This sequence was shot in a single take, a remarkable feat. Stan was justly proud of it.)

In order to get peace, Victor has his piano sent to a tree house high above an Alpine gorge, attainable only by a swinging rope bridge. The boys are sent to transport it, but Stan isn't an awful lot of help in his present condition. He isn't quite aware of the piece of fruit that Ollie knocks out of his hand, leading it to further adventure bouncing off Ollie and ultimately smacking the unfortunate Edward.

They huff and they puff getting it up the side of the mountain glen.

They look over the cliff—far, far below. Ollie tells Stan to test the rope bridge, which he promptly does, running out to the tree house and back. On his return, Stan says, "Say, listen, I'm not going across that bridge." When told that he has just done so, he faints. They begin to carry the piano across, Ollie steps on the dolly they are using to haul it, and crashes headfirst through the bridge. Stan pulls him back. Ollie tests the rest of the bridge slats, going all the way over to the tree house.

Ollie confidently tells Stan that from now on it's going to be easy sailing. As Ollie returns to the piano, a door in the tree house opens and a gorilla (Charles Gamora) comes out, following Ollie. "I see a monkey," whispers Stan. "Well, it doesn't surprise me a bit," Ollie tells him. "If you don't quit drinking that brandy you'll be seeing pink elephants." The gorilla bedevils Ollie gently from behind: lifting his hat from his head, scratching his leg. "Everything ain't just all right," Ollie says, looking back, seeing nothing of the gorilla who has sat down demurely behind him. The gorilla finally slaps him heartily on the back, and Ollie shouts out in shock. In an excess of whimsy, the gorilla begins to swing the bridge to and fro in an ever-increasing arc. It breaks, the gorilla and the piano fall into the valley far below, and the boys cling to the bridge, which hangs like a rope ladder from the perilous cliff.

Stan gets clear and, in helping Ollie up, he is distracted by the St. Bernard going by with another full barrel of brandy. Stan knows where his most immediate needs are, and he follows the dog, leaving Ollie to howl with indignation as he clings to the battered bridge.

Ollie has fallen deeply in love with Anna who he believes to be a simple, peasant girl. Stan verifies his condition for him: "Look at the silly, sloppy look on your face." Ollie is much moved by this. Stan also asserts Anna loves Ollie in return. "How do you know?" "Any dumbbell can tell that," Stan says with the air of one who should know. He recommends that Ollie serenade his ladylove "like the gay caviars used to do in the olden days." Ollie does so that very night, first reciting a poem to Anna: "If you love me like I love you, I'd love you better than Irish stew. Boo-boop-a-doo!" "I wrote that," Stan says proudly. Ollie wants to take Anna to the Alpenfest tomorrow; she suggests he come visit her next morning at sunrise to hear a plan she is projecting.

Ollie then sings "Let Me Call You Sweetheart," Stan accompanying on the tuba. The chef pours down his scorn in the form of cold water. He says Anna is *his* girl, and to stay away or he'll skin him alive. "Get out!," he shouts at them.

The Alpenfest commences with all hands singing "I Can't Get Over the Alps." Stan and Ollie attired as Gypsies, replete with bounteous false moustaches, drive into the courtyard of the hotel with Anna, now in the guise of a Gypsy dancer. Everyone watches a flag-tossing dance, and Ollie introduces Anna as Romany Rose, "the greatest prima donna that ever trilled a cantata." She sings "Gypsy Song." On a balcony above, Victor watches her and sends Edward down to bring the Gypsy up to his room. Edward is stung by this disloyalty to Anna but Victor says, "You fool, don't you recognize her? That *is* Anna."

The boys deliver Anna to Victor's room, but he insists on bringing her in alone, hanging a Do Not Disturb sign on the door.

The chef encounters the boys on the stairs: "I thought I told you two not to come back here." Stan turns to Ollie, "You know what? He thinks we're us. Isn't that silly?" The chef chases them all over the hotel—and the three of them do an in-and-out sequence in the kitchen lockers until the chef is caught, his arms hung out of the locker-door holes and tied together in a knot. The boys return to Victor's room, where Ollie is shocked to find Victor and Anna embracing and infinitely more shocked to learn they are married. "I thought you told me that I had her right in the palm of my hand?," Ollie says to Stan. "Well, you did have," Stan says with studious illogicality, "but you didn't play your cards right. Remember I told you. If you—" "Oh, get out."

As the chorus sings "Yo-Ho-Dee-O-Lay-Hee," the boys leave the hotel for new adventures, only to be confronted by a remembrance of one just past. The gorilla has somehow made it out of that deep gorge and now, considerably battered, growls menacingly at them. The boys run swiftly down the road. The gorilla swings a crutch around and around his head until it spins off far into the distance, knocking the boys down. The gorilla jumps up and down in an ecstasy of satisfaction.

Production Sidelights

Note: One of *Swiss Miss*'s highlights—carrying the piano across the Alpine gorge—is manifestly hilarious but because of inexplicable studio interference part of the sequence does not make sense. As originally conceived by Stan, a bomb was planted in the piano by the chef who, jealous of Anna's husband, hoped to finish him off by triggering the bomb to explode when a certain key was struck. It was planned that the many twistings and turnings of Stan, Ollie, and the gorilla, especially the accidental falls of the intoxicated Stan against the keys, would add strength to an already suspenseful scene. For some incredible reason during the editing (Stan was not consulted), the bomb footage was removed, and the scene in its present form contains meaningless shots of Stan crashing against the keys.

Several other interesting scenes were cut from the final footage. One is a humorously macabre nightmare scene in which Ollie accidentally shaves off his nose and his big toe and, in helping reattach them, Stan puts the toe where the nose should be, and vice versa. It results in such esoterica as Ollie's foot sneezing and a classic remark of Stan's: "Well, now whenever you get a shave, you can get a manicure at the same time."

One might forgive the cutting of these scenes, but it is totally indefensible to have cut an enchanting ten-minute musical sequence in which Stan and Ollie demonstrate a wide variety of Rube Goldbergish mousetraps to the proprietor of the cheese shop. All that is left of the sequence is the very end of it, still retained in the film, and the following still of Stan and Babe rehearsing the songs with composer Marvin Hatley at the piano, and with bespectacled Charles Judels, who plays the proprietor of the cheese shop.

Stan and Marvin Hatley at the piano. Leaning against the piano, Walter Woolf King; the young man at the right is Hal Roach, Jr.

Alan Mowbray, then working in a Roach film on an adjacent set, drops over for a visit with a fellow countryman.

Hal Roach's daughter, Margaret, as a Swiss extra, hugs the brandy-toting St. Bernard.

Stan as candid-camera fiend and a mulish friend.

On location: Babe's stand-in, Charlie Phillips; Stan; Babe; Stan's stand-in, Ham Kinsey.

BLOCK-HEADS

1938

58 minutes—Sound
Released August 19, 1938, by M-G-M
Produced by Hal Roach
Associate producer, Hal Roach, Jr.
Production managed by
Sidney S. Van Keuran
Directed by John G. Blystone
Photographed by Art Lloyd
Photographic effects by Roy Seawright
Edited by Bert Jordan
Original story and screenplay by
Charles Rogers, Felix Adler,
James Parrott, Harry Langdon,
and Arnold Belgard
Sound by Hal Bumbaugh
Music direction by Marvin Hatley

Stan Laurel	Himself
Oliver Hardy	Himself
Big-game hunter	Billy Gilbert
Mrs. Gilbert	Patricia Ellis
Mrs. Hardy	Minna Gombell
James	James C. Morton
Wizened man on stairs in top hat and tails	James Finlayson
Tough guy in apartment	Harry Woods
His son	Tommy (Butch) Bond
French aviator	Jean del Val
National Soldiers Home superintendent	Henry Hall
"Come on, lug, get out of that chair"	Sam Lufkin
Bemused long-haired clerk	Harry Strang

Military officer in trenches	William Royle
Midget in elevator	Harry Earles
Reporter in Billy Gilbert's home	Max Hoffman, Jr.
Lulu	Patsy Moran
Pedestrian	Ed Brandenberg
Soldier in trenches	Jack Hill
Bits	George Chandler Harry Stubbs
Stunt double for Stan Laurel	Ham Kinsey
Stunt double for Oliver Hardy	Cy Slocum
Bass voice-over for midget	Billy Bletcher
Part cut from final release print:	
Dowager seated near stairs	Zeffie Tilbury

(Academy Award nomination for "Best Original Score," by Marvin Hatley.)

With the AEF in France, 1917. Private Laurel is ordered by his commanding officer (William Royle) to stay in the trench and guard this post until relieved from duty. The company is going over the top in a sweeping attack.

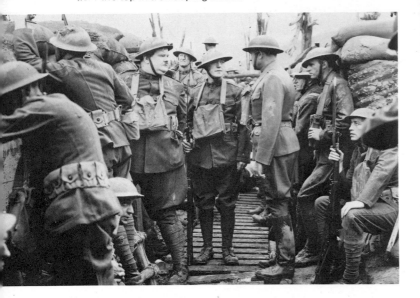

"Gee, I wish I was going with you," says Stan. "Take care of yourself, won't you?" "Don't worry about me, Stan," his pal assures him. "I'll be back. We'll *all* be back." The whistle blows, the battle begins, all hell breaks loose in no-man's-land. Time passes, indeed 1918 passes, all the years up to 1938 pass—and we see Stan still faithful to his charge, gun on shoulder, walking sentry go, his feet encased in burlap. His pacing has hollowed out another trench. After blowing a few cracked notes on the bugle, he goes to the dugout, takes out a can of beans, shakes it into his mess kit and tosses the can over to a small mountain of empty bean cans. An airplane is heard; Stan runs to a machine gun and shoots. Minutes later the pilot leans over the trench and learns to his astonishment that this "block-head" has been at his post for 20 years after the cessation of hostilities. Stan admits that things have been kind of quiet lately.

The Hardys are lovebirding it because this is their first wedding anniversary. Ollie asks for an extra dollar with his allowance today—"It's to be a surprise!"—and Mrs. Hardy (Minna Gombell) generously gives him a dollar and a *quarter.* He bids good-bye to his little "fig newton," and in the hall meets Mrs. Gilbert (Patricia Ellis). Ollie explains the reason for his obvious happiness and learns she, too, is celebrating—her husband's return after two months hunting in Africa. She and Ollie fall to their knees to pick up newspapers she dropped; Ollie takes them up for her as her husband (Billy Gilbert) appears in the hall. He is returning home aggressively with his elephant gun. Confused, Ollie starts to take Mrs. Gilbert into her apartment, comes back, removes his hat, puts the papers on his head, exchanges them for his hat, and leaves with a flustered laugh. Billy is not amused.

Down the hall Ollie encounters the porter reading a paper that contains a hilarious story about a fellow who stayed in the trenches for 20 years after the war, not knowing it was over. "I can't imagine anybody being *that* dumb," says Ollie. In delayed reaction, he admits, "Oh, yes I can," checks the paper, and goes directly to the National Soldiers Home.

At the home Stan, searching for a place to read his newspaper on the grounds, notices a wheelchair. It has a shortened leg support on one side for a crippled soldier, so Stan is forced to sit on the chair with his right leg doubled under him. Ollie approaches, sees Stan's truncated limb, and shakes his head sadly. The two chums greet each other effusively, and in telling Stan about his wife's cooking abilities, Ollie says, "You just wait 'til you put your legs under that table...er...pardon me. You just wait 'til you put your *leg* under that table..." Ollie describes all the wonders of Mrs. Hardy's culinary arts. "Any beans?," asks Stan. "You can have beans if you want 'em. You can have anything in the world you want." Ollie insists that Stan go with him. "My home is your home. I'm never going to let you out of my sight again." "Do you remember how dumb I used to be?," asks Stan. Ollie remembers. "Well, I'm better now."

And he does, to Stan's bemused wonder, grunting, stumbling, to the Hardy car. After they fall down while trying to get in, Stan helps Ollie to his feet, brushes him off, and walks around the car. "Why didn't you tell me you had two legs?," he asks indignantly. "Well, you didn't ask me," says Stan. "You're *better* now," says Ollie witheringly. Ollie's car is stuck between another car and a huge truck. Ollie asks Stan to move the latter forward, and Stan mounts its cab.

He shifts gears, and the rear of the truck rises, dumping its entire load of sand on Ollie. When Stan comes to the car, he finds it buried, Ollie's head barely above a fat sand hill. Ollie sighs and Stan begins to dig him out.

Stan wants to get a drink of water from a faucet across the road and makes a move to get up. "Well, how can you get over to that faucet?," Ollie asks. *He* will go over and get the hose. He gives it to Stan, walks back to turn on the faucet and the resulting blast hits him full in the back. "Hey," a veteran (Sam Lufkin) says to Stan, "come on, lug. Get out of that chair... That's my buddy's chair and I want it." Ollie says he'll give it to him when he's good and ready. The veteran hits Ollie smartly and asks if he's ready. "On second thought—*yes*. Don't exert yourself, Stanley, I'll carry you."

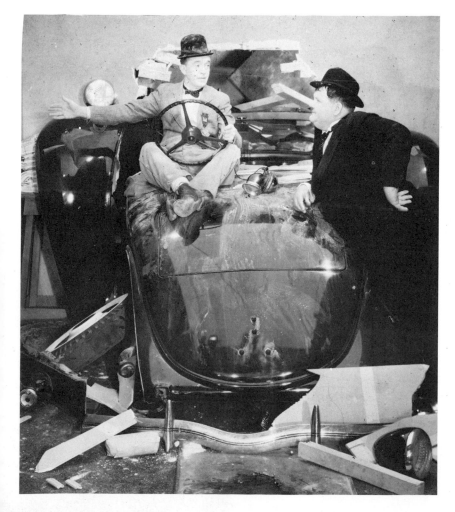

Back at the Gilbert apartment, Billy is telling engrossed reporters how he bagged the biggest boar in India. When his gun jammed (he says), he jumped to one side, just keeping cool ("I had a chill in my back"), took out both revolvers, and let the beast have it, "zix und zix." He boasts that he never brings them back alive, he brings himself back alive. After similar tales of derring-do, he excuses himself to go down to the gun shop. "I'm having a new gun made especially for me. I mean for the *elephants.*"

At his garage, Ollie proudly shows Stan how their automatic door opener works: one simply drives over a signal plate in the ground and the door swings open. Stan asks to try it. He drives the car forward at a frenzied pace, misses the plate completely, smashes through the door, and comes to befuddled rest.

In the apartment house, the elevator is out of order and they must walk up 13 floors. Halfway up, Ollie says it will take them just a jiffy longer. When Stan asks how far a jiffy is, Ollie replies that it is about three shakes of a dead lamb's tail. "Hmm!," says Stan, "I didn't think it was so far. Surprising, the distance." As they are resting on the staircase for a moment, a formally dressed gentleman (James Finlayson) demands they get out of his way, calls Ollie an overstuffed pollywog, and at Ollie's taking umbrage, marches with him all the way downstairs to settle this on the field of honor. Fin finally admits Ollie is not an overstuffed pollywog, he is "an inflated blimp." "That's different," says Ollie, but he is taken aback by the laughter of the crowd around him. The disputants push and shove, and finally Fin's handbag hits Ollie in the head, breaking all the ample liquid goods therein. Ollie lies flat on his back, and when Stan (who has been recruiting an audience for the scrap) appears to ask him what happened, his pal announces, "The fight is over."

After encountering an old flame of Ollie's, who admits she has sent an indiscreet note to his apartment, unaware that he was married, the boys hurry upstairs where a kid (Tommy Bond) playing football in the hall drop-kicks it into Ollie's face. Ollie kicks the ball downstairs and the boy's tough dad (Harry Woods) tells Ollie to go downstairs and bring the ball *up*. Exhausting minutes later, Stan and Ollie appear, puffing up the stairs. They give the ball to the kid, and when he bends down to kick it, Stan carefully kicks him. The dad reappears, kicks Ollie; Stan kicks the dad; the dad kicks Ollie again and starts back inside. Stan taps the man on the shoulder, and as he turns, Stan holds out his fist—and hits him with the other one. The man stands immobile—Stan taps him again, and he falls back board-stiff as his son looks on in wonder. Ollie kicks the ball downstairs with finality. In the hallway outside the Hardy apartment Stan takes a glass of water out of his pocket and starts to drink. "Why don't you put some *ice* in it?," Ollie asks sarcastically. Realizing a good idea when he hears one, Stan reaches into his pocket, pulls out several cubes, and drops them in the glass. Fortunately the note from Ollie's girl friend was misdelivered to the Gilbert's, and Ollie gratefully retrieves it. After "door-key" difficulty, the boys prepare to enjoy their arrival in the apartment; Ollie finds his wife has gone shopping. After making sure it's allowed, Stan prepares to smoke. He cups his hand like a pipe, pours tobacco into it, tamps it, lights it, and contentedly puffs on his thumb, blowing out smoke and coughing a bit. Ollie is amazed to the point of exasperation, as he always is, with these bits of Laurel white magic. Mrs. Hardy enters in a rage, is distinctly unimpressed with Ollie's old pal—a "knickknack" she terms him—and storms out to her mother's.

"We'll show her," says Ollie as he prepares to fix the meal he's promised Stan, who is sent to light the oven. Stan goes to the kitchen, turns on the gas, and looks for a match. He comes out and asks Ollie for one. "Any time I want something done right, I always have to do it myself," sighs Ollie as he strikes a match and walks into the kitchen. During the rocking explosion that follows, Stan runs downstairs and outside; Ollie surveys the wreckage sadly. Mrs. Gilbert comes in to help; Stan drifts back; and Ollie strongly needs a drink of the punch that his wife has prepared for this festive day. In the wrecked kitchen Ollie finds the full punch bowl, the only thing unscathed, resting in perfect balance on a slim upturned table leg. He tells Stan to get some glasses, walks carefully out of the kitchen holding the punch bowl high—and steps on a rolling pin. Crashing into the next room, he drenches Mrs. Gilbert with the punch. Going home to change her dress, she finds her apartment is locked, and the only thing available at the Hardy's for her to change into while her dress is drying seems to be a pair of Ollie's pajamas. Mrs. Hardy is heard approaching. Ollie frantically hides Mrs. Gilbert by making her sit in the posture of a chair and throwing a slipcover over her. The Hardys have a spirited battle, climaxed by her walking out again.

The boys hide Mrs. Gilbert in a trunk. Mrs. Hardy roars back, the argument flares again. Billy returns to his apartment. Overhearing the argument, he learns that Mrs. Hardy considers Stan to be the cause of the breakup of her happy home. She leaves to call the police, and when Billy wanders over, Stan tells him that Ollie has a girl concealed in the trunk, "so he asked me to help..."

Laughing confidentially, Billy says, "What do you want to bring them into your own home for? That's ridiculous. Why don't you come with me sometime? I know where there's a whole bunch of blondes ... Why do you think I go to Borneo all the time? You got to come with me sometime." His wife rises grimly from the trunk. Billy smiles at her and says, "You, too ... MY WIFE!" He runs into his apartment, picks up a gun and chases the boys out of the apartment into a courtyard. As he follows them between buildings, shooting as he goes, men jump from windows on both sides.

Note: This is the same ending as in *We Faw Down* of 1928. *Block-Heads'* ending was shot during Stan's absence from the studio (doubles were employed), and he was bitterly opposed to it when he finally saw it. The ending he wanted would have been much funnier, even if slightly macabre: the film would have ended with Billy chasing them, shooting wildly, followed by a terminal shot of Stan and Ollie in separate trophy mounts over Billy's fireplace. Ollie turns to Stan and says heavily, "Well—here's *another* nice mess you've gotten me into."

Production Sidelights

(Shots Between Scenes, *Block-Heads*
Hal Roach Studios, Culver City, California, 1938)

Babe discussing script matters with Charley Rogers.

The beginning of the punch bowl scene, from a lighting man's view.

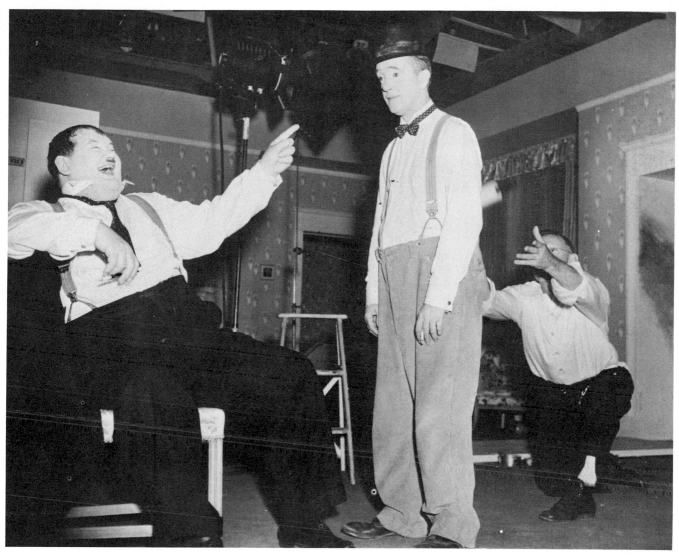

A grip (studio stagehand), just out of camera range, ready to receive Stan in a backward fall.

Stan had a birthday party given him on the set, June 16, 1938. He was 48 that day.

Birthday party. Harry Langdon, Stan, Hal Roach, Jr., Pat Ellis, Babe.

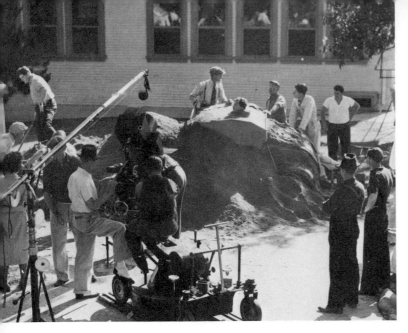

Long shot of the dump truck scene.

Babe preparing to enter the car for the climax of the dump truck scene.

Propman Bob Saunders packs Babe in for the dump truck scene.

Stan, Minna Gombell, and Babe.

Quite simply—three giants of film comedy: Stan Laurel, Harry Langdon, Oliver Hardy.

THE FLYING DEUCES

1939

69 minutes—Sound

Released October 20, 1939,
by RKO-Radio Pictures

Produced by Boris Morros
for RKO-Radio Pictures

Production managed by Joe Nadel

Directed by A. Edward Sutherland

Second unit direction by Robert Stillman

Photographed by Art Lloyd

Aerial photography by Elmer Dyer

Photographic effects by Howard Anderson

Edited by Jack Dennis

Original story and screenplay by
Ralph Spence, Alfred Schiller,
Charles Rogers, and Harry Langdon

Chief pilot and technical advice
by Frank Clarke

Production advice by Rudolph Mate

Art direction by Boris Leven

Sketch of Laurel and Hardy in
an opening scene by Harry Langdon

Sound by William Wilmarth

Musical direction by Edward Paul

Music compositions by John Leipold
and Leo Shuken

Stan Laurel . . . . Himself
Oliver Hardy . . . . Himself
Georgette . . . . Jean Parker
Francois . . . . Reginald Gardner
Jailer . . . . James Finlayson

The commandant . . . . Charles Middleton
Corporal . . . . Clem Wilenchick/Crane Whitley
Sergeant . . . . Jean del Val
Truck driver who delivers
laundry . . . . Rychard Cramer
Innkeeper . . . . Michael Visaroff
Georgette's girl friends . . . . Monica Bannister
Bonnie Bannon
Mary Jane Carey
Christine Cabanne
Pilot . . . . Frank Clarke
Legionnaires knocked out by
corks . . . . Eddie Borden
Sam Lufkin
Other Legionnaires . . . . Kit Guard
Billy Engle
Jack Chefe

Stan and Ollie are in Paris, the former anticipating a return home, but Ollie speaks of mysterious plans of his own. Stan warns his pal that if they don't go back soon they'll lose their jobs at the fish market in Des Moines, Iowa. Over a glass of milk and two straws, Stan tells Ollie he must be hiding something. (Stan's autograph appears on this and a subsequent still.)

Back at their hotel the charming Georgette (Jean Parker) thanks Ollie for the gifts of flowers and candy. He sent them, he says, because he thought she would like to smell something while eating. Upstairs, a few minutes later, Ollie confesses to Stan that he loves this exquisite lass. Stan agrees that she is "a swell dish," a designation that deeply offends Ollie who regards the girl as the future Mrs. Hardy. Minutes later, Ollie is telling Georgette, "You're going to marry me—that is, if you don't mind." She rather does mind because there is Someone Else. Ollie is crushed but Stan consoles him by saying that there is "no use crying over split milk." "I want to be a-*lone*," Ollie says.

Back upstairs, Ollie sighs that this blow comes at a time when he needs "something real, something wholesome, something *tender*." Stan urges him to try a nice, fat, juicy steak. Ollie cannot even be consoled with sweetmeats.

Indeed, Ollie has the vapors, and in the administration of smelling salts, goes into a tantrum when the bottle sticks to his nose. Severely practical, Stan says, "Why, if I felt as bad as you do, I'd drown myself." An idea is thereby implanted. Meanwhile, the newspaper headlines read: "Man-eating shark escapes—ferocious fish battles keeper in Paris Aquarium—believed at large in Seine; boaters, swimmers beware."

If Ollie is going to commit suicide in order to forget Georgette, it is sound Laurel and Hardy logic that Stan go with him. Stan doesn't quite see this at first, but Ollie patiently explains that, left alone, Stan would be unprotected. "Why," Ollie says, "people would stare at you and wonder what you are—and I wouldn't be there to tell them." In speaking of possible reincarnation, Ollie would like to come back as a horse. Stan would rather come back as himself: "I always got along swell with me." An officer of the Foreign Legion (Reginald Gardiner) happens by and convinces Ollie that the legion is the sovereign balm for hurt hearts. Ordered to throw the rock away, Stan (having untied himself meanwhile) does so and Ollie gurgles down in the river. Helped up by Stan, Ollie's posterior is severely scored by the escaped shark swimming by.

The legion never had two merrier—or less able— recruits.

They quickly reduce order to disorder...

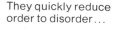

...and disorder to chaos.

They are summarily brought into the presence of their stern commandant (Charles Middleton) who gives them a full idea of the magnitude of their daily tasks and the diminutiveness of their pay—three cents a day. The boys refuse to have any part of this—for anything under 25 cents a day.

They are sent to do a mountain of laundry, and Stan earnestly advises Ollie at least to *pretend* to forget Georgette, thus giving them warrant to leave the legion. Ollie sits down, tries to forget, but Stan goes into a long litany of praise about Georgette's beauty, insisting that it would be hard indeed to forget her. In addition to the laundry the boys are also told to peel a truckload of vegetables. "Stanley," Ollie says, "I feel something coming over me. Why, I've forgotten Georgette completely." In preparing to depart the legion they unknowingly knock over a small fire that completely consumes the vast pile of laundry.

Back in mufti, they do not find the commandant in his office. Leaving him a stern note of farewell, they walk through the post courtyard where an orchestra is playing "Shine On, Harvest Moon"—which Stan dances...

...and Ollie sings—to pleasant appreciation. In the interim the commandant, having seen the burning laundry, leads a search party for the boys.

Stan and Ollie find themselves on the airfield at the moment Georgette lands. Thrilled that she has come back to him, Ollie rushes up to find that Georgette's Someone Else is her husband, Francois, the very man who urged him to join the legion. The commandant appears, and in answer to Ollie's asking if he received the note, replies grimly that the note has become the boys' death warrant.

As deserters, they are hustled strenuously into their cell by the guard (the ineffable James Finlayson). They are to be shot at sunrise; Stan offers the hope that it will be cloudy tomorrow. While casually picking at his bedsprings, Stan discovers that they emit musical tones. Setting up the springs à la Harpo Marx, he fervently strums "The World Is Waiting for the Sunrise." Ollie's camera-looks are heartrending, but by the second chorus he cannot resist tapping his foot appreciatively. Suddenly a note is thrown through the window, telling them of a tunnel under their cell.

...which they quickly find. But Stan wonders if they are allowed to do this.

Once in the tunnel, they dig upward and burrow into a wine cellar, which gives them freedom and unexpected access to Georgette's bedroom. They hide in a wardrobe but Stan sneezes, toppling their hiding place. Georgette screams and faints.

They put her on the bed and try to revive her assiduously—a scene that greets Francois as he comes into her room. The boys run off, and the entire post is after them. The boys run back into their cell and reenter the tunnel, followed by many soldiers. On reaching the wine cellar, Stan and Ollie shoot erupting champagne corks at their pursuers and escape to an airplane hangar.

They hide in an airplane that takes off when its controls are accidentally manipulated. They fly everywhere around the post in eccentric and totally unbelievable patterns, ending their adventure with...

...a direct dive to the ground. Stan crawls out of the wreckage but we see a superimposition of Ollie, winged, going heavenward and waving to Stan. Fade-out, fade in. Stan is walking along a country road when he hears Ollie calling him. The voice comes from a derbied horse in the field. "Ollie, is that really you?," Stan asks. "Of course it's me" is the reply. "Gee, I'm glad to see you!," Stan says as he puts his arms around the horse.

Production Sidelights

The script girl on *The Flying Deuces* was a beautiful young lady, Virginia Lucille Jones. She met Babe during the making of the picture and married him in March the following year. This is the wedding picture. They had 17 deeply happy years together before his death in 1957.

At the 1939 public announcement by Boris Morros of the reuniting of Laurel and Hardy for the forthcoming *The Flying Deuces*. A Laurel contract dispute with Hal Roach had threatened to separate the boys.

Stan and Babe at lunch with director Eddie Sutherland.

A Chump At Oxford

1940

42 minutes (American release); 63 minutes (European release)—Sound

Released February 16, 1940, by United Artists

Produced by Hal Roach

Associate producer, Hal Roach, Jr.

Production managed by Sidney S. Van Keuran

Directed by Alfred Goulding

Photographed by Art Lloyd

Photographic effects by Roy Seawright

Edited by Bert Jordan

Original story and screenplay by Charles Rogers, Felix Adler, and Harry Langdon

Art direction by Charles D. Hall

Set decorations by William L. Stevens

Wardrobe supervision by Harry Black

Sound by William Randall

Musical score by Marvin Hatley

Stan Laurel/Legendary Lord Paddington	Stan Laurel
Oliver Hardy	Himself
Meredith	Forrester Harvey
Dean Williams	Wilfred Lucas
Bank president James Finlayson	Forbes Murray
Jenkins, the dean's servant	Frank Baker
Student ghost	Eddie Borden
Prankish students:	
Jones	Peter Cushing
Hector	Charlie Hall
Brown	Gerald Fielding
Cecil	Victor Kendall
Johnson	Gerald Rogers
Hodges	Jack Heasley
Bank robber	Rex Lease
Officer	Stanley Blystone
Cabdriver	Alec Harford

Additional cast in the European (longer) version:

Baldy Vandevere	James Finlayson
Mrs. Vandevere	Anita Garvin
Receptionist at Sterling Employment Agency	Vivien Oakland
Chauffeur	James Millican
Officer	Harry Bernard
Driver for street sweeper	Sam Lufkin*
Pierre the cook	Jean de Briac
Tow-truck driver	George Magrill

*Working in last of his 39 films with Laurel and Hardy.

(Title is a burlesque on *A Yank at Oxford*, released two years earlier, with Robert Taylor.)

379

As usual, firmly rooted in the ranks of the unemployed, Stan and Ollie go to an employment agency, where they learn a posh family needs the services of a maid and butler. Under the soubriquets of Ollie and Agnes, they get the jobs (Stan in giddy drag) but their informal approach to their work at a formal dinner party sends them back among the jobless. (During the dinner party, Stan repeats the "serve the salad undressed" routine from *From Soup to Nuts* of 1928.)

Stan and Ollie find themselves literally in the gutter—but *employed*. They speculate how wonderful it would be if they had education enough to bring them farther up in the world— say, to the sidewalk.

As they rest on the steps of a bank to eat lunch, Stan throws his banana peel carelessly to one side, on the theory that he'll be cleaning it up anyway.

A bandit robbing the bank slips on the peel during a getaway, is apprehended...

...and the bank president hails the boys as heroes. When he asks how he can repay them, Ollie mentions their need of schooling. "If it's education you want," the president says, "you shall have the finest that money can buy." The boys think about it and Stan says, "Well, it'll save us the trouble of going to night school."

They find themselves in a hansom cab on an Oxford Street— wearing Eton suits. When it's pointed out by a student that they're dressed for Eton, Stan says, "Well, that's swell. We haven't eaten since breakfast."

Ollie asks a fellow student if he could direct them to "the head teacher." "The dean?," asks the student; "yes—but one must have a pass, *but* to get a pass one must see the pass professor, *and* in order to see the pass professor one must go through 'that hedge over there…'" And " … when you enter there," the prankster continues, "you go to the right, then to the left, then to the right again, and then to the right again. Then after you've been to the right you keep going right until you come to the left turn again. Then you go right again until you find yourself left on the right side."

Not realizing the prankster has diverted them into a maze, which is designed to confuse, the boys are very confused before they begin and awfully confused by the time they have carried their luggage only partway through the leafy labyrinth.

A group of students have decided to "rag" Stan and Ollie, and one of their number dresses up as a fairly handsome ghost, frightening the boys to near-debility.

The students intensify their kidding of the American chumps by pretending to be professors. (Fourth from the left, behind the fake moustache, is a young Peter Cushing, some time away from his fame as a perennial Dr. Frankenstein.) The "professors" escort Stan and Ollie to their new home—actually the private quarters of the dean.

The boys partake of all the amenities the dean's quarters affords. "No wonder people go to school," says Stan. "Nice place to live in like this—and no flies or nothin'." When Dean Williams (Wilfred Lucas) appears…

...he is given a jolly splash of seltzer water in the face and several choice insults. He finally convinces the boys he *is* the dean—and *not* a "dizzy" Dean, as Ollie suggests.

The pranksters, hiding behind a screen, try to edge it to the door but the dean's valet enters, knocking it down, revealing the miscreants. The dean thunders that they shall be expelled for this, "the most disgraceful outrage in the history of Oxford." One of the students turns vengefully on the boys and utters the foulest word he knows: "Snitchers!"

The pranksters resolve to get back at Stan and Ollie because, as one student avers passionately, "That's one thing we won't tolerate in Oxford—snitching!" Meanwhile the boys go to their proper quarters where their valet Meredith (Forrester Harvey) is astounded when he sees Stan. "Your lordship," Meredith asks excitedly, "don't you remember me, sir?" Stan, he says, is actually Lord Paddington, the greatest athlete and finest scholar Oxford ever knew. Ollie laughs, saying Stan is the dumbest guy he ever knew, and Stan completely concurs. But Meredith is not to be swayed. In this very room after Lord Paddington had defeated Cambridge, he was standing at the window acknowledging the plaudits of the entire student body, when the window slipped, hitting him severely on the head. After he came to, memory gone, he wandered away from the university.

As Meredith explains the strange history of Lord Paddington, the chanting of vengeful students can be heard outside: "Fee, fie, foh, fum. We want the blood of an American. Be he alive or be he dead, we'll crush his bones to make our bread. Fee, fie, foh, fum. We'll beat those Yankees like a drum." It is the students' chant of revenge, says Meredith. Someone has violated the ethics of the student body, and now they are coming to hound the offender out of Oxford. Stan is watching at the window when it cracks down upon his head, restoring his memory instantly. Once more he is the dashingly cool and supremely intelligent Lord Paddington.

The students come into the room. "We're going to take off your britches," one says, "and run you out of Oxford." "What? Take off my britches in the presence of Meredith?," asks his lordship with cold hauteur. After the students call him a snitcher, Stan glacially asks Meredith to hold his handkerchief. Lord Paddington's unusual mannerism of wiggling his ears strenuously when very angry now manifests itself, an overture of catastrophe. The students rush him, and one by one we see them sailing out of Stan's window as Ollie cowers on a ledge outside. Some of the students land in a pool, the rest are bounced in a blanket by other students. The dean runs into Stan's room and he, too, is shot through the window. Ollie reenters the room only to suffer the fate of all the others.

Ollie doesn't like his treatment, but Lord Paddington at the moment can only be bothered with considering the proper way his hankie fits up his sleeve. 383

Having no other source of income, Ollie must become Lord Paddington's manservant. The dean enters deferentially to congratulate his lordship on all the wonderful things he has accomplished since his return to Oxford. The dean asks his lordship how he tolerates Ollie's obtuseness. Lord Paddington explains, " . . . He's got a jolly old face, you know. Breaks the monotony and helps fill up the room." The dean—to Ollie's mounting incredulity—asks his lordship, "Professor Einstein has just arrived from Princeton and he's a bit confused about his theory . . . He wondered if you could straighten him out." Stan agrees to give Einstein a few moments—on Ash Wednesday.

Lord Paddington censures Ollie for the inferior tea he serves him and for his posture. This is too much for Ollie who breaks into angry exasperation and declares his intention to go back to America. The student body outside serenades Lord Paddington with choruses of "For He's a Jolly Good Fellow," and as he goes to the window to acknowledge the tribute, the sash crashes down on him again, restoring him to essential Stan-hood. Ollie exults at his old pal's return to vacuity and hugs him heartily.

Production Sidelights

Stan touching up his makeup.

Charley Rogers, the great Harry Langdon (working as a screenwriter for the film), Babe, and Stan playing a game between shots.

"Saps At Sea"

57 minutes—Sound
Released May 3, 1940, by United Artists
Produced by Hal Roach
Production managed
by Sidney S. Van Keuran
Directed by Gordon Douglas
Photographed by Art Lloyd
Photographic effects by Roy Seawright
Edited by William Ziegler
Original story and screenplay
by Charles Rogers, Felix Adler,
Gil Pratt and Harry Langdon
Art direction by Charles D. Hall
Set decorations by William L. Stevens
Wardrobe supervision by Harry Black
Boats and marine work by Benton Roberts
Sound by Elmer R. Raguse
and William B. Delaplain
Compositions used in incidental music
scoring by Marvin Hatley and Le Roy Shield

Stan Laurel . . . . Himself
Oliver Hardy . . . . Himself
Dr. J. H. Finlayson . . . . James Finlayson*
Mixed-up plumber . . . . Ben Turpin
Nick Grainger . . . . Rychard Cramer
Professor O'Brien . . . . Eddie Conrad
Mr. Sharp . . . . Harry Hayden
Apartment desk clerk. . . . . Charlie Hall**
Switchboard operator . . . . Patsy Moran
Officers . . . . Gene Morgan
Charles A. Bachman
Bud Geary
Jack Greene
Berserk victim . . . . Eddie Borden
Captain McKenzie . . . . Robert McKenzie
Newsboy . . . . Ernie Alexander

*Working in last of his 33 films with Laurel
and Hardy.
**Working in last of his 47 films with Laurel
and Hardy.

Mrs. O'Riley . . . . Mary Gordon
Man beneath auto . . . . Jack Hill†
Pedestrian . . . . Walter Lawrence
Harbor Police officer . . . . Carl Faulkner
Store dress extras . . . . Harry Evans
Ed Brady
Mother . . . . Patsy O'Byrne
Sharing role as the little girl
with the "Mama" doll. . . . . Francesca Santoro
Jackie Horner
Harbor Patrol captain . . . . Harry Bernard‡
Workmen at horn factory . . . . Sam Lufkin
Constantine Romanoff
Goat . . . . Narcissus

† Working in last of his 34 films with Laurel
and Hardy.
‡ Working in last of his 26 films with Laurel
and Hardy.

(Working titles: *Jitterbugs* and *Two's Company.*)

A horn factory has certain inbuilt work hazards for souls (like Ollie) sensitive to sound. Here at Sharp and Pierce Horn Manufacturing Company, Mr. Sharp (Harry Hayden) asks Ollie to tune the G-minor horn. The resulting cacophony upsets the delicate Hardy constitution rousingly, and he succumbs to a nervous breakdown.

Getting in their car to go home, unrelenting fate decrees that the boys have an encounter with a stuck horn and a balky engine. The engine, it is discovered, will run only when placed in the backseat.

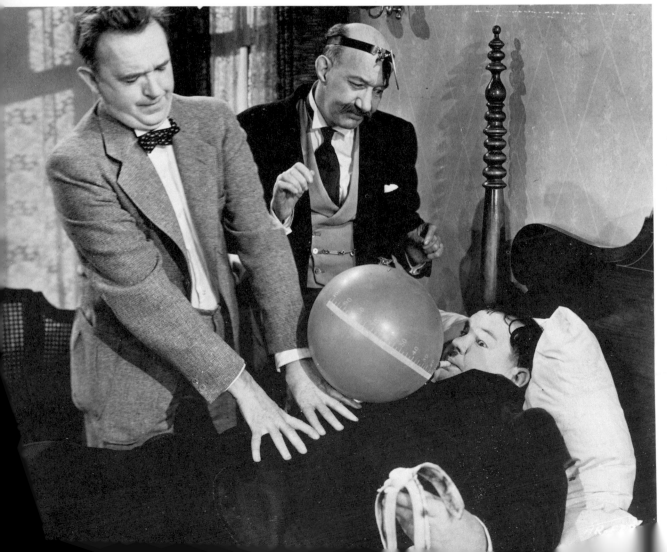

The good doctor (James Finlayson) examines Ollie and tests his lungs with an invention of his own. The results are disastrous: Ollie has a galloping case of hornophobia. "In fact," Fin tells him, "you're on the verge of hornomania!" The doctor's prescription is an ocean voyage and steady consumption of goat's milk.

The boys' apartment building is in functional chaos best illustrated by a neighbor lady showing Stan and Ollie her music-playing refrigerator and her ice-covered radio. This state of reversal is also true of the boys' apartment where the plumbing, electricity, and gas are all awry. How awry is evidenced by this chaos, which occurred when they tried to light the gas.

The maintenance man (Ben Turpin) listens to the voluminous complaints and says—very logically for him—"It looks all right to me."

While Ollie goes downstairs to give the maintenance man a piece of his mind, Stan has his music lesson. Ollie, returning with a large black eye, hears the Laurel horn and goes berserk. Stan hides in the closet, leaving his teacher to take the brunt of the Hardy fury. Later, thinking the coast is clear, Stan opens the closet door, which knocks Ollie right out of their second-story window.

In his precipitate exit, Ollie stays his descent by grabbing the outside telephone wires, while Stan rushes downstairs to place a mattress below his pal as he hangs above. As Stan rushes by the front desk, he pauses to ask the desk man (Charlie Hall), "Where's the alley?" The cryptic reply is "Out in the street." The telephone girl (Patsy Moran) looks on sympathetically.

Aftermath of the "rescue" by Stan. The mattress is placed in the back of the car that Stan hopes to drive beneath the dangling Ollie. Instead, Stan drives through the brick wall of their building, reverses, and backs up sedately over Ollie who, in the interim, has crashed down to the ground.

Wanting the best of both worlds, the boys hire a boat that they plan to keep tied to the dock during their stay at sea. Their goat friend is named Narcissus.

Their first night "at sea" Stan reads Ollie to sleep with literature he finds particularly suitable for his chum. The Laurel trombone is nearby, for clandestine practice.

During the night, Nick Grainger (Rychard Cramer), a vicious fugitive from the law, finds refuge on the boat. The goat, having been put ashore, chews the mooring rope and by morning the ship is out at sea. Nick greets the boys with a sneering "Excuse me, jitterbugs." Ollie haughtily orders Nick off the boat, and tells Stan to get a cop.

The boys discover that they are at sea, and also encounter a new member of the crew—Nick's gun, which he has named "Nick, Jr." Big Nick also rechristens the boys: Ollie is named "Dizzy" and Stan, "Dopey." Big Nick and Nick, Jr., order the boys to rustle up some grub.

Having no food on board, the boys vengefully substitute various items for a lavish menu: string becomes spaghetti; red paint becomes tomato sauce; sponge becomes meat balls; soap becomes cheese; kerosine wick becomes bacon; talcum powder is cooked into biscuits; and coffee is brewed from tobacco. Nick spies on these secret proceedings, and at dinner time forces Stan and Ollie to eat their own repast.

The boys try to force it all down. Then Stan, in a rare moment of thoughtful inspiration, plays his trombone, knowing that Ollie's consequent flare-up is bound to have some positive results. Running amok, Ollie throws coffee in Nick's face and the boys scent victory—when the trombone, comes apart. The splenetic Nick is set to rip Ollie apart when Stan gets the horn fixed. They are dominating Nick again when the horn breaks apart once more, and in a protracted chase, Nick angrily follows Ollie all over the boat. But Ollie bests Nick and the harbor police arrive.

In recapitulating Nick's capture to the captain of the harbor patrol (Harry Bernard), Stan again blows the horn and Ollie goes wild—with sad consequences to the captain. As Stan and Ollie are being led to prison, the captain asks the two guards which cell Nick Grainger is in. The film fades out to the strains of "Home Sweet Home."

Production Sidelights

Musical clowning on the set.

Career Turnabout

In 1940 the long and profitable association of Laurel and Hardy with Hal Roach came to an end. In retrospect it is so easy to say that the boys should have remained on the Roach lot where—despite occasional irrational studio interference with Stan's creative work—they were happy.

But in 1940 Stan was sensibly convinced that at the very least the future of Laurel and Hardy should be in the hands of Laurel and Hardy. From their earliest days at the studio, both Stan and Babe had been under individual contracts with Roach, each contract terminating at a different time. In this way Roach was able to control the team's destinies in any way he liked. It would be too much to say that he played one against the other; but keeping both men apart contractually was a shrewd business move. Stan explained it.

Keeping us under separate contracts meant that Roach could control us completely, bargain with each of us individually. Whereas if we were a team contractually, if we were a legal entity, he would find it much more difficult to maneuver a deal to his special advantage. Now, I don't mean Hal was ever dishonest with us, or tried to gyp us. We were always well paid. But we could have made more money and had greater freedom if we had been legally a team long before we were.

In 1939, at the end of his contract, Stan, determined never again to sign a contract unless it coincided with Babe's, so informed Roach. Babe's contract had some months to run, and in the interim Roach teamed Babe with Harry Langdon in an undistinguished film, *Zenobia*. In that year also, Stan and Babe joined to do *The Flying Deuces,* an enjoyable effort, for an independent producer, Boris Morros, who released through RKO. Early in 1939 Roach signed Stan and Babe to do two films, *A Chump at Oxford* and *Saps at Sea*. These were completed by the spring of 1940.

What Laurel and Hardy now entered into was a five-year period of agonizing upset and frustrations. It has been suggested by one scholar that the eight films Laurel and Hardy made for Twentieth Century-Fox and Metro-Goldwyn-Mayer were stridently inferior because the boys were tired and played out by 1940. On the contrary, in that year Stan and Babe were psychologically and physically at their apex. Stan's personal life, long complicated by marital discords, seemed to be stabilized by 1940 because he was divorced that year from the most contentious of his wives, the Russian dancer-singer known as Illeana. (There was to be another unfortunate brief marriage a year later, but in 1940 he was happily unaware of that.) Moreover by 1940 Stan felt euphoric at what he considered to be his newly won creative freedom. (Again, he was mercifully unaware of the future.)

Babe, too, after well-publicized difficulties with his first wife, Myrtle, found a personal happy ending in his marriage to Virginia Lucille Jones in 1940. This was an enduring marriage.

Also, by 1940 Stan had created a large stock of comedic ideas and plot concepts, never used during the Roach days, that he was eager to film. And finally, 1940 was the year Stan and Babe formed their own company, Laurel and Hardy Feature Productions. Brimming with enthusiasm, they were set to go all kinds of lively places.

They went nowhere. Artistically, they were stopped before they began. When Stan started *Great Guns* (1941),

Noted entertainers leave in the "Flying Showboat" for a two-week tour of Caribbean bases to present shows for Army and Navy men, October 1941. Left to right, front row: Lawrence Phillips of Camp Shows Inc., cameraman Frank Muto, Eddie Dowling, president of Camp Shows Inc., Louis Polanski; on the ramp: Ray Bolger, Mitzi Mayfair, Stan, Jane Pickens, John Garfield, Benay Venuta, Babe.

their first film for Twentieth Century-Fox, he found to his shocked surprise that he was not to be consulted about the film's content. This was to be the pattern for the remaining films they did from 1940 to 1945. "We had no say in those films," he said bitterly, "and it sure looked it." Had Stan been consulted, these eight films would have been completely worthy of Laurel and Hardy. Instead, studio writers either conceived their own weak and pointless gags or threw in old Laurel and Hardy gags from the Roach days, gags that Stan was forced to use despite his pleas that they be updated and given his reshapings and emendations. He was ignored.

Seven of these eight films—*Great Guns* (1941), *A-Haunting We Will Go* (1942), *Air Raid Wardens* (1943), *The Dancing Masters* (1943), *The Big Noise* (1944), *The Bullfighters* (1945), and *Nothing But Trouble* (1945) —are artistic disgraces. *Jitterbugs* (1943) at least had an endurable story line, tasty production values, and young Vivian Blaine. Stan was revolted by the experience. "What was there for us but to get out?," he asked. "We had done too many films in our own way for us to keep taking anything like that, so we gave up the ghost. It was sickening."

The second tour abroad, a London hotel, 1947.

Stan and Babe, free of the trauma of their four-year experience with Twentieth Century-Fox, celebrating 20 years as a team, 1947.

Stan and Ida—a valid happy ending, 1946.

Val Parnell, right, producer for the Royal Command Variety Performance at the London Palladium, instructs his leading performers: Babe and Stan, and below, left to right: Jimmy Gold, Bud Flanagan, Charlie Naughton, and Jimmy Nervo (of the Crazy Gang), November 3, 1947.

Fortunately for Stan's mental equilibrium, his personal life found total happiness in 1946 with his marriage to Ida Kitaeva Raphael, a White Russian concert singer. They were to have 20 deeply happy years together before Stan's death.

After the Fox-M-G-M debacle, Stan and Babe were understandably wary of rushing into a working situation without foreknowledge. So in 1947, Stan was delighted at the opportunity to appear in the form of entertainment that first had nourished him and helped form his comedic talents—British music hall. He and Babe happily toured theatres in England, Ireland, and Scotland for several months in a sketch Stan wrote. They returned to the States high in hope that somewhere a studio might be ready to offer them work—on the comedians' terms. But the old Hollywood was in its initial death throes. In 1950 a producing company in France offered Stan and Babe the chance to do a film unfettered by restrictions, and they accepted eagerly. They were given full working freedom; moreover, France was a country devoted to Laurel and Hardy. To make the offer even more attractive, they were told the film was to be done quickly—in 12 weeks. It took 12 months.

During the making of *Atoll K,* Stan became seriously ill and could only work in half-hour spurts and just a few times a day. The director was incompetent and the gag writers were lazy. Stan said of it, "It was an abortion. Part of the cast was talking French, some were talking Italian, and there were the two of us, the stars, talking English. Nobody—and that included the director and us—knew what the hell was going on."

Atoll K was Laurel and Hardy's last film.

GREAT GUNS

1   1941

74 minutes / Sound / Released October 10, 1941, by Twentieth Century-Fox / Produced by Sol M. Wurtzel for Twentieth Century-Fox / Directed by Montague (Monty) Banks / Photographed by Glen MacWilliams / Edited by Al de Gaetano / Original screenplay by Lou Breslow / Art direction by Richard Day and Albert Hogsett / Set decorations by Thomas Little / Costumes by Herschel / Sound by W.D. Flick and Harry M. Leonard / Musical direction by Emil Newman.

Stan Laurel Himself / *Oliver Hardy* Himself / *Overly protective aunts: Martha* Mae Marsh, *Agatha* Ethel Griffies / *Ginger Hammond* Sheila Ryan / *Dan Forrester* Dick Nelson / *Sergeant Hippo, D.I.* Edmund MacDonald / *Captain Baker* Kane Richmond / *Selective Service doctor* Charles Arndt / *Dr. Hugo Schickel* Ludwig Stossel / *Post cook* Dick Rich / *General Burns* Russell Hicks / *Recruit at corral* Billy Benedict / *Recruit at target practice* Dave Willock / *Postman* Irving Bacon / *Mess-hall draftee extra* Chet Brandenberg / *Soldier customer at Hammond's Photo Shop* Alan Ladd. (Clearly inspired by *Buck Privates*, a Universal feature with Bud Abbott and Lou Costello, which was made in the same year.)

Pampered young millionaire Dan Forrester (Dick Nelson) is inducted into the army, and his two faithful henchmen, Stan and Ollie, enlist to take care of him. Dan, however, turns out to be surprisingly self-reliant, and the boys find they need all of what they possess in the way of wits to protect themselves from the army—particularly tough Sergeant Hippo (Edmund MacDonald).

When the boys' pet crow, Penelope, also decides on an army career, they have a difficult time keeping her out of Hippo's way. Meanwhile, Dan falls in love with pretty Ginger Hammond (Sheila Ryan) who runs a photo shop on the post. Stan and Ollie think she is after Dan's money and they attempt to dissolve the affair. Inevitably they discover Ginger is not a gold digger (she already has a heart full of the stuff), so the boys encourage the two young people.

Annual maneuvers occupy the entire camp, and Stan and Ollie are captured by the "enemy." But Dan and Penelope cooperate by coming to the rescue.

A-Haunting We Will Go

1   1942

67 minutes / Sound / Released August 7, 1942, by Twentieth Century-Fox / Produced by Sol M. Wurtzel for Twentieth Century-Fox / Directed by Alfred Werker / Photographed by Glen MacWilliams / Edited by Alfred Day / Original story by Lou Breslow and Stanley Rauh / Screenplay by Lou Breslow / Art direction by Richard Day and Lewis Creber / Set decorations by Thomas Little / Costumes by Herschel / Sound by Arthur von Kirbach and Harry M. Leonard / Musical direction by Emil Newman.

Stan Laurel Himself / *Oliver Hardy* Himself / *Dante the Magician* Harry A. Jansen / *Margo* Sheila Ryan / *Tommy White* John Shelton / *Doc Lake* Don Costello / *Frank Lucas* Elisha Cook, Jr. / *Police Lieutenant Foster* Ed Gargan / *Attorney Malcolm Kilgore/ Federal dick Steve Barnes* Addison Richards / *Porter* Mantan Moreland / *Waiter* Willie (Sleep 'n' Eat) Best.

Once again in devitalized financial condition, Stan and Ollie, after being thrown out of a boxcar on their way to Florida, find themselves in a small community. Picked up as vagrants, they are given 24 hours to clear out of town. They read an advertisement in the local newspaper that offers free transportation to Dayton and a $50 bonus. But the offer has certain conditions: they must serve as escorts for a coffin and see that the deceased arrives safely in the Ohio city.

What Stan and Ollie do not know is that their employers are gangsters and that the so-called corpse, Darby Mason, is actually a live fugitive from the law, hiding in the coffin. The gangsters must whisk Darby into Dayton clandestinely to collect a $150,000 inheritance awaiting him there. On the same train with Darby and the boys is Dante, the magician, and his entourage, including his assistant, Margo (Sheila Ryan), and his business manager, Tommy White (John Shelton). While the cargo is being loaded on the train, Stan and Ollie's casket is mislabeled as one of Dante's trick boxes.

On the way to Dayton, Stan and Ollie are tricked by confidence men who sell them an "Inflato," a putative money-manufacturing machine. Now thoroughly penni-

less, the boys must depend on the benign Dante to help them out financially. Arriving in Dayton, Stan and Ollie are paid for delivering the coffin, and they go to Dante's theatre to repay his loan to them. Amused by their zaniness, Dante hires the boys as comedy relief for his magic act. Meanwhile the gangsters have discovered that the coffin containing Darby is actually one of Dante's boxes. They come to the theatre to find their precious "corpse."

But Darby would have been in trouble anyway. The lawyer handling his "inheritance" is actually a federal agent, and this worthy helps capture the gangsters backstage at the theatre. The prime movers in the capture, however, are Stan and Ollie who, in their sure and bumbling way, round up the bad guys. The boys win a $500 reward with which they propose to buy a *genuine* moneymaking machine.

A piquant little moment in comedy film history. Two years after Stan and Babe left the Hal Roach Studios, they again meet Roach's daughter, Margaret—the blonde girl looking down—now working for Twentieth Century-Fox under the name of Diane Rochelle.

The Tree in a Test Tube
1943

United States Government Defense Reels Series / One reel / Silent, with narration, synchronized music and sound effects / filmed in 16mm Kodachrome color / Released early in 1943 / Produced by the Department of Agriculture, Forest Service, at Twentieth Century-Fox / Directed by Charles McDonald / Photographed by A.H.C. Sintzenich / Edited by Boris Vermont / Sound by Reuben Ford / Music by Edward Craig.

Stan Laurel Himself / *Oliver Hardy* Himself / *Offscreen interlocutor* Pete Smith / *Narrator for unrelated second portion of film* Lee Vickers.

The slightness of Laurel's and Hardy's involvement in the film is proved by the fact that they did their part in it during a lunch-hour break—as a contribution to the war effort. They do not speak.

Pete Smith, in voice-over, asks the boys "to show the audience how much wood the average person totes." Stan and Ollie run after the car, and Smith says, "Oh plains just how many articles they possess are wood-based: a newspaper, spectacle rims, fountain pens, billfold, Mrs. Laurel's stockings (in the billfold), cigarette case and holder, hat sweatband, pipe, penknife—and the contents of a suitcase: slippers, shoes, belt, witch hazel, cascara, toilet case, mirror backing, brushes, soap container, razor holder, writing paper, pajamas, items of clothing, and the suitcase itself. Ollie at one point indicates Stan's head.

The boys simply let the items serve as the focus for Smith's commentary, and after he thanks them, a car drives off with their belongings on the rear bumper. Stan and Ollie run after the car, and Smith says, "Oh well, they need the exercise anyway. G'bye now."

The rest of the film consists of factory, laboratory, and military scenes emphasizing the need for the United States to develop new uses for, and industries from, its forests.

Air Raid Wardens
1943

67 minutes / Sound / Released April, 1943, by M-G-M / Produced by B. F. Zeidman for M-G-M / Directed by Edward Sedgwick / Photographed by Walter Lundin / Edited by Irvine Warburton / Original screenplay by Martin Rackin, Jack Jevne, Charles Rogers, and Harry Crane / Art direction by Cedric Gibbons / Associate art direction by Harry McAfee / Set decorations by Edwin B. Willis and Alfred Spencer / Technical advice by Florence Maher / Sound by Douglas Shearer / Musical score by Nathaniel Shilkret.

Stan Laurel Himself / *Oliver Hardy* Himself / *Joe Bledsoe, exasperated moving man* Edgar Kennedy / *Peggy Parker* Jacqueline White / *Dan Madison* Horace / Stephen McNally / *Major Scanlon* Russell Hicks / *Millicent Norton* Nella Walker / *J. P. Norton* Howard Freeman / *Eustace Middling* Donald Meek / *Rittenhause* Henry O'Neill / *Captain Biddle, principal of the high school* Paul Stanton / *Charlie Beaugart* Robert Emmett O'Connor / *Moving men* Lee Phelps, Martin Cichy / *Warden* Bert Moorhouse / *Heydrich* Don Costello / *Joseph* William Tannen / *Night watchmen* Forrest Taylor, Edward Hearn / *Lem* Milton Kibbee / *Herman* Phil Van Zandt / *Otto* Frederic Worlock / *Waitress* Betty Jaynes / *Huxton officer* Howard Mitchell / *Johnson* Jack Gardner / *Butler* Charles Coleman / *Barbershop patron* Jules Cowles / *Bank secretary* Rose Hobart / *Filling station attendant* Nolan Leary / *Boy* Walter Coughlin / *Gymnasium extra* Robert (Bobby) Burns / *Bits* Joe Yule, Sr., Constance Purdy / *Dog* Daisy.

War is just a new brand of headache for the firm of Laurel and Hardy, erstwhile dealers in fertilizer, in the up-and-coming town of Huxton.

They are bankrupt anyhow. They try the pet shop business, then a cycle store, but each is equally unlucky. They close down to enlist, leaving a note tacked to the door for their creditors.

No branch of the armed services can find a use for their talents, however, and they volunteer as air raid wardens. Dan Madison is editor of the local paper and chief of civilian defense. He and his ace reporter and fiancée, Peggy Parker, welcome the boys into the newly formed organization. Not so, however, the town banker, J. P. Norton, and his haughty wife, Millicent. In fact, Norton threatens to resign unless Laurel and Hardy are ousted.

At this stage, Eustace Middling, a newcomer in Huxton, takes over the recently vacated store to sell radios. Joe Bledsoe, the local moving man, installs his wares over the unavailing protests of the partners.

This is the situation when Madison orders a test air raid alarm. Laurel and Hardy, by now first aid specialists, are to bring in casualties, bandage their imaginary wounds, and see that lights are out during the test air raid. They immediately encounter two difficulties—banker Norton and moving man Bledsoe. First they make the banker a "casualty." He is strapped to a plank, mauled and hauled to the receiving station—all in the best of humor on their part, but not on his. Then when they call on mover Bledsoe to switch off his lights, he objects—strenuously—finally closing the argument with a well-wielded beer bottle. When the authorities find the wardens, they are completely out—with the bottle beside them. That gives banker Norton his opportunity. The evidence is overwhelming and the wardens are dismissed for drunkenness.

Justice triumphs when a special air raid test is planned for the benefit of Major Scanlon, chief of civilian defense. Norton is to stage an "incident" at a designated time. At this psychological moment, Laurel and Hardy overhear Middling and a grim stranger called Rittenhause plotting to sabotage the magnesium plant. In a spectacular surprise move, they upset the plot and bring the surprised civilian defenders to the plant where the saboteurs are captured.

Jitterbugs  1943

74 minutes / Sound / Released June 11, 1943, by Twentieth Century-Fox / Produced by Sol M. Wurtzel for Twentieth Century-Fox / Directed by Malcolm St. Clair / Photographed by Lucien Andriot / Special photographic effects by Fred Sersen / Edited by Norman Colbert / Screenplay by Scott Darling / Art direction by James Basevi and Chester Gore / Set decorations by Thomas Little and Al Orenbach / Costumes by N'Was McKenzie / Dances staged by Geneva Sawyer / Sound by E. Clayton Ward and Harry M. Leonard / Musical direction by Emil Newman / Lyrics and music by Charles Newman and Lew Pollack.

Stan Laurel Himself / *Oliver Hardy* Himself / *Susan Cowan* Vivian Blaine / *Chester Wright* Robert (Bob) Bailey / *Dorcas* Lee Patrick / *Old-timer, and the shill in league with con man Bailey* Francis Ford / *Malcolm Bennett* Douglas Fowley / *Henry Corcoran* Robert Emmett Keane / *Tony Queen* Noel Madison.

Stan and Ollie, a two-man Jitterbug band, run out of gas on a desert road, stranding them and their beat-up trailer. An enterprising young man, Chester Wright (Bob Bailey), rescues them, and beguiles them into thinking that he possesses a formula for turning water into gasoline. He cons them into partnership, and they leave to sell the pills at a nearby carnival. At the carnival Stan's and Ollie's band attracts a great crowd that dances up a simoom. One of the spectators is Susan Cowan (Vivian Blaine) who entrances Chester, and vice versa.

The gasoline pills are selling furiously when their worthlessness is discovered, and the crowd threatens Stan and Ollie. Chester, posing as a sheriff, "arrests" the boys and spirits them away. Susan is accidentally locked in their trailer. Susan tells the boys her mother has invested $10,000 in a land deal, and Chester recognizes the real estate men, from a photograph, as a pair of swindlers. The boys and Chester determine to help recover the money for Susan's mother, so they trail the con men to New Orleans where Susan gets a singing job on a showboat belonging to one of the crooks.

In order to entice the con men, Stan (very convincingly) dons woman's attire and becomes Susan's wealthy aunt from Boston; Ollie joins the plot by becoming a millionaire oozing Southern gallantry. The boys, between them, manage to recover the money for Susan's mother but they are trapped by the crooks before they can flee. Imprisoned on the showboat, Stan and Ollie rescue Susan from the crooks but the ship starts down the river during a melee and runs amok. The boys try to stop it, only increasing its speed. Chester arrives in a police launch, halts the boat, and apprehends the crooks. Stan and Ollie fall in the river.

In this film Laurel and Hardy play more or less "straight" roles, which is a blessing because their natural charm helps disguise the weakness of the script. Babe Hardy has a particularly felicitous opportunity to play a character close to his own in real life—an old-fashioned Southern gentleman.

THE DANCING MASTERS
1943

63 minutes / Sound / Released November 19, 1943, by Twentieth Century-Fox / Produced by Lee Marcus for Twentieth Century-Fox / Directed by Malcolm St. Clair / Photographed by Norbert Brodine / Special photographic effects by Fred Sersen / Edited by Norman Colbert / Screenplay by W. Scott Darling / Suggested by a story by George Bricker / Art direction by James Basevi and Chester Gore / Set decorations by Thomas Little and Al Orenbach / Costumes by N'Was McKenzie / Sound by Bernard Freericks and Harry M. Leonard / Musical direction by Emil Newman / Music by Arthur Lange.

Stan Laurel Himself / *Oliver Hardy* Himself / *Mary Harlan* Trudy Marshall / *Grant Lawrence* Robert (Bob) Bailey / *Wentworth Harlan* Matt Briggs / *Mrs. Louise Harlan* Margaret Dumont / *George Worthing* Allan Lane / *Unimpressed mother* Daphne Pollard / *Harlan's butler* Charley Rogers / *Vegetable man* Hank Mann / *Featherstone* Emory Parnell / *Auctioneer* Robert Emmett Keane.

Stan and Ollie own and operate a dancing school—a formidable anomaly when one considers that they know dancing as well as they know the binomial theorem in Urdu. Moreover, customers are as scarce as one-armed brain surgeons. The final indignity their business suffers is that the boys are forced to take "accident insurance" from a group of accident-prone gangsters.

Stan and Ollie's favorite student is Mary Harlan (Trudy Marshall) whose parents exceedingly dislike Mary's boyfriend, Grant Lawrence (Bob Bailey). Grant has invented a new flamothrowing machine that he hopes Mary's father will finance for production once it has been seen in operation. To help Grant Stan and Ollie pretend the machine is theirs and in the test demonstration of it destroy not only the military objective but the Harlan house and the flamethrower itself.

Distraught, the boys decide to finance Grant's creation of another flamethrower. Ollie recalls the availability of an insurance policy that will pay $10,000 for a broken leg, and he promptly insures both Stan's limbs. Stan is led through a series of not-so-merry misadventures by Ollie—who breaks his *own* leg in the process.

THE BIG NOISE ▮ 1944

74 minutes / Sound / Released October, 1944, by Twentieth Century-Fox / Produced by Sol M. Wurtzel for Twentieth Century-Fox / Directed by Malcolm St. Clair / Direction assistance by Caston Class / Photographed by Joe MacDonald / Special photographic effects by Fred Sersen / Edited by Norman Colbert / Screenplay by W. Scott Darling / Art direction by Lyle Wheeler and John Ewing / Set decorations by Thomas Little and Al Orenbach / Costumes by Yvonne Wood / Makeup by Guy Pearce / Sound by Bernard Freericks and Harry M. Leonard / Musical direction by Emil Newman / Music by David Buttolph and Cyril J. Mockridge.

Stan Laurel Himself / *Oliver Hardy* Himself / *Capsule-happy Egbert Hartley* Bobby/Robert Blake / *The drunk* Jack Norton / *Mrs. Mayme Charlton* Veda Ann Borg / *Evelyn, Mayme's niece* Doris Merrick / *Alva P. Hartley* Arthur Space / *Aunt Sophie Manner* Esther Howard / *Hartley's father* Robert Duddley / *Attendant at train depot* Francis Ford / *Train conductor* Charles C. Wilson / *Mugridge* George Melford / *Charlton* Frank Fenton / *Jim Hartman* James Bush / *Dutchie Glassman* Phil Van Zandt / *Man in upper berth* Del Henderson / *German military officer* Louis Arco / *Japanese military officer* Beal Wong / *Officer on motorcycle* Edgar Dearing / *Patent Officials: Manning* Selmer Jackson, *Digby* Harry Hayden / *Cabdriver* Julie Carter / *Bits* Sarah Edwards, Emmett Vogan, Ken Christy, Billy Bletcher.

Stan and Ollie are detectives (through the courtesy of a mail-order house) who are hired to guard a potent new explosive in the home of its inventor, Alva Hartley (Arthur Space). The boys are a bit befuddled by the complexities of Alva's ultramodern house with its capsule meals and disappearing furnishings. Alva's seven-time widowed sister-in-law (Esther Howard) develops a strong yen for Ollie. She is amiability itself except for a disturbing habit of roaming around the house in her sleep armed with a sharp carving knife.

Thugs attempt to steal the explosive and sell it to the enemy. Stan and Ollie take the bomb and carry it off to Washington, foiling the gangsters in the process. At one point the boys become unwitting passengers in a remote-controlled plane sent up by the army as a practice target. But after Stan and Ollie unexpectedly and unpremeditatedly capture an enemy submarine, they conclude their mission satisfactorily.

The best moment in this sublimely indifferent film is a redoing of Laurel and Hardy's two-men-in-a-berth gag from *Berth Marks* (1929). It is not an unqualified success because their hearts weren't in it. Stan would have preferred a new gag but deferred to pressure from Fox executives who insisted on the old laugh-getter. "Then let's improve it," Stan said. He pointed out that the gag would be made funnier by placing the berth in an airliner hitting air pockets, thus further complicating arm and leg entanglements. The Fox studio rudely told Stan that the gag was to be done the old way. As a result, the inherent humor in the sequence is attenuated and strained.

Time-Almost-Goes-By-Department: Edgar Dearing, who plays a motorcycle cop in the film, was the irate motorcycle cop in Laurel and Hardy's classic *Two Tars* of 1928.

THE BULLFIGHTERS ▮ 1945

69 minutes / Sound / Released May 18, 1945, by Twentieth Century-Fox / Produced by William Girard for Twentieth Century-Fox / Directed by Malcolm St. Clair / Direction assistance by Jasper Blystone / Photographed by Norbert Brodine / Special photographic effects by Fred Sersen / Edited by Stanley Rabjohn / Original screenplay by W. Scott Darling / Art direction by Lyle Wheeler and Chester Gore / Set decorations by Thomas Little and Al Orenbach / Costumes by Bonnie Cashin / Makeup by Ben Nye / Sound by Arthur von Kirbach and Harry M. Leonard / Musical direction by Emil Newman / Music by David Buttolph.

Stan Laurel Himself / *Don Sebastian* Stan Laurel / *Oliver Hardy* Himself / *Señorita Tangerine* Margo Woode / *Hotshot Coleman* Richard Lane / *Larceny Nell/Hattie Blake* Carol Andrews / *Conchita* Diosa Costello / *El Brillante* Frank McCown/Rory Calhoun / *Richard K. Muldoon* Ralph Sanford / *Mr. Gump* Irving Gump / *Texas delegate to the Bricklayer's Convention* Edward Gargan / *Girl in Spanish costume* Lorraine de Wood / *Prosecuting attorney* Emmett Vogan / *Master of ceremonies* Roger Neury / *Bullfighters* Guy Zanette, Robert W. Filmer / *Real bullfighters* Francisco Reyas, Daniel Rea / *Brawny attendant* Max Wagner / *Waiters* Julian Rivero, Jose Portugal / *Judge* Gus Glassmire / *Mr. McCoy* Hank Worden / *Mexican officers* Steve Darrell, Jose Dominguez / *Pancho* Ralph Platz / *Hotel Clerk* Raphael Storm / *Luis, the maître d'* Jay Novello / *Bits* Cyril Ring, Paul Kruger, Henry Russell, Edgar Mason.

Once again Stan and Ollie are private detectives—this time on the trail of the infamous Larceny Nell (Carol Andrews). They follow her to Mexico where, to his befuddled surprise, Stan finds he is actually a double of the brilliant Spanish matator, Don Sebastian. Don Sebastian's great rival is El Brillante (Frank McCown/Rory Calhoun) who sneeringly refers to Stan as "Mickey Mouse."

After a number of stupendously boring complications, Stan is forced to take the place of the real Don Sebastian in the bullring. Stan has a number of close calls while fleeing the taurine terror, but we are not so lucky. This film remains an unrelieved bore—a thing of patches and shreds, using scrap background clips from the Fox film, *Blood and Sand,* completed by the studio in 1941.

Nothing But Trouble

1945

70 minutes / Sound / Released March, 1945, by M-G-M / Produced by B.F. Ziedman for M-G-M / Directed by Sam Taylor / Direction assistance by Bert Glazer / Photographed by Charles Salerno, Jr. / Edited by Conrad A. Nervig / Original screenplay by Russell Rouse and Ray Golden / Additional dialogue by Bradford Ropes and Margaret Gruen / Art direction by Cedric Gibbons and Harry McAfee / Set decorations by Edwin B. Willis and Jack Bonar / Research and technical advice by Felix Berstein / Costume supervision by Irene / Sound by Douglas Shearer and Thomas Edwards / Musical score by Nathaniel Shilkret.

Stan Laurel Himself / *Oliver Hardy* Himself / *Basil Hawkley, wealthy socialite* Henry O'Neill / *Mrs. Elvira Hawkley* Mary Boland / *King Christopher* David Leland / *Ronetz* John Warburton / *Prince Prentiloff of Marshovia* Mathew Boulton / *Mrs. Flannagan* Connie Gilchrist / *Prince Saul* Philip Merivale / *Italian restauranteur* Paul Porcasi / *French restaurateur* Jean de Briac / *Officers* Joe Yule, Sr., Eddie Dunn, Forbes Murray, Ray Teal / *Zoo attendants* Howard Mitchell, Steve Darrell / *Ocean liner passenger* William Frambe / *Periwinkle* Garry Owen / *Mulligan* Robert Emmett O'Connor / *Jailer* Robert Emmett Homans / *Royal couriers* William J. Holmes, Mayo Newhall, Toby Noolan / *Doolittle* Chester Clute. (Working title: *The Home Front*.)

Stan and Ollie are chef and butler for a wealthy couple (Mary Boland and Henry O'Neill). The couple invite to dinner King Christopher of Orlandia (David Leland), a boy monarch now in exile, and his wicked uncle, Prince Saul (Philip Merivale). Stan and Ollie go out to buy a steak but on their way are diverted by children playing football. One of the lads is King Chris who has fled from a murderous underling of Prince Saul. Stan and Ollie take Chris under their wing, concealing him in the home of the wealthy couple. Stan and Ollie steal a piece of horsemeat from the lion in the zoo to replace the steak they forgot to buy. No one at the formal dinner can cut the "steak," including Prince Saul who leaves when he gets word that King Chris has disappeared.

Fired, Stan and Ollie take Chris with them to a mission, where a vagrant, recognizing the boy from a newspaper picture, calls the police. Stan and Ollie are jailed as kidnappers, and Chris is returned to his uncle. After Chris pleads for the boys' freedom, Prince Saul craftily hires them as butler and chef for a reception at which Prince Saul plans to have a salad containing a poison capsule served to his majesty. Stan and Ollie switch salads, believing Chris entitled to the largest one, and Prince Saul gets the poisonous one. Saul sees this and leaves, pretending a nervous breakdown, and Ollie inadvertently places the poison capsule in a caviar canapé.

Chris uncovers the poison plot and confronts his uncle who draws a gun, ordering Stan, Ollie, and Chris to jump from a window high above ground. Chris jumps first, landing on a painter's platform. He summons the police. The painters remove the platform. Prince Saul, about to make Stan and Ollie jump, picks up the poisoned canapé and eats it. He collapses as Chris and the police run in to rescue Stan and Ollie from the window ledge.

ATOLL K

1950

98 minutes (European releases); 82 minutes (American release) / Sound / Released in France, November 21, 1951, by Les Films Sirius / A French-Italian coproduction of Les Films Sirius (Paris), Franco-London Films S.A. (Paris), and Fortezza Film (Rome) / Associate producer Raymond Eger / Production managed by Paul Joly / Directed by Leo Joannon and John Berry / Direction assistance by Isabelle Kloukowski and Jean-Claude Eger / Special direction assistance by Alf Goulding / Photographed by Armand Thiraro and Louis Nee / Edited by Raymond Isnardon.

Stan Laurel Himself / *Oliver Hardy* Himself / *Cherie Lamour, singer* Suzy Delair / *Kokken Antoine* Max Elloy / *Mrs. Dolan* Suzet Mais / *The mayor* Felix Oudart / *Captain Dolan* Robert Murzeau / *Lieutenant Jack Frazer* Luigi Tosi / *Alecto* Michael Dalmatoff / *Giovanni Copini* Adriano Rimoldi / *Fortune hunters and subversives* Charles Lemontier, Simone Voisin, Olivia Hussenot, Lucien Callamand, Robert Vattier, Gilbert Morfau, Jean Verner, Andre Randall, C. May, R. Legris. (Working title: *Atoll*.) (Produced during 1950 and 1951, but not released outside of France and Italy until 1952 when Equity issued it in the United Kingdom as *Escapade*, and Franco-London issued it in the U.S. as *Robinson Crusoe-Land*, with Paul Frees [as English narrator] added to the cast. Reissued in the U.S. in 1954 by Exploitation Productions as *Utopia*. Both American releases were cut by approximately two reels.)

Laurel and Hardy's last film, to put it pleasantly, is a mess. Occasionally a nice mess, but mostly a messy mess.

Stan and Ollie inherit an island in the Pacific. They sail for their anticipated paradise, but a tempest intrudes on their plans and they are forced to seek shelter on a deserted atoll where they live in the style of Robinson Crusoe. With the help of singer Cherie Lamour (Suzy Delair) and her boyfriend, surveyor Jack Fraser (Luigi Tosi), Stan and Ollie are carried away with the idea that their

atoll can become a modern-day Utopia. Plans are made for the establishment of their ideal republic, and all seems well until Jack discovers uranium on the atoll. Unfortunately this news spreads wide and far and the little island is overrun by fortune seekers and opportunists. A crook tries to take over the government and all is slapstick chaos until good order prevails.

There are occasional good gags in *Atoll K* but the fun is always diminished by the sight of Stan's illness etched in deep lines on his face. In the early days of making *Atoll K* he began to lose weight and suffered from a persistent urinary difficulty. Added to this worry was another one — a very real (and, as it turned out, fully justified) apprehension about the inadequacy of the film's writers and director. After an operation in Paris that removed a prostate growth, Stan returned to location (near Cannes) and painfully, slowly, completed the film. In later years, after his health had been restored, he wished he had refused to complete it.

Final Footage

For those who love Laurel and Hardy it would be unendurable to think that *Atoll K* was their final contribution to the world of entertainment.

After a period of enforced rest, they returned once again to tour British music halls and for this, their last appearance, Stan wrote a wildly funny sketch, *Birds of a Feather,* which delighted their audiences. This 25-minute routine has Stan and Ollie finding the ultimate in euphoric employment as professional whiskey tasters. Most of the sketch occurs in a hospital room to which Ollie has been confined after his first day of work. So pleased had he been with his new job that he took a couple of doubles to celebrate; this, in turn, made him so happy that he decided to leap out the window and fly around with the birds. Upon learning of this, head bandaged, supine on a bed of pain, Ollie asks Stan indignantly, "Well, why didn't you stop me?" "Well," Stan says, "I was celebrating too, and I thought you could do it." The rest of the sketch is a series of hilarious misadventures with an eccentric doctor and a silly nurse.*

Following their tour in 1954, Stan and Babe returned to California where, after a frustratingly fallow period, they were once more in demand. Hal Roach, Jr., son of their old boss, had become aware of the high run frequency of Laurel and Hardy films on television across the country, and he contracted with the boys for a series of hour-long films in color. This project was a particular joy to Stan, who was given carte blanche in structuring the films. He outlined a series to be called *Laurel and Hardy's Fabulous Fables,* fashioned in the spirit of the English music-hall pantomimes he had always loved and in which he had made his professional debut as a teenager. The atmosphere of the new films was to be that of the never-never land of the fairy story and the children's book.

Stan had finished the scenario for their first film as well as a number of gags for the others when he was felled by a minor stroke. Nonetheless, he continued writing and concentrating on physical exercises to restore a lame leg to full use. Then Babe had a stroke, a heavy, degenerating one, from which he did not recover. He died August 7, 1957.

On tour, the climax of their music-hall sketch based on their 1930 film, *Night Owls,* England, 1952.

Shaken and depressed by the death of his old friend and partner, Stan ultimately found the perfect consolation. Out of respect for the work he and Babe had created together, Stan resolved never to perform again, but he maintained the partnership by continuing to fashion gags for Laurel and Hardy as in the days of their greatness. This work was not only consolation for Babe's loss but it insured that Stan's magnificent comedic sense was kept in continual stimulation.

In consequence, Laurel and Hardy did not die until Stan did, on February 23, 1965. They had been together 38 years.

*This sketch, together with three others Stan wrote, is in *The Comedy World of Stan Laurel* by John McCabe (New York: Doubleday, 1974).

Hal Roach, Jr., and his dad flank their prize comedians at the site of some merry catastrophes, Lake Laurel and Hardy. Dedication ceremony courtesy of "This Is Your Life," December 1954.

As the years went on, the smile never dimmed.

The Sons of the Desert

When he was writing the authorized biography, *Mr. Laurel and Mr. Hardy,** John McCabe became aware of a growing and vibrant interest in the boys among his fellow members of The Lambs club in New York. Actors and directors are particularly fond of Laurel and Hardy because of the sheer virtuosity of their performing skills. But anyone who has worked professionally in comedy appreciates the craft of Laurel and Hardy with special enthusiasm because of the team's bone-deep professionalism.

Realizing that those who loved Laurel and Hardy were not only legion but needed an intramural focus for their affections, McCabe asked Stan if he would mind the establishment of an organization devoted to Laurel and Hardy patterned along the lines of The Baker Street Irregulars, the Sherlock Holmes club. When Stan learned that the new group would have celebration as its essential theme, he thoroughly approved and even helped write the group's constitution.

McCabe discussed the logistics of founding the group with artist Al Kilgore, who suggested its name. After drawing up the Constitution, McCabe sent it to Stan, who gave it two delightful emendations.

Constitution

Article I

The Sons of the Desert is an organization with scholarly overtones and heavily social undertones devoted to the loving study of the persons and films of Stan Laurel and Oliver Hardy.

Article II

The founding members are Orson Bean, Al Kilgore, John McCabe, Chuck McCann and John Municino.

Article III

The Sons of the Desert shall have the following officers and board members who will be elected at an annual meeting:

Grand Sheik

Vice-Sheik
(Sheik in charge of vice)

Sub-Vice-Vizier
(Sheik-Treasurer, and in charge of sub-vice)

Grand Vizier
(Corresponding Secretary)

Board Members-at-Large
(This number should not exceed 812.)

Article IV

All officers *and* Board Members-at-Large shall sit at an exalted place at the annual banquet table.

Article V

The officers and Board Members-at-Large shall have absolutely no authority whatever.

Article VI

Despite his absolute lack of authority, the Grand Sheik or his deputy shall act as chairman at all meetings, and will follow the standard parliamentary procedure in conducting same. At the meetings, it is hoped that the innate dignity, sensitivity and good taste of the members assembled will permit activities to be conducted with a lively sense of deportment and good order.

Article VII

Article VI is ridiculous.

Article VIII

The Annual Meeting shall be conducted in the following sequence:
 a. Cocktails
 b. Business meeting and cocktails
 c. Dinner (with cocktails)
 d. After-dinner speeches and cocktails
 e. Cocktails
 f. Coffee and cocktails
 g. Showing of Laurel and Hardy film
 h. After-film critique and cocktails
 i. After-after-film critique and cocktails
 j. Stan has suggested this period. In his words: "All members are requested to park their camels and hire a taxi; then return for 'One for the desert!'"

Article IX

Section "d" above shall consist in part of the following toasts:
 1—"To Stan" 2—"To Babe" 3—"To Fin" 4—"To Mae Busch and Charlie Hall —who are eternally ever-popular."

Article X

Section "h" above shall include the reading of scholarly papers on Laurel and Hardy. Any member going over an 8½-minute time limit shall have his cocktails limited to fourteen.

Article XI

Hopefully, and seriously, The Sons of the Desert, in the strong desire to perpetuate the spirit and genius of Laurel and Hardy, will conduct activities ultimately and always devoted to the preservation of their films and the encouragement of their showing everywhere.

Article XII

There shall be member societies in other cities called "Tents," each of which shall derive its name from one of the films.

Article XIII

Stan has suggested that members might wear a fez or blazer patch with an appropriate motto. He says: "I hope that the motto can be blue and grey, showing two derbies with these words superimposed: 'Two Minds Without a Single Thought.'" These words have been duly set into the delightful escutcheon created for The Sons of the Desert by Al Kilgore. They have been rendered into Latin in the spirit of Stan's dictum that our organization should have, to use his words, "a half-assed dignity" about it.
We shall strive to maintain precisely that kind of dignity at all costs—at all times.

* New York: Doubleday, 1961; New York: Signet Paperback, New American Library, 1968.

The Sons flourish under Al Kilgore's splendid coat of arms:

At last count, in addition to the parent Tent in New York, there are Tents in Detroit, Michigan; St. Paul-Minneapolis, Minnesota; Lane County, Oregon; Los Angeles, California; the Connecticut Valley (including much of Massachusetts); Toronto, Ontario; Decatur, Illinois; Richmond, Virginia; Cleveland, Ohio; San Diego, California; Boston, Massachusetts; Daytona Beach, Florida; eastern New Jersey; Huntington Beach, California; Seattle, Washington; Washington, D.C.; Syracuse, New York; Chicago, Illinois; Philadelphia, Pennsylvania; Calgary, Alberta; Saginaw-Flint-Bay City, Michigan; Miami, Florida; and one Tent in a prison—the Connecticut Correctional Institution at Somers—appropriately designated by its members as the "Pardon Us" Tent.

The name of the group derives, of course, from *Sons of the Desert,* the 1933 film in which the boys pledge their loyalties to a national lodge fashioned along the lines of the Shriners. Stan, seeing The Sons take their fledgling steps, was severe on just one point, "In addition to having a half-assed dignity about it, the only thing I really insist on is that everybody have a hell of a lot of fun." His wish has been warmly—one could easily say flamboyantly—honored.

The caricatures of Laurel and Hardy by Al Kilgore, which have been reproduced frequently since 1960 in books and articles about the boys, were especially dear to Stan:

**849 OCEAN AVENUE
SANTA MONICA, CALIF.**

AUGUST 23rd 1960

My Dear Al:

Very many thanks for your charming letter and the magnificent caricatures of Babe and me. Only wish I were able to express fully my deep appreciation for your gracious gesture. Believe me, I was really touched when I read your letter, so beautifully expressed. Again, my humble thanks for your courtesy and those sentiments.

The drawing is wonderful, Al. A work of art. I naturally have seen many of them through the years, but none to compare to this. I can't tell you how thrilled I am. Many of my friends have great admiration for your work; they are delighted. Am having a special frame made for it and will treasure and cherish it as long as I live.

All for now, Al.

My warmest regards and every good wish to your kind self and family.
Good luck and God bless.
Sincerely always:

Stan.

STAN LAUREL

400